# Blue-tongued Skinks

## Contributions to the Knowledge of
## *Tiliqua* and *Cyclodomorphus*

# Blue-tongued Skinks

## Contributions to the Knowledge of *Tiliqua* and *Cyclodomorphus*

**Edited by**
**Robert Hitz, Glenn M. Shea, Andree Hauschild, Klaus Henle & Heiko Werning**

with contributions by 13 authors

129 color photographs, 13 sketches
16 distribution maps

Matthias Schmidt Publications

Cover photographs:
Top left and right: *Tiliqua rugosa rugosa*
Bottom: *Tiliqua occipitalis*
Photographs: O. Daniel

Based on a translation from the German original by Herprint International cc, P.O.Box 14241, Bredell 1623, South Africa

ISBN 3-931587-34-7

© 2004 by Matthias Schmidt Publications for the English language edition.
    Matthias Schmidt Publications is part of: Natur und Tier – Verlag GmbH
    An der Kleimannbrücke 39/41, D-48157 Münster
    Layout: Sibylle Manthey, Berlin
    Printed by: Veiters, Riga

Original publication in German under the title „Blauzungenskinke" © 2000 by Natur und Tier – Verlag, Matthias Schmidt, Münster, ISBN 3-931587-33-9

# Contents

# Contents

# Foreword

Skinks are the largest family of lizards in the world with nearly 1200 species. They occur throughout most parts of the world, but are most diverse in the tropics and southern hemisphere. Because of this distribution, skinks are poorly known to most herpetologists and other naturalists, who for the most part live and work in the temperate regions of the northern hemisphere.

However, if there is one group of skinks that almost all herpetologists and many naturalists are likely to recognize, no matter where they live, it is the bluetongue skinks of the genera *Tiliqua* and *Cyclodomorphus*. Although these animals are indigenous to Australia and the neighboring islands to the north, they have a long history of being kept in captivity throughout the world. This is probably due to the ease with which they can be kept, and this, in turn, is probably due to their large size. Large size has probably put them beyond the reach of many usual lizard predators, thereby leading to their being relative passive in temperament. Their size may also help buffer them against extreme conditions such as the occasional lack of food and water. And large size may have also permitted the evolution of their omnivorous habits, a feature which allows them to get by on almost any kind of food, plant or animal.

Bluetongues are not only interesting from an aesthetic point of view, they are also interesting scientifically. This is because of the great diversity represented in so few species. For example, bluetongues range in size from the relatively "small" Adelaide pygmy bluetongue, *Tiliqua adelaidensis,* with a maximum snout-vent length of 97 mm to the very large eastern bluetongue, *T. scincoides,* with a maximum snout-vent length of 371 mm. They range in shape from the slender northern sheoak skink, *Cyclodomorphus michaeli,* to the stocky shingleback, *Tiliqua rugosa.* This wide range of sizes and shapes invites speculation about what determines these basic morphological features in evolution. Similarly, litter sizes range from one to three large young in the shingleback, *Tiliqua rugosa,* up to as many as 67 much smaller young in the pink-tongued skink, *Cyclodomorphus gerrardii.* Hence any theory that seeks to account for the number and size of offspring in lizards has virtually an entire laboratory just in the 16 species of bluetongues alone. Even the wide variety of food habits in the group may help provide insights into how diet changes with size among species.

Despite the widespread interest in bluetongues, there has never been a book that brings together all the information on these animals in one place. However, thanks to Andree Hauschild, Klaus Henle, Robert Hitz and Glenn Shea, we now have that book in the form of "Blue-tongued Skinks, Contributions to the Knowledge of *Tiliqua* and *Cyclodomorphus"*. This book will certainly assist keepers seeking basic information on the husbandry of these animals, and hopefully, it will also stimulate further discoveries in their basic biology.

Author's address
Allen E. Greer
The Australian Museum
6 College St.
Sydney, New South Wales 2000
Australia

# Preface

With this book the editors intend to reach every terrarium enthusiast, herpetologist, and staff of zoological gardens, who, just like they do, find particular enjoyment in working with blue-tongued skinks. The contributions in this book are meant to support everybody interested in their efforts and provide encouragement to intensify the study of all biological aspects of the species of *Cyclodomorphus* **and** *Tiliqua.*

The present book is an attempt to compile and present a large portion of the currently existing knowledge on subjects such as biology, husbandry and the propagation of these animals. This goal has attracted a good number of experienced authors who represent both herpetological science and terrarium hobby.

The total of 30 individual contributions on *Tiliqua* and *Cyclodomorphus* form a pool of information that makes it imperative to work on its scientific as well as popular-scientific expansion.
This is also very much in the interest of the observed animals, both in the wild, where they and their habitats must be protected and conserved, and in the terrarium of the enthusiast, where their living conditions must be appropriate.

Blue-tongued skinks are rather long-lived, large-sized lizards that can justifiably be considered "personalities". They are by no means replaceable objects of a vivarium collection. Those who may ponder the acquisition of these animals have to take into consideration that they are about to engage themselves in a long term partnership as the life expectancy of many individuals may come close to 20 years. For the captive animals it would obviously be highly beneficial if they were not subjected to a change of ownership. Such commitment rewards the owner with the animals displaying their full range of behavioral patterns, and he will also experience - similar to small mammals - a mutual relationship.

One major aspect of the long term successful keeping obviously is the endeavor to propagate the animals kept in captivity, and it is fortunate that many zoological gardens and private breeders have dedicated themselves with great enthusiasm to this form of nature conservation, i.e. through captive propagation. Having animals on display for the enjoyment of the public has today taken a back seat, much rather is emphasis placed on the optimization of keeping conditions to a level where it eventually leads to successful reproduction. The last decade can look back on particularly remarkable successes, and this was by no means due to lucky circumstances. Responsible terrarium keeping has revealed numerous elements of the biology of blue-tongued skinks which will lastly also benefit their survival in their natural environments. It demonstrates that terrarium keeping is not only sensible, but also a necessity - we can only protect what we know and love.
In the 30 contributions contained in this book we will share all our knowledge on the ecology, husbandry and breeding of bluetongues. Careful reading will reward you with a plentitude of new information which, added to your own experiences, will encourage you to focus on as yet unsolved problems and work towards their solution. The editors would greatly appreciate your feedback in this respect and hope to have laid a foundation for a book that can be continuously expanded over time.

Grevenbroich, Thal, Leipzig, Sydney, Berlin, in the spring of 2000
Andree Hauschild, Klaus Henle, Robert Hitz, Glenn M. Shea and Heiko Werning

**Preface to the English edition**
The first edition of this book, in German language, found widespread acceptance among both hobbyists and herpetologists interested in *Tiliqua* and *Cyclodomorphus* all over Europe. A German magazine (DATZ) nominated it "Book of the year 2000". The publishers therefore decided to also realize an English edition. It is hoped that this book will so provide the non-German speaking readership with actual, comprehensive information on blue-tongued skinks and stimulate an intensified work with these fascinating creatures.

Thal, Sydney in the summer of 2002
Robert Hitz, Glenn M. Shea

# Acknowledgements

The editors and authors would like to express their sincere thanks to all who have contributed to the evolution and realization of the present book.
A word of special thanks is due to our publisher, Matthias Schmidt (Münster, Germany). He has shown courage in that he offered the means to realize a book project which may be considered "for specialists only".
The great helpfulness of Christian Schwartz (Leinsweiler, Germany) must not go unmentioned, for we owe to him the import from Australia and conversion of Glenn Shea's dissertation which was available only in the form of many hundreds of microfiches. Finally we want to also thank Sibylle and Ulrich Manthey (Berlin, Germany) for the competent and well contrived layout.
The following persons (listed in alphabetical order) have supported us in various ways:
Markus Becker (Bedburg) helped us out with artwork inspired by Aboriginal art on rather short notice, Melanie Burgartz (Grevenbroich-Kapellen) assisted with dictation, stenorette and word processing, O. Daniel (Buxtehude) made available to us his excellent photographs, Pavel German (Sydney, Australia) sent us photographs of New Guinean biotopes, Ken Griffiths (Engadine, Australia) made available photographs of *T. nigrolutea* and *T. rugosa aspera,* Raymond Hoser (Doncaster, Australia) sent us slides of *C. gerrardii,* Isabelle Kosmalla (Grevenbroich, Germany) made translations from Dutch, Christian Langner (Münster, Germany) allowed us to use his photographs of *T. gigas* from Irian Jaya, Dr. Michael Meyer (Herne, Germany) translated some contributions from Australia for the German original edition, Alexander Niedermair (Traun, Austria) supplied us with information on and slides of *Tiliqua gigas,* David Pearson contributed with valuable information on the conservation of bluetongues, Miklos Schiberna (Stuttgart, Germany) tackled the conversion of the numerous hand drawn distribution maps on the computer, Pete Weis (Talahassee, Florida, USA) made available to us photographs of Indonesian blue-tongued skinks, and, last but not least, did Frank Bambang Yuwono (Jakarta, Indonesia) provide valuable information and slides of Indonesian blue-tongued skinks with locality data.

**Acknowledgements to the English edition**
The editors and authors would like to thank cordially all who have contributed to the realization of the present English edition, first of all again our publisher, Matthias Schmidt (Münster, Germany). Special thanks should be expressed to Claudia Stieneker, trilingual secretary, NTV Publishing Company (Münster, Germany) for her dynamic support concerning this book and to Thomas Ulber, Herprint International (Bredell, South Africa) for his excellent translation work.

# History and systematics

GLENN M. SHEA

**Key words: Reptilia: Sauria: Scincidae:** *Tiliqua, Cyclodomorphus,* **history, systematics, hybrids**

The large size and phlegmatic nature of blue-tongued skinks have placed them among the lizards most familiar to the people in their native countries, and among the most popular terrarium lizards worldwide. Within Australia, bluetongues are well-known to the Aborigines, and feature in their legends, art, diet and traditional medicine (BENNETT 1834, DUNBAR 1943-44, JOHNSTON 1943, MOUNTFORD 1965, SERVENTY 1970, DOUGLAS & OLDMEADOW 1972, MCCARTHY 1976, FYFE 1985). They were the first Australian lizards reported by European explorers (DAMPIER 1729) and the first Australian lizards to be formally described and named (HUNTER 1790). Preserved specimens from eastern Indonesia reached Europe as early as in 1787 (GEVERS 1787, HOUTTUYN 1787), and specimens were seen and collected in Australia by a number of early expeditions, including the voyages of James COOK in 1777 (EDEN 1787), George VANCOUVER in 1791 (VANCOUVER 1798), Nicolas BAUDIN in 1801 (PÉRON 1807), Matthew FLINDERS in 1801 (FLINDERS 1814), Louis DE FREYCINET in 1819 (QUOY & GAIMARD 1824), Philip Parker KING in 1821 (GRAY 1827), and Robert FITZROY (with Charles DARWIN as naturalist) in 1836 (NICHOLAS & NICHOLAS 1989).

By the second half of the 19th century, they were being exhibited in zoos both in Australia (RIX 1978) and Europe (FRASER 1862, SAUVAGE 1875, 1879), and were commonly being imported to Europe from Australia for the pet trade (VON FISCHER 1882, BATEMAN 1897). Although early attempts to keep bluetongues outside Australia were often unsuccessful (BREHM 1883, BERG 1897, BOULENGER 1914, SCHNEIDER 1941), particularly in the case of the shingleback *(Tiliqua rugosa),* husbandry techniques improved as a result of greater familiarity with the Australian environment and climate, and captive breeding was soon reported, both in Europe (BOULENGER 1914, HAUCHECORNE 1929) and Australia (LE SOUËF 1918).

The combination of large size and ease of handling and husbandry has resulted in bluetongues being used extensively in comparative physiological, biochemical, immunological, pathological, anatomical and biomechanical studies. One study even explored the possibility, happily not followed, of using bluetongues to detect human pregnancy (JORGENSEN & WELCH 1953). In the early 1960s, large numbers of shinglebacks were collected for physiological research at two Adelaide institutions (TYLER 1962) and later for commercial trade. Such uncontrolled exploitation of wild populations led to legislative protection of reptiles in South Australia in 1972 (TYLER et al. 1976), a pattern repeated more recently in the legislative protection given to the New Guinea bluetongue *(Tiliqua gigas)* by the Indonesian government.

Despite the large numbers of experimental laboratory studies, there have been few studies of the ecology of most species of bluetongue. Much of the accumulated knowledge of the ecology of bluetongue species is from serendipitous observations by naturalists and reptile keepers, beginning with natural history observations by PÉRON (1807) and NIND (1832). The most extensively studied species is the shingleback, which has been studied in New South Wales (HENLE 1990, MACMILLEN et al. 1989) and Western Australia (FERGUSSON & ALGAR 1986, SHEA 1989, BAMFORD 1980), although the most extensive studies of the species are by Professor Michael BULL and his team at Flinders University in South Australia (BULL 1978, 1987, 1988, 1990, 1994, 1995, BULL & BAGHURST 1998, BULL & PAMULA 1996, BULL & SATRAWAHA 1981, BULL et al. 1991, 1993a, b, 1994, DUBAS & BULL 1991, 1992, MAIN & BULL 1996, SATRAWAHA & BULL 1981). YEATMAN (1988) studied comparative ecology of three species in sympatry in southeastern South Australia, although her results have yet to be published, and MILNE (1999) has studied the ecology of the Adelaide pygmy bluetongue *(Tiliqua adelaidensis)*.

Bluetongues are members of the family Scincidae (skinks). Skinks are the largest family of lizards, with more than 1000 species worldwide. Skinks are characterised by the development of compound plates of bone (osteoderms) within the scales, giving the large overlapping scales a strength and rigidity not present in other lizards. Within this family, bluetongues belong to the subfamily Lygosominae, characterised by the development of a secondary bony palate in the roof of the mouth, a fusion of the frontal bones, and the development of ventral projections from the frontal to the palatine bones (GREER 1970, 1986). Lygosomine skinks include the majority of all skinks worldwide and all skinks native to Australia and New Guinea. Two major species groups are recognizable within the Lygosominae: the *Eugongylus* and the *Sphenomorphuis* groups which together incorporate the majority of species and genera (GREER 1979). There are, however, a small number of genera which do not form part of these two groups, and the evolutionary relationships between these are as yet poorly understood. The blue-tongued skinks belong to these "other" genera.

The most recent study (SHEA 1990) identified the blue-tongued skinks as an evolutionary lineage of their own, the *Tiliqua* lineage, and recognised two genera within this lineage: *Tiliqua* (also named *Cyclodus* during last century), the true bluetongues, and *Cyclodomorphus* (previously *Omolepida),* the slender bluetongues. This classification has not been universally accepted, and some authors (e.g., COGGER 1992, EHMANN 1992, HAUSCHILD & GASSNER 1995) have treated one species, the pink-tongued skink, which was placed by SHEA in the genus *Cyclodomorphus,* as a distinct genus *(Hemisphaeriodon).* However, the features which have been identified as distinguishing this species from *Cyclodomorphus* are either also present in other *Cyclodomorphus* species (e.g., a prehensile tail) or are primitive features which do not indicate evolutionary relationship (e.g., relatively longer limbs). A close relationship between the pink-tongued skink and the sheoak skinks within *Cyclodomorphus* is also suggested by a shared tongue flicking behaviour, which is not present in other *Cyclodomorphus* species.

A second species, the shingleback *(Tiliqua rugosa)* was for over a century, since its first scientific description, treated as a distinct genus, variably spelled *Trachydosaurus* or *Trachysaurus.* However, more recently it has been shown on the basis of immunological (HUTCHINSON 1980) and anatomical (MITCHELL 1950, SHEA 1990) studies, to be part of the genus *Tiliqua,* albeit a highly specialised member of the genus.

The *Tiliqua* lineage is defined mostly on characters of the skeleton and dentition. All *Cyclodomorphus* and *Tiliqua* species have an increased number of trunk (presacral) vertebrae (32 or more, in contrast to 26-27 in their closest relatives), a reduction in the number of bones in the fingers and toes (at a minimum, loss of one phalanx in the fourth finger and the fourth and fifth toes), contact between the squamosal and jugal bones in the skull, loss of a lacrimal bone in the skull, a well-developed projection from the ectopterygoid bone reaching the palatine bone, and enlargement of the teeth in the posterior part of the mouth. This latter feature is most prominent in juveniles, where the seventh or eighth maxillary tooth from the front and the tenth dentary tooth from the front are much larger than the others. Externally, the features of the skeleton are evident as a relatively long body and short digits, with the third and fourth digits being equal in length. The other external feature characteristic of the *Tiliqua* lineage is an increased number of scales over the temporal region, produced by the division of the larger scales of other skinks.

Within the *Tiliqua* lineage, the genus *Tiliqua* (true bluetongues) is defined by a lack of differentiation of broad nuchal scales on the nape and the presence of a row of large subocular scales completely separating the supralabial scales from the lower eyelid, while the genus *Cyclodomorphus* (slender bluetongues) is defined by the presence of only three supraocular scales, due to a fusion of the second and third supraoculars of other species (in *Tiliqua* there are three or four, but when three are present, the reduction is generally due to fusion of the first and second), reduction in the number of ear lobules (absent or only one or two lobules present along the anterior margin of the ear), and a differently shaped contact between the frontal, nasal and maxillary bones of the skull. The genus *Tiliqua* generally includes large, robust species, while *Cyclodomorphus* species are generally smaller and more slender.

Seven species of *Tiliqua* are currently recognized. Because they are large and conspicuous, and generally easily distinguishable, these were mostly described during the 19th century when the first specimens reached Europe. However, it is only relatively recently, since 1955, that more detailed studies have considered patterns of variation within each species, allowing the recognition of subspecies. The most recent and thorough analysis of patterns of geographic variation within *Tiliqua* was made by SHEA (1992), in a yet-to-be published thesis. This study recognised subspecies in three species, with three new

subspecies to be described. In order to provide formal names to these subspecies, abbreviated descriptions of the new subspecies were presented in the German edition of this book (2000), with an English version being published here. A full analysis of the patterns of geographic variation, demonstrating that the new subspecies do not simply represent artificial segments of clinal variation, will be published elsewhere.

**The species and subspecies of *Tiliqua* are:**

*Tiliqua adelaidensis* (PETERS, 1863) - Adelaide Pygmy Bluetongue

*Tiliqua gigas gigas* (SCHNEIDER, 1801) - Northern New Guinea Bluetongue

*Tiliqua gigas evanescens* SHEA, 2000 - Southern New Guinea Bluetongue

*Tiliqua gigas keyensis* (OUDEMANS, 1888) - Kei Islands Bluetongue

*Tiliqua multifasciata* STERNFELD, 1918 - Centralian Bluetongue

*Tiliqua nigrolutea* (QUOY & GAIMARD, 1824) - Blotched or Southern Bluetongue

*Tiliqua occipitalis* (PETERS, 1863) - Western Bluetongue

*Tiliqua rugosa aspera* (GRAY, 1845) - Shingleback or Sleepy Lizard

*Tiliqua rugosa rugosa* (GRAY, 1825) - Common Bobtail or Shingleback

*Tiliqua rugosa konowi* (MERTENS, 1958) - Rottnest Island Bobtail

*Tiliqua rugosa palarra* SHEA, 2000 - Shark Bay Bobtail

*Tiliqua scincoides scincoides* (HUNTER, 1790) - Eastern Bluetongue

*Tiliqua scincoides chimaerea* SHEA, 2000 - Sunda Islands Bluetongue

*Tiliqua scincoides intermedia* MITCHELL, 1955 - Northern Bluetongue

**Two groups can be recognised among these species.**

The first group consists of *Tiliqua scincoides* and *Tiliqua gigas* and their subspecies. These two species share a loss of the primary temporal scales, replaced by anterior extensions of the secondary temporals so that the anteriormost temporal scales are much longer than tall. Additionally, they alone retain fracture planes in the vertebrae of the tail throughout life, enabling tail loss (caudal autotomy) and regeneration. These two species are so similar that they have been regarded as only subspecifically distinct by some authors. However, the two species may be differentiated by the following characters. *Tiliqua gigas* has generally fewer paravertebral scales (the longitudinal row of scales along the midline of the back, counted from the first scale behind the parietal, to the last scale anterior to the level of the anterior edge of the hindlimbs, when these are held at right angles to the body) and more subcaudal scales (counted along the ventral midline of the tail, on original tails only). Although there is some overlap between the species in each count, the ratio of subcaudal scales/paravertebral scales gives nearly complete separation of the two species, with values of less than 0.90 for 98% of *T. scincoides,* and 99% of *T. gigas* having values greater than 0.95. Additionally, most *T. gigas* have the dorsal body scales, particularly on the posterior part of the body, with angulate free margins, sometimes even keeled, while all populations of *T. scincoides* have smoothly rounded free margins to the dorsal body scales. In coloration, *T. gigas* have the forelimbs black to brown above, either uniform or with small paler spots, while most populations of *T. scincoides* (including those geographically closest to *T. gigas*) have pale gray to fawn forelimbs. There may also be a difference in tongue pigmentation. The few live

**Fig. 1** Albino *Tiliqua scincoides scincoides*                    Photograph: K. Griffiths

**Fig. 2** Albino *Tiliqua scincoides scincoides*.                    Photograph: P. Horner

specimens of *Tiliqua gigas* I have examined have the base of the tongue pink, and the tip blue, while all specimens of *T. scincoides* have the tongues completely blue.

The second group consists of *Tiliqua multifasciata* and *Tiliqua occipitalis*. Both species have the first few rows of scales posterior to the parietals much longer than wide (broader than long, like the more posterior scales, in other species). Again, the general similarity of these two species led to early authors considering them only subspecifically distinct. However, they differ in body proportions, coloration and scalation (fewer supralabial, ventral and subcaudal scales in *T. multifasciata*).

The evolutionary relationships of the other *Tiliqua* species remain poorly known. *Tiliqua adelaidensis* is particularly enigmatic. This species is much smaller than the other *Tiliqua*, and has a combination of features shared with both *Tiliqua* and *Cyclodomorphus*, as well as a few generally primitive characters.

Together, true bluetongues are found throughout Australia, from the coast to the arid centre, and from sea level to the Snowy Mountains, in almost all habitats, from desert to wet forest. Outside of Australia, they occur in the lowlands of New Guinea and adjacent islands (possibly absent from the extensive swamplands of southern Irian Jaya), and in the eastern Indonesian islands. All confirmable records are east of Wallace's Line. A few early literature records from Java and Sumatra (DUMÉRIL & BIBRON 1839, BOULENGER 1887, WERNER 1909) have not been confirmed by more recent collections, and are presumed to

**Fig. 3** *Tiliqua occipitalis,* adult, from 13.3 miles south of Bow Hill, South Australia      Photograph:  G. Shea

**Fig. 4**  *Tiliqua adelaidensis,* pair                                                Photograph:  M. Hutchinson

be erroneous, due either to confusion of localities of early expeditions, or the citation of points of shipping as collection locality. With the exception of *Tiliqua rugosa,* which is in extensive contact with both *Tiliqua occipitalis* and *Tiliqua scincoides,* overlap of the distributions of the species is limited or absent. Hybrids have been bred in captivity between *Tiliqua scincoides* and *Tiliqua nigrolutea* (Figs. 5 and 6), and between *Tiliqua scincoides* and *Tiliqua rugosa* (Fig. 7). Although LONGLEY (1941, 1944) reported that hybrids between the first two species were fertile, he also reported a high mortality among the offspring. First generation hybrids of the same cross in the author's collection also showed high mortality, together with a high incidence of abnormalities. Three wild-caught adult lizards have been collected in eastern South Australia that appear to be hybrids, two between *Tiliqua scincoides* and *Tiliqua rugosa,* which are similar in appearance to captive-bred hybrids, and one between

**Fig. 5** Hybrid *Tiliqua scincoides* × *Tiliqua nigrolutea,* juvenile     Photograph: G. Shea

**Fig. 6** Hybrid *Tiliqua scincoides* × *Tiliqua nigrolutea.*     Photograph: G. Shea

**Fig. 7** Hybrid *Tiliqua scincoides scincoides* × *Tiliqua rugosa aspera*
Photograph: G. Shea

**Fig. 8** Hybrid *Tiliqua nigrolutea* × *Tiliqua rugosa aspera*,
found near Mt. Gambier, South Australia
Photograph: G. Shea

*Tiliqua rugosa* and *Tiliqua nigrolutea* (Fig. 8). Although MERTENS (1950) suggested that Longley's records of hybridisation might indicate that *T. nigrolutea* and *T. scincoides* are only subspecifically distinct, hybridisation between bluetongue species appears to be a rare event, and does not imply that the species are not genetically distinct.

Until recently, only three species of *Cyclodomorphus* were recognised: *C. gerrardii, C. casuarinae* and *C. branchialis*. However, recent studies by SHEA (1995) and SHEA &

MILLER (1995) have led to both of the latter two species being divided. Currently, the following species and subspecies of slender bluetongue are recognised:

*Cyclodomorphus branchialis* (GÜNTHER, 1867) - Western Gill-necked Skink

*Cyclodomorphus venustus* SHEA & MILLER, 1995 - Eastern Gill-necked Skink

*Cyclodomorphus celatus* SHEA & MILLER, 1995 - South-western Slender Bluetongue

*Cyclodomorphus maximus* (STORR, 1976) - Kimberley Slender Bluetongue

*Cyclodomorphus melanops melanops* (STIRLING & ZIETZ, 1893) - Northern Spinifex Slender Bluetongue

*Cyclodomorphus melanops elongatus* (WERNER, 1910) - Southern Spinifex Slender Bluetongue

*Cyclodomorphus melanops siticulosus* SHEA & MILLER, 1995 - Nullarbor Slender Bluetongue

*Cyclodomorphus casuarinae* (DUMÉRIL & BIBRON, 1839) - Tasmanian Sheoak Skink

*Cyclodomorphus michaeli* WELLS & WELLINGTON, 1984 - Northern Sheoak Skink

*Cyclodomorphus praealtus* SHEA, 1995 - Alpine Sheoak Skink

*Cyclodomorphus gerrardii* (GRAY, 1845) - Pink-tongued Skink

Slender bluetongues are restricted to Australia. The sheoak skinks and the pinktongue are distributed along the east coast and ranges south of Cooktown in wet forests, heaths and tussock grasslands, although the distribution is not continuous. The northern sheoak skink is sympatric with the pink-tongued skink at several localities along the central coast of New South Wales, but the species are otherwise allopatric in eastern Australia. The more western slender bluetongues are also largely allopatrically distributed, inhabiting dry or seasonally dry parts of western and central Australia. Because of the lack of contact between wild populations, and the few opportunities for captive interbreeding (only the pink-tongued skink is commonly kept in captivity), hybridisation is not known between slender bluetongue species.

The distinctive enlarged teeth of both genera of bluetongues, first noted by Richard OWEN (1840-1845), have allowed a number of fossils to be recognised. These are mostly from Pleistocene and Recent deposits, and have been referred to living species. However, a small species, *Tiliqua pusilla,* has been described (SHEA & HUTCHINSON 1992) from early Middle Miocene deposits (15 million years before present) at Riversleigh in northern Australia. A second fossil from South Australia of slightly greater age has also been reported (ESTES 1984), although this specimen has remained undescribed.

The evolutionary relationships of the *Tiliqua* lineage remain poorly known. Studies of blood protein similarity using immunological techniques (HUTCHINSON 1980), chromosomal studies (DONNELLAN 1991) and morphology (GREER 1979) have suggested that the bluetongue lineage is related to the genus *Egernia,* another Australian and New Guinean genus, and more distantly to *Corucia,* the Solomon Islands Tree skink. Further evidence in support of this claim comes from an instance of captive hybridisation between *Tiliqua gigas* and *Egernia cunninghami* (ROSE 1985). The nature of the evolutionary relationship between the *Tiliqua* lineage and *Egernia* is not known. Because *Egernia* is not defined by shared derived characters, it is possible that the *Tiliqua* lineage arose from within *Egernia.* Preliminary immunological studies (BAVERSTOCK & DONNELLAN 1990) suggested that *Tiliqua rugosa* and *Egernia frerei* last shared a common ancestor about 12 million years ago, although the existence of *Tiliqua pusilla* in the middle Miocene indicates that this estimate is too short. An understanding of how short will require additional fossil material.

**Fig. 9** *Egernia cunninghami,* here a thoroughbred, can be crossbred with *Tiliqua gigas* under terrarium conditions  Photograph: U. Manthey

## Literature

BAMFORD, M.J. (1980): Aspects of the population biology of the Bobtail Skink, *Tiliqua rugosa* (GRAY). – B.Sc.(Hons.) thesis, Murdoch University, 184 pp.

BATEMAN, G.C. (1897): The Vivarium, being a practical guide to the construction, arrangement, and management of vivaria, containing full information as to all reptiles suitable as pets, how and where to obtain them, and how to keep them in health. – L. Upcott Gill, London, 424 pp.

BAVERSTOCK, P.R. & S.C DONNELLAN (1990): Molecular evolution in Australian dragons and skinks: a progress report. – Memoirs of the Queensland Museum 29(2): 323–331.

BENNETT, G. (1834): Wanderings in New South Wales, Batavia, Pedir Coast, Singapore, and China; being the journal of a naturalist in those countries, during 1832, 1833, and 1834. Vol. I. – Richard Bentley, London, 440 pp.

BERG, J.(1897): Zur Kenntnis der Stummelschwanzechse (*Trachysaurus rugosus*). – Der Zoologische Garten 38(9): 277–279.

BOULENGER, E.G. (1914): Reptiles and batrachians. – J.M. Dent & Sons, London, 278 pp.

BOULENGER, G.A. (1887): Catalogue of the Lizards in the British Museum (Natural History). Vol. III. Lacertidae, Gerrhosauridae, Scincidae, Anelytropidae, Dibamidae, Chamaeleontidae. – British Museum, London. 575 pp. + xl pl.

BREHM, A.E. (1883): Brehms Thierleben. Allgemeine Runde des Thierreichs. Dritte Abtheilung – Kriechthiere, Lurche und Fische. Erster Band. – Verlag des Bibliographischen Instituts, Leipzig, 673 S.

BULL, C.M. (1978): Dispersal of the Australian reptile tick *Aponomma hydrosauri* by host movement. – Australian Journal of Zoology 26(4): 689–697.

– (1987): A population study of the viviparous Australian lizard, *Trachydosaurus rugosus* (Scincidae). – Copeia 1987(3): 749–757.

– (1988): Mate fidelity in an Australian lizard *Trachydosaurus rugosus*. – Behavioural Ecology and Sociobiology 23(1): 45–49.

– (1990): Comparisons of displaced and retained partners in a monogamous lizard. – Australian Wildlife Research 17(2): 135–140.

– (1994): Population dynamics and pair fidelity in Sleepy Lizards. – Pp. 159–174 in VITT, L.J. & E.R. PIANKA (eds.): Lizard Ecology. Historical and Experimental Perspectives. – Princeton University Press, Princeton, 403 pp.

– (1995): Population ecology of the Sleepy Lizard, *Tiliqua rugosa*, at Mt Mary, South Australia. – Australian Journal of Ecology 20(3): 393–402.

BULL, C.M. & B.C BAGHURST (1998): Home range overlap of mothers and their offspring in the Sleepy Lizard, *Tiliqua rugosa*. – Behavioural Ecology and Sociobiology 42(5): 357–362.

BULL, C.M., G.S. BEDFORD & B.A. SCHULZ (1993): How do Sleepy Lizards find each other? – Herpetologica 49(3): 294–300.

BULL, C.M., M. DOHERTY, L.R. SCHULZE & Y. PAMULA (1994): Recognition of offspring by females of the Australian skink, *Tiliqua rugosa*. – Journal of Herpetology 28(1): 117–120.

BULL, C.M., A. MCNALLY & G. DUBAS (1991): Asynchronous seasonal activity of male and female Sleepy Lizards, *Tiliqua rugosa*. – Journal of Herpetology 25(4): 436–441.

BULL, C.M. & Y. PAMULA (1996): Sexually dimorphic head sizes and reproductive success in the Sleepy Lizard *Tiliqua rugosa*. – Journal of Zoology 240: 511–521.

BULL, C.M., Y. PAMULA & L. SCHULZE (1993): Parturition in the Sleepy Lizard, *Tiliqua rugosa*. – Journal of Herpetology 27(4): 489–492.

BULL, C.M. & R. SATRAWAHA (1981): Dispersal and social organisation in *Trachydosaurus rugosus*. – Pp. 24 in BANKS, C.B. & A.A. MARTIN (eds.): Proceedings of the Melbourne Herpetological Symposium. – Zoological Board of Victoria, Melbourne, 199 pp.

COGGER, H.G. (1992): Reptiles and amphibians of Australia. – Reed Books, Chatswood, NSW, 775 pp.

DAMPIER, L. (1729): A Voyage to New Holland, & c. in the year 1699. – J & J Knapton, London.

DONNELLAN, S.C. (1991): Chromosomes of Australian lygosomine skinks (Lacertilia: Scincidae) I. The *Egernia* group: C-banding, silver staining, Hoechst 33258 condensation analysis. – Genetica 83(3): 207–222.

DOUGLAS, M. & D. OLDMEADOW (1972): Across the Top and other places. – Rigby, Adelaide, 200 pp.

DUBAS, G. & C.M. BULL (1991): Diet choice and food availability in the omnivorous lizard, *Trachydosaurus rugosus*. – Wildlife Research 18(2): 147–155.

– (1992): Food addition and home range size of the lizard *Tiliqua rugosa*. – Herpetologica 48(3): 301–306.

DUMÉRIL, A.M.C. & G. BIBRON (1839): Erpétologie Générale ou Histoire Naturelle Complète des Reptiles. Vol. 5. – Librairie Encyclopédique de Roret, Paris, 854 pp.

DUNBAR, G.K. (1943–44): Notes on the Ngemba tribe of the central Darling River, western New South Wales. – Mankind 3(5): 140–148; (6): 172–180.

EDEN, W. (1787): The history of New Holland, from its first discovery in 1616, to the present time. With a particular account of its produce and inhabitants; and a description of Botany Bay: also, a list of the naval, marine, military, and civil establishment. To which is prefixed, an introductory discourse on banishment. – 2nd Edn. John Stockdale, London, 254 pp.

EHMANN, H. (1992): Encyclopedia of Australian animals. Reptiles. – Collins Angus & Robertson, Pymble, NSW, xv + 495 pp.

ESTES, R. (1984): Fish, amphibians and reptiles from the Etadunna Formation, Miocene of South Australia. – Australian Zoologist 21(4): 335–343.

FERGUSSON, B. & D. ALGAR (1986): Home range and activity patterns of pregnant female skinks, *Tiliqua rugosa*. – Australian Wildlife Research 13(2): 287–294.

FLINDERS, M. (1814): A voyage to Terra Australia; undertaken for the purpose of completing the discovery of that vast country, and prosecuted in the years 1801, 1802, and 1803, in His Majesty's Ship the Investigator, and subsequently in the armed vessel Porpoise and Cumberland schooner. With an account of the shipwreck of the Porpoise, arrival of the Cumberland at Mauritius, and imprisonment of the commander during six years and a half in that island. Vol. I. – G. and W. Nicol, London, cciv + 269 pp.

FRASER, L. (1862): List of vertebrated animals living in the Gardens of the Zoological Society of London. – Longman, Green, Longmans and Roberts, London, v + 100 pp.

FYFE, G. (1985): Some notes on sympatry between *Tiliqua occipitalis* and *Tiliqua multifasciata* in the Ayers Rock region and their associations with Aboriginal people of the area. – Herpetofauna 15(1): 18–19.

GEVERS, A. (1787): Museum Geversianum sive index rerum naturalium continens instructissimam copiam pretiosissimorum omnis generis ex tribus regnis naturae objectorium quam dum in vivis erat magna diligentia multaque cura comparavit vir amplissimus. – P. & J. Holsteyn, Rotterdam, iv + 659 pp.

GRAY, J.E. (1827): Reptilia. – Pp. 424–434 in KING, P.P.: Narrative of a survey of the intertropical and western coasts of Australia. Performed between the years 1818 and 1822. Vol. II. – John Murray, London, 637 pp.

GREER, A.E. (1970): A subfamilial classification of scincid lizards. – Bulletin of the Museum of Comparative Zoology 139(3): 151–184.

– (1979): A phylogenetic subdivision of Australian skinks. – Records of the Australian Museum 32(8): 339–371.

– (1986): Lygosomine (Scincidae) monophyly: a third, corroborating character and a reply to critics. – Journal of Herpetology 20(1): 123–126.

HAUCHECORNE, F. (1929): Zuchterfolge bei der Blauzunge (*Tiliqua scincoides*) im Zoologischen

Garten zu Halle. – Der Zoologische Garten (n.s.) 2(1/3): 50–51.

HAUSCHILD, A. & GAßNER, P. (1995): Skinke im Terrarium. – Landbuch Verlag, Hannover, 197 S.

HENLE, K. (1990): Notes on the population ecology of the large herbivorous lizard, *Trachydosaurus rugosus*, in arid Australia. – Journal of Herpetology 24(1): 100–103.

HOUTTUYN, M. (1787): Catalogus van eene uitmuntende Verzameling van allerley Soorte van Dieren en Dierlyke Zaaken, tot ophelderding der Natuurlyke Historie in meer dan dertig jaaren vergaderd en, volgens het Samenstel van den wydberoemden Linnaeus, in orde geschikt. – Amsterdam, viii + 170 pp.

HUNTER, J. (1790): The Scincoid, or Skinc-formed Lizard. – S. 242–243 in WHITE, J.: Journal of a Voyage to new South Wales with sixty-five plates of non descript animals, birds, lizards serpents, curious cones of trees and other natural productions. – J. Debrett, Piccadilly, 299 pp.

HUTCHINSON, M.N. (1981): The systematic relationships of the genera *Egernia* and *Tiliqua* (Lacertilia: Scincidae). A review and immunological reassessment. – Pp. 176–193 in BANKS, C.B. & MARTIN, A.A. (eds.): Proceedings of the Melbourne Herpetological Symposium. Zoological Board of Victoria, Melbourne, 199 pp.

JOHNSTONE, T.H. (1943): Aboriginal names and utilization of the fauna in the Eyrean region. –Transactions of the Royal Society of South Australia 67(2): 244–311.

JORGENSEN, L. & J.B.st.V. WELCH (1953): Pregnancy test: Australian reptiles as test animals. – Medical Journal of Australia 40(II)(15): 564–565.

LE SOUEF, D. (1918): The Blue-tongued Lizard. – Victorian Naturalist 35(1): 15.

LONGLEY, G. (1941): Notes on some Australian lizards. – Proceedings of the Royal Zoological Society of New South Wales 1940–41: 30–35.

– (1944): Notes on a hybrid blue tongue lizard. – Proceedings of the Royal Zoological Society of New South Wales 1943–44: 23–24.

MACMILLEN, R.E., M.L. AUGEE & B.A. ELLIS, (1989): Thermal ecology and diet of some xerophilous lizards from western New South Wales. – Journal of Arid Environments 16(2): 193–201.

MAIN, A.R. & C.M. BULL (1996): Mother-offspring recognition in two Australian lizards, *Tiliqua rugosa* and *Egernia stokesii*. – Animal Behaviour 52: 193–200.

MCCARTHY, F.D. (1976): Rock art of the Cobar pediplain in central western New South Wales. – Australian Aboriginal Studies. Research and Regional Studies (7): 1–163 + 78 figs.

MERTENS, R. (1950): Über Reptilienbastarde. – Senckenbergiana 31(3–4): 127–144 + pl. i–iii.

MILNE, T.I. 1999. Conservation and ecology of the endangered pygmy bluetongue lizard *Tiliqua adelaidensis*. Ph.D. thesis, Flinders University of South Australia. vii + 313 pp.

MITCHELL, F.J. (1950): The scincid genera *Egernia* and *Tiliqua* (Lacertilia). – Records of the South Australian Museum 9(3): 275–308 + pl. xxiii.

MOUNTFORD, C.P. (1965): Ayers Rock, its people, their beliefs and their art. – Angus & Robertson, Sydney, 216 pp.

NICHOLAS, F.W. & J.M. NICHOLAS (1989): Charles Darwin in Australia. – Cambridge University Press, Cambridge, 175 pp.

NIND, S. (1832): Description of the natives of King George's Sound (Swan River Colony) and adjoining country. – Journal of the Royal Geographical Society of London 1: 21–51.

OWEN, R. (1840–1845): Odontography; or, a treatise on the comparative anatomy of the teeth; their physiological relations, mode of development, and microscopic structure, in the vertebrate animals. – 2 vols. Hippolyte Bailliere, London, 655 pp. + 150 pl.

PÉRON, F. (1807): Voyage de Découvertes aux Terres Australes, exécuté par ordre de Sa Majesté l'Empereur et Roi, sur les Corvettes le Géographe, le Naturaliste, et la Goelette le Casuarina, pendant les Années 1800, 1801, 1802, 1803 et 1804. Vol. I. – Imprimerie Impériale, Paris, 496 S.

QUOY, J.R.C. & P. GAIMARD (1824): Zoologie. – in DE FREYCINET, L.: Voyage autour du monde, entrepris par Ordre du Roi, sous le ministère et conformément aux instructions de s. exc. M. le Vicomte du Bouchage, secrétaire d'état au Département de la Marine, exécuté sur les corvettes de S.M. l'Uranie et la Physicienne, pendant les années 1817, 1818, 1819 et 1820. – Pillet Aîné, Imprimeur-Libraire, de l'Imprimerie Royale, Paris, 712 S.

RIX, C.E. (1978): Royal Zoological Society of South Australia 1878–1978. – Royal Zoological Society of South Australia Inc., Adelaide, 247 pp.

ROSE, S. (1985): Captive breeding of Cunningham's Skink. – The Vipera (South Western Herpetological Society, U.K.) 1(8): 14–22.

SATRAWAHA, R. & C.M. BULL (1981): The area occupied by an omnivorous lizard, *Trachydosaurus rugosus*. – Australian Wildlife Research 8(2): 435–442.

SAUVAGE, E. (1875): De quelques reptiles d'Australie. – La Nature 3(II)(106): 22–26.

– (1879): Les Cyclodes. – La Nature 7(I)(310): 367–368.

SCHNEIDER, K.M. (1941): Über Fettlager im Schwanz der Krusten- (*Heloderma* Wiegm.) und Stutz-Echse (*Trachydosaurus* GRAY). – Der Zoologische Garten 13(3/4): 236–247.

SERVENTY, V. (1970): Dryandra. The story of an Australian forest. – A.H. & A.W. Reed, Sydney, 205 pp.

SHEA, G.M. (1989): Diet and reproductive biology of the Rottnest Island Bobtail, *Tiliqua rugosa konowi* (Lacertilia, Scincidae). – Herpetological Journal 1(8): 366–369.

– (1990): The genera *Tiliqua* and *Cyclodomorphus* (Lacertilia: Scincidae): generic diagnoses and systematic relationships. – Memoirs of the Queensland Museum 29(2): 495–519.

– (1992): The systematics and reproduction of bluetongue lizards of the genus *Tiliqua* (Squamata: Scincidae). – 4 Vols. Ph.D. thesis, University of Sydney.

– (1995): A taxonomic revision of the *Cyclodomorphus casuarinae* complex (Squamata: Scincidae). – Records of the Australian Museum 47(1): 83–115.

SHEA, G.M. & M.N. HUTCHINSON (1992): A new species of lizard (*Tiliqua*) from the Miocene of Riversleigh, Queensland. – Memoirs of the Queensland Museum 32(1): 303–310.

SHEA, G.M. & B. MILLER (1995): A taxonomic revision of the *Cyclodomorphus branchialis* species group (Squamata: Scincidae). – Records of the Australian Museum 47(3): 265–325.

TYLER, M.J. (1962): Unusual observations on the lizard *Tiliqua* (*Trachysaurus*) *rugosa* (Gray). – South Australian Naturalist 37(2): 22–23.

TYLER, M.J., G.F. GROSS, C.E RIX & R.W. INNS (1976): Terrestrial fauna and aquatic vertebrates. – Pp. 121–129 in TWIDALE, C.R., M.J. TYLER &

B.P. WEBB (eds.): Natural history of the Adelaide region. Royal Society of South Australia Inc., Adelaide, 189 pp.

VANCOUVER, G. (1798): A voyage of discovery to the North Pacific Ocean, and round the world, in which the coast of north-west America has been carefully examined and accurately surveyed. Undertaken by His Majesty's command, principally with a view to ascertain the existence of any navigable communication between the North Pacific and North Atlantic oceans; and performed in the years 1790, 1791, 1792, 1793, 1794, and 1795, in the Discovery sloop of war, and armed tender Chatham, under the command of Captain George Vancouver. – 3 Vols. G.G. & J. Robinson, London.

VON FISCHER, J. (1882): Die Stummelschwanz-Eidechse (*Trachydosaurus asper*) in der Gefangenschaft. – Der Zoologische Garten 23(7): 206–210.

WERNER, F. (1909): Neue oder seltnere Reptilien des Musée Royal d'Histoire naturelle de Belgique in Brüssel. – Zoologische Jahrbücher. Abteilung für Systematik, Geographie und Biologie der Tiere 28(3): 263–288.

YEATMAN, E.M. (1988): Resource partitioning by three congeneric species of skink (*Tiliqua*) in sympatry in South Australia. – Ph.D. thesis, Flinders University of South Australia, 459 pp.

Author's address:
Dr. Glenn M. Shea
Faculty of Veterinary Science
University of Sydney
New South Wales 2006
Australia

# The role of the genus *Tiliqua* in the daily life of the Aborigines: Myths, totem and food resource

ANDREE HAUSCHILD

**Key words: Reptilia: Sauria: Scincidae:** *Tiliqua,* **Australia, Aboriginal myths, legends, food resource**

**Why the blue-tongued skink has a blue tongue** (Aboriginal tale)
*An old man was very sick and asked his friend, the lizard, to run to the ocean and urgently bring back ink from the squid which was required to cure him from his bad illness. When the lizard arrived at the ocean, he called the squid and asked him for a little bit of ink for his sick friend. The squid was in charitable mood and offered the lizard to help himself from his full bladder of ink. But in all his hurry the lizard had forgotten to bring a vessel for the ink so the only way to transport the ink was in his mouth. Then he ran back so fast that he nearly ground off his legs. But eventually he arrived just in time to save his friend from certain death. Since then these skinks have blue tongues and very, very short legs ...*

More than 50,000 years ago the forefathers of the Aborigines began to settle for good on the fifth continent. Coming from Southeast Asia this process took a couple of thousand years. Although the sea level was at that time some 150 m lower than today, they still had to cross about 70 km of open sea which must be considered an outstanding achievement considering the means available at that time. When asked after their origin, Aborigines will inevitably start talking (they have never developed a written language) about Dream time. This is a conception of time in which future, present and past become one. Aborigines regard themselves as the descendants of ancestors who once created the universe (LAWLOR 1993).

**Fig. 1** Squid lets the skink have his ink for the sick man

© Markus Becker / Bedburg

According to Aboriginal belief their ancestors created a world during "Dream time" which originally was inhospitable and barren. The earth was flat and housed no people, animals or plants. Under the surface slept the ancestors, the Dream time creatures. When they awoke they rose from the ground and began to roam the entire land. Where they passed they left valleys and ravines, mountains, boulders, and trees. Men were formed from loam and clay, and strong winds blew life into them. The ancestors wandered through the land during the day and laid down in the evenings to sleep and in their Dreams would make up all the adventures and occurrences that were to happen the next day. When the ancestors had finished their work they went away, some of them into the sky in order to become the sun, the moon or a star, some went back to where they had come from (LAWLOR 1993). Since times immemorial these actions of the ancestors have been remembered in ceremonies, symbolism, and tales. To ensure that nature will continue to produce life around them, the Australian aboriginals endeavor to keep in touch and strengthen their contact with the Dream time by performing certain rituals and ceremonies. The life of the Aborigines did of course not only consist of singing songs, telling tales and dancing, that is the creative reactivation of the Dream time, but also of a more practical transposition for the daily survival (LAWLOR 1993). The aboriginal people did not know about the cultivation of soil, but rather were nomads who sustained themselves from what Nature had to offer. Their survival is ensured basically by their detailed knowledge of their environment. Even today they know exactly the effects of the seasonal changes, are intimately acquainted with the landscape, have an expert knowledge of the plants, and are ardent observers of animals.

Their ceremonies include the portrayal of animals in movement, gesticulation and miming - results of ancient old experience and intense observation. Aborigines consider all animals and plants to be embodiments of their Dream time ancestors. Animals are god-like beings which receive compensation for their death by being reborn in spirit

**Fig. 2** Sources of food and trails for hunters and gatherers                        © Markus Becker / Bedburg

(ILGENSTEIN 1990). For the Aborigines living in the Australian outback eating has remained a holy deed until today. The killing, dissecting and processing of an animal is subjected to certain rules which, if violated, may bring about severe punishment. Totem animals may never be killed. Persons who have a certain animal as a family symbol may never kill or even consume this animal. These rules may differ substantially from tribe to tribe or from region to region, or may even be abandoned (MORTON 1991).

Aboriginal hunters (men) acquired large game animals, including kangaroo and emu. Hunting these required an important amount of persistence and substantial skills, lots of practice, and a profound knowledge of the ways of the animals. The men were armed with spears and spear throwers when they and their dogs left camp for a hunt early in the mornings. Their hunting strategies varied from using fire and pits, hounding, to battues in which also the children and women could participate by driving game towards the men who lay in ambush. The success of a hunt often depended very much on the skills of the trained dogs (DOMEIER 1993).

The "bounty" acquired by women and children made up about 80% of the food available to a tribe. Their contributions included fruit, berries, mushrooms, seeds and roots, but also small marsupials, snakes, lizards and insects. On average one woman would collect approximately 5 kg of vegetarian food in a time span of about four and a half hours (DOMEIER 1993). Fresh tracks were followed right to the hiding place of a reptile or marsupial from which it would then be flushed or dug out with a digging stick. The hunters would sneak up on birds and arboreal lizards, e.g. the frill-necked lizard *Chlamydosaurus kingii*, and kill it with a stone or boomerang. Large areas of bush were often cleared with fire to flush out the game hiding in it. This type of clearing had a secondary side effect on the vegetation in that it enabled a large number of hard-husked seeds of edible plants to germinate that need the heat of a fire. The so-called "fire stick farming" therefore encourages plant growth which in turn attracts animals.

In the late afternoons the Aborigines would assemble for a common meal during which the day's proceeds were distributed. Reptiles, like *Tiliqua multifasciata*, for example, were always roasted "medium" over an open fire (SCROBOGNA 1980). This short braising ensured that the "juice" stayed in the meat and the innards could be removed easier. The animal was then taken from the fire, the belly slit open with a sharp stone blade and the intestines pulled out with the fingers. Spoked on a freshly cut branch the skink would then be roasted over the fire until it was crisp.

Before the arrival of the new colonists the Australian continent buzzed with flora and fauna. Game was plentiful to no compare, and rivers, lakes and the ocean teemed with fish and other aquatic animals. Hunters and collectors were able to secure a balanced, varying and diverse diet easily. It is now estimated that a substantial portion of the original megafauna of Australia has succumbed to the pressure of aboriginal hunting. Their fire management, which was performed rather intensely for their hunting, has also contributed considerably to the change of ecosystems. It was a hard life at that time, full of shortages and dangers.

Eventually, the immigration of European settlers then gave rise to a speedy increase in the clearing of forests, pollution of the water courses, and an uncontrolled urbanization which naturally had various negative effects on the Aborigines and their daily chores (DOMEIER 1993).

Many Aborigines have, more or less voluntarily, retreated to reservations in the Northern Territory, Western Australia, and, on a smaller scale, in Queensland and South Australia. There they try to maintain the ways of their ancestors. But although they have access to a knowledge gathered over 50,000 years of tradition, this will help them only to a limited extent today - a "back into Dream time" is possible only with significant limitations.

## Literature

DOMEIER, I. (1993): Akkulturation bei den westlichen Aranda in Zentralaustralien. – Mundus Reihe Ethnologie, Bd. 63, Bonn (Holos Verlag), 404 S.

ILGENSTEIN, G. (1990): Die Steinzeitmenschen von Australien. – Fischer Verlag, 111 S.

LAWLOR, R. (1993): Am Anfang war der Traum: die Kulturgeschichte der Aborigines. – München (Droemersche Verlagsanstalt Th. Knaur Nachf.), 450 S.

MORTON, J. (1991): Black and white totemism: conservation, animal symbolism. – Pp. 21–52 in Australia´s People and Animals in Todays Dreamtime. Ed by D.B.Croft. Praeger: New York.

SCROBOGNA, B. (1980): Die Pintubi. Am Ende der Steinzeit. – Berlin, Frankfurt/M., Wien (Ullstein Verlag), 246 S.

Author's address
Andree Hauschild
Narzissenweg 7
D-41516 Grevenbroich, Germany

# Functionality of the blue tongue in blue-tongued skinks (*Tiliqua* sp.)

ANTHONY HERREL

**Key words: Reptilia: Sauria: Scincidae:** *Tiliqua:* **tongue, coloration, function, defensive behavior**

The lizard tongue is part of a complex integrated system (hyolingual apparatus) that can be used for a variety of functions. Its structure and use have always fascinated biologists. In the early 20th century the tongue structure was considered an important characteristic in the classification of lizards. Consequently, the first comprehensive classification of lizards (CAMP 1923) was primarily based on exactly such differences in tongue structure and use in lizards: while the more primitive groups have a fleshy, broad tongue that is mainly used during feeding (Ascalabota, mainly chameleons, agamids, iguanids, geckos), the more derived groups have a narrow, elongated tongue that is predominantly used for chemoreceptive purposes (Autarchoglossa, see also UNDERWOOD 1971, SCHWENK 1988). Although scincid lizards are generally considered to be autarchoglossans, they do not show the extreme specializations of the tongue for chemoreception observed, for example, in varanids.

Even nowadays the tongue is sometimes used as a systematic character, one example being the case of the genus *Tiliqua*. Lizards of this genus are characterized by a dark, often blue tongue (hence the vernacular name bluetongues). One species of the genus clearly forms an exception. The pink tongued skink *(Tiliqua gerrardii)* has, as indicated by its common name, generally a pink tongue as an adult (GREER 1989). Still the young animals are born with a dark tongue (BARNETT 1977, ROBERTSON 1980) which gradually looses its color in the adults (STEPHENSON 1977). However, some confusion exists as these lizards are sometimes also characterized as belonging to a separate genus (*Hemisphaeridion,* GREER 1989, COGGER 1992) or to the genus *Cyclodomorphus* (SHEA in COGGER 1992). All the other lizards of the genus are born with a darkly colored tongue and keep this color for the rest of their life.

One of the most frequently asked questions related to bluetongues is what the function of the blue tongue color in these lizards might be. One of the most important functions of the tongue in lizards in general is its assistance in feeding. Lizards of the genus *Tiliqua* do not only use their tongue to transport prey through the buccal cavity (GANS et al. 1985), but also to pick up food items (GANS et al. 1985, KIENE et al. 1996, pers. obs.). Similarly, the tongue is of prime importance for drinking, where it is used to lap up water. During both drinking and prey prehension, the tongue is extended from the mouth, makes contact with the food item or water and is subsequently withdrawn. Still, as tongue prehension is only used while capturing stationary or immobile food items, the coloration of the tongue seems trivial in this respect. One other important function of the tongue in scincid lizards is chemoreception (COOPER 1994). In order to sample chemicals from the environment the tongue is elongated, extruded from the mouth, flicked through the air and withdrawn. Still, no plausible explanation for the blue coloration of the tongue during tongue flicking can be identified.

Apart from its function during foraging, feeding and drinking, the tongue (actually the whole hyolingual apparatus) is also used for behavioral purposes. The best known examples in this respect are the extension of a brightly colored dewlap as in *Anolis* lizards (GREENBERG 1977) and the flying dragons (*Draco* sp.) from Southeast Asia, and the frill erection of bearded and other dragons (CARPENTER & FERGUSON 1977, THROCKMORTON et al. 1985, BELS et al. 1994). Both types of display are mediated by the action of the hyolingual apparatus which causes an extension of the throat region. Usually such display behavior is used in social interactions with conspecifics, as in anoles, or for defensive purposes as in the case of the bearded dragons.

Most explanations for the blue coloration of the tongue in *Tiliqua* are of a similar nature. Generally, a defensive function is attributed to it, as the tongue is used in display actions during defensive behaviors. Most accounts indicate that the defensive display of *Tiliqua* skinks is very characteristic and stereotyped. Usually the animals flatten the body, and face the intruder. Next they open the mouth widely, extrude the tongue and start hissing loudly (CARPENTER & MURPHY 1978). During such defensive display, the animals may even lunge at a predator, attack and bite.

Two functions of this behavior are provided in literature. Firstly, by the fierce hissing, and the orientation of the animal towards the predator, the latter may confound the lizard (partially due to the crossbanded color pattern) with a death adder (*Acanthophis* sp., GREER 1989). However, this explanation can

only be validated for those species with a crossbanded pattern (e.g., *T. occipitalis* or *T. scincoides*). Secondly, by turning towards the threat, opening the mouth and sticking out the bright blue tongue (contrasting vividly with the pink mouth), the predator might simply be scared off (SHEA 1998). Clearluy, whereas the first explanation does not provide any explanation for the blue coloration of the tongue, the second one does. Some support for the second hypothesis can also be found by examining the functional characteristics of the threat behavior. During such threat display, the leaf shaped lingual pad of the flexible tongue can be lifted by pulling the hyoid apparatus forward. Next the tongue is tilted over and past the mandibular symphysis (GANS et al. 1985, pers. obs.). As during these actions the tongue is actively flattened, spread out, and protruded from the mouth, its visibility is greatly increased. Additionally, with blue and red being complementary colors, the contrast and visibility are increased further.

Still, although the explanation that the blue coloration of the tongue serves to deter predators seems plausible, evidence to support it is purely circumstantial. One contradicting argument is the absence of the dark coloration of the tongue in one of the *Tiliqua* species (*T. gerrardii*). If the coloration has a positive effect on predator deterrance, then the predation on *T. gerrardii* should be greater than on congeneric species. An alternative explanation might be that this is only of importance in juvenile lizards which are clearly more vulnerable, and for which predation pressures are usually higher. As the defensive display is even present in near term, but not yet born, young (WAKEFIELD 1956), this indicates that the behavior is innate and not learned. It supports the hypothesis that defensive display might be more crucial for newborn and young animals. If the blue tongue coloration is predominantly functional in juveniles, then *T. gerrardii* also

**Fig. 1** *Tiliqua rugosa aspera* from Dalby / QLD.          Photograph:  Raymond Hoser

fits the general *Tiliqua* pattern, which gives further support for the hypothesis. Nevertheless, to test this hypothesis the effect of the tongue coloration on the predation rate should be quantified in the field for both adult and juvenile lizards by experimental manipulation of the tongue coloration.

An alternative hypothesis might be that the blue tongue and the typical display behavior serves a role during the mating season when male-male combat is usually fierce (in *T. rugosa* this is the result of their mate guarding strategy; BULL 1994). If the tongue coloration and display can be used to judge the "quality" of conspecifics, actual combat might be avoided. Again this hypothesis should be tested by field observations of mating and combat in several species of *Tiliqua*.

One last hypothesis is that the blue coloration is due to simple phylogenetic inertia. This implies that the blue tongue color arose in the predecessor of the whole genus (by accident or not) and just persisted throughout the further evolution of the lineage.

## Literature

BELS, V.L., M. CHARDON & K.V. KARDONG (1994): Biomechanics of the hyolingual system in squamata. – Advances in Comparative and Environmental Physiology 18: 197–236.

BARNETT, B. (1977): Additional notes on new-born Centralian Bluetongues (*Tiliqua multifasciata*). – Vict. Herp. Soc. Newsletter 1: 10.

BULL, C.M. (1994): Population dynamics and pair fidelity in sleepy lizards. – in L.J. VITT & E.R. PIANKA (eds.): Lizard Ecology. – Princeton University Press, Princeton: 159–174.

CAMP, C. (1923): Classification of the lizards. – Bull. Amer. Mus. Nat. Hist. 48: 289–481.

CARPENTER, C.C. & G.W. FERGUSON (1977): Variation and evolution of stereotyped behavior in reptiles. – Pp. 335–554 in C. GANS & D.W. TINKLE (eds.): Biology of the Reptilia Vol. 7. – Academic Press, New York.

CARPENTER, C.C. & J.B. MURPHY (1978): Tongue display by the common bluetongue (*Tiliqua scincoides*, Reptilia, Lacertilia, Scincidae). – J. Herpetol. 12: 428–429.

COGGER, H.G. (1992): Reptiles and amphibians of Australia. – Cornell University Press, New York, 775 pp.

COOPER, W.E. (1994): Prey chemical discrimination, foraging mode and phylogeny. – Pp. 15–16 in VITT, J. L. & E.R. PIANKA (eds.): Lizard Ecology – Historical and Experimental Perspectives. – Princeton (Princeton University Press).

GANS, C., F. DE VREE & D. CARRIER (1985): Usage pattern of the complex masticatory muscles in the shingleback lizard, *Trachydosaurus rugosus*: a model for muscle placement. – Am. J. Anat. 173: 219–240.

GREENBERG, N. (1977): A neuroethological study of the display behavior in the lizard *Anolis carolinensis* (Sauria, Iguanidae). – Am. Zool. 17: 191–201.

GREENE, H.W. (1994): Antipredator mechanisms in reptiles. – Pp. 1–152 in C. GANS & R.B. HUEY (eds.): Biology of the Reptilia Vol. 16. – Branta Books, Ann Arbor.

GREER, A.E. (1988): Biology and evolution of Australian lizards. – Surrey Beatty & Sons Pty Ltd.: 264 pp.

KIENE, T.L., K.V. KARDONG & V.L. BELS (1996): Evolution of lizard feeding systems: testing a model. – Am. Zool. 36: 116A.

ROBERTSON, P. (1980): Captivity mating of pink tongue skinks (*Tiliqua gerrardii*). – Vict. Herp. Soc. Newsletter 18: 11–12.

SCHWENK, K. (1988): Comparative morphology of the lepidosaur tongue and its relevance to squamate phylogeny. – Pp. 569–598 in ESTES, R. & G. PREGILL (eds.): Phylogenetic relationships of the lizard families. – Stanford University Press, Stanford.

SHEA, G. M. (1998): Blue tongued lizards in New South Wales. – http://www.austmus.gov.au/is/sand/bluetoun.html.

STEPHENSON, G. (1977): Notes on *Tiliqua gerrardii* in captivity. – Herpetofauna 9: 4–5.

THROCKMORTON, G., S.J. DE BAVAY, W. CHAFFEY, B. MERROTSKY, B.S. NOSKE & R. NOSKE (1985): The mechanism of frill erection in the bearded dragon *Amphibolurus barbatus* with comments on the jacky lizard *A. muricatus* (Agamidae). – J. Morphol. 183: 285–292.

UNDERWOOD, G. (1971): A modern appreciation of Camp's "Classification of the lizards". – Introduction to reprint by SSAR.

WAKEFIELD, N.A. (1956): Blue-tongued lizards and instinct. – Vict. Nat. 72: 143–144.

Author's address
Dr. Anthony Herrel
University of Antwerp
2610 Antwerp, Belgium

# A contribution to the functional morphology of the organs in the body cavity of *Tiliqua*

MARKUS LIMBERGER

**Key words: Reptilia: Sauria: Scincidae: *Tiliqua:* anatomy, functional morphology**

Anatomy is the science of the structure of the body and its inner organs. Looking at the genus *Tiliqua* from an anatomical viewpoint, the inner structure of its members appears fairly clearly arranged and simple in comparison to that of other reptiles. The individual organs do not show any remarkable specializations, but are rather simple in their construction. Their arrangement in relation to each other, the so-called topography, also exhibits no extraordinary features. Accordingly, there is very little to be found on the inner structure of these animals in the existing literature. Those notes which exist all deal with one or another section of their anatomy, usually in the context of a comparative study of one particular organ system in various species, with examples being the papers by RAU (1924), ROGERS (1967) or IVERSON (1980). A more comprehensive description of a representative of this genus is, however, as yet wanting. In this conjunction I may take the opportunity to refer to my dissertation which is at present in preparation.

The anatomy of this genus takes on an entirely new and interesting perspective if one leaves the way of comparative viewpoint traditionally trodden in vertebrate zoology and instead tries to understand how the anatomy of these animals "works", that is if one deals with the so-called functional morphology. In the case of *Tiliqua* one attribute soon becomes apparent which I would like to term plasticity. This is meant to refer to the possibility to vary the size and position of organs without afflicting the organism and without significant changes to the

exterior morphology. More simply you could also talk of a "distortion of the body contents". This phenomenon is, of course, present in all animals to a certain extent, but what is so astounding in *Tiliqua* is the large degree of this plasticity.

If, for example, the space available in the body cavity for the lung of a mammal is reduced by a tumour or an accumulation of fluid, the animal will, depending on the extent of the loss of space, develop a more or less severe shortness of breath. Or to give another example: an overfed dog stores fat in its subcutaneous tissue. The result is that it changes its body shape, it "appears fat". The anatomy of these animals therefore obviously has only a small degree of plasticity, since in the first case scenario it results in an affliction of the organism, and in the second it leads to an alteration of the exterior appearance.

In order to place these examples in a relation to the situation found in *Tiliqua,* I will have to start off with a brief description of the structure and position of the lung as it plays a major role in the high plasticity of *Tiliqua.* Its anatomy has been described earlier, i.e. by MILANI (1894) and WOLF (1933). The structure of this lung is relatively simple. In principle it consists of two sacs which have no structures that would help to increase their inner surfaces other than a honeycomb-like relief. Such a type of lung must seem rather ineffective and primitive since it relies only on a relatively small surface available for the exchange of gases. In comparison, by a division

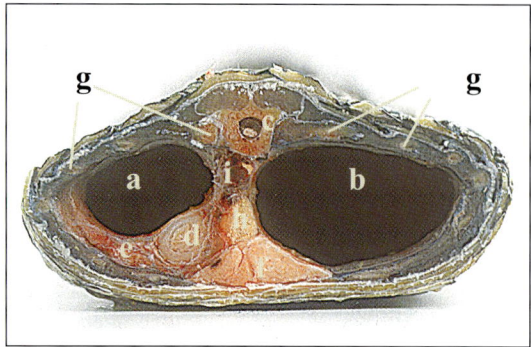

**Fig. 1** Cross section of *Tiliqua rugosa,* viewed from caudal, cut about 2.5 cm behind midbody
a - left lung; b - right lung; c - vertebral column; d - stomach; e - midgut; f - fat; g - ribs; h - right testis; i - spleen        Photograph: M. Limberger

of the lung volume into various chambers and niches other reptiles achieve a substantial enlargement of the usable surface. By being equipped with alveoli ("lung bubbles") the lungs of mammals are divided even more finely. The downside of such a complex lung structure is, as was demonstrated by the first example, that it responds very sensitively to a reduction of the space normally available to it. The simple sac-like lungs of *Tiliqua,* on the other hand, are able to vary their volume to a surprising extent without experiencing problems in their functioning as a breathing organ. Provided with sufficient space they take on the shape of two cylinders which are positioned to the left and right of the body's longitudinal axis with their anterior ends being situated in the shoulder girdle region. They extend to the posteriormost quarter of the body length. In Fig. 1, which shows a cross cut at midbody of *Tiliqua rugosa,* they appear as nearly circular objects that take up a large portion of the picture. If, however, the space occupied by them is required by other organs, their posterior sections will be compressed to form flat, airless flaps. It is only the anterior thirds of the lungs that are always filled with air and so ensure breathing. These observations correspond well

with the anatomy of the lung. The honeycomb-like relief mentioned before is well developed only in the anterior portion of the lung while it gradually disappears more posteriorly. A similar situation is found as far as the blood supply is concerned (WOLF 1933). Accordingly, the lung of *Tiliqua* can be sectioned in two parts which differ in both function and anatomy. The anterior section is more differentiated in its structure and has a better blood supply: it primarily serves the purpose of breathing. The posterior part has a comparatively simpler structure: its main function is to compensate for fluctuations in the size of other organs. This means that, next to its original and main function as a breathing organ, the lung has taken on another task. It represents some kind of volume equalizer within the body cavity.

Now, which are the organs whose fluctuations the lung has to compensate for? It is mainly the gastro-intestinal tract. Its space requirements within the body cavity fluctuate depending on its contents and activity. A central role in this is played by the hindgut. In contrast to all other sections of the intestines it is never entirely empty and therefore maintains a substantial volume, even in specimens that have not been feeding for a longer period of time. Fig. 2 shows its position and size in such an animal: it lies as an elongated, centrally positioned "pipe" in the posteriormost third of the body with its thickest point matching the left lung (Fig. 1) in diameter. Fully active the section of the hindgut anterior to the fat bodies will occupy a significantly larger space, an example for the volume and position of such an active intestinal tract is shown in Fig. 3. Being stretched lengthwise the hindgut may extend forward over the midbody mark, and change its direction by approaching the left body wall. Simultaneously its volume will increase, pushing the lung out of the central body section in the process.

The other part of the digestive tract which is subjected to substantial changes in volume is the stomach. Situated in the center of the body it is a direct continuation of the esophagus. In specimens with an inactive digestive tract it runs, like the latter, about along the body longitudinal axis: this is well recognizable in Figs. 1 and 2. During normal activity of the digestive tract the stomach is, however, dislodged from this position by the hindgut and pressed towards the left body wall. As the stomach represents some kind of storage space for the intestine which supplies the subsequent sections of the intestine with portions of nutrition, its contents and, accordingly, its space requirements vary greatly. In relation to the cross section area of the stomach in Fig. 1, it may extend to four times this volume. In its anterior section this increase in size is done at the expense of the left lung, while in its posterior part it leads to a competitive situation with the hindgut. The latter may be forced by a greatly filled stomach into the left half of the body, an impression of which is given by the illustration published by Jacobshagen (1937).

The fluctuations of the volume of the midgut, which represents the link between stomach and hindgut, are, by comparison, rather minor. Forming a series of coils the midgut is situated below the stomach and anterior hindgut. As the midgut has relatively thin walls it will collapse similar to an empty hose when it is empty. Figure 1 shows parts of such collapsed midgut coils. However, because it only turns into a relatively thin pipe even when filled, and therefore does not consume very much space, it will not cause a significant displacement of other organs.

Besides the fluctuations of the volume of the digestive tract, the lung can also compensate to a certain extent for those of the liver and fat bodies. The volumes of these organs are corre-

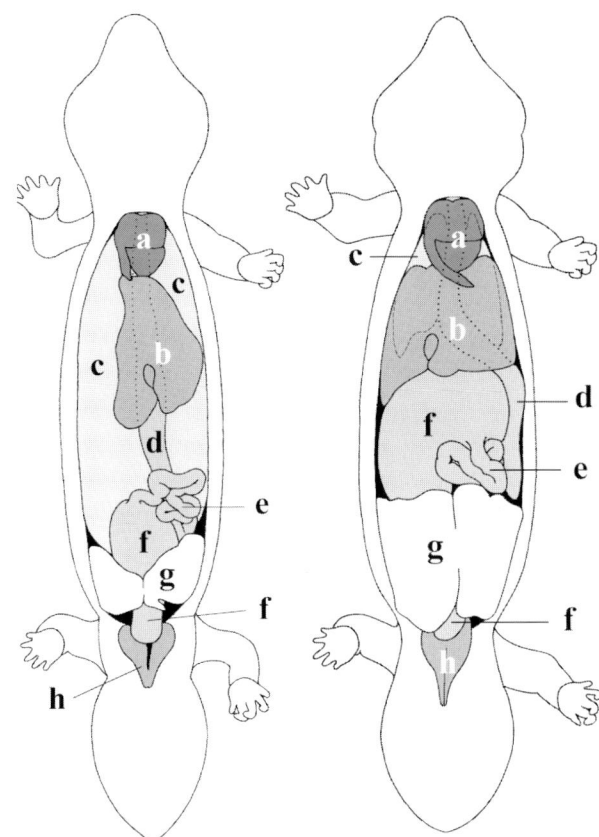

Example of the organ topography of *Tiliqua rugosa,* ventral view - from left to right:
**Fig. 2** in a specimen with an inactive intestinal tract, small liver and small fat bodies
**Fig. 3** in a specimen with an active intestinal tract, large liver and well developed fat bodies
a - heart; b - liver; c - lung; d - stomach; e - midgut; f - hindgut; g - fat body; h - kidneys. The position of the esophagus, situated behind liver and heart is indicated by a dotted line.
Sketches: M. Limberger

lated to the state of health and nutrition of *Tiliqua.* It is likely that there is also a connection to the reproductive cycle.

The liver is situated in the anterior half of the body immediately behind the heart and below esophagus and stomach. In specimens with a comparatively small liver it occupies in cross section together with stomach about the same space which in Fig. 1 is claimed by the fat bodies, testes and the visible portions of the intestine. At no place will it occupy the entire width of the body cavity, as Fig. 2 illustrates. In contrast, a large liver may claim the entire width of the anterior third of the body and expand so much towards the back that the space available to the lung and stomach is reduced to a narrow gap beneath the ribs.

The space requirements of the two fat bodies can be even more extreme. They flank the hindgut on both sides in the posterior portion of the body. Furthermore, they form a strip of fat which rests on the belly wall and so wedges itself between the latter and the hindgut. The anterior portion of this strip of fat is visible in Fig. 1. Figures 2 and 3 demonstrate that the volume of these fat bodies may vary substantially. In an extreme scenario they may expand right up to the center of the body so that almost the entire posterior part of the animal's body cavity is filled by these fat bodies. Save for the posterior section of the hindgut all organs including the lungs are then evicted from this area. In contrast to the overfed dog mentioned earlier, shinglebacks thus put on volume inwards rather than outwards. Together with a large liver the fat bodies act like a press, exposing the portions of the intestine situated in the center of the body (including the anterior sections of the hindgut), and the other organs situated in this region, to pressure from two sides. These have therefore no other option than to move towards the back where they completely displace the lungs.

Such drastic increases of the liver, and the fat bodies in particular, also result in signs visible from the outside: the animal will appear deformed and bloated particularly in its posterior part. It is obvious then that the compensation capabilities of the lungs have been exceeded. A similar situation arises at an advanced stage of gravidity. Nevertheless, it remains noteworthy to which extent these animals are able to compensate the increased space requirements of an organ and so hide it from detection from the outside. This extraordinary plasticity of the anatomy is certainly an interesting and remarkable characteristic of the genus *Tiliqua*. Shape, position and expansion of the organs exhibit such a large amount of variability that it actually becomes impossible to treat "their anatomy" as a constant property. Much rather must the anatomy of each and every individual be understood as one of many possible conditional and adaptive forms.

## Literature

IVERSON, J.B. (1980): Colic modifications in iguanine lizards. – J. morphol. 163: 79–93.

JACOBSHAGEN, E. (1937): Mittel- und Enddarm. – S. 563–724 in BOLK, L., E. GÖPPERT, E. KALLIUS & W. LUBOSCH (Hrsg.): Handbuch der vergleichenden Anatomie der Wirbeltiere, Bd. 3. – Berlin, Wien (Urban & Schwarzenberg): 1018 S. – Nachdruck 1967, Amsterdam (A. Shert Co.)

LIMBERGER, M. (in Vorb.): Topographische Anatomie und Funktionsmorphologie der Leibeshöhle bei den Gattungen *Tiliqua* und *Corucia*. – Diss. in prep., TU-Darmstadt.

MILANI, A. (1894): Beiträge zur Kenntnis der Reptilienlunge, 1. Teil (Lacertilia). – Zool. Jb. Vol. 7, Abt. Anat. Heft 1: 545–593.

RAU, A.S. (1924): Observations on the anatomy of the heart of *Tiliqua scincoides* and *Eunectes murinus*. – J. Anat. London 59: 60–71.

ROGERS, D.C. (1967): The structure of the carotid bifurcation in the lizards *Tiliqua occipitalis* and *Trachydosaurus rugosus*. – J. Morph. 122: 115–130.

WOLF, S. (1933): Zur Kenntnis von Bau und Funktion der Reptilienlunge. – Zool. Jb. Jena Anat. 57: 139–190.

Author's address
Markus Limberger
Schumannstr. 29
D-63500 Seligenstadt, Germany

# Sex identification in blue-tongued skinks
# (Sauria: Scincidae: *Tiliqua*)

ROBERT HITZ and THOMAS ZIEGLER

**Key words: Reptilia: Sauria: Scincidae: *Tiliqua*, sex, sex identification**

## Introduction

Sex identification in reptiles is not only of fundamental importance for their successful keeping and breeding, but also for ecological and ethological studies in the field. Depending on the reptile taxa there are various methods of sex identification, with a general review having been published by, among others, HONEGGER (1978) and for squamate reptiles by ZIEGLER & BÖHME (1996a, b). As far as terminology is concerned it should be mentioned that sex identification (or sex recognition) refers to sexing whereas the often employed term "sex determination" actually implies the biological process of the formation of the one or the other sex.

Besides primary sexual differences, i.e. those relating directly to the genital organs, many reptiles also exhibit to a varying extent secondary sexual characteristics which may appear as differences of their external morphology or coloration. By lacking such readily recognizable, external sex indicative characteristics, in many other reptiles, however, sex identification is problematic. This is also the case in the almost monomorphous skinks of the genus *Tiliqua*. It is therefore the aim of this contribution to present the various sex identification methods in blue-tongued skinks and to discuss their practicability and reliability.

## 1. External morphology

While the evaluation of external morphological features (external structural characteristics) and/or coloration is in principle an easy method for the identification of the sexes everybody is able to perform without any further technical assistance, it is difficult to apply in the case of the almost monomorphous representatives of the genus *Tiliqua*. Certain differences do exist, but these are hardly recognizable in juveniles and also not always distinct in adults (Fig. 1).
One external morphological characteristic is the shape of the head with male skinks usually possessing larger, i.e. more massive or more compact, heads than females. According to JONES (1987) the head of male *Tiliqua* is as

**Fig. 1** Pair of *T. nigrolutea,* highland morph, male above, female below          Photograph: R. Hitz

wide or wider than the body whereas it is narrower in females. More detailed information on the differences in body proportions of numerous species of *Tiliqua* can be found in SHEA (1992), and for *T. rugosa* aspera in BULL & PAMULA (1996) (comp. Table 1). Besides differences in their body proportions SHEA (1992) also discovered numerous differences in the scalation between the sexes. However, although the mean values differ, the range of absolute numbers overlap in part so substantially that these features are of limited use for the identification of a sex.

Finally, another form of sex identification on the basis of external morphology is the evaluation of the thickness of the ventral base of the tail which, due to the retracted hemipenes is slightly wider in male specimens. But also this method does not necessarily lead to reliable results as skinks usually have a strong base of the tail anyway with a firm and hard scalation.

In general it must be stated that an identification of the sexes based on the external morphology can provide reliable results only in the case of subadult and adult specimens and should, if possible, be based on a comparison with identified representatives of both sexes. It should furthermore be taken into consideration for such an evaluation that in species with very large distribution ranges (e.g. *T. r. aspera*) local variation is possible.

**Table 1** Sexual dimorphism in blue-tongued skinks, compiled from data published by SHEA (1992) with additions by the senior author

| Species / Subspecies | Total length or Snout-vent length | Body proportions | | |
|---|---|---|---|---|
| *T. adelaidensis* | ♀ > ♂ * | ♂ with longer heads than ♀ **** | | |
| *T. g. gigas* | ♀ slightly > ♂ * | ** | | |
| *T. g. evanescens* | ♀ slightly > ♂ * | ** | | |
| *T. g. keyensis* | sample size too small for comparison | | | |
| *T. multifasciata* | TL ♀ > ♂ * | ♀ with tail < ♂ * | | |
| *T. nigrolutea* Highland morph | ♀ > ♂ * | ** | ♀ with thicker tails than ♂ (pers. obs. senior author) | |
| *T. nigrolutea* Lowland morph | ♀ > ♂ * | ** | ♂ head width > ♀ * | |
| *T. occipitalis* | no data | ** | ♀ with broader heads and slightly larger eyes than ♂ | |
| *T. r. rugosa* | no differences | ** | ♀ with shorter, broader tails than ♂ | |
| *T. r. aspera* | no differences | ** | ♀ with shorter, broader tails than ♂ ♀ with broader heads than ♂ | |
| | | *** | | |
| *T. r. konowi* | no differences | ** | | |
| *T. r. palarra* | no differences | ♀ with shorter heads and smaller hind legs than ♂. Sample size small! | | |
| *T. s. scincoides* | ♀ slightly > ♂ * | ** | | |
| *T. s. intermedia* | ♀ slightly > ♂ * | ** | | |
| *T. s. chimaerea* | sample size too small for comparison | | | |

Abbreviations: TL = total length; * = adults; ** in proportion to the snout-vent length subadult and adult females have shorter heads, shorter snouts, longer bodies, broader hips, shorter legs and shorter tails than males; *** = BULL & PAMULA (1996) found females with shorter and narrower heads than males in the population of the Mt. Mary region; **** = HUTCHINSON (pers. comm. 1998)

It should always be borne in mind that the common practice of sex identification based on external morphology may not produce a reliable result, even if the examined specimens are fully grown. To eliminate the relatively high unreliability or error ratio we can only recommend using another method of sex identification for confirmation.

## 2. External (secondary) genital organs (hemipenes / hemiclitores)

Until a few years ago it was supposed that only male squamates (Squamata), i.e. lizards and snakes, were equipped with pairs of copulatory organs. While studying cases of sexual dimorphism, various authors found, however, similar structures in females which could not be referred to properly (for a synopsis of the literature see ZIEGLER & BÖHME 1997). For these female structures, corresponding at a smaller scale to the male hemipenes, BÖHME (1995) eventually coined the term hemiclitores. Like the hemipenes the equally paired and evertible hemiclitores rise from the posterior section of the cloaca and are retracted into the base of the tail by the retractor muscle when inactive. Especially with regard to the identification of the sexes the existence of female copulatory organs, neglected for a very long time, should in future be paid more attention (comp. ZIEGLER & BÖHME 1996a, b, 1997).

In the case of *Tiliqua* the inverted hemiclitores of an adult female are notably smaller and many times narrower than the hemipenes of a male specimen. The hemiclitores, which are caudally connected to the retractor muscle, are also distinctly shorter (Fig. 2). This is admittedly very difficult to examine in a live animal, but the points of emergence of these copulatory organs at the ventral base of the tail also provide a clue. Naturally, in the smaller hemiclitores these are less voluminous and finer than in the hemipenes. Comparing specimens of about the same snout-vent length, the everted hemiclitores appear less than half as long as the hemipenes, they are distinctly more

**Fig. 2 Left:** ventral view of the cloacal region of a female *T. s. scincoides* (ZFMK 49319, cave Beach, Jervis Bay, NSW, SVL 31.3 cm, TL 18.2 cm) with the inverted right hemiclitoris exposed.
**Right**: ventral view of a male *T. s. scincoides* (ZFMK 26804, Sydney, SVL 31 cm, TL 17.5 cm) with inverted left hemipenis exposed.
Photograph:   T. Ziegler
Abbreviations: SVL = snout-vent length; TL = tail length

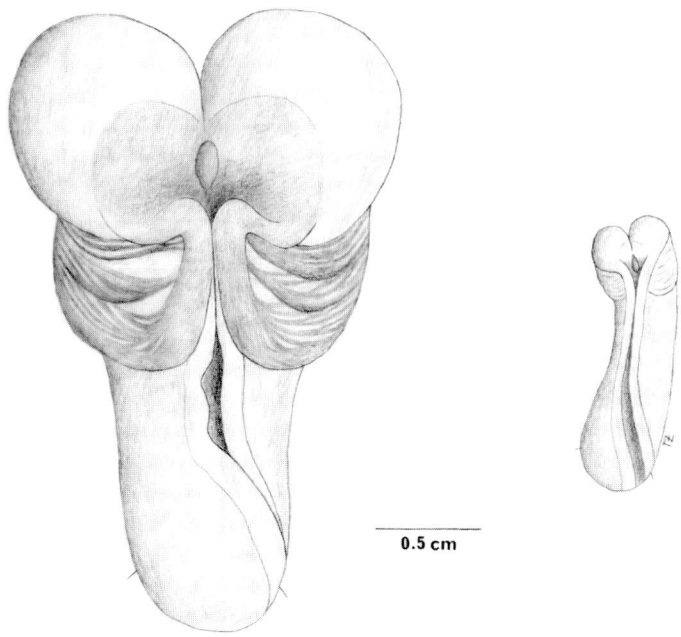

0.5 cm

**Fig. 3** Subsequently everted hemipenis and hemiclitoris, respectively, of the specimens of *T. s. scincoides* shown in Fig. 2 scaled to size for equal snout-vent lengths.
Left: tourniqueted right hemipenis of ZFMK 26804 (HPL about 3-3.5 cm). Right: right hemiclitoris of ZFMK 49319 (HCL about 1.1-1.2 cm). Both in sulcal view.                                                  Sketches: T. Ziegler
Abbreviations: HPL = hemipenis length; HCL hemiclitoris length

its pocket. However, as was described in the previous paragraph, it is known meanwhile that the hemiclitores are also evertible, although this is extremely rarely observed. Nevertheless one should, for precision's sake, replace the commonly used term "everting the hemipenes" with "everting the copulatory organs". If this method is successful and the organ, or at least its base (Fig. 4) can be everted, the thickness of the organ, its lumen, and the distinctiveness of the sperm groove usually provide a fairly good clue whether this is a hemiclitoris or a hemipenis and, thus, whether the specimen is a female or a male. A precondition obviously is that the examiner has an adequate knowledge of the genital structures and has looked at and compared material before. This method is probably also limited for the use in adult specimens, in particular because differences in the respective features will be very difficult to discern in the case of juveniles. Finally will the attempt to force the copulation organs out not always be successful, so that the evaluation will be limited to the organ lumen.

slender and less voluminous. Despite the delicacy of the hemiclitores a more detailed examination will reveal that they show at least indications of the structures also present in the hemipenes (Fig. 3).

**Eversion of the hemipenes:**
This method was described in detail for *Tiliqua r. rugosa* by WAGNER & RICHARDSON (1988). Such manipulation is best performed in an animal that is at its activity temperature. By exerting pressure on the ventral side of the base of the tail it is attempted to extrude at least one of the two hemipenes from

**Adspection of the blood vessels in the cloacal slit:**
Lifting the cloacal shields also provides a view at the blood vessels Arteria and Vena cloacalis and penis, respectively (in a female specimen clitoridis, accordingly) which supply the hemipenes and hemiclitores (comp. MAJUPURIA 1970). These blood vessels can be made to swell

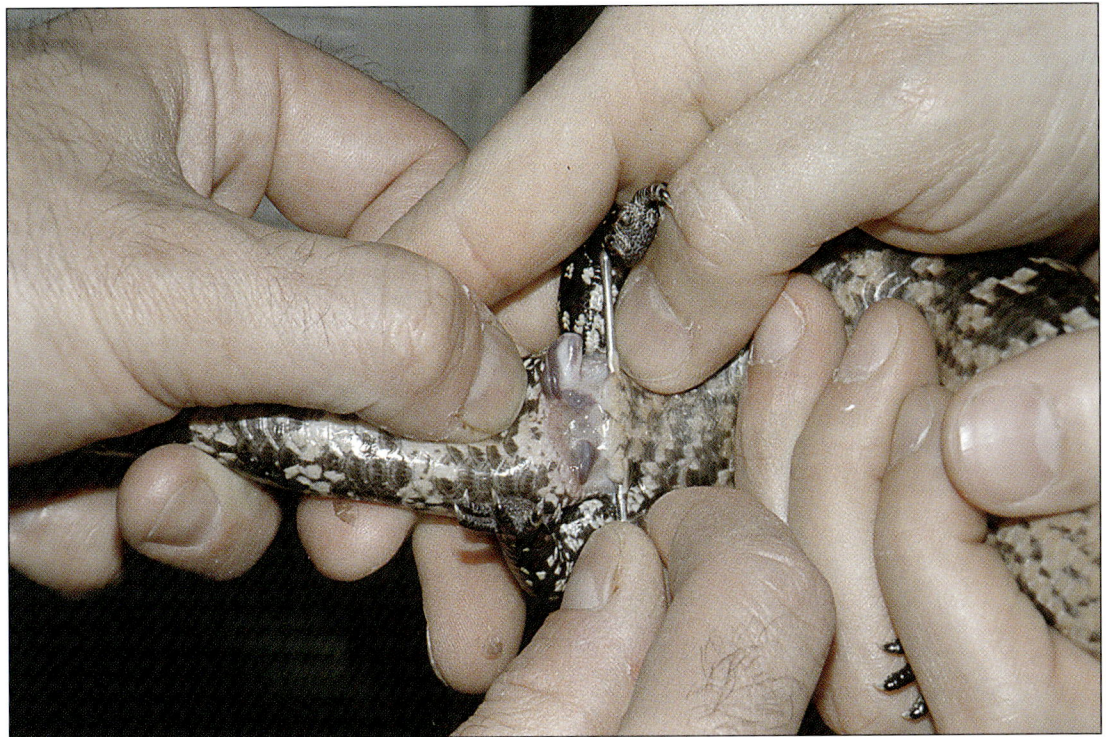

**Fig. 4** Cloacal region of a subadult male *T. gigas*. Clearly recognizable are the partially everted right hemipenis and the distinct blood vessels in the cloacal slit that are swollen as a result of pressure exerted on the base of the tail.                                                                                               Photograph: R. Hitz

by exerting pressure on the base of the tail. They then appear more pronounced in male than in female specimens (Fig. 4). This method is said to be also successful in the case of juvenile specimens (EBBERT pers. comm.).

**Probing:**
In this method a fine olive-headed probe is carefully inserted through the cloaca into the inactive and therefore inverted, that is retracted, copulatory organs. The depth of penetration then indicates the length of the respective organ, with higher values corresponding with hemipenes and lower ones with the smaller and shorter hemiclitores. The only problem encountered here is that the size ratio does not appear to be constant in all squamates, and that they

still have to be studied for most taxa. It must also be taken into consideration that the depth of penetration may be influenced by numerous factors, such as the state of tensing up of the animal, which may lead to unprecise or often even incorrect results (comp. ZIEGLER & BÖHME 1996a, b, 1997).

TREMPER (1985) reported about good probing results for *T. multifasciata*, *T. nigrolutea*, *T. s. scincoides* and *T. s. intermedia*, whereas the depth of penetration was undifferentiated in male and female specimens of *T. gigas*. HITZ (1984) apparently noted sex-correlated differences in the penetration depth in *T. gigas*, *T. nigrolutea*, *T. scincoides* and *T. rugosa*, but was later (HITZ unpubl.) unable to verify the results for many specimens by other sex identification methods. JOGER et al. (1986) eventually were the first to provide evidence of the unreliability of probing for the genus *Tiliqua* in that they were able to disprove the findings of probing in *T. rugosa* by subsequent hormonal analyzes. In closing it must be said that although this method of sex identification is based on a sensible principle, its practicability is rather limited due to the high number of incorrect results.

## 3. Internal (primary) genital organs (testes / ovaries)

### Genital endoscopy:
This method of identifying the sex is most successful in the cases of subadult and adult specimens. It is the only alternative when more simple methods have failed to produce a trustworthy result.

A genital endoscopy is done by making a small surgical incision on the flank through which an arthroscope (as is used in humane medicine) is inserted to provide a view of the primary genital organs, i.e. testes (testicles) and ovaries, respectively (Fig. 5). The method was described in detail by SCHILDGER & WICKER (1987, 1989, 1992). It is unfortunately not suitable for use on juveniles as their internal genital organs (gonads) are visually hard to differentiate. It is only for the very experienced examiner that he is able to identify females at a juvenile stage on the basis of the presence of oviducts and the craniodorsad (forward and up) orientated oviductal ligaments - structures which are obviously absent in males (HÄFELI 1994, SCHILDGER 1995). There is no information available as yet on the point of time from which the sexes of juveniles of *Tiliqua* species can be distinguished.

The success of a genital endoscopy calls for a particular dietic preparation of the animals. Depending on their states of nutrition they have to undergo a period of fasting of four to six weeks prior to the scheduled examination

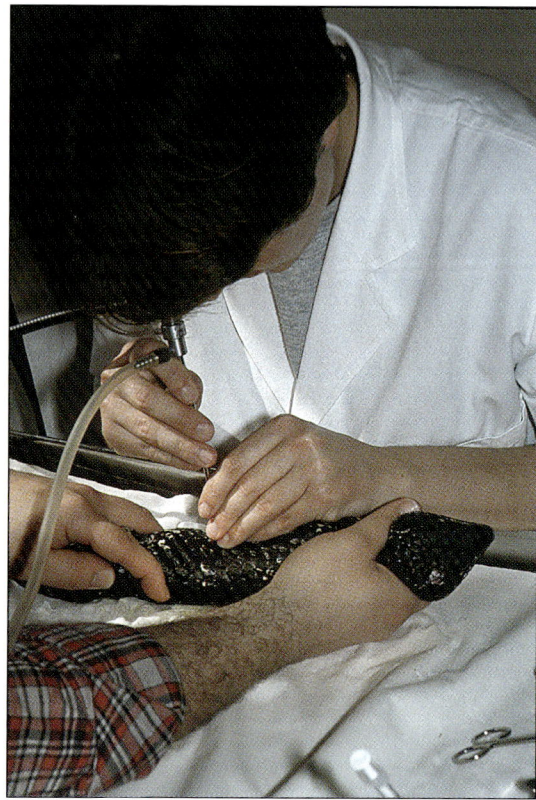

**Fig. 5** Sex endoscopy in a *T. rugosa aspera*
Photograph: R. Hitz

in order to avoid a situation where the access of the optical instrument to the gonads is obstructed by a full gut or overly large abdominal fat bodies. Water must also be withheld for three to seven days before the examination in order to ensure a small urinary bladder. Calm and "tame" specimens may be operated under local anesthesia only, but a short general anesthesia is actually the better alternative. Such a surgical procedure can only be performed by an experienced veterinarian.

### Sonography (ultrasound) and radiography (X-ray):
These so-called graphic procedures are unsuitable for routine sexing of reptiles (SCHILDGER

et al. 1993). While testes are not detectable by a sonography, the follicles on the ovaries of females only become recognizable if they are larger than one millimeter in diameter. This implies that the usability of this method is limited to distinguishing sexually mature females from immature females and males. Sonography can be used, though, to confirm a suspected pregnancy of a female.

A radiographic examination will produce interpretable pictures only in the case of a female with follicles with a diameter of ten millimeters or more. Ovarial and testicular tissue cannot be made visible with this method.

## 4. Observation of various biological aspects

### Behavior:

Specific behavioral patterns may help to recognize the sexes during the mating season. Adult males of about the same size and with similar blood testosterone levels will usually attack each other when they meet. If a female crosses the path of a male, it will usually be examined olfactorily by the latter, before mating may be attempted. On the other hand are smaller males or those with a low testosterone level often ignored by a dominant specimen in captivity or even treated as if they were females. In the most extreme case a dominant male may even attempt to mate with a subordinate specimen of the same sex.

Although the behavior can provide valuable clues as to the sexual identity of specimens in field studies, it should be treated with care in captivity where various factors may have an influence on the behavior.

### Presence of hemipenis exuviae:

ZIEGLER & BÖHME (1996b) already discussed hemipenis exuviae (hemipenis molts) in the light of misinterpretations (also compare the interpretation as "expired sperm" in HAUSCHILD & GASSNER 1995) and with regard to sex identification. Hemipenis exuviae can only be identified with confidence if they are of a certain minimum size, simply because the epithel of the smaller hemiclitores is also shed. This phenomenon has so far only been observed in subadult and adult male, but not in female, blue-tongued skinks.

The hemipenis exuviae of, for example, *Tiliqua nigrolutea* appear as about two to three centimeter long, white, club shaped objects which are often excreted together with feces and uric acid concrements, but also indepen-

**Fig. 6** Freshly deposited hemipenis exuviae of *T. nigrolutea,* discharged together with fecal matter and uric acid concrements        Photograph: R. Hitz

dently from these (Fig. 6). They appear as a fine negative "cast" of the hemipenis lumen that are jelly-like immediately after having been excreted and dry up very quickly. An interesting observation is one made by the senior author whose male *T. nigrolutea* (highland morph) and *T. r. aspera* excreted hemipenis exuviae at intervals of only a few days or even daily during the mating season. This discarding of hemipenis exuviae at an increased frequency was, however, not correlated with a normal shedding of the entire body. It was furthermore observed that the exuviae were excreted without simultaneous defecation and promoted through an intense "wiping" of the cloaca on the ground.

Therefore, if a subadult or adult blue-tongued skink produces hemipenis exuviae independently from a general shedding, it is beyond doubt that it is a male specimen.

## Excretion of yolk masses:

If adult specimens of *Tiliqua* discharge yolk during the course of a year, they are sure to be of female sex. The excreted yolk is the result of infertile eggs that have failed to develop further within the ovaries. The orange yellow material may be firm and egg-shaped, but can also be dissolved and aqueous. This phenomenon is occasionally observed some months after ovulations have occurred (pers. obs. senior author).

## 5. Laboratory methods

**Plasma or serum testosterone evaluation:**
This is an expensive method based on an analysis of the sexual hormones present in the blood. It can only be used in adult specimens. The blood sample is taken from the Vena coccygea ventralis on the ventral side of the tail (SAMOUR et al. 1984), a procedure which has to be performed by a veterinarian. JOGER et al. (1986) found values of < 0.5 ng (nanogram) testosterone/ml serum in female *T. rug-*

*osa* whereas male specimens had values of > 2.5 ng testosterone/ml serum. DÖBELI & HITZ (unpubl.) recorded similar results during respective studies on *T. r. aspera* in 1985. They also examined two four month old juveniles which were found to possess levels of 0.13 and 0.14 ng testosterone/ml plasma, respectively. These values thus are even lower than those of various females examined.

This method can probably be used in all species of *Tiliqua,* although no other studies have become known. It is also still uncertain whether the results are indicative throughout the year. As JOGER et al. (1986), however, took samples of (captive) specimens irrespective of the stage of their reproductive cycles, it can be presumed that the values differ among males and females at all times of the year.

## Fecal steroid patterns:

Due to the problems attached to hormone analyses from blood samples, a non-invasive method has also been developed. It is based on the identification of hormones in urine and fecal samples. DÖBELI et al. (1992) were the first to report about the quantitative presence of sexual steroid hormones and their metabolites (metabolic products) in the feces of reptiles. While the sampling process is easy and entirely harmless for the animal concerned (collection of feces), the analyses in the laboratory, described in detail by DÖBELI et al. (1992) and CASARES (1995), are extremely laborious. If the method is to be used for the identification of sexes, three or four different hormones, or hormone metabolites, have to be identified since females also excrete the male sexual hormone testosterone. These are testosterone, estradiol-17ß, estrone, and pregnandiol-3a-glucuronid. The hormonal values obtained are used to form quotients which are then evaluated. In the case of birds, for example, the quotient "(estrone + estradiol / testosterone) x 100" gives an indication of the sex. Smaller values point to males, higher ones indicate females. It is most unfortunate that respective studies have not been pursued beyond an initial stage for the species of *Tiliqua* (DÖBELI unpubl.) although a large number of samples were collected for just this purpose. One question to be answered during these studies would have been as to from which age sex identification is possible on the basis of fecal steroids.

## Chromosomes:

Blue-tongued skinks possess diploid sets of chromosomes with 2 n = 32 chromosomes (DONNELLAN 1991). Since no heteromorphous sex chromosomes can be found, sex identification based on chromosomal patterns must fail. At least in theory, however, it could be possible that specific cytological research (e.g. by a sex-linked staining of parts of the chromosomes) would be successful.

## DNA technology:

The possible proof of sex-indicative DNA sequences could, at least for some reptile taxa, be the method of a reliable sex identification of the future, as has already been realized in the case of birds (HALVERSON 1990). One of the problems that is bound to be encountered is the fact that most birds possess sex chromosomes whereas many lizards, including the species of *Tiliqua,* lack these. It would be ideal if the required samples could be taken by non-invasive methods such as smears from the oral mucous membranes.

## Projections

As has been demonstrated above a number of methods are available for the identification of the sexes within the genus *Tiliqua.* Every method has its advantages, but unfortunately also its disadvantages - not only for the user, but also for the animal concerned. These must be balanced against each other as to their efficiencies. Every keeper or scientist should therefore give preference to that method, or better a combination of methods, which promise the best possible results. The terrarium keeper will often be satisfied with practising a little patience in order to improve the odds for a successful sexing, which may in the end even become unnecessary when he is surprised with a litter.

## Literature

BÖHME, W. (1995): Hemiclitoris discovered, a fully differentiated erectile structure in female monitor lizards (*Varanus* spp.) (Reptilia: Varanidae). – J. Zool. Syst. Evol. Res., 33: 129–132.

BULL, C.M. & Y. PAMULA (1996): Sexually dimorphic head sizes and reproductive success in the Sleepy Lizard *Tiliqua rugosa*. – J. Zool., London, 240: 511–521.

CASARES, M. (1995): Untersuchung zum Fortpflanzungsgeschehen bei Riesenschildkröten (*Geochelone elephantopus* und *G. gigantea*) und Landschildkröten (*Testudo graeca* und *T. hermanni*) anhand von Ultraschalldiagnostik und Steroidanalysen im Kot. – Zool. Garten N. F. 65(1): 50–76.

DÖBELI, M., M. RÜHLI, M. PFEIFFER, A. RÜBEL, R. HONEGGER & E. ISENBÜGEL (1992): Preliminary results on faecal steroid measurements in tortoises. – The First International Symposium on Faecal Steroid Monitoring: 73–83.

DONNELLAN, S.C. (1991): Chromosomes of Australian lygosomine skinks. – Genetica, 83(3): 207–222.

HÄFELI, W. (1994): Endoskopische Geschlechtsbestimmung juveniler Schildkröten. – Verh. ber. Erkrg. Zootiere., 36: 159–162.

HALVERSON, J. (1990): Avian sex identification by recombinant DNA technology. – Proc. Annual Meeting of Ass. of Avian Vet., Phoenix, AZ: 256–262.

HAUSCHILD, A. & P. GAßNER (1995): Skinke im Terrarium. – Hannover (Landbuch Verlag), 197 S.

HITZ, R. (1984): Geschlechtsbestimmung bei Echsen der Gattungen *Tiliqua* und *Trachydosaurus* mittels der Sondenmethode (Sauria: Scincidae). – Salamandra, Bonn, 20(1): 39–42.

HONEGGER, R.E. (1978): Geschlechtsbestimmung bei Reptilien. – Salamandra, 14(2): 69–79.

JOGER, U., E. WALLIKEWITZ & A. HAUSCHILD (1986): Hormon- und serochemische Untersuchungen zur Bestimmung des Geschlechtes und zur Überprüfung des Gesundheitszustandes bei *Trachydosaurus rugosus* (GRAY, 1827). – Salamandra, Bonn, 22(1): 21–28.

JONES, S. (1987): A report on a reproducible and sustainable system for the captive propagation of the genus *Tiliqua* GRAY 1825. – Pp. 17–25 in COOTE, J. (ed.): Reptiles. – Proceedings of the 1986 U.K. Herpet. Societies Symposium on Captive Breeding. – London (British Herpet. Soc.).

MAJUPURIA, T.C. (1970): The muscles, blood vessels and nerves of the cloaca and copulatory organs of *Uromastyx hardwickii*, GRAY, together with the mode of eversion of the hemipenis, the copulation and the sexual dimorphism. – Zool. Anz., 184: 48–60.

SAMOUR, H.J., D. RISLEY, T. MARCH, B. SAVAGE, O. NIEVA & D.M. JONES (1984): Blood sampling techniques in reptiles. – The Veterinary Record, 12: 472–476.

SCHILDGER, B.-J. (1995): Endoskopische Untersuchungen des Urogenitaltraktes bei Reptilien. – Verh. ber. Erkrg. Zootiere, 37: 305–308.

SCHILDGER, B.-J. & R. WICKER (1987): Endoskopische Geschlechtsbestimmung bei *Trachydosaurus rugosus*. (GRAY, 1827). – Salamandra, Bonn, 23(2/3): 97–105.

– (1989): Sex determination and clinical examination in reptiles using endoscopy. – Herp. Review, 20(1): 9–10.

– (1992): Endoskopie bei Reptilien und Amphibien – Indikationen, Methoden, Befunde. – Der praktische Tierarzt, 1992/6: 516–526.

SCHILDGER, B.-J., M. KRAMER, H. SPÖRLE, M. GERWING & R. WICKER (1993) : Vergleichende bildgebende Ovardiagnostik bei Echsen am Beispiel des Chuckwallas (*Sauromalus obesus*) und des Arguswarans (*Varanus panoptes*). – Salamandra, Bonn, 29(3/4): 240–247.

SHEA, G.M. (1992): The systematics and reproduction of bluetongue lizards of the genus *Tiliqua* (Squamata: Scincidae). – Ph.D. thesis, University of Sydney, 4 Vols.

TREMPER, R.L. (1985): An improved technique for sexing skinks of the genus *Tiliqua*. – 9th Intern. Herp. Symp. on Capt. Prop. & Husb., San Diego: 171–174.

WAGNER, E. & D. RICHARDSON (1988): Breeding the Shingleback Skink, *Trachydosaurus rugosus*. – The Vivarium, California (American Federation of Herpetoculturists), 1(2): 40–41.

ZIEGLER, T. & W. BÖHME (1996 a): Neue Erkenntnisse zur Geschlechtsunterscheidung bei squamaten Reptilien. – Kleintierpraxis, 41(8): 585–590.

– (1996 b): Zur Hemiclitoris der squamaten Reptilien: Auswirkungen auf einige Methoden der Geschlechtsunterscheidung. – herpetofauna, Weinstadt, 18(101): 11–19.

– (1997): Genitalstrukturen und Paarungsbiologie bei squamaten Reptilien, speziell den Platynota, mit Bemerkungen zur Systematik. – Mertensiella (Supplement zu Salamandra), Rheinbach, 8: 207 S.

Authors' addresses:

Dr. Robert Hitz
Am Mülibach 8
CH-9425 Thal, Switzerland

Dr. Thomas Ziegler
Zoologisches Forschungsinstitut und Museum Alexander Koenig
Adenauerallee 160
D-53113 Bonn, Germany

# On the genital morphology of blue-tongued skinks (Scincidae: Lygosominae: *Tiliqua*)

Thomas Ziegler and Wolfgang Böhme

**Key words: Reptilia: Sauria: Scincidae: Lygosominae: *Tiliqua, Cyclodomorphus, Corucia, Egernia*, genital morphology**

## Introduction

This chapter has the goal of portraying the poorly known genital structures of the species of *Tiliqua* and discuss them in a systematic context. The genus *Tiliqua* is presently understood as containing the Australian species *T. adelaidensis, T. multifasciata, T. nigrolutea, T. occipitalis, T. rugosa* and *T. scincoides,* as well as *T. gigas* which is native to New Guinea and eastern Indonesia (a.o. WILSON & KNOWLES 1992). It is obvious that the species of *Tiliqua* can only be compared and characterized as a related cluster if they can be distinguished from their most closely related neighboring genera, in this case *Cyclodomorphus* (or *Hemisphaeriodon,* respectively) as well as *Corucia* and *Egernia*. While the former were previously included in the genus *Tiliqua,* the shingleback *(T. rugosa)* was until recently placed in a monotypic genus, *Trachydosaurus* (comp. COGGER 1992, EHMANN 1992).

Genital morphology features have been shown to be useful taxonomic-phylogenetic markers between species as well as between genera in various groups of lizards (BÖHME 1988, ZIEGLER & BÖHME 1997), so that such an approach promised to be interesting also for blue-tongued skinks. It must be said, though, that due to time, material and space constraints it has not been possible to perform a comprehensive study of the subject given the framework of this book. The following results and discussions should therefore be understood as a first

step towards subsequent studies. It nevertheless appears to be a useful addition to the variety of the aspects dealt with in the present monograph of blue-tongued skinks.

## Material and methods

Our studies were based on the genital organs of 25 specimens (24 males, 1 female) representing 11 species (*Tiliqua:* 6; for comparisons *Cyclodomorphus* and *Corucia* 1 each, *Egernia* 3) all being part of the herpetological collection of the Zoologisches Forschungsinstitut und Museum Alexander Koenig (ZFMK) in Bonn, Germany. We used freshly everted copulatory organs as well as those which had to be everted subsequent to a longer period of preservation in alcohol (for the method see PESANTES 1994, ZIEGLER & BÖHME 1997). We refrained from performing further preparation work on apically incompletely everted genital samples due to the partly very thin and thus easily damaged skin of the apex. In all cases the in part basally twisted copulatory organs were detached from the body and pumped with 70% alcohol before examination in order to attain a turgid condition. It has to be taken into account that due to the preparation method the subsequently everted genital samples (marked * in the text) appear distinctly more elongated as opposed to stout or twisted in freshly everted genitals.

The terminology used here follows BÖHME (1988) and ZIEGLER & Böhme (1997) with the

45

following abbreviations being used: SVL: snout-vent length; TL: tail length; HPL, resp. HCL: hemipenis and hemiclitoris length, respectively.

## Genital morphology

### *Tiliqua scincoides*

ZFMK 26804*: Australia, Sydney (SVL: 31, TL: 17.5, HPL: ca. 3-3.5 cm)
ZFMK 26805*: Australia, Sydney (SVL: 25.2, TL: 14.5, HPL: ca. 2-2.5 cm)
ZFMK 49318*: Australia, NSW: 4 km N Goolgowi (SVL: 29, HPL: ca. 3 cm)
ZFMK 49319*: Australia, NSW: Cave Beach,

Jervis Bay (SVL: 31.3, SL: 18.2, HCL: ca. 1.1-1.2 cm)

Hemipenes of ZFMK 26804 (Fig. 1) elongate, unpigmented. Sperm groove bordered with distinct lips that rise almost straight from a basal arc to the apex and each laterally flank the two apical lobes (strongly inflated in turgid condition) below the terminal apex. This bilateral expansion of the sperm groove is guided by the equally laterally directed sulcus lips. Where the two apical lobes meet sulcally and the sperm groove extends laterally onto the two lobes, an elongate point of tissue is recognizable with the closely surrounding tissue of the two apical

**Fig. 1** Basally tourniqueted right hemipenis of *Tiliqua scincoides* (ZFMK 26804) in turgid state. Left: sulcal view; right: asulcal view.                                     Sketch: T. Ziegler

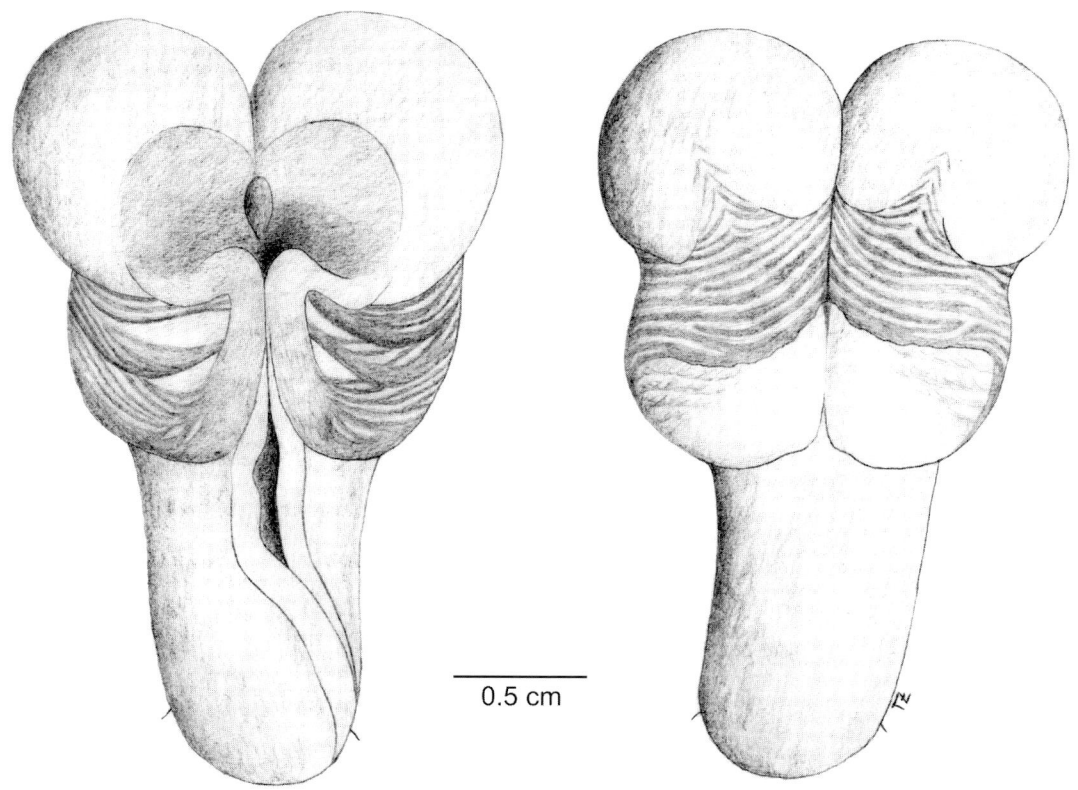

0.5 cm

lobes appearing reinforced. Asulcally, the transitory area between the truncus and apex is at a turgid state marked by two enormously inflated, thin-skinned rises which meet centrally at an inconspicuously compacted tissue seam. Some irregular plicae (petala sensu SAVAGE 1997) already run along each of the outer margins of the two rises, but are relatively difficult to discern. Above these two enormously inflated rises the actual plica ornamentation stretches laterally up to the sulcus, dorsally reaching the two apical lobes at the center of the asulcal side. These plicae are differentiated from the truncus by a puffy tissue seam which is particularly obvious asulcally. Both ends of this tissue seam rise on the sulcal side from the sulcus lips in the basal apex region, then turns towards the base, only to turn sidewards at the transition to the truncus and run to the middle of the asulcal side where it again turns upwards. Asulcally the plicae rise apically in the middle between the two apical lobes, then run obliquely towards the base - circumventing a basally expanding tissue area that is not visible in the drawing - eventually turning laterally, or sulcally, respectively, by following the course of the tissue seam; at the transition line from the asulcal to the sulcal side the plicae rise once more steeply on the lateral side, only to descend again on the sulcal side, finally ending centrally in the outer sulcus lip region. Due to the partly irregularly connected plicae the plica ornamentation is difficult to characterize. It remains noteworthy, though, that the altogether slightly more than 10 plicae, which each run in a curved fashion from the outer sulcus lips to the asulcal side, are grouped on the sulcal side in three larger plica compartments that are separated from each other by more or less plica free areas. Furthermore, the top ones of the about 15 asulcal plica rows extend up to the center of the two apical lobes with each one forming an inverted V. The pedicel appears smooth without any further ornamentation.

This description also applies to the hemipenes of ZFMK 26805 and ZFMK 49318, although fewer plicae are discernible on the smaller hemipenes of ZFMK 26805. The right hemiclitoris of ZFMK 49319 also shows the hemipenial structure in principle, although the plicae are hardly visible due to the organ being much smaller, i.e. less than half as long and distinctly less voluminous than the hemipenes of ZFMK 26804 (for more detailed data on this subject see the chapter on sex identification in this book).

### Tiliqua adelaidensis
ZFMK 46066*: Australia (SVL: 7.9, TL: 6.2, HPL: ca. 0.7-0.8 cm)

Comparing the available, distinctly smaller and apically partly destroyed right hemipenis of *T. adelaidensis* with that of *T. scincoides,* a similar structure cannot be overlooked. Like in *T. scincoides,* numerous plicae run from the outer sulcus lips to the asulcal apical region, but a more precise description is rendered impossible by the state of the only available genital sample. It is noteworthy, though, that, as a result of terminal lateral course of the sulcus lips, the two apical lobes are also enormously bulged and inflated laterally.

### Tiliqua gigas
ZFMK 48567: New Guinea (SVL: 25, TL: 24, HPL: ca. 2-2.5 cm)
ZFMK 50427: New Guinea (SVL: 22.7, TL: 16.7, HPL: ca. 2 cm)

The available hemipenes of *T. gigas* correspond largely with those of *T. scincoides.* It is only that the plica ornamentation of the right hemipenis of ZFMK 48567 (Fig. 2) appears to be sectioned in four plica compartments sulcally, in contrast to the left hemipenis which is, however, incompletely everted apically. A tendency to form four rather than three plica compartments is also notable on the two apically not fully everted hemipenes of ZFMK 50427.

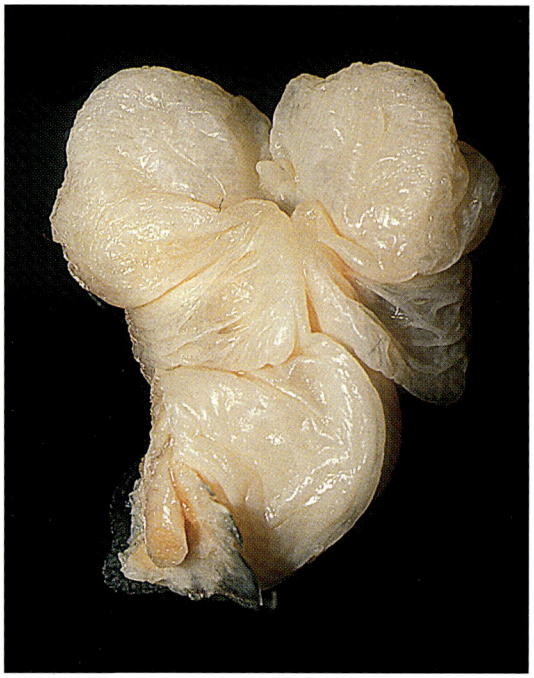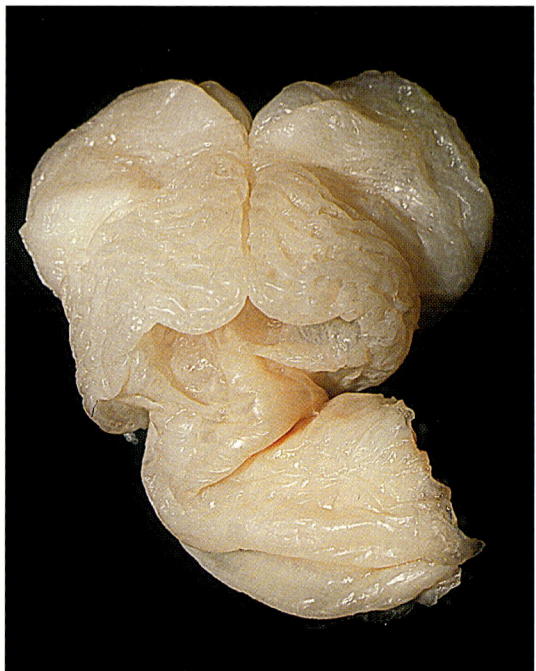

**Fig. 2**  Partly turgid right hemipenis of *Tiliqua gigas* (ZFMK 48567). Left: sulcal view; right: asulcal view.
Photograph:  T. Ziegler

### Tiliqua multifasciata
ZFMK 45788: Australia, WA, Port Headland
(SVL: 21.5, TL: 8.5+, HPL ca. 2 cm)

The hemipenes of ZFMK 45788 are apically
not completely everted, but nevertheless correspond largely with the hemipenes of  *T.
scincoides*. Of particular note are the enormously inflated asulcal rises which are distinctly covered with numerous plicae. The
plicae on the sulcal side also appear to be
grouped in four rather than three compartments.

### Tiliqua nigrolutea
ZFMK 66592*: Australia,  NSW, Blue Mountains (SVL: 28.5, TL: 14.7, HPL: 3-3.5 cm)

The available hemipenes of the highland
morph of *T. nigrolutea* (Fig. 3) correspond

well in their general appearance with those of
*T. scincoides,* save for the plicae being more
numerous and more distinctly discernible on
the two asulcally strongly inflated rises. Also,
there are more inverted V-shaped plicae running towards the center of the two apical lobes
asulcally. On the sulcal side there are only two
plica compartments recognizable which spare
out a large plica-free window in the center.

### Tiliqua rugosa
ZFMK 14300: Australia (SVL: 26.3, TL: 6,
HPL: ca. 1.5-2 cm)
ZFMK 50022*: Australia, NSW, Kinchega NP
(SVL: 30.5, SL: 6.5, HPL: ca. 2.5 cm)

The hemipenis samples of *T. rugosa* correspond
fairly well with those of *T. scincoides*. Cope
(1896) had already made incidental notes on
the hemipenis of *Trachysaurus* (= *Trachydo-*

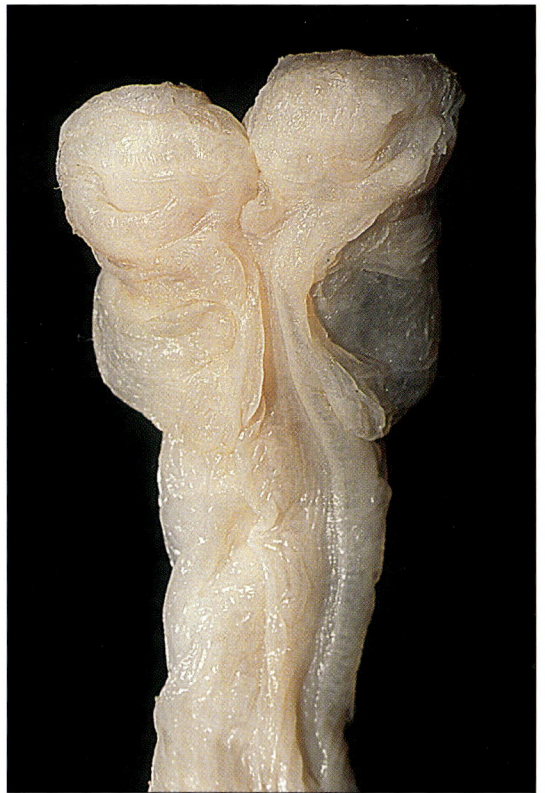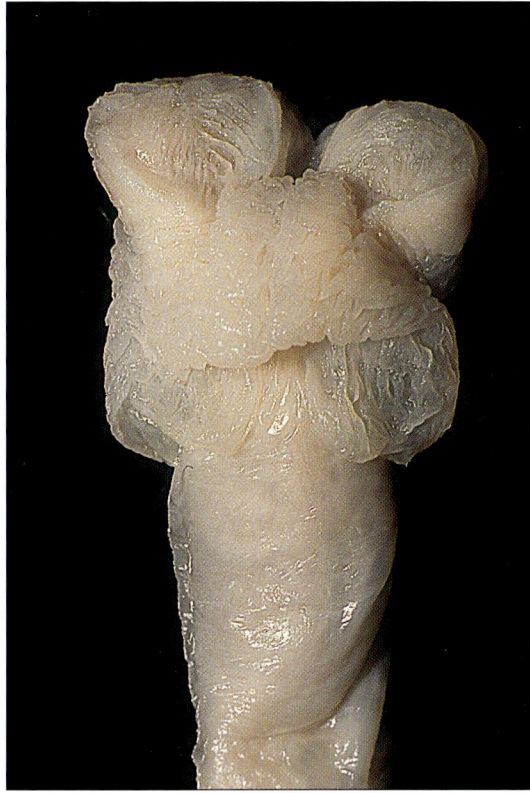

**Fig. 3** Partly turgid right hemipenis of *Tiliqua nigrolutea* (ZFMK 66592). Left: sulcal view; right: asulcal view. Note the elongated shape of the subsequently everted organ (the differences in length of the apical lobes are a result of an incomplete eversion). Photograph: T. Ziegler

*saurus,* implying *Trachydosaurus rugosus,* today *Tiliqua rugosa*): "Here the laminae diverge from the sulcus proximad and turn to a horizontal direction, meeting opposite the sulcus in a chevron directed distad."

### Cyclodomorphus gerrardii
ZFMK 49848, ZFMK 51418, ZFMK 65614: Australia (SVL: 15.3-21, TL: 18.5- 25.3, HPL: ca. 1-1.5 cm)

Although the available genital samples of *Cyclodomorphus gerrardii* clearly follow the structural pattern of the hemipenes of *T. scincoides* (Fig. 4), both the apical lobes are less distinct and less rounded. Furthermore are the two sulcus lips less laterally orientated apically, but rather run more obliquely upwards where they end in a bulged manner similar to the two apical lobes. On the sulcal side a wide plica free field is spared out above the most basal one of the 3 plica compartments.

### Corucia zebrata
ZFMK 50421, ZFMK 50486, ZFMK 50713, ZFMK 54295-9: Solomon Islands (SVL: 25-29.5, TL: 32.5-38, HPL: ca. 2-2.5 cm)

Following the principle structural pattern of the currently available genital samples of rep-

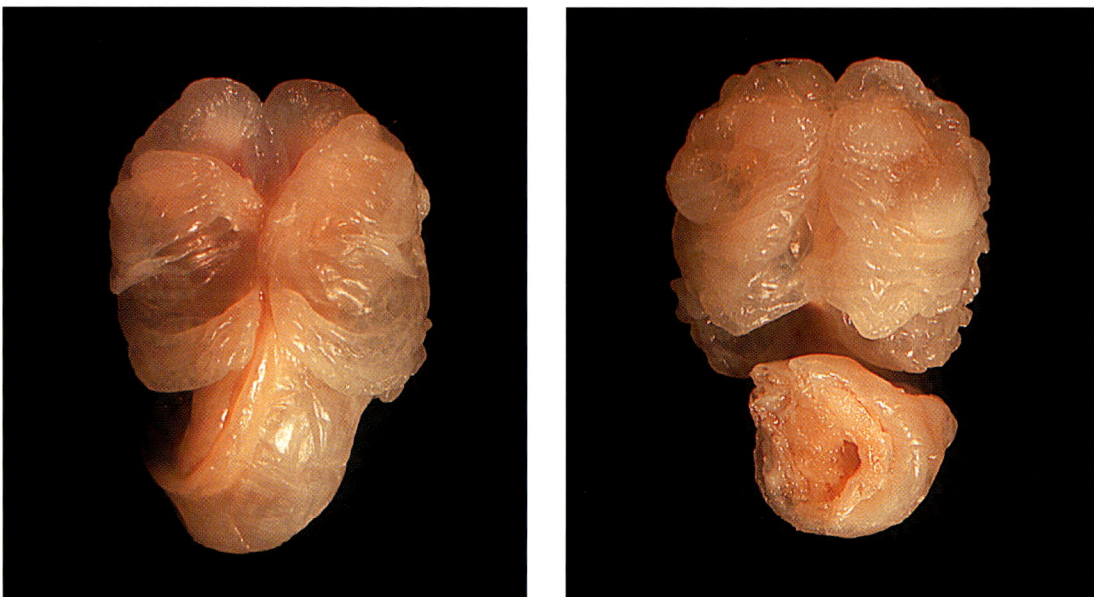

**Fig. 4** Largely turgid left hemipenis of *Cyclodomorphus gerrardii* (ZFMK 65614, Australia, SVL 15.3, TL 18.5, HPL ca. 1.5 cm). Left: sulcal view; right: asulcal view. Photograph: T. Ziegler

**Fig. 5** Left hemipenis of *Corucia zebrata* (ZFMK 50421, Solomon Islands, Guadalcanal, SVL 29.5, TL 36.5, HPL ca. 2.5 cm) in turgid state. Left: sulcal view; right: asulcal view. Asulcally the bloated and protruding tissue seam above the two mightily bloated rises largely shrouds the few plicae. Sketch: T. Ziegler

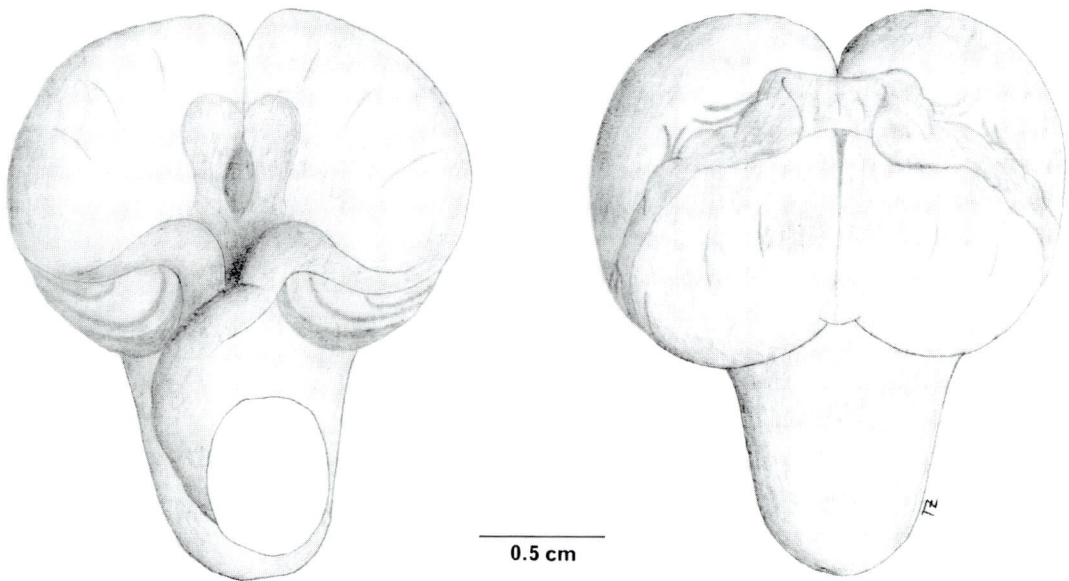

0.5 cm

resentatives of the genus *Tiliqua,* the hemipenes of *Corucia zebrata* (Fig. 5) exhibit significantly fewer and hardly distinct plicae. Basically, there are each only three singular plicae visible sulcally, which branch out, partly in an irregular fashion, asulcally. Above the enormously developed asulcal seam there are only a few plicae, of which the upper ones run almost in an inverted V-shape and hardly recognizable to the center of the apical lobes. Fully everted the apical lobes are enormously expanded and inflated, as are the two asulcal rises, whose outer margins hardly show, or even lack, plica-like structures.

### Egernia spp.

ZFMK 47901: *E. depressa,* ZFMK 45949: *E. hosmeri,* ZFMK 53796: *E. margaretae*

Only a few, partly incompletely everted, partly poorly preserved hemipenes of about 0.6 to 1 cm in length were available for comparisons. Notwithstanding these constraints these show a structure related to the genital samples of *Tiliqua,* including numerous plicae which run from the sulcus lips to the apical asulcal side, an apically diverging sperm groove, the inflated, although in *Egernia* spp. differently shaped, apex that does not end with two distinctly developed lobes - compare BÖHME (1988) - and the two asulcally inflated rises.

### Discussion

With regard to a polarisation of the character states, an ornamentation with numerous plicae has to be considered primitive, whilst a reduction of the numbers of plicae indicates a derived condition according to BÖHME (1988). Following BÖHME (l.c.) an entire or unbranched hemipenis is also to be interpreted as primitive. GREER (1979) categorized the entirely everted hemipenes of Australian Lygosominae into the "basically columnar hemipenis" of the *Egernia* and *Eugongylus*

group ("with a relatively short, columnar base and a slightly bulbous or bilobed cap"), and the "deeply bifurcated hemipenis" of the *Sphenomorphus* group ("with a long narrow base and two equally long bifurcations").

Also with regard to the respective illustrations 11 to 15 in GREER (l.c.) it becomes obvious that the present *Tiliqua* hemipenes, as well as those of *Cyclodomorphus, Corucia* and *Egernia,* all correspond with the former hemipenis type despite the hemipenes of *Tiliqua* and *Corucia* forming two distinct inflated lobes apically.

As a result of the small number and partly poor state of the genital samples of *Egernia* currently available to us it is not possible to produce a comprehensive evaluation of the character states, although the differently structured apex of the *Egernia* hemipenis already suggests the more distant systematic position from *Tiliqua* that could be expected. Compared with *Tiliqua, Cyclodomorphus* and *Egernia,* the few, hardly pronounced plicae of the hemipenis of *Corucia zebrata* must be considered reduced and therefore represent a derived state (sensu BÖHME 1988). Together with the numerous adaptive apomorphies they serve as an autapomorphy that can be used to validate the genus *Corucia.*

The phylogenetic relationships of the genus *Cyclodomorphus* (or *Hemisphaeriodon* , respectively), which was temporarily included in *Tiliqua,* can also not entirely be clarified based on the now available study of their genital morphology. Referring to the results from immunological studies obtained by HUTCHINSON (1980) which showed distinct differences between the species *gerrardii* and representatives of the genus *Tiliqua,* the different formation of the apex of the hemipenes of *Cyclodomorphus gerrardii* does, however, at least not contradict its exclusion from the genus *Tiliqua.*

If one now compares the hemipenes of the present species of *Tiliqua* among each other, one finds a common structural design, but on closer inspection partly also interspecific differences. It must be stated, though, that the small sample size necessitates further studies using a larger number of genital samples of a better quality to demonstrate as to how far these differences are constant, i.e. whether they can definitely be considered specifically indicative. This will then also facilitate a phylogenetic analysis within the genus. It would be particularly important to clarify as to how far the development of the plica ornamentation - with its numerous, partly irregular, and hardly describable reticulations among the plicae - is subject to certain rules or varies intraspecifically (compare in this respect the development of the sulcal plica compartments in *T. gigas*).

It remains noteworthy that the hemipenes of *T. rugosa* fit perfectly in the overall picture of the genital morphology of *Tiliqua*. This also supports the findings by HUTCHINSON (1980) who demonstrated on the basis of serum-immunological electrophoresis a close phylogenetic relationship of the species *rugosa* - which was temporarily assigned to a monotypic genus, *Trachydosaurus* - with the genus *Tiliqua*. The closeness of this relationship to the genus *Tiliqua* is furthermore apparent from the hybridization of *T. rugosa* with *T. nigrolutea* as well as with *T. scincoides* (SHEA 1992, HAUSCHILD & GASSNER 1995). This criterion corresponds with the generic concept of DUBOIS (1988) who, among others, tried to use infertile hybridization for establishing a more objective definition of the category genus.

DUBOIS, A. (1988): The genus in zoology: a contribution to the theory of evolutionary systematics. – Mém. Mus. natn. Hist. nat., Paris, (zool.) 140: 1–122.

EHMANN, H. (1992): Encyclopedia of Australian animals. Reptiles. – Angus & Robertson, Pymble/New South Wales, 495 pp.

GREER, A. E. (1979): A phylogenetic subdivision of Australian skinks. – Records of the Australian Museum 32 (8): 339–371.

HAUSCHILD, A. & P. GAßNER (1995): Skinke im Terrarium. – Landbuch-Verlag, Hannover, 197 S.

HUTCHINSON, M. N. (1980): The systematic relationships of the genera *Egernia* and *Tiliqua* (Lacertilia: Scincidae). A review and immunological reassessment. – in BANKS, C. B. & A. A. MARTIN (eds.): Proc. Melbourne Herp. Symp. – Melbourne: 176–193.

PESANTES, O. S. (1994): A method for preparing the hemipenis of preserved snakes. – J. Herpetol. 28 (1): 93–95.

SAVAGE, J. M. (1997): On terminology for the description of the hemipenes of squamate reptiles. – Herp. Journal 7: 23–25.

SHEA, G. M. (1992): The systematics and reproduction of bluetongue lizards of the genus *Tiliqua* (Squamata: Scincidae). – Dissertation, Universität Sydney.

WILSON, S. K. & D. G. KNOWLES (1992): Australia's reptiles. – Collins, Sydney, 447 pp.

ZIEGLER, T. & W. BÖHME (1997): Genitalstrukturen und Paarungsbiologie bei squamaten Reptilien, speziell den Platynota, mit Bemerkungen zur Systematik. – Mertensiella, Rheinbach 8: 1–207.

## Literature

BÖHME, W. (1988): Zur Genitalmorphologie der Sauria: funktionelle und stammesgeschichtliche Aspekte. – Bonn. zool. Monogr. 27: 1–176.

COGGER, H. G. (1992): Reptiles and Amphibians of Australia. – 5th edition. Reed books Pty. Ltd., Chatswood/NSW, 755 pp.

COPE, E. D. (1896): On the hemipenes of the Sauria. – Proc. Acad. Nat. Sci. Philadelphia 48: 461–467.

Authors' addresses
Dr. Thomas Ziegler
Prof. Dr. Wolfgang Böhme
Zoologisches Forschungsinstitut und Museum Alexander Koenig
Adenauerallee 160
53113 Bonn, Germany

# Complications observed during pregnancy and birth in blue-tongued skinks

ROBERT HITZ

**Key words: Reptilia: Sauria: Scincidae: *Tiliqua*, pathology, pregnancy, birth**

## Introduction

Pregnancy and birth occasionally bring about complications in blue-tongued skinks kept under terrarium conditions. These include inflammation of the ovaries and oviducts as a result of abnormal yolk production, malformed juveniles, stillborn youngs, and dystokia (obstruction preventing birth). Respective experiences have been made with *T. gigas* (UNVERZAGT pers. comm.), the highland morph of *T. nigrolutea* (HITZ pers. obs., RÖHE pers. comm.), *T. occipitalis* (RÖHE pers. comm.), *T. rugosa aspera* (HITZ pers. obs., SCHIBERNA pers. comm.), *T. scincoides intermedia* (HAUSCHILD pers. comm.), and *T. s. scincoides* (TURNER 1996, UNVERZAGT pers. comm.).

For a better understanding of this chapter some information on vivipary, placentation, and the female reproductive cycle may prove useful.

## Viviparity and placentation

The members of the genus *Tiliqua* belong to the "truly livebearing" reptiles. They possess a pair of oviducts which lead from the ovaries to the cloaca where each side has its own opening in the so-called urodeum of the cloaca (LIMBERGER pers. comm.). During ovulation eggs charged with a lot of yolk migrate into the oviducts. They do not form egg shells, but instead parts of the egg membranes, which envelop embryo and yolk partly or fully (chorion and allantois), come into contact with the mucous membrane of the oviduct. This means that the oviducts become the place of placentation in the case of a pregnancy and therefore correspond in their function with

the uterus of a mammal. One could also say: "the oviducts serve the pregnant blue-tongued skink as "uteri". The upper layer of the chorioallantois and that of the uterus degenerate in part so that the motherly and embryonic blood vessels come into close contact, and the motherly and embryonic parts of tissue attach over large surface areas. This simple form of placentation is called allanto-placentation (FLYNN 1923, WEEKES 1935), or, using a more recent nomenclature, chorioallantois-placentation (STEWART & BLACKBURN 1988). The yolk sac membrane also unites with the uterus wall, a phenomenon called omphaloplacenta ("yolk sac placenta"). The species of *Tiliqua* so far studied in this respect (*T. s. scincoides*, FLYNN 1923, *T. nigrolutea* and *T. s. scincoides*, WEEKES 1935) therefore show a combined form of placentation, i.e. a chorioallantois placenta and an omphaloplacenta. The developing embryo is, on one side, fed from the yolk sac, and, on the other side, there is a metabolic exchange via the blood vessels in the placentation zone. The amount of yolk of eggs produced by the livebearing species of *Tiliqua* is, by the way, equal to that of comparable oviparous (egg laying) lizards. During birth the egg membranes detach themselves from the uterus walls which, due to the simple connection does not cause any bleeding.

## The female reproductive cycle (ovarian cycle)

According to LICHT (1972), female reptiles show less variation in their ovarian cycle (breeding cycle) than male specimens in their testicular cycle. This was also found to be true for the species of *Tiliqua* as was shown through studies done by SHEA (1992). During most of the year only small follicles can be traced on the ovaries, indicating a low degree of ovarian activity. The weeks preceding a breeding season are then marked by a rapid growth of these follicles as a result of changes in the environment which in turn triggers hormonal activities. Simultaneously, yolk is synthesized in the body and deposited in the follicles. The peak of the mating season is eventually the time when mating, fertilization and ovulation take place. The ripe eggs migrate into the ovaries during ovulation, where fertilization, placentation and eventually the embryonic development take place. Subsequent to this period of time a regression (involution) of the non-ovulated follicles can be observed, and gravid specimens develop corpora lutea. Infertile eggs are usually discharged during birth in liquidized or compact form (Fig. 1). Their yolk serves the simultaneously born juveniles and the mother as food (BULL et al. 1993).

As was mentioned above, the reproductive cycle is primarily driven by environmental cues (DUVALL et al. 1982, MATZ 1984), the most

important of which is the temperature (DUVALL et al. 1982). This is certainly also the case in species of *Tiliqua* from moderate and subtropical zones, whereas in species from tropical regions it appears that, besides temperatures, moisture levels also play a role as triggers because in these species the seasonality of reproduction can be linked to the changes between dry and rainy season.

### Ovariitis (ovarial inflammation) and salpingitis (inflammation of the oviduct)

Terraria are often marked by an insufficient gradient between places of high and those of low temperature. This prevents the animals kept from observing an optimum thermoregulation. At the same time the drop of the temperatures at night is far too insignificant over long periods of the year. These unnatural temperature conditions cause a malfunction of the vitellogenesis (production of yolk) so that overly large masses of yolk are deposited in the follicles. In an ideal scenario these excessively large eggs are discharged after ovulation, or after the normal gestation period during the birth of the juveniles, or separately.

In unfavorable cases such masses of yolk may, however, degenerate (caseate) within the ovaries or oviducts. The result is then a severe inflammation within the ovary or the affected oviduct. This inflammation and the resorption of toxic protein catabolites (products of decomposition) lead to a severe disturbance of the general health status of the affected animal. Diseased females discontinue feeding, behave apathetic, and breathe with difficulty. The diagnosis is then based on recent history (breeding season, observed matings, increase in body volume) and confirmed by a radiographic (X-ray) examination during which the possible presence of other problems is excluded. The only viable measure is then the immediate surgical removal of the degenerated yolk masses by Cesarean section with a subsequent treatment of the animal with an appropriate antibiotic (e.g. enrofloxacin)

**Fig. 1** Two normal-sized yolk masses of infertile eggs deposited by a *T. nigrolutea* during birth
Photograph: R. Hitz

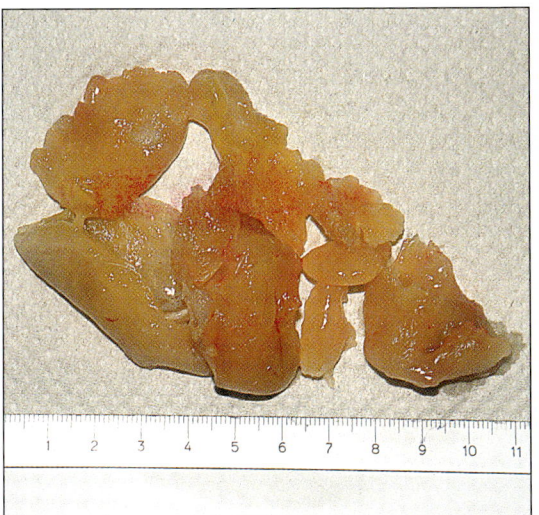

**Fig. 2** Abnormally large yolk masses surgically removed from a *T. nigrolutea* by cesarean section
Photograph: R. Hitz

**Fig. 3** *T. nigrolutea,* highland morph, malformed baby
Photograph: R. Hitz

plus a supply with an electrolyte-glucose-amino acid solution. Affected animals may, however, just die unexpectedly.

If the oversized yolk masses do neither cause an inflammation nor an intoxication (poisoning), they may become an absolute dystokia (Fig. 2). In this case the animal will show labor activity for a prolonged period of time without parturition or yolk being discharged. Again, the only way to save the female is by immediate Cesarean section.

## Malformations

Malformed juveniles (Fig. 3) are an occasional occurrence with contortions of the vertebral column being most frequent. Heavily bent, stiffened juveniles cannot be borne naturally, but have to be delivered by Cesarean section. ROSS & MARZEK (1994) named as causes for the development of deformations, too high or too low keeping temperatures as well as inbreeding. It can also not be excluded that food shortages, poisons, inappropriately applied medication, hazardous radiation, and spontaneous mutations in the genetic material may cause malformations.

## Stillborn juveniles

An embryo may perish at any point of time before or during birth. This phenomenon has been observed in captive kept *T. nigrolutea* (pers. obs.), as well as in *T. nigrolutea* and *T. s. scincoides* (TURNER 1996). ROSS & MARZEK (1994) again presumed as possible causes too low or too high environmental temperatures, whilst TURNER (1996) took a more generalized standpoint and suggested the cause to be captivity related stress.

If normally formed juveniles perish only during birth, a disturbed labor process is usually the reason, more precisely an incorrect position of one or more fetuses within the birth canals. Exceedingly large yolk masses may also hinder the birth of young and so lead to their demise. If a birth does not proceed normally, emergency aid by a veterinarian is required.

## Obstetrics for blue-tongued skinks

Female blue-tongued skinks usually give birth during the day when they have reached their activity temperature (BULL et al. 1993, HITZ pers. obs.). If no juvenile has been born within one hour subsequent to regular contractions of the abdomen at short intervals and after the breaking of water was observed, veterinarian assistance is indicated. A radiographic examination will be able to show why the birth is delayed.

If uterine inertia is diagnosed, it may be based on a calcium deficiency and can be overcome through an injection with a generally compatible calcium preparation (ZWART 1995). If this measure does not bring about the expected success, an injection of the labor hormone oxytocin is given 1-2 hours later (dosage: 1-2 International Units per 1000 g body mass). Furthermore, a lubricant may be instilled in the birth canal. If all these actions do not lead to the birth of at least one juvenile within 1-2 hours, a Cesarean section becomes inevitable (Fig. 4).

The operation is performed under general anesthesia. Since the injectable anesthetic ketaminhydrochloride, dosed at 20-60 mg/kg BM (SCHILDGER et al. 1993, ZWART 1995), commonly employed for many reptiles, results only in an insufficiently deep narcosis, the gas isofluran should be administered in addition (or as exclusive anesthetic) via a tracheotube directly into the breathing system (SCHILDGER pers. comm. 1995). The animal is fixed in dorsal recumbancy and its body cavity opened by a paramedian longitudinal cut (one centimeter off the ventral midline) at the border between the center and hind thirds of the body. Some specialists do not stitch up the opened oviduct after the contents have been removed as the margins of the wound should close rapidly without as-

**Fig. 4** Cesarean section in a *T. scincoides intermedia* to retrieve a stillborn baby

Photograph: A. Hauschild

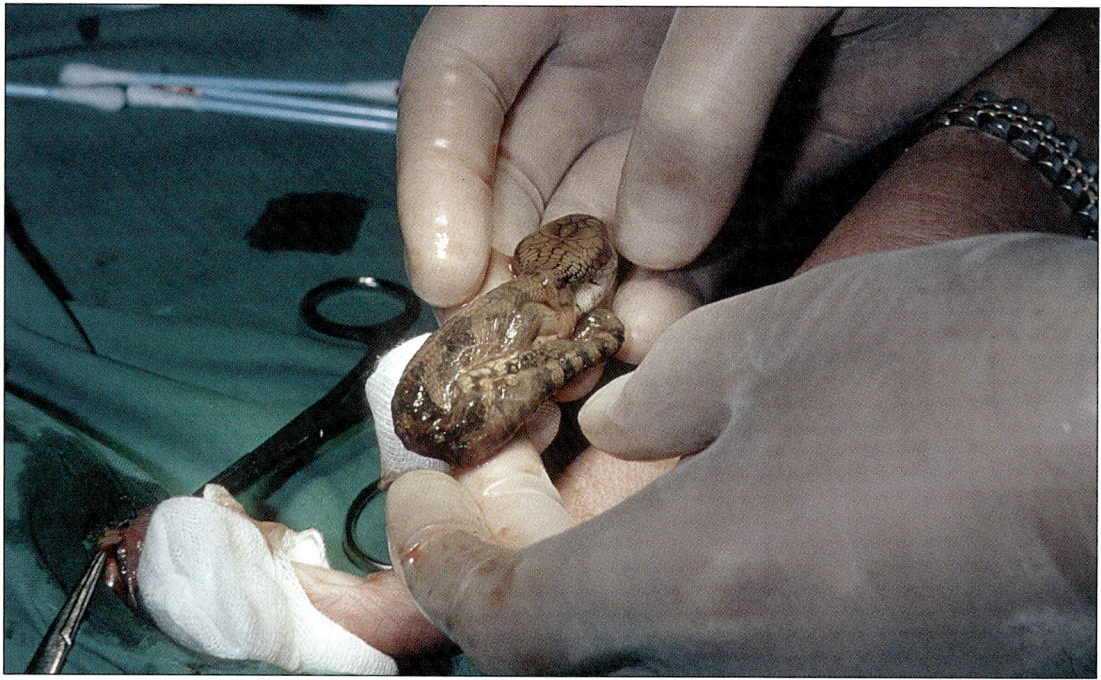

sistance. The author prefers to apply an oviduct suture with fine, resorbable suture material in order to eliminate the possibility of future abdominal pregnancies (one such case is known in *T. nigrolutea* [RÖHE pers. comm.]). The cut in the scaly ventral skin is stitched up with non-resorbable suture material in protruding U-seams. The patient is then supplied with a broad-band antibiotic (enrofloxacin for example) for the following 5-7 days. Accounting for the slowly progressing healing process the stitches may only be removed after four weeks. Normally formed juveniles obtained in the process do usually not require further medical attention.

## Frequency of the described complications

No relevant information exists as to the situation in nature. SHEA (pers. comm. 1996) mentioned that the dissection of some wild caught gravid specimens of *T. scincoides* revealed mummified embryos in the oviducts. The author has access to data obtained from 16 births in the highland morph of *T. nigrolutea* under terrarium conditions with various terrarium keepers. In total 42 juveniles were born, with an average of 2.6 (1-5) juveniles per litter. The following complications were noted: stillborn fetuses in two births, malformations in four births, abnormal yolk masses in three births. Two cases were marked by more than one of the mentioned complications. Complications were observed in six out of sixteen (that is 37.5%!) births. In three of sixteen births a Cesarean section was necessary.

No such quantitative information is available for the other species of *Tiliqua* mentioned in the introduction besides *T. nigrolutea*. It cannot be excluded that the described pathological phenomena are more rare in blue-tongued skinks of tropical origin since the temperature regime in a terrarium may come closer to the situation in their natural environment as opposed to the case of animals from moderate and subtropical regions. It remains to be hoped that husbandry conditions closer to the optimum will eliminate the mentioned problems in future.

## Literature

BULL, C.M., Y. PAMULA & L. SCHULZE (1993): Parturition in the Sleepy Lizard, *Tiliqua rugosa*. – Journal of Herpetology, 27: 489–492.

DUVALL, D., L.J. GUILLETTE JR. & R.E. JONES (1982): Environmental Control of Reptilian Breeding Cycles. – Pp. 201–231 in GANS, C. & B. HUE (edts): Biology of the Reptilia. – Vol. 13.

FLYNN, T.T. ( 1923 ): On the occurrence of a true allantoplacenta of the conjoint type in an Australian lizard. – Records of the Australian Museum, 14(1): 72–77 .

LICHT, P. (1972): Environmental physiology of reptilian breeding cycles: Role of temperature. – General and Comparative Endocrinology, Supplement 3: 477–488.

MATZ, G. (1984): La réproduction des reptiles et les facteurs de son induction. – Acta Zoologica et Pathologica Antverpiensia, 78: 33–68.

ROSS, R.A. & G. MARZEK (1994): Riesenschlangen – Zucht und Pflege. – Ruhmannsfelden (bede-Verlag), 245 S.

SCHILDGER, B.-J., R. BAUMGARTNER, W. HÄFELI, A. RÜBEL & E. ISENBÜGEL (1993): Narkose und Immobilisation bei Reptilien. – Tierärztl. Prax., 21: 361– 376.

SHEA, G.M. (1992): The systematics and reproduction of bluetongue lizards of the genus *Tiliqua* (Squamata: Scincidae). – Ph.D. thesis, University of Sydney, 4 Vols.

STEWART, J.R. & D.G. BLACKBURN (1988): Reptilian placentation: Structural diversity and terminology. – Copeia, 4: 839–852 .

TURNER, G. (1996): Some litters of the eastern blue-tongued skink *Tiliqua scincoides scincoides* (Scincidae). – Herpetofauna, 26(2): 39–47.

WEEKES, H.C. (1935): A review of placentation among reptiles with particular regard to the function and evolution of the placenta. – Proceedings of the Zoological Society of London, 2: 625–645.

ZWART, P. (1995): Echsen. – S. 809–858 in GABRISCH, K. & P. ZWART (Hrsg.): Krankheiten der Heimtiere. – Hannover (Schlütersche), 1000 S.

Author's address
Dr. Robert Hitz
Am Mülibach 8
CH-9425 Thal, Switzerland

# A contribution to the feeding of blue-tongued skinks

CAROLIN DENNERT

**Key words: Reptilia: Sauria: Scincidae: *Tiliqua, Cyclodomorphus*, diet**

The diet of bluetongues in their natural environment is composed of a wide variety of plant and animal foods. With the exception of the snail-eating pink-tongued skink, *Cyclodomorphus gerrardii,* they may therefore be considered omnivores. Skinks belong to those reptiles in which the sense of smell is well developed. This sense plays an important role in the locating and ingestion of food (HALPERN 1992). Bluetongues also have well developed teeth which are situated on the rims of both the lower and upper jaws. The transportation of food towards the throat is facilitated by movements of the tongue and forward jerks of the head (MARCUS 1983, PORTER 1972). Assisted by press-choking movements of the head and neck the food is forwarded to the stomach. The latter has the elongate shape of a cigar and possesses extraordinarily distendable walls. The length of the intestinal tract equals about the SVL in both *Tiliqua rugosa* and *T. scincoides.* Two thirds of it represent the midgut and one third the hindgut. The slim midgut of *T. rugosa* is coiled, whereas the wide hindgut runs almost in a straight line (LIMBERGER 2000). Although the gastrointestinal tract of reptiles is rather short in comparison with that of a mammal, the lingering period of the food is often much longer. Observations made by LIMBERGER (2000) indicate that *Tiliqua* spp. are able to digest food of animal origin through enzymatic action in the midgut as efficiently as plant fiber materials are digested with the aid of micro-organisms in the voluminous hindgut.

The portrayed situation was sketched from a specimen that had not eaten for several days.

**Fig. 1** Topography of esophagus and the gastro-intestinal tract in *Tiliqua rugosa*    Sketch: C. Dennert

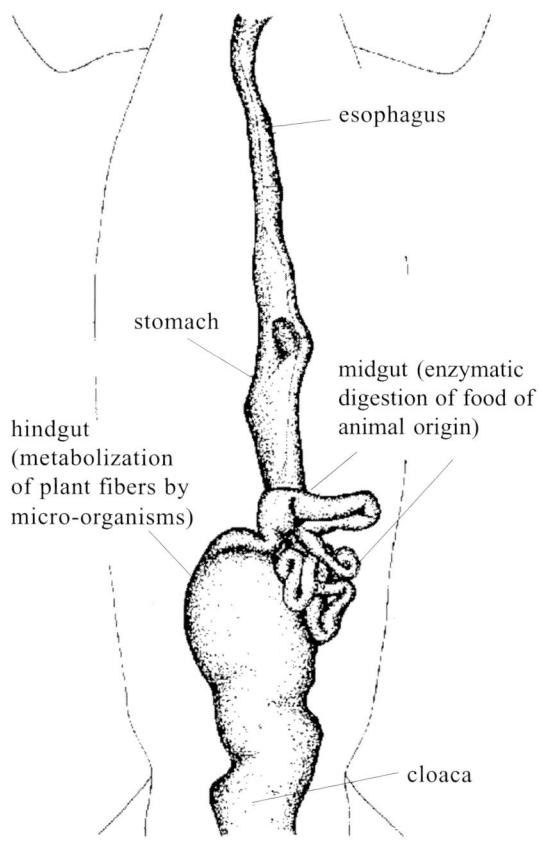

esophagus

stomach

midgut (enzymatic digestion of food of animal origin)

hindgut (metabolization of plant fibers by micro-organisms)

cloaca

It corresponds well with observations made on the digestive tract of *Tiliqua scincoides* (after LIMBERGER 2000).

## Components of the ration

In their natural environment most species of blue-tongued skinks consume variable amounts of feeder plants (including fruit) plus a variable amount of animal prey. Their food spectrum is usually very broad. Blue-tongued skinks readily accept a multitude of fruit and vegetables also under the conditions of a ter-

rarium. Their diet also includes feeder animals such as crickets, grasshoppers, beetles, roaches, snails as well as pink mice. Besides these staple feedstuffs, moist (tinned) cat and dog food, commercial baby food (on a basis of fruit, vegetables or meat), and fruit yoghurt are eagerly consumed (JONES 1987, WALLS 1995). An overview of the food spectrum of various species of *Tiliqua* is given in Table 1 below.

This overview is meant to draw an approximate picture of commonly used feedstuffs that are accepted by bluetongues. Various species will also occasionally feed on carrion in nature.

**Table 1** Food spectrum of bluetongues in nature and captivity

continued on next page

| Feedstuffs of animal origin | *Tiliqua* sp. | *Cyclodomorphus casuarinae* | *Cyclodomorphus gerrardii* | *Tiliqua gigas* | *Tiliqua nigrolutea* | *Tiliqua occipitalis* | *Tiliqua rugosa* | *Tiliqua scincoides* |
|---|---|---|---|---|---|---|---|---|
| **Vertebrates and products of these** | | | | | | | | |
| pink mice | ● | ❖ | ● | A | ❖ | ❖ | ❖ | ● |
| meat (beef, poultry) | ● | ❖ | ● | ❖ | ❖ | – | ❖ | – |
| innards | ❖ | – | A | ● | ❖ | – | ❖ | ❖ |
| birds, fledglings | ❖ | – | – | ❖ | – | ❖ | □ | – |
| egg, raw and boiled | ● | – | – | ❖ | – | – | ❖ | ❖ |
| fish | □ | – | □ | ● | – | – | – | ❖ |
| **Invertebrates** | | | | | | | | |
| crickets | ● | ❖ | – | J | ❖ | – | ❖ | ● |
| locusts | □ | ❖ | – | – | □ | ❖ | ❖ | ❖ |
| beetles | □ | ❖ | – | | ❖ | – | ● | – |
| roaches | □ | ❖ | – | ❖ | ❖ | ❖ | ❖ | ❖ |
| spiders | □ | ❖ | – | | ❖ | – | □ | – |
| earth worms | □ | ❖ | □ | ❖ | – | – | ❖ | ❖ |
| snails, slugs | ❖ | ❖ | ● | ● | □ | ❖ | ❖ | ● |
| crustaceans | ❖ | | – | ● | – | – | □ | A |

❖ = readily taken in nature and in a terrarium; ● = commonly taken / preferred item; □ = occasional; J = for juveniles; A = for adults;

| Source | 1) | 2) | 3) | 4) | 5) | 6) | 7) | 8) |
|---|---|---|---|---|---|---|---|---|

**Table 1** (continued)  Food spectrum of bluetongues in nature and captivity

| Feedstuffs of plant origin | Tiliqua sp. | Cyclodomorphus casuarinae | Cyclodomorphus gerrardii | Tiliqua gigas | Tiliqua nigrolutea | Tiliqua occipitalis | Tiliqua rugosa | Tiliqua scincoides |
|---|---|---|---|---|---|---|---|---|
| Percentage (%) of plant matter in ration | 0 | – | N/A. | 0 | 0 | N/A. | 0 | 0 |
| juveniles | N/A. | – | N/A. | 0 | 0 | N/A. | 0 | 40 (20*) |
| fruit in general | ● | – | ❖ | ❖ | ❖ | ❖ | ❖ | ❖ |
| berries preferred | – | – | | – | – | ❖ | ● | ❖ |
| vegetables | ● | – | J | ❖ | ❖ | □ | ● | ❖ |
| vegetable flakes | – | – | ❖ | ❖ | – | – | – | ❖ |
| wild herbs | □ | – | – | ❖ | ❖ | ❖ | ❖ | ❖ |
| sprouts | □ | – | – | ❖ | ❖ | – | – | ❖ |
| mushrooms | – | – | – | ❖ | ❖ | – | □ | A |
| flowers | – | – | – | – | □ | ❖ | ● | ❖ |
| oat, wheat bran | □ | – | – | ❖ | – | – | ❖ | ❖ |
| **Feedstuffs for other animals** | | | | | | | | |
| dog food, moist | □ | ❖ | – | ● | □ | – | ❖ | – |
| cat food, moist | □ | – | – | ● | □ | – | ❖ | □ |

❖ = readily taken in nature and in a terrarium;   ● = commonly taken / preferred item;   □ = occasional; J = for juveniles; A = for adults; n.a. = nicht in der Literatur angegeben

| Source | 1) | 2) | 3) | 4) | 5) | 6) | 7) | 8) |
|---|---|---|---|---|---|---|---|---|

**Key to sources: 1)** FRYE (1991), HITZ (1989, in litt.), JONES (1987), MUDRACK (1969), PETERS (1986), RÖHE (1997, verb. comm.), ROGNER (1994), SWITAK (1986), **2)** JUSCHKA (1998, verb. comm.), **3)** HAUSCHILD (1988), JONES (1987), MILES (1973), MUDRACK (1974), MÜNSCH (1980), PETERS (1976), SUHR (1967), ZWINENBERG (1976), **4)** GASSNER (1998, in litt.), HAUSCHILD (1998, in litt.), HAUSCHILD & GASSNER (1995), JUSCHKA (1998, verb. comm.), **5)** HAUSCHILD & GASSNER (1995), HITZ (1998, in litt.), **6)** HAUSCHILD & GASSNER (1995), **7)** DUBAS & BULL (1991, 1992), FRYE (1991), GROSS (1989, 1998, in litt.), HAUSCHILD & GASSNER (1995), HOUBA (1959), JUSCHKA (1998, verb. comm.), RÖHE (1997, verb. comm.), SHEA (1989), **8)** GASSNER (1998, in litt.), HAUSCHILD & GASSNER (1995), JUSCHKA (1998, verb. comm.), * UNVERZAGT (1998, in litt.)

Less common feedstuffs offered in terrarium keeping include caterpillars, mealworms and giant mealworms, mussel meat and calamaris, chopped one-day chicks, also dry food for dogs, and commercial mixed feedstuffs for reptiles, various seeds, rice, buckwheat, and nectar. The offered innerts include beef and chicken heart, and occasionally beef liver. Bluetongues are in general appreciative subjects in a terrarium and easily adjust to outlandish feedstuffs. This is unfortunately also the reason why in many publications mention is made of an occasional feeding with "very human" foodstuffs. Such would comprise puddings and chocolate creme, flour-based foods, red groats, fruit desserts, whipped cream, white bread soaked in sugar water, and others. The gusto with which these foods are consumed should, however, never tempt the keeper to spoil his animals with such treats more often than very occasionally. From a perspective of proper animal alimentationthese items should actually be cut out entirely. In general a very diverse menu should be created in order to prevent deficiency related diseases, particularly metabolic bone diseases in juveniles. Vegetarian and animalian feeds may be offered in alternation or in mixed rations. According to HITZ (1989, pers. comm.) a mixed ration for omnivorous skinks could be composed of 75% individual feedstuffs of plant origin (50% fiber-rich vegetables, 25% fruit), complemented with 25% lean meat (beef heart or turkey hen). No matter whether vegetarian food is alternated with feedstuffs of animal origin or mixed rations are offered - it should always be ensured that the individual components complement each other in a sensible manner. Particular attention must be paid to the calcium content of the ration and the ratio between calcium and phosphorus. Rations with a calcium content of more than 1%, but less than 2%, in the dry mass appear appropriate, and the calcium/phosphorus ratio should range around 1.5 : 1. It would therefore be sensible to compensate feedstuffs with a low calcium content (e.g. feeder insects, beef and fowl meat, fruit and vegetables) and/or feedstuffs with a particularly high phosphorus content (e.g. wheat bran, sprouts) by adding calcium-rich components (e.g. dandelion and other wild green feeds, pink

**Fig. 2** A blue-tongued skink from Indonesia feeding

Photograph: A. Hauschild

mice, dogs flakes). If necessary, a calcium deficiency can be compensated by adding grated cuttlefish shell or ground egg shells. Minced mice, rats or one-day chicks are therefore much more appropriate than a piece of beef heart or fowl meat.

A high content of raw fiber favors the microbial activity in the large intestine and thus has positive effects on the intestinal fauna and the texture of the feces. The latter then tend to be firmer and drier, resulting in less spoiling of the terrarium and its substrate in particular (JONES 1987). To assist with the evaluation of various feedstuffs the table at the end of this chapter provides an overview of the nutritional composition of a variety of consumables which are used for feeding bluetongues. This overview should make it simple to compose a balanced diet.

**Fig. 3** A blue-tongued skink on a blueberry pie
Photograph: M. Juschka

The raising of juveniles requires particular attention. Fed with the right foods they thrive beautifully, but CHAUMONT (1964) also reported about losses among captive bred bluetongues due to deficiency related diseases that involved spinal curvature. He presumed that an insufficient calcium supply and a lack of UV-irradiation were responsible. The calcium requirements of juveniles should be covered by a content of about 2% calcium in the dry mass of the ration, provided the calcium/phosphorus ratio is balanced. Supplying juveniles, or even adults, with vitamin $D_3$, for example via tablets, requires utmost care as an overdosage in conjunction with an oversupply with calcium can result in calcium deposits in the inner organs. A weekly supply of 100 I.U. vitamin $D_3$ per kilogram body mass has proved beneficial in the rearing of juveniles of other genera. No information exists on the permeability of the skin of live skinks for UV-radiation, but this does not suggest that a regular exposure to UV-radiation from suitable UV-lamps (e.g. Osram Ultra VitaLux® 300 watts) would have negative effects.

## Feeding praxis

The size of feeder animals should be chosen according to the size of the skink (WALLS 1995). Live feeder animals, flying invertebrates in particular, should be offered preferably directly from forceps. This method prevents that individual specimens may establish themselves in the terrarium or the apartment and become a pest. It also provides the keeper with an overview of the amounts ingested by the individual bluetongue and enables him to distribute food sensibly among a group kept together. Terrestrial invertebrates can be offered in a bowl with steep smooth walls. If a terrarium is occupied by several individuals, the use of several food bowls helps to prevent aggression. In general the keeper has to ensure that every member of a group receives an appropriate portion (HITZ 1983). Animal protection laws in some countries may prohibit the use of live vertebrates, e.g. live pink mice, as food.

## Feeding time and frequency

In general feeding should take place when the skinks have reached their preferred body temperature. Juveniles require food on a daily basis. With increasing age and body mass a more restrictive feeding routine is recommended and feeding intervals should be prolonged. Fed daily ad libitum bluetongues show a tendency to gigantism and obesity with negative consequences to their life expectancy and fertility. Adult specimens should therefore be fed twice or three times per week with the feeding intervals changing according to the season. Depending on seasonal inactivity a period of non-availability of food is to be inserted (JONES 1987): according to the seasonal rhythm chosen for many captive kept *Tiliqua* spp. (northern or southern hemisphere) the southern Australian springtime corresponds with the months of autumn at northern latitudes. During the spring months the animals should enjoy generous rations at warm and dry conditions. Fully grown specimens are then fed twice a week, while during the hot and dry summer months as well as during the warm and dry autumn, food is made available rather sparsely. The terraria should be kept cool with no, or only very little, food being offered in winter (HITZ 1998, in litt).

## Drinking water

Most species of blue-tongued skinks originate from arid habitats and drink rather rarely (MATTISON 1991). Nevertheless should drinking water always be accessible and is best made available in a water bowl. This source of water is usually readily accepted with the animals learning quickly to drink from it. If the bowl is large enough, it may also be used for occasional bathing. The bowl should be cleansed on a daily basis in order to prevent a proliferation of micro-organisms.

## Details of the feeding regime for *Tiliqua rugosa*

The shingleback represents an exception among the genus of the blue-tongued skinks as its diet in nature includes animal components only on an occasional basis. Analyses of the composition of feces deposited by free ranging specimens confirm that this is a predominantly herbivorous species. With one exception, only metabolic products of plant matter were found, usually with high portions of berries, various wild herbs and yellow flowers. Individual samples showed that beetles or carrion had been consumed (HENLE 1990). Field studies have furthermore revealed that the diet consists mainly of flowers (85%) in spring. The content of berries reaches 66% in summer and decreases to about 30% in autumn. The rest is made up of flowers and leaves. In addition to that terrestrial snails *(Theba pisana)* are consumed, more rarely small skinks and fledgling birds, possibly also carrion or grasshoppers (DUBAS & BULL 1991). Nevertheless, this omnivore is a predominantly herbivorous species. The diet for juveniles may thus include a portion of up to 20% of feedstuffs of animal origin, whereas in adults it should never exceed 10% (DUBAS & BULL 1991, 1992, GROSS 1998, in litt.). In nature a selection of plants is consumed during the day with no particular preferences for certain plant species being apparent. The availability of food varies in type and quantity with the changes of the seasons. Spring offers *Tiliqua rugosa* a bounty of foodstuffs which gradually decreases during summer and autumn. This correlates to a decrease in the activity of the animals. The feeder plants become fewer and more widely scattered (DUBAS & BULL 1991, 1992).

In nature *Tiliqua rugosa* is in constant movement searching for and ingesting food., and 12 minutes of each day are spent on average with food ingestion. Feeder plants are never consumed entirely (HENLE 1990). Considering the feeding habits of free ranging shinglebacks their diet in captivity should by all means be kept as varying as possible. This also helps to prevent deficiency based diseases. As an example, a ration may therefore consist of 40% banana, 20% apple, 10% tomato and 10% flowers and berries freshly collected from the wild, to which may be added a maximum of 20% moist dog food (DUBAS & BULL 1991, 1992).

**Table 2** Overview of the composition of some feedstuffs of plant and animal origin used for the feeding of bluetongues continued on next page

| Individual feedstuffs of animal origin | | Dry mass per 100 g oS | Raw nutrients | | | Calzium | Phosphorus | Ca/P-ratio | Source |
|---|---|---|---|---|---|---|---|---|---|
| | | | Raw protein | Raw fat | Raw fiber | | | | |
| | | | in % of the dry mass | | | | | | |
| **Invertebrates** | | | | | | | | | |
| crickets (twin-spotted) | *Gryllus bimaculatus* | 28 | 68,2 | 12,8 | o.A. | 0,4 | 0,9 | 0,5 | |
| locusts | *Locusta migratoria* | 33 | 71 | 13,9 | o.A. | 0,38 | 0,65 | 0,6 | 1) |
| earthworms | *Lumbricus terrestris* | 16,3 | 61,4 | 5,5 | o.A. | 0,8 | 0,9 | 0,9 | |
| snails | *Helix pomatia* | 18,1 | 70,6 | 6,6 | o.A. | o.A. | o.A. | o.A. | 2) |
| mealworms | *Tenebrio molitor* | 37,2 | 45,8 | 42,4 | o.A. | 0,01 | 0,27 | 0,04 | 1) |
| giant mealworms | *Zophobas morio* | 42,7 | 48,2 | 41,5 | o.A. | 0,04 | 0,56 | 0,07 | |
| shrimps (North Sea) | *Crangon crangon* | 21,6 | 86,1 | 6,7 | o.A. | 0,4 | 1 | 0,4 | |
| mussels | *Mytilus edulis* | 16,8 | 58,6 | 8 | o.A. | 0,2 | 1,5 | 0,1 | 2) |
| cephalopods | *Sepia* sp. | 19 | 84,7 | 4,7 | o.A. | 0,1 | 0,8 | 0,2 | |
| **Vertebrates** | | | | | | | | | |
| pink mice | | 20,4 | 69,1 | 19,6 | o.A. | 1,9 | 1,9 | 1 | 1) |
| one-day chicks | | 22 | 68,2 | 18,2 | o.A. | 1,3 | 1 | 1,3 | 3) |
| of chicken: | egg | 25,9 | 49,8 | 43,2 | o.A. | 0,2 | 0,8 | 0,3 | |
| | meat | 29,4 | 75,5 | 21,1 | o.A. | 0,05 | 0,7 | 0,1 | 2) |
| | heart | 25,7 | 67,3 | 22,7 | o.A. | 0,1 | 0,6 | 0,1 | |
| of beef: | mince | 39,4 | 58,1 | 35,5 | o.A. | 0,02 | 0,9 | 0,02 | 2), 3) |
| | heart | 24,5 | 68,6 | 24,5 | o.A. | 0,04 | 0,9 | 0,04 | 2) |
| | liver | 30,1 | 65,4 | 10,3 | o.A. | 0,02 | 1,2 | 0,02 | 2) |
| **Dog and cat foods** | | | | | | | | | |
| dog flakes | (on average) | 92 | 13 | 4,1 | 1,8 | 1,1 | 0,6 | 1,7 | |
| dog food, moist | minimum content | 22 | 41,8 | 19,1 | 0,9 | 1,8 | 1,8 | 1 | |
| | maximum content | 20 | 60 | 25 | 4 | 7,5 | 5,5 | 1,4 | |
| dog food, dry | minimum content | 90 | 21,1 | 8,9 | 2,8 | 0,8 | 0,8 | 1 | 3) |
| | maximum content | 80 | 30 | 18,8 | 5 | 2,3 | 1,5 | 1,5 | |
| cat food, moist | minimum content | 20 | 42,5 | 17,5 | 1 | 0,9 | 0,8 | 1,1 | |
| | maximum content | 18 | 63,9 | 33,3 | 2,8 | 4,1 | 2,2 | 1,9 | |

oS = original substance

Source:
1) DENNERT (1997); 2) SOUCI et al. (1993); 3) MEYER & HECKÖTTER (1986); 4) GEIGY (1968)

**Table 2** (continued) Overview of the composition of some feedstuffs of plant and animal origin used for the feeding of bluetongues

| Individual feedstuffs of plant origin | | Dry mass per 100 g oS | Raw protein | Raw fat | Raw fiber | Calzium | Phosphorus | Ca/P-ratio | Source |
|---|---|---|---|---|---|---|---|---|---|
| | | | | Raw nutrients | | | | | |
| | | | | in % of the dry mass | | | | | |
| **Vegetables** | | | | | | | | | |
| buckwheat | *Fagopyrum esculentum* | 87,2 | 10,4 | 2 | 4,2 | 0,02 | 0,3 | 0,1 | |
| champignons | *Agaricus bisporus* | 9,3 | 29,5 | 2,6 | 21,8 | 0,1 | 1,3 | 0,1 | 2) |
| Chinese coleslaw | *Brassica chinensis* | 4,6 | 25,9 | 6,5 | 41,3 | 0,9 | 0,7 | 1,3 | |
| oat flakes | | 90 | 13,9 | 7,8 | 6 | 0,1 | 0,4 | 0,1 | |
| carrot | *Daucus carota* | 11,8 | 8,3 | 1,7 | 30,8 | 0,35 | 0,3 | 1,2 | |
| dandelion (leaves) | *Taraxacum offinalis* | 14,3 | 17,8 | 4,3 | 10,5 | 1,1 | 0,5 | 2,3 | 2), 4) |
| mungo bean sprouts | | 6,9 | 46,4 | 4,3 | 18 | 0,1 | 0,7 | 0,1 | |
| rice, polished, cooked | | 22 | 8,9 | 0,7 | oA | 0,01 | 0,2 | 0,1 | |
| soy bean sprouts | | 14,4 | 38,4 | 7,1 | 16,5 | 0,2 | 0,5 | 0,4 | 2) |
| sunflower | *Helianthus annuus* | 93,4 | 24,1 | 52,5 | 6,7 | 0,1 | 0,7 | 0,2 | |
| tomato | *Lycopersicon esculentum* | 5,8 | 16,4 | 3,6 | 16,4 | 0,1 | 0,3 | 0,5 | |
| wheat sprouts | | 88,3 | 30,1 | 10,4 | 20 | 0,1 | 1,2 | 0,1 | |
| wheat bran | | 88,5 | 16,8 | 5,3 | 51,3 | 0,05 | 1,5 | 0,03 | |
| zucchini | *Cucurbita pepo* | 7,8 | 20,5 | 5,1 | 13,8 | 0,4 | 0,3 | 1,3 | |
| **Fruit** | | | | | | | | | |
| apple | *Malus sylvestris* | 14,7 | 2,3 | 3,9 | 13,7 | 0,05 | 0,1 | 0,6 | |
| banana | *Musa sapientum* | 26,1 | 4,4 | 0,7 | 7 | 0,03 | 0,1 | 0,3 | |
| strawberry | *Fragaria sp.* | 10,5 | 7,8 | 3,8 | 15,5 | 0,2 | 0,3 | 0,9 | |
| red currant | *Ribes rubrum* | 15,3 | 7,4 | 1,3 | 22,9 | 0,2 | 0,2 | 1,1 | |
| pear | *Pyrus communis* | 15,7 | 3 | 1,8 | 20,8 | 0,1 | 0,1 | 0,7 | 2) |
| kiwi | *Actinidia chinensis* | 16,2 | 6,2 | 3,9 | 13,1 | 0,2 | 0,2 | 1,2 | |
| orange | *Citrus aurantium* | 14,3 | 7 | 1,4 | 11,2 | 0,3 | 0,2 | 1,8 | |
| peach | *Prunus persica* | 12,5 | 6,1 | 0,9 | 15,4 | 0,1 | 0,2 | 0,3 | |
| plum | *Prunus domestica* | 16,3 | 3,7 | 1 | 9,7 | 0,1 | 0,1 | 0,8 | |
| gooseberry | *Ribes grossularia* | 12,7 | 6,3 | 1,2 | 23,2 | 0,2 | 0,2 | 1 | |
| grape | *Vitis vinifera* | 18,9 | 3,6 | 1,5 | 7,9 | 0,1 | 0,1 | 0,9 | |

oS = original substance

Source:
1) DENNERT (1997); 2) SOUCI et al. (1993); 3) MEYER & HECKÖTTER (1986); 4) GEIGY (1968)

The diet management for *Tiliqua rugosa* is handled very differently by individual keepers. RÖHE (1998, pers. comm.) stated that a porridge consisting of runner beans, dandelion, kiwi, and egg shell has produced excellent results in the keeping of *Tiliqua rugosa*. Feeding plant based food twice a week could also be alternated with feedstuffs of animal origin (HITZ 1983). JUSCHKA (1998, pers. comm.) achieves a seasonal variation by supplying his shinglebacks with a plant based diet during the two months following hibernation, then mainly food of animal origin for three to four months, which is thereafter complemented with dandelion flowers. Prior to hibernation the diet is again changed to primarily herbivorous.

## The food specialist *Cyclodomorphus gerrardii*

The snail-eating pink-tongued skink *Cyclodomorphus gerrardii* is an unusual food specialist. In its natural habitat its diet consists primarily of terrestrial snails with both snails and slugs being accepted. The adult specimens kept by MILES (1973) accepted only snails and slugs whereas banana and minced meat were rejected. The animals were fed twice a week with five large snails or slugs each. Many slugs display warning colors that signal their unpalatable taste. However, the pink-tongued skink overcomes this problem in a remarkable manner. Once a slug is sighted and approached, the skink is able to produce a foamy lining in its mouth by opposing movements of the upper and lower jaws. This may be a defense strategy that protects the mucous membranes in its mouth from direct damage caused by the ingestion of actually unsavory slugs. If no snails or slugs are available during the winter months, animals kept in terraria may also be fed with crustaceans (e.g. mussels), the occasional pink mouse, fresh meat, or moist food for cats. These alternative feedstuffs are, however, much less eagerly accepted than molluscs (JONES 1987, MATTISON 1991). A ration for juveniles in the terrarium could be composed of small snails and slugs, minced meat, banana and tomato (MILES 1973).

In order to keep the removal of snails from nature at a low level, and to ensure a constant supply, breeding feeder snails is a good idea. Common land and garden snails, such as *Cepaea nemoralis* and *C. hortensis* in Europe, but also agate snails *(Achatina fulica),* are suitable for this purpose. It must be said, though, that the space and work requirements for a snail farm are relatively great in comparison as these animals have long development cycles and are only moderately productive. Agate snails furthermore demand a substantial investment in appropriate feeds. A detailed guide to breeding snails can be found in FRIEDERICH & VOLLAND (1992).

## Literature

BIRD, D. M. & S. K. HO (1976): Nutritive values of whole animal diets for captive birds of prey. – Raptor Res. 10: 45–49.

CHAUMONT, F. (1964): Die Aufzucht der jungen Blauzungenskinke. – DATZ 1964: 28–29.

DENNERT, C. (1997): Untersuchungen zur Fütterung von Schuppenechsen und Schildkröten. – Hannover, Tierärztl. Hochschule, Diss., 190 S.

DUBAS, G. & C. M. BULL (1991): Diet choice and food availability in the omnivorous lizard *Trachydosaurus rugosus*. – Wildl. Res. 18(2): 147–155.

– (1992): Food addition and home range size of the lizard *Tiliqua rugosa*. – Herpetologica, 48(3): 301–306.

FRIEDERICH, U. & W. VOLLAND (1992): Futtertierzucht. – 2. Aufl., Ulmer, Stuttgart: 188 S.

FRYE, F. L. (1991): Nutrition. A Practical Guide for Feeding Captive Reptiles. – In F. L. FRYE (Hrsg.): Reptile Care. An Atlas of Diseases and Treatments. – T.F.H. Publications, Neptune City, N.J., Bd. 1, 325 pp.

GEIGY, J. R. (1968): Wissenschaftliche Tabellen. – Geigy Eigenverlag, Basel, 742 S.

GROSS, J. (1989): Pflege, Geschlechtsbestimmung und Zucht der Tannenzapfenechse, *Trachydosaurus rugosus*. – DATZ 42(10): 612–613.

HALPERN, M. (1992): Nasal Chemical Senses in Reptiles: Structure and Function. – in: GANS, C. & D. CREWS (Hrsg.): Biology of the Reptilia. – Bd. 18. Physiology E. University of Chicago Press, Chicago: 423–524.

HAUSCHILD, A. (1988): Bemerkungen zu Haltung und Nachzucht des Schneckenskinks *Tiliqua gerrardii* (GRAY, 1845). – Salamandra, Bonn, 24(4): 248–257.

HAUSCHILD, A. & P. GAßNER (1995): Skinke im Terrarium. – Landbuch-Verlag, Hannover, 197 S.

HENLE, K. (1990): Notes on the Population Ecology of the Large Herbivorous Lizard, *Trachydosaurus rugosus*, in Arid Australia. – J. Herp. 24(1): 100–103.

HITZ, R. (1983): Pflege und Nachzucht von *Trachydosaurus rugosus* (GRAY, 1827) im Terrarium. – Salamandra, Bonn, 19(4): 198–210.

HOUBA, J. (1959): *Tiliqua rugosa* (GRAY). – AT 6: 176–177.

JONES, S. (1987): A report on reproducible and sustainable system for the captive propagation of the genus *Tiliqua* GRAY 1825. – In COOTE, J. (Ed.): Reptiles. – Proceedings of the UK Herpetological Societies Symposium on Captive Breeding. British Herpetological Society, London: 1–97.

LIMBERGER, M. (2000): Topographische Anatomie der inneren Organe des Rumpfes bei Skinken der Gattungen *Tiliqua* und *Corucia* (Reptilia: Lacertilia: Scincidae) unter Verwendung der Kernspintomographie als Methode in der Wirbeltieranatomie. TU Darmstadt, 140 S.

MARCUS, L. C. (1983): Amphibien und Reptilien in Heim, Labor und Zoo. – Enke, Stuttgart, 184 S.

MATTISON, C. (1991): Keeping and Breeding Lizards. – Blandford Press, Poole, England, 224 pp.

MEYER, H. & E. HECKÖTTER (1986): Futterwerttabellen für Hunde und Katzen. – 2. Aufl., Schlütersche, Hannover, 48 S.

MILES, T. (1973): Measurements and notes on adult and juvenile Pink Tongues Skinks (*Tiliqua gerrardi*). – Herpetofauna, Sydney, 6(1): 116–117.

MUDRACK, W. (1969): Einiges über Pflege und Zucht von Blauzungenskinken im Zimmerterrarium. – Aqua. Terra 6(2): 23–24.

– (1974): Der Rosazungenskink – eine terraristische Kostbarkeit. – Aquarienmagazin 8(10): 407–411.

MÜNSCH, W. (1980): Erfahrungen mit dem Schneckenskink *Tiliqua gerrardii*. – Das Aquarium 133: 371–374.

PETERS, U. (1967): *Tiliqua gerrardii* und *Tiliqua casuarinae*, zwei wenig bekannte Echsen. – AT, Jena, Leipzig, 3: 94–96.

– (1986): Australische Skinke. Acht Arten werden vorgestellt. – Das Aquarium 206: 436–440.

PORTER, K. R. (1972): Herpetology. – Saunders, Philadelphia, London, 524 pp.

ROGNER, M. (1994): Echsen: Haltung, Pflege und Zucht im Terrarium. Bd. 2. – Ulmer, Stuttgart, 270 S.

SHEA, G. M. (1989): Diet and Reproductive Biology of the Rottnest Island Bobtail, *Tiliqua rugosa konowi* (Lacertilia, Scincidae). – Herp. J. 1: 366–369.

SOUCI, S. W., W. FACHMANN & H. KRAUT (1993): Die Zusammensetzung der Lebensmittel. Nährwert-Tabellen. – 4. Aufl., Wissenschaftliche Verlagsgesellschaft, Stuttgart, 1091 S.

SUHR, E. (1967): Ein seltener Australier, leicht zu pflegen: *Tiliqua gerrardii*. – AT Jena, Leipzig: 14.

SWITAK, K. H. (1986): Zwei Echsen aus Australien: Tannenzapfen- und Blauzungenskink. Verhalten und Pflegeansprüche. – Aquarienmagazin 20(7): 296–299.

WALLS, J. G. (1995): Skinke im Terrarium. – bede, Ruhmannsfelden, 65 S.

ZWINENBERG, A. J. (1976): Der Schneckenskink *Tiliqua gerrardii* (GRAY). – Aquaria, St. Gallen, 23(8): 123–126.

Author's address
Dr. med. vet. Carolin Dennert
Hünxer Str. 194
46537 Dinslaken, Germany

# The biology of *Tiliqua rugosa aspera* (Gray, 1845)

## Robert Hitz and Klaus Henle

**Key words: Reptilia: Sauria: Scincidae: *Tiliqua: Tiliqua rugosa aspera*, Australia, biology, description, distribution, ecology, reproduction.**

## Description

The shingleback is very easily distinguished from all other lizards in the world by its round, often slightly thickened, and dorsally flattened tail and the name-giving, much enlarged scales that are arranged like the imbricate scales of a fir cone. Reaching up to 34 cm in snout-vent length (SVL) and 1103 g body mass (Henle unpubl.) the eastern shingleback ranks among the largest forms of blue-tongued skinks. The length of the tail makes up only 14.5 to 30% of the SVL (n = 648). The head is massive and distinctly wider than the body. The legs are relatively short. The scales are very large and strongly ossified; 19-27 rows of these are counted around midbody. The length between the shoulders and the insertion of the hind legs is covered by 12-22 scales. The ventral scales are flat and number 52-76 between axilla and insertion of the hind legs. The underside of the tail is covered with 11-20 scale rows (all data from Shea 1992). The coloration is highly variable, ranging from uniformly blackish brown to earth brown with irregular, more or less large, yellow blotches. In general the margins of the scales, particularly at their ends, are substantially lighter than the centers of the individual scales; often the scales show yellow tips. The yellow coloration may fuse to form larger blotches. The ventral side is usually cream colored or yellowish, often with a more or less distinct pattern of dark, brown dashes and bands. This dark pattern may even replace the light ventral coloration entirely.

## Geographic variation

The darkest shinglebacks are found in the east of their distribution range; here they may even appear black. These specimens also reach the maximum body size. In the west of the range the animals are smaller and lighter in color, often exhibiting a yellow ground color on the back. Between these two extremes at both ends of the distribution range, numerous intermediate forms exist (Shea 1992). For example, the shinglebacks living in the Kinchega National Park, situated in the west of New South Wales, reach significantly higher body masses than specimens from South Australia (Bull 1987, Henle 1990).

While the scalation of animals from the mainland shows hardly any geographic variation, some island specimens may differ substantially. Higher as well as lower numbers of scale rows than on the mainland may be counted here (Shea 1992), a phenomenon also known from many other island populations of lizards (e.g. Henle & Klaver 1986). Island populations also display a reduced genetic variability (found in allozyme studies) as opposed to mainland populations and therefore differ among each other more than mainland populations (Sarre et al. 1990).

## Differentiation from other subspecies

The eastern shingleback lizard *(Tiliqua rugosa aspera)* differs from all other subspecies by having a particularly short, very thick tail with a low number of subcaudal scales (usually < 17 versus usually ≥ 16 in the other subspecies), fewer scale rows along the vertebral line of the back (18-31, rarely >28, versus 23-38), a particularly wide head, a moderately distinct ear opening, and a dark dorsal surface of the body in which light circumferential bands are absent (SHEA 1992).

## Sex identification

**Exterior sexual dimorphism:** Distinguishing male and female shinglebacks is very difficult. Both sexes grow to about the same size and also reach maturity at a similar size. Although males and females differ with regard to the average values of a number of scalation traits, the absolute values overlap so much that these traits are practically useless for the identification of the sex of an individual animal.

The most promising method for sex identification is still based on head and body shapes. Mature males always have shorter bodies, but longer tails and smaller eyes than females. The body appears longer in females than in males (SCHNEIDER 1941, HORN 1980, SARRE & DEARN 1991). According to BULL & PAMULA (1996) males also have a tendency of developing wider heads, but this does not apply throughout the entire distribution range (SHEA 1992). Geographical variation (SHEA 1992, HITZ pers. obs.) proves to be a substantial obstacle here, in particular when specimens of different origins are compared with one another. It must be said in any case that the identification of the sexes on the basis of external traits is very difficult and requires a lot of experience to produce acceptably reliable results.

**Other methods of distinguishing between sexes:** A detailed description of the various suitable methods for sexing can be found in the chapter "Sex identification in blue-tongued skinks (Sauria: Scincidae: *Tiliqua*)" by HITZ and ZIEGLER in this book.

## Distribution

*Tiliqua rugosa aspera* inhabits the arid regions of eastern Australia, south of a line extending from Clermont via Aramac, Birdsville, the Lake

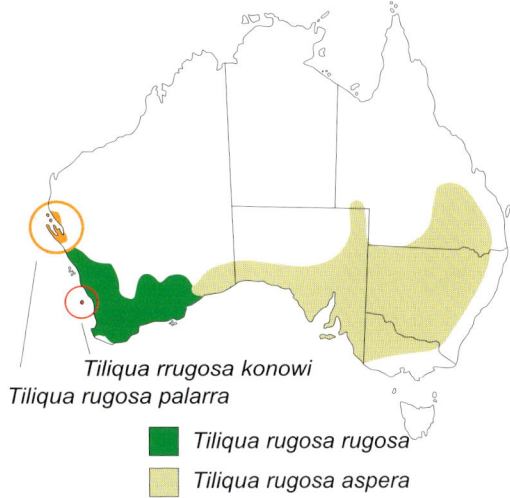

Tiliqua rrugosa konowi
Tiliqua rugosa palarra

■ Tiliqua rugosa rugosa
▫ Tiliqua rugosa aspera

**Fig. 1** Geographical distribution of *Tiliqua rugosa* and its subspecies

Bring region, and 98 km N of Loongama, to a point 112 km north of Rawlinna. In the east it touches the Great Diving Range and just penetrates the Australian Capital Territory (ACT). To the west its distribution range stretches up to 40 km west of Caiguna and the Naretha District, followed by a transitory zone with the nominal form, *T. r. rugosa,* farther to the west. Furthermore it is present on numerous islands off the South Australian coast (SHEA 1992). The large distribution range of *Tiliqua rugosa aspera* is reflected by various common names, used by the population, e.g. shingleback, sleepy lizard, stumpy-tailed lizard or boggi (SHEA pers. com. to the senior author).

## Ecology

**Natural habitat:** *Tiliqua rugosa aspera* lives in a wide variety of biotopes, ranging from open, semi-arid grasslands, through bushy savannas, Maireana-steppes (salt-tolerant shrubs of the family Chenopodiaceae; Fig. 2), mallee (open stands of bushy, 2-5 m tall species of *Eucalyptus* and *Acacia*), up to various open *Eu-*

**Fig. 2**  Natural habitat of *T. r. aspera* in the Kinchega National Park, New South Wales. The rotting branches in the foreground serve as hiding places.　　Photo: K. Henle

*calyptus* and *Casuarina* forests and gallery forests along rivers (SHEA 1992). They are largely absent in areas marked by expansive floodplains even if these have been dry for several years (HENLE 1989, 1990). They can even be found in gardens and parks of urban areas and on agriculturally used fields (for a respective bibliography see SHEA 1992).

*Tiliqua rugosa aspera* lives almost exclusively in flat country, on red laterite soil (Fig. 2) as well as on eroded gray sandstone. It is also encountered on heavily compacted rises, but rather rarely on mobile sand dunes, or on stony or rocky hills (SHEA 1992, HENLE unpubl.).

*Tiliqua rugosa aspera* finds shelter beneath bushes and bark, in hollow branches of large fallen trees (Fig. 2), in the burrows of rabbits, and among dense tussocks of grass. Perched between desiccated pieces of dead bark,

**Fig. 3**  Despite their size shinglebacks are well camouflaged among dry bark and disintegrating branches (Kinchega National Park, New South Wales).　　Photograph: K. Henle

branches and disintegrating trunks of dead bushes and trees it is fairly well camouflaged, even if it basks in the open (Fig. 3). The skink also makes use of pieces of corrugated iron, railway sleepers, fence poles, and a variety of other materials used by humans to find shelters

(HENLE 1990, SHEA 1992). The latter is one reason why it is found particularly often and easy in the surrounds of homesteads in the Australian Outback, where man-made structures offer more hiding places than the natural habitat.

**Diet:** The eastern shingleback is predominantly herbivorous. BROWN (1991) determined the plant ratio to account for 93.7% of its food volume. In an analysis of fecal samples of 12 specimens 11 consisted exclusively of plant matter (HENLE 1990). The red, yellow and green berries of the dwarf shrub *Enchylaena tomentosa* (Fig. 4) and the yellow flowering cruciferous plant *Brassica tournefortii* obviously enjoyed a particular popularity as these always constituted large portions of the food. The rest included various other herbs, even the poisonous black nightshade *(Solanum nigrum)*. Plants of the goosefoot family (Chenopodiaceae) were avoided, probably because the species present in the study area contain high concentrations of salt. The animal content was limited to remains of black beetles (Tenebrionidae). The natural food spectrum, however, also includes other insects, mainly in the form of caterpillars, as well as terrestrial snails, and small vertebrates such as small skinks and fledgling birds (DUBAS & BULL 1991). Occasionally a shingleback will be seen feeding on carrion as well (Henle unpubl.).

Numerous publications deal with the feeding of *Tiliqua rugosa aspera* in captivity. A comparative overview of the feeding regime for the species of *Tiliqua* under terrarium conditions

**Fig. 4**   The dwarf shrub *Enchylaena tomentosa,* and its berries in particular, are a favorite food for shinglebacks.
Photograph:  K. Henle

is provided in the chapter "A contribution to the feeding of blue-tongued skinks" by DENNERT in this book. Further references relative to the feeding habits in nature and in captivity can also be found in GREER (1989) although it is not clear for every publication quoted by him to which subspecies it may be referable. On the other hand, there is presumably little variation among the feeding habits of the various subspecies.

**Predators, parasites, mortality and life expectancy:** Owing to their body size and armor, shinglebacks have few natural enemies. These appear to be limited to the wedge-tailed eagle *(Aquila audax)*, large lace monitors *(Varanus varius)* and the introduced red foxes *(Vulpes vulpes)*, while large cats *(Felis cato)* may also pose a danger to juveniles. During their development shinglebacks lose the ability for a caudal autotomy which is still present in juveniles (ARNOLD 1988).

The most important cause of death is probably physiological stress (hunger and thirst) (BRADSHAW 1986, HENLE 1990), and it is common to find skeletal remains of shinglebacks amidst the sparse bushes of their natural habitat. In the course of one particularly hot summer several freshly deceased adult and subadult specimens were found which did not show signs that any predator whatsoever could have been involved (HENLE 1990). Furthermore one will very often find specimens dead on roads - this is most likely the most common cause of death in the vicinity of public roads (HENLE 1990).

Free ranging shinglebacks are often heavily infested with ticks (BULL 1978, BULL et al. 1989, HENLE 1990). Unicellular parasites (Protozoa) are equally known to plague these animals (JOHNSTON 1932).

Juveniles have substantially lower survival chances than adults (BULL 1987, HENLE 1990), and only a few (16%) of them will make it through to the spring following their birth (BULL 1995). Adult animals, on the other hand, have a low mortality rate and a high life expectancy; BULL (1987) estimated that *Tiliqua*

*rugosa aspera* may live to an age of more than 20 years in nature.

**Annual rhythm and thermoregulation:** It appears as though male and female specimens awake from their hibernation simultaneously. At least, there is no indication to the contrary in the existing literature. BULL et al. (1991) noted merely that there is an asynchronous seasonal activity during the course of a year notable among the sexes, with more males being found in the field in spring, and more females in summer after the mating season. The mating season of *T. rugosa aspera* falls into the Australian spring. The longest period of time during which matings may be observed is given by BULL (1988) who stated September through December, with the highest frequency occurring from late October through mid-November (BULL et al. 1991). Shinglebacks are most active during their mating season. Activity is furthermore closely correlated to the availability of herbal food (HENLE 1990). Times during which food is scarce are spent with inactivity. Day time temperatures probably also have a certain influence on the activity level of a shingleback population, albeit respective field studies on this subject have as yet failed to produce conclusive results (HENLE 1990). At least during winter the animals are generally inactive, although particularly warm days may trigger a low degree of activity and can cause them to leave their shelters (HENLE unpubl.).

In general - like with all reptiles - temperatures play a major role. The preferred body temperature of shinglebacks ranges between 29.5 and 36°C with most studies on this subject appearing to refer to the nominate subspecies of the shingleback (overview in GREER 1989). Active shinglebacks (both the nominate form and *T. r. aspera*) have been encountered in nature with body temperatures of 25 to 35.9°C (LICHT et al. 1966, BENNETT & JOHN-ALDER 1986). Below 20-22°C the thyroid gland, being the central controlling gland for the metabolism, shuts down its activity (HULBERT & WILLIAMS 1988). If the temperatures drop below 3.5-5°C, a life threatening situation arises (nominate subspecies and *T. r. aspera*) (SPELLERBERG 1972, BENNETT & JOHN-ALDER 1986). Values exceeding 43°C are equally lethal for eastern shinglebacks (BENNETT & JOHN-ALDER 1986).

**Population size, density and home range size:** Shinglebacks are relatively evenly spaced in their natural habitats. They are therefore relatively spread out and relatively common in their habitats. Densities in Kinchega National Park in western New South Wales were estimated at about 1 individual/ha amounting to a biomass of 0.8 kg/ha (HENLE 1990). The study area of BULL (1987) in southern Australia was home to 2.7 individuals/ha with a biomass of 1.6 kg/ha. Weighing 575 g on average, his specimens were substantially more lightweight than those in Kinchega National Park which weighed 821 g on average. The maximum mass of 755 g established by BULL (1987) did not even reach the average value of the Kinchega specimens (HENLE 1990), let alone come close to the maximum mass of 1103 g established for the latter. If the ground is covered with a layer of fine sand, the home ranges of individual shinglebacks can be tracked on the basis of the characteristic spoors (Fig. 5). Detailed data, however, can only be obtained through a process of monitoring individually marked specimens or with the aid of telemetry. Although shinglebacks can wander long distances, they rarely venture out for more than 100 m, and all specimens were in fact tracked down within a range of < 500 m of the point of first encounter (HENLE 1990). In a southern Australian population the home ranges of individual *T. r. aspera* covered surface areas of between 100 and 50,000 m$^2$ with an average of slightly less than 4,000 m$^2$ (SATRAWAHA & BULL 1981). These ranges may overlap and are not defended against conspecifics.

## Reproductive biology

As far as its reproductive biology is concerned *Tiliqua rugosa* belongs to the well-studied spe-

**Fig. 5** Typical tracks left by *T. r. aspera* in the sand of the Kinchega National Park, New South Wales.
Photograph: K. Henle

cies of lizards. Two groups of Australian scientists have in particular been focusing on this subject for the past 20 years. While BOURNE and his team have been studying its reproductive physiology and hormonal functions especially, BULL and his colleagues have been concentrating on its reproductive biology from an ecological and ethological angle. Both groups of scientists worked with the subspecies *T. r. aspera*. Other excellent sources for information on the reproductive biology are the works by SHEA (1992) and GREER (1989). Pieces in the puzzle of the reproductive biology of this lizard have, however, also been contributed and published by various other authors within and without Australia. Fig. 6 provides an overview of the reproductive cycle of the eastern shingleback lizard. This information, which includes numerous personal observations (HITZ), is the subject of the following paragraphs.

**The male sexual cycle:** The testes of *T. r. aspera* show varying lengths and changes in their turgor (state of tissue tension) depending on the season (SHEA 1992). During summer and early autumn (from December through late March) the testes are small, flattened and limp. From the mid of autumn (from April through June) they increase slightly in volume, and

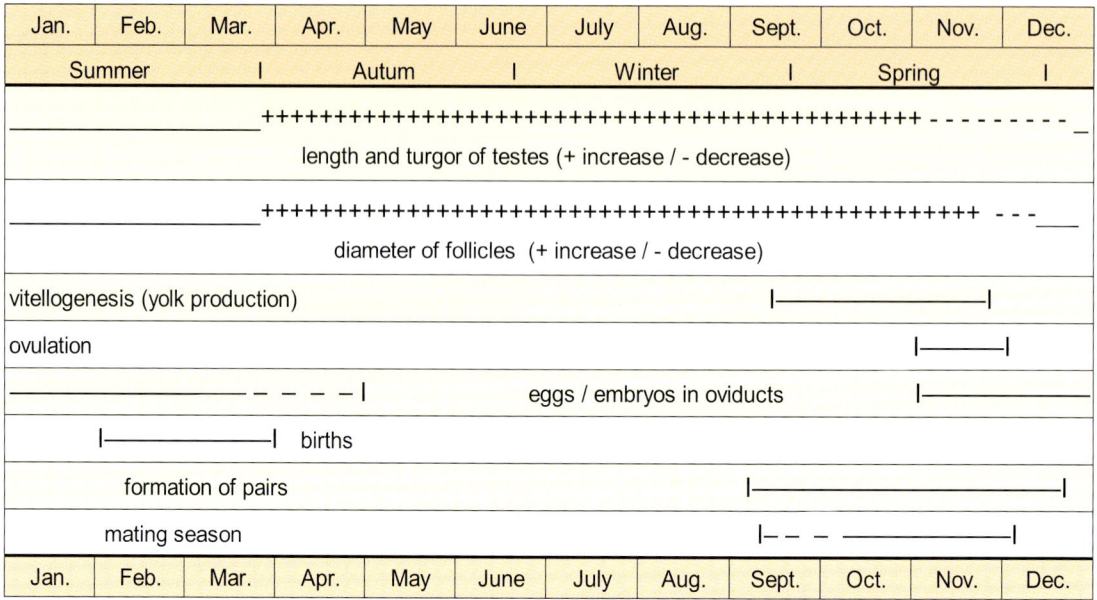

| Jan. | Feb. | Mar. | Apr. | May | June | July | Aug. | Sept. | Oct. | Nov. | Dec. |
|------|------|------|------|-----|------|------|------|-------|------|------|------|
| Summer | | I | Autumn | | I | Winter | | I | Spring | | I |

length and turgor of testes (+ increase / - decrease)

diameter of follicles  (+ increase / - decrease)

vitellogenesis (yolk production)

ovulation

eggs / embryos in oviducts

births

formation of pairs

mating season

| Jan. | Feb. | Mar. | Apr. | May | June | July | Aug. | Sept. | Oct. | Nov. | Dec. |
|------|------|------|------|-----|------|------|------|-------|------|------|------|

**Fig. 6** Chronological course of the reproductive cycle of *Tiliqua rugosa aspera* (after BULL 1988; BULL et al. 1991; SHEA 1992).

between mid-winter and spring (from July through October) both length and turgor increase substantially. This swollen state is then maintained during spring (from October through November). A regression of the testes is then observed in late spring (November through December) resulting in their shrinking in length and diameter and a reduced turgescence. The changes in the testes correspond with the levels of concentration of testosterone and epitestosterone in the testicular tissue and blood plasma (BOURNE & SEAMARK 1975, 1978, BOURNE et al. 1986b). This annual reproductive cycle fits the Type III of LICHT (1972).

The male reproductive cycle of *T. r. aspera* reaches its peak in the mating season in spring. Under the circumstances of a terrarium this point of time becomes evident by the excretion of fine hemipenis exuviae during the 4-5 week long mating season (Fig. 7) (HITZ pers. obs.). The males often discharge these exuviae when they leave their overnight shelters in the

morning, even without simultaneous defecation, and this process is accompanied by an intense rubbing of the cloaca against the soil. The biological function of this phenomenon is as yet unexplained.

Adult males will occasionally engage in fights when they encounter each other during the mating season (Fig. 8). BULL & PAMULA (1996) reported that such fights were relatively rarely observed (less than 20 observations during 13 years of field studies). The opponents will then take hold of the antagonist's head and try to roll him on his back. Some fights may last for more than 15 minutes. In a terrarium such fight may result in severe damage if the fighting males are not separated as quickly as possible.

**The female sexual cycle:** The diameters of the follicles are smallest in summer (December through February), and many females will be gravid at this time (SHEA 1992). The follicles then grow slowly and continually during autumn and winter, with an accelerated growth in spring (end of September through early November) during which time the follicles are also charged with yolk. From end of October the mature follicles are ovulated with a subsequent gravidity. If a female is not mated during this time, a regression of the follicles is observed. It is, however, also possible that females which have ovulated, but have not been impregnated, discharge the unused yolk masses after the completion of the normal term of gravidity.

**Fig. 7** Hemipenis exuviae of *T. r. aspera* in a terrarium
Photograph: R. Hitz

**Synchronization of the sexes**: As *T. r. aspera* originates from regions where winters are relatively cold, it is very probably this cool period which provides a deciding stimulus for reproductive cycles of both sexes and their synchronization (DUVALL et al. 1982, HITZ pers. obs.). For the terrarium keeper this means that a cool hibernation period is essential. Reproduction will be successful if males and females are hibernated simultaneously. Under terrarium conditions male *T. r. aspera* do not shed in spring before mating begins, unlike, for example, *T. nigrolutea* which does so at least in captivity (HITZ pers. obs.).

**Partner bonding, mating, monogamy:** While these lizards live basically solitary for most of the year - although up to four adult individuals may occupy larger hiding places (HENLE 1990)

**Fig. 8** Fighting males of *T. r. aspera* in a terrarium                    Photograph: R. Hitz

**Fig. 9** *T. r. aspera* mating in a terrarium
Photograph: R. Hitz

- they form pairs that stay closely together almost continuously for six to eight weeks during the mating season. Their typical spoors in the sand indicate that males and females may follow each other often over long distances (HENLE unpubl.). During this time the pairs are frequently found in close physical contact, or at least within a radius of 50 cm to each other. The male will test the willingness of the female to mate by touching the latter's body in various places with the tip of the mouth. This probably serves a gathering of olfactory cues (pheromones). The male will also attempt to mate.

If, under terrarium conditions, the period of hibernation is followed by a three week long transitory period of increasing illumination intensity, warmth and food supply, matings will be observed four to six weeks after hibernation. Over a period of seven years three females were observed ready to mate on $7.9 \pm 5.9$ (1-17, n = 10) days (HITZ unpubl.). During this time the female may even take over the active role and try to stimulate the male by nudging him with the snout, biting him gently, and rubbing her cloaca and tail on the ground. On average each female mated $3.9 \pm 2.8$ (1-10, n = 10) times per mating season.

Copulations were witnessed by HITZ (1983) under terrarium conditions. The male will place a mating bite on the lateral occiput, on the side of the neck, or on the body above a front leg of the female (Fig. 9). Once the bite is positioned properly the male will push his base of the tail with the cloaca turned upwards from the side opposite to the bite below that of the female and in doing so insert one of his hemipenes. Copulation takes about 1-2 minutes after which the male will ease his bite, and both animals will separate. No signs of an actual courtship could be observed.

If a female is not ready to mate, she will shake off the male through vigorous wriggling if the latter is at all able to place a mating bite. Once a male has received such a message signalling the end of the mating season in the terrarium, he will not try to mate again in the same season. In nature this marks the point of time (during the course of the month of November) when the partners separate again and return to their solitary lifestyles (BULL 1988, BULL et al. 1991).

The formation of monogamous pairs which come together in every mating season over many years (five to seven years have been documented until now) has among reptiles only been documented from *T. rugosa*. Although the presence of monogamy during a reproductive period was suspected by STAMPS as early as in 1983 for large lizards with overlapping home ranges, it is somewhat surprising that a case of monogamy that lasts over many years is found in a species whose individuals live largely solitarily for the rest of the year. Lasting partnerships primarily involve larger, older males, whereas smaller, younger males tend to swap females or lose them through fights to other males, until they eventually manage to establish a stable partnership (BULL 1990). Among younger males those with broader heads are significantly more often paired up than those with more slender heads (BULL & PAMULA 1996). Young males with broader heads (better "offensive armory") may therefore win a female through fights at an earlier stage than others.

The pairs employ three strategies to find together again after a time of separation (BULL et al. 1993a). For one, they are able to pick up olfactory cues (pheromones). These are given off from the skin or from cloacal glands. BULL et al. (1993a) presumed the presence of one highly volatile and one less volatile component. The lumbering component marks spoors on the ground, while the volatile one charges the air with olfactory cues. The lizards would actively search for one another by following these two types of pheromones. The third strategy involves the revisiting of places the partner is known to frequent. It is usually the male that searches for the female, but females have also been observed searching for their partner.

During the mating season the bonding between the partners is very intense. SHARRAD (1995) reported about one male which stayed for a longer period of time with his female after the latter had been killed on a road and even tried to mate with it. Such case of necrophilous behavior has otherwise been documented only for a species of monitor (LAMBIRIS 1966).

Whether copulations outside the bonded partnership occur in nature is as yet unknown (COOPER et al. 1997), but at least this is possible under terrarium conditions. One of the authors (HITZ) had one male mating with three different females during the mating season of 1986. The male displayed a preference for one particular female which could, however, be broken by replacing this specimen with another.

**Pregnancy:** Like all members of the genus *Tiliqua, T. r. aspera* is live bearing. Placentation takes place in the form of an allanto-placentation (FLYNN 1923, WEEKES 1935), or as a chorioallantois-placentation following more recent nomenclature (STEWART & BLACKBURN 1988). As with most vertebrates the hormone progesterone appears to play an important role in the course of a gravidity (BOURNE et al. 1986a).

Duration of pregnancy takes the four to five months from November through March, but may also extend into April (bibliography in SHEA 1992). For three captive females one of the authors (HITZ) recorded an average gestation period (inferred from the day the last mating was observed to the day of birth) of 135 ± 15 days (116-159, n = 8). The average gestation period amounted to 139.8 ± 14.6 days (123-159, n = 5) when a single young was born. It was shorter in the case of twins, that is on average 127.2 ± 12.9 days (116-142, n = 3). This shows that, like with other animal species, the duration of gravidity may be influenced to a small extent by the number of embryos.

Gravid females tend to spend the vast majority of the day at the warmest spots of their terrarium. This corresponds well with field observations in which it was notable that females became more active than males from late November (BULL et al. 1991), indicating that they were obviously more commonly encountered in the sun.

An interesting phenomenon was observed in the terrarium of one of the authors (HITZ) when a female gave birth to two healthy babies on dates six days apart. This female had been receptive during the previous mating season for 11 days suggesting that ovulations in both ovaries possibly took place at different points of time.

During their pregnancies the females continue feeding right until shortly before giving birth. They increase in circumference and mass. Towards the end of the term the animals often breathe heavily with the back rising and falling in a distinct manner. Captive gravid females showed increases of mass during the gestation period of 150 to 230 g, with start-off weights right after the completion of hibernation of 600-700 g rising to 760-900 g right before giving birth. Similar values were recorded by BULL et al. (1993b) who noted average masses of 838.5 ± 41.7 g. With a mean mass of 730.0 ± 85.5 g females carrying a single offspring were lighter than those carrying twins which weighed 871.1 ± 44.9 g on average. In some cases no exterior signs of pregnancy are visible.

Abnormal courses of a pregnancy have so far not been documented from nature. In captivity, one or more embryos may occasionally perish towards the end of the full term, though, or sizable amounts of yolk may accumulate in the oviducts which will inevitably lead to the death of the female concerned if they are not removed surgically in time.

**Birth and parental care:** In their native Australia, *T. r. aspera* give birth in autumn, with most young being born in the month of March (BULL 1995). In captivity, births preferably take place during the later hours of noon when the female and her environment have warmed up nicely. An impending birth may announce itself already days before the actual event in the form of strong muscular contractions of the body at intervals of 30 seconds minimum (BULL et al. 1993b). In a terrarium the female will then seek cover in her hiding place where she will excavate a shallow ditch by shovelling substrate away with the front and hind legs (HITZ 1983).

Heavy contractions appear again shortly before birth. The female will then stretch her hind legs straight backwards and lift her pelvic region, hind legs and tail. This is followed by the release of approximately 10 ml of amniotic fluid upon which the head of a baby will appear from the cloaca under more intensive contractions. This causes the inner embryonic membrane to tear so that more amniotic fluid seeps out. Another 4-5 intensive contractions expel the rest of the juvenile. The intervals between the individual contractions are 5-10 seconds long, the entire expelling process is completed within 40-50 seconds.

Right after birth the mother nudges and licks the newborn. Being attached to the navel the newborn drags the placenta with it and is therefore no longer physically connected with its mother. It will consume the placenta and remains of the yolk sac, which both still contain yellow yolk material, shortly after its birth. It may also happen that the mother ingests parts of the placenta (HITZ 1983). Shortly thereafter the young will shed its skin in small shreds and also consume these pieces. In all of the births observed the babies were born stretched out with the head first. In one case, a juvenile was born 15 minutes after the first one.

BULL et al. (1993b) discussed a variety of possible biological functions and the importance of these yolk reserves for the newborns. For one, they might serve them as energy reserves since food may often be very scarce in late summer and autumn. Well nourished juveniles may also stay in their hiding places where they are safer from predators. Furthermore they may have an energy reserve in the case of an early onset of winter. These energy reserves may equally bridge the time span the young animals need to establish a functioning intestinal flora for the digestion of plant matter. The last mentioned hypothesis appears the most likely one to us as, although the availability of food may be very variable, it is closely correlated to the amount of precipitation which is highly variable but aseasonal in the distribution range of *T. r. aspera* (see, e.g., ROBERTSON et al. 1987). The temperatures, on the other hand, remain at a level that permits activity for at least another 1.5-2 months. Lastly, there are only a few predators that prey upon shinglebacks (comp. paragraph "Predators, parasites, ...", p. 72).

Mothers are able to distinguish their own babies from those of other mothers, and juveniles can recognize their own mothers among strange animals (MAIN & BULL 1996). Olfactory cues probably play an important role in this. The presence of mother-child recognition suggests that family groups represent a component in the social organization of this species, at least during the early stages of juvenile development. This fact may also be interpreted that a certain degree of parental care (staying together of newborns and mothers, protection of the newborn by the mother) exists in *T. rugosa* (Fig. 10). During the first spring following their birth the juveniles roam within relatively small home ranges which overlap widely with that of their mothers (BULL & BAGHURST 1998). Despite this spatial proximity juveniles and mothers could, however, never be observed together.

**Litter size:** Overviews of the existing literature were published by GREER (1989) and SHEA (1992). According to these authors, a litter may consist of 1 to 5 juveniles with litters of 4 or 5 probably representing very rare exceptions. Females in the material examined by SHEA contained an average of 2.2 ± 0.7 yolked follicles, yolk masses, or embryos in the oviducts during the reproductive season (1-4, n = 95).

**Fig. 10** *T. r. aspera,* mother with two newly born babies
Photograph: K. Griffiths

Litters of four babies only occurred in mothers with an SVL of 28.2 cm and more. BULL et al. (1993b) and BULL (1995) mentioned an average litter size of 2.15 babies per litter (1-3) for the population of the Mt. Mary region in South Australia. A total of eleven juveniles were obtained by one of the authors (HITZ unpubl.) from eight births by three females within seven years amounting to an average of 1.4 ± 0.5 (1-2, n = 8). This average value for a captive environment therefore is significantly lower (by 35-37%) than the above mentioned values from nature. A reason for this might be that the management of the reproduction under terrarium conditions is not quite perfect yet.

**Newly born juveniles**

According to SHEA (1992) the body sizes (SVL) of newly born juveniles of various populations vary as to their minimum values: 153 mm in the east, 127 mm in the south, and 133 mm in the west. GREEN (1995) reported about juveniles born as quadruplets with respectable SVL values between 142 and 148 mm, while the twins of another litter measured 169 and 172 mm, respectively. HITZ (unpubl.) noted an average SVL of 150 ± 6 mm (134-157, n = 11) in captive born juveniles. The average mass at birth (juvenile inclusive ingested placenta) was given by BULL et al. (1993b) to be 106.4 ± 4.5 g in the case of twins, and 107.3 ± 5.1 g for singles. In GREEN's (1995) litter of quadruplets, the babies weighed only 50-65 g. One of the authors (HITZ unpubl.) noted an average weight of 125.5 ± 17.6 g (100-150 g, n = 11). These values suggest that the smaller average litter size in captivity may be compensated by a larger offspring body mass. It is possible, though, that this phenomenon is merely the result of a greater food supply in captivity.

**Maturity**

In the species of *Tiliqua,* sexual maturity is correlated with a minimum size and a minimum body mass (JONES 1987). The size at which *T.*

*r. aspera* become mature varies greatly from population to population (BULL 1987, HENLE 1990, SHEA 1992). Shinglebacks mature at 450 g body mass in South Australia (BULL 1987), whereas they need to attain 695 g in Kinchega National Park in western New South Wales (HENLE 1990). Under terrarium conditions the masses on reaching maturity were recorded to be 720-800 g in males and 660-690 g in females (HITZ unpubl.).

The average SVL of mature male specimens ranges around 293 mm, and 295 mm for females in the east, 282 and 284 mm, respectively, in the southeast, 271 and 271 mm, respectively, in the center of the distribution range, and 250 and 246, respectively, in the west. The differences between male and female sizes were not significant in any of the populations examined (SHEA 1992). In his studies of the Mt. Mary population BULL (1995) classified specimens exceeding 28 cm SVL as adult since pairs of these lizards almost exclusively measured 28 cm SVL and more. To grow to this size the animals living there require 3 - 5 years. In Kinchega, western New South Wales, HENLE (1990) observed a male specimen, which presumably reached maturity in his second year of life, at an estimated age of about 19 months.

FERGER (pers. comm.) reported on a captive bred female of *T. rugosa rugosa* which gave birth to a young in its third year of life, and one of the authors (HITZ) witnessed attempts to mate in a 3.5 year old captive bred pair. The female failed to conceive and later expelled a large yolk mass. The earliest signs of sexual activity could be noted in an eleven-month-old male juvenile, which discharged hemipenes exuviae in its terrarium. By means of intense feeding and a shortened period of hibernation it is possible in captivity to push juveniles of *Tiliqua* to maturity within a very short time span. JONES (1987), for example, reported on a female juvenile of *T. gigas* which gave birth to babies at an age of only 18 months.

## Frequency of reproduction

SHEA (1992) deduced from the dissection of female *T. r. aspera* that these would be able to reproduce year after year, but that some (ca. 30%) do not participate in the annual reproduction every year. The reason for a biennial breeding rhythm could be that some females are unable to regain an appropriate condition for another gravidity by the next spring. Biennial rhythms could also be demonstrated by BULL (1995) in the field and by HITZ (unpubl.) in captivity, and it is possible that even longer rhythms exist elsewhere. BULL (1995) estimated that 50% of all females of his population reproduce annually. Based on an average litter size of 2.15 this translates into 1.07 juveniles per female and year.

Under the conditions of a terrarium there may be an alternation of annual and biennial rhythms (HITZ unpubl.). A female with three births displayed both rhythms, whereas two others only showed a one year rhythm. Interestingly enough a female in biennial mode may exhibit receptiveness and mate without developing embryos afterwards.

In summary it can be said that a large pool of information exists on the reproductive biology of *T. r. aspera* from both the field and captivity. A successful propagation of this lizard is well possible under terrarium conditions if the basic requirements of the animals are fulfilled (comp. chapter "On the husbandry and breeding of *Tiliqua rugosa aspera* (GRAY, 1845)").

## Literature

ARNOLD, E. N. (1988): Caudal autotomy as a defense. – Pp. 235–273 in GANS, C. & R. B. HUEY: Biology of the Reptilia. – New York (Alan R. Liss): 235–273.

BENNETT, A. F. & H. JOHN-ALDER (1986): Thermal relations of some Australian skinks, Sauria: Scincidae. – Copeia, 1986: 57–64.

BOURNE, A. R. & R. F. SEAMARK (1975): Seasonal changes in 17b-hydroxysteroids in the plasma of a male lizard (*Tiliqua rugosa*). – Comp. Biochem. Physiol., 50 B: 515–536.

– (1978): Seasonal variation in steroid biosynthesis by the testis of the Lizard *Tiliqua rugosa*. – Comp. Biochem. Physiol., 59 B: 363–367.

BOURNE, A. R., B. J. STEWART & T. G. WATSON (1986a): Changes in blood progesterone concentration during pregnancy in the lizard *Tiliqua (Trachydosaurus) rugosa*. – Comp. Biochem. Physiol., 84A: 581–583.

BOURNE, A. R., J. L. TAYLOR & T. G. WATSON (1986b): Annual cycles of plasma and testicular androgens in the lizard *Tiliqua (Trachydosaurus) rugosa*. – General Comp. Endocrin., 61: 278–286.

BRADSHAW, S. D. (1986): Ecophysiology of Desert Reptiles. – Sydney (Academic Press.), 324 pp.

BROWN, G. W. (1991): Ecological feeding analysis of south-eastern Australian scincids (Reptilia: Lacertilia). – Aust. J. Zool., 39: 9–29.

BULL, C. M. (1978): Dispersal of the Australian reptile tick *Aponomma hydrosauri* by host movement. – Aust. J. Zool., 26(4): 689–697.

– (1987): A population study of the viviparous Australian lizard, *Trachydosaurus rugosus* (Scincidae). – Copeia, 1987: 749–757.

– (1988): Mate fidelity in an Australian lizard *Trachydosaurus rugosus*. – Behav. Ecol. Sociobiol., 23(1): 45–49.

– (1990): Comparisons of displaced and retained partners in a monogamous lizard. – Aust. Wildl. Res., 17(2): 135–140.

– (1995): Population ecology of the sleepy lizard, *Tiliqua rugosa*, at Mt Mary, South Australia. – 2nd World Congress of Herpetology. – Aust. J. Ecol., 20: 393–402.

BULL, C. M. & B. C. BAGHURST (1998): Home range overlap of mothers and their offspring in the sleepy lizard, *Tiliqua rugosa*. – Behav. Ecol. Sociobiol., 42(5): 357–362.

BULL, C. M., G. S. BEDFORD & B. A. SCHULZ (1993a): How do sleepy lizards find each other? – Herpetologica, 49(3): 294–300.

BULL, C. M., D. BURZACOTT & R. D. SHARRAD (1989): No competition for resources between two tick species at their parapatric boundary. – Oecologia, 79: 558–562.

BULL, C. M., A. MC NALLY & G. DUBAS (1991): Asynchronous seasonal activity of male and female sleepy lizards, *Tiliqua rugosa*. – J. Herpetol., 25(4): 436–441.

BULL, C. M. & Y. PAMULA (1996): Sexually dimorphic head sizes and reproductive success in the sleepy lizard *Tiliqua rugosa*. – J. Zool., London, 240: 511–521.

BULL, C. M., Y. PAMULA & L. SCHULZE (1993b): Parturition in the sleepy lizard, *Tiliqua rugosa*. – J. Herpetol., 27: 489–492.

COOPER, S. J. B., C. M. BULL & M. G. GARDNER (1997): Characterization of microsatellite loci from the socially monogamous lizard *Tiliqua rugosa* using a PCR-based isolation technique. – Molecular Ecol., 6: 793–795.

DUBAS, G. & C. M. BULL (1991): Diet choice and food availability in the omnivorous lizard *Trachydosaurus rugosus*. – Wildl. Res., 18(2): 147–155.

DUVALL, D., L. J. GUILLETTE & R. E. JONES (1982): Environmental control of reptilian breeding cycles. – Pp. 201–231 in GANS, C. & F. H. POUGH: Biology of the Reptilia. Vol. 13: Physiology D: Physiological Ecology. – London (Acad. Press).

FLYNN, T. T. (1923): On the occurrence of a true allantoplacenta of the conjoint type in an Australian lizard. – Rec. Aust. Mus., 14(1): 72–77.

GRAY, J. E. (1845): Catalogue of the Specimens of Lizards in the Collection of the British Museum. – London (Trustees of the British Museum), 289 pp.

GREEN, D. (1995): A comparison of three litters in the shingleback lizard, *Trachydosaurus rugosus*. – Herpetofauna, 25(1): 42–43.

GREER, A. E. (1989): The Biology and Evolution of Australian Lizards. – Chipping Norton, NSW (Surrey Beatty & Sons Pty Ltd.), 264 pp.

HENLE, K. (1989): Ecological segregation in an assemblage of diurnal lizards in arid Australia. – Acta Œcol. Œcol. Gener., 10: 19–35.

– (1990): Notes on the population ecology of the large herbivorous lizard, *Trachydosaurus rugosus*, in arid Australia. – J. Herpetol., 24(1): 100–103.

HENLE, K. & C. J. J. KLAVER (1986): *Podarcis sicula* (RAFINESQUE-SCHMALTZ, 1810) – Ruineneidechse. – S. 254–342 in BÖHME, W.: Handbuch der Reptilien und Amphibien Europas. Bd. 2/II: Echsen (Sauria) III: Lacertidae III: *Podarcis*. – Wiesbaden (Aula-Verlag).

HITZ, R. (1983): Pflege und Nachzucht von *Trachydosaurus rugosus* GRAY, 1827 im Terrarium.

(Sauria: Scincidae). – Salamandra, Bonn, 19(4): 198–210.

HORN, H. -G. (1980): Bisher unbekannte Details zur Kenntnis von *Varanus varius* auf Grund von feldherpetologischen und terraristischen Beobachtungen (Reptilia: Sauria: Varanidae). – Salamandra, Bonn, 16(1): 1–18.

HULBERT, J. A. & C. A. WILLIAMS (1988): Thyroid function in a lizard, a turtle, and a crocodile compared with mammals. – Comp. Biochem. Physiol. 90A: 41–48.

JOGER, U., E. WALLIKEWITZ & A. HAUSCHILD (1986): Hormon- und serochemische Untersuchungen zur Bestimmung des Geschlechtes und zur Überprüfung des Gesundheitszustandes bei *Trachydosaurus rugosus* GRAY, 1827. – Salamandra, Bonn, 22(1): 21–28.

JOHNSTON, T.H. (1932): The parasites of the „stumpytail" lizard, *Trachydosaurus rugosus*. –Trans. Roy. Soc. S. Aust. 56: 62–70.

JONES, S. (1987): A report on a reproducible and sustainable system for the captive propagation of the genus *Tiliqua* GRAY, 1825. – Pp. 17–25 in COOTE, J.: Reptiles. – Proceedings of the 1986 U.K. Herpetological Societies Symposium on Captive Breeding. – London (British Herpet. Soc.).

LAMBIRIS, A.J. (1966): Observation on Rhodesian reptiles. – J. Herpetol. Assoc. Africa, 2: 33–34.

LICHT, P. (1972): Environmental physiology of reptilian breeding cycles: Role of temperature. – Gen. Comp. Endocrin., Suppl. 3: 477–488.

LICHT, P., W.R. DAWSON, V.H. SHOEMAKER & A.R. MAIN (1966): Observations on the thermal relations of Western Australian lizards. – Copeia, l: 97–110.

MAIN, A.R. & C.M. BULL (1996): Mother-offspring recognition in two Australian lizards, *Tiliqua rugosa* and *Egernia stokesii*. – Anim. Behav., 52: 193–200.

ROBERTSON, G., J. SHORT & G. WELLARD (1987): The environment of the Australian sheep rangelands. – Pp. 14–34 in CAUGHLEY, G., N. SHEPHERD & J. SHORT: Kangaroos, their Ecology and Management in the Sheep Rangelands of Australia. – Cambridge (Univ. Press.).

SARRE, S. & J.M. DEARN (1991) : Morphological variation and fluktuating asymmetry among insular populations of the sleepy lizard, *Trachydosaurus rugosus*. – Aust. J. Zool., 39: 91–104.

SARRE, S., T.D. SCHWANER & A. GEORGES (1990): Genetic variation among insular populations of the sleepy lizard, *Trachydosaurus rugosus* GRAY (Squamata: Scincidae). – Aust. J. Zool., 38:603–616.

SATRAWAHA, R. & C.M. BULL (1981): The area occupied by an omnivorous lizard, *Trachydosaurus rugosus*. – Aust. Wildl. Res., 8(2): 435–442.

SCHNEIDER, K.M. (1941): Über Fettlager im Schwanz der Krusten- (*Heloderma* WIEGM.) und Stutzechse (*Trachydosaurus* GRAY). – Zool. Garten, 13(3/4):236–247.

SHARRAD, R.D. (1995): Necrophilia in *Tiliqua rugosa*: A dead end in evolution? – West. Aust. Nat., 20(1): 33–35.

SHEA, G.M. (1992): The Systematics and Reproduction of Bluetongue Lizards of the Genus *Tiliqua* (Squamata: Scincidae). Vol. 1–4. – Sydney (Ph.D. thesis, University of Sydney).

SPELLERBERG, I.F. (1972): Temperature tolerances of southeast Australian reptiles examined in relation to reptile thermoregulatory behavior and distribution. – Oecologia, 9: 23–46.

STAMPS, J.A. (1983): Sexual selection, sexual dimorphism and territoriality. – Pp. 169–204 in HUEY, R.B., E.R. PIANKA & T.W. SCHOENER (eds.): Lizard Ecology. Studies of a Model Organism. – Cambridge (Harvard University Press), 501 pp.

STEWART, J.R. & D.G. BLACKBURN (1988): Reptilian placentation: Structural diversity and terminology. – Copeia, 1988: 839–852.

WEEKES, H.C. (1935): A review of placentation among reptiles with particular regard to the function and evolution of the placenta. – Proc. Zool. Soc. London., 1935: 625–645.

Authors' addresses
Dr. Robert Hitz
Am Mülibach 8
CH-9425 Thal, Switzerland

Dr. Klaus Henle
Department of Conservation Biology and Natural Resources, Centre for Environmental Research, UFZ Leipzig-Halle
Permoserstr. 13, D-04318 Leipzig, Germany

# On the husbandry and breeding of *Tiliqua rugosa aspera* (GRAY, 1845)

ROBERT HITZ

Key words: Reptilia: Sauria: Scincidae: *Tiliqua: Tiliqua rugosa aspera,* Australia, husbandry, breeding

## Introduction

*Tiliqua rugosa aspera* is a very popular terrarium animal in Europe and the United States and used to be imported from Australia in large numbers before restrictive legislation came into effect. The popularity of these lizards is due to their interesting appearance, their easy-to-fulfil husbandry requirements, and their longevity. Although they were kept without problems for many years in terraria up until the early eighties, they did not disclose all of their biological potential. This situation was based on a number of fundamental errors as to the understanding of their husbandry requirements and a lack of certain basic conditions. In his terrarium book NIETZKE still stated in 1978 that *T. rugosa* would not require a cool overwintering period.

When the author had the fortune of being able to acquire two juvenile pairs of *T. r. aspera,* the information provided by two authors in particular was taken really seriously: BUSTARD (1970) and STETTLER (1978). As a precondition for the successful propagation and raising of amphibians and reptiles in the terrarium STETTLER named optimum keeping conditions (emulation of the natural environmental factors). It would be imperative to take into consideration the seasonal changes of the environmental influences (availability of food, changes of climate) which would then trigger matings. These environmental influences are very nicely lined out in BUSTARD (1970). As a consequence the author was the first to propagate *T. r. aspera*

on a regular basis in Europe by emulating the seasonal rhythm of the southern hemisphere in the animals' terraria. The strict adherence to a cool period of overwintering proved to be of particular importance (HITZ 1983). Subsequently there were a number of reports about the successful keeping and breeding of these lizards, in Europe by JONES (1987) and GROSS (1989), in the US by WAGNER & RICHARDSON (1988) and CARD (1993). A detailed account of the husbandry and propagation was published by HAUSCHILD & GASSNER (1995). At the same time an increasing amount of data became available in specialized literature (see chapter "The biology of *Tiliqua rugosa aspera* (GRAY, 1845)"). The present contribution is meant to portray the husbandry and breeding of *T. r. aspera* based on all existing literature and the author's own experiences.

## Individual vs. group keeping

In their natural habitat the individuals of *T. r. aspera* live solitarily in very large home ranges and only come together during the mating season. These home ranges may stretch over surface areas of between 100 and 50,000 m² (SATRAWAHA 1980) with an average of a little less than 4,000 m² (BULL et al. 1991). Although these areas may overlap and although they are not defended against conspecifics, it will appear logical that a continuous housing of several specimens in a terrarium measuring between 0.5 and several square meters must inevitably lead to perma-stress resulting in psychic hebetude. JONES (1987) therefore recommended housing these lizards individually. FERGER (pers. comm. 1997), however, also had good breeding results with *T. r. rugosa* of which 3-5 well harmonizing specimens were kept together in well structured terraria. That the presence of conspecifics is tolerated, or perhaps even coveted, under certain circumstances in nature also, is demonstrated by observations made by HENLE (1990) who found up to four adult specimens of *T. r. aspera* in larger hiding places. The author was successful in keeping these lizards in pairs. In summary the experiences made until now suggest an individual keeping outside the mating season, at maximum a keeping in pairs.

## Housing

In Europe and North America *T. r. aspera* are mainly kept in indoor terraria. Combining this mode of keeping with a temporary stay outdoors (or in fresh air), at times when the climatic conditions correspond with the chosen annual rhythm, is possible and sensible. In suitable regions, such as southern Europe and South Africa, and obviously within the natural distribution range in Australia, the skinks can be kept outdoors throughout the year.

## Terrarium

With *T. r. aspera* being a ground dwelling lizard, its terrarium should offer as much ground space as possible whereas the height of the cage is of secondary importance. Some countries have laws in effect that regulate the captive keeping of wild animals and these may also include minimum sizes for a terrarium. In Germany, for example, dimensions of 200 × 140 × 100 cm would be recommended (l × w × h; based on 6 × 4 × 3 times SVL, with a maximum SVL of 34.1 cm [SHEA 1992]). The preconditions necessary for a successful propagation may, however, be fulfilled already in much smaller terraria. JONES (1987) suggested terraria of 60 × 60 × 30 cm (l × w × h), and HITZ (1983) successfully bred shinglebacks in cages measuring 90 × 60 × 40 cm (l × w × h) and 100 × 50 × 45 cm, respectively. Where relevant legislation exists, the keeper should adhere to it.

## Decoration of the terrarium

Various types of sand may be used as substrate. The author made good experiences with quartzite with a granulation of 1.0-1.5 mm. Finer sand tends to stick to the animals' mouths, nostrils, and eyes, whereas a coarser substrate causes excessive wear of the claws on the toes of the front feet from digging. Suitable hiding places can be created from arched pieces of bark, ridging tiles, or massive, but low rock constructions. Various rocks can be used to create an agreeable general appearance. Suitable plants for larger terraria are found among aridophilous species which may have to be protected from the skinks by strategically placed rocks. Plastic plants are an alternative, particularly in smaller cages, and are equally appreciated by the animals for cover they provide. The decoration should be planned in a manner so that its structure makes it impossible for the inhabitants to overview the entire interior from any one point. This encourages them to roam around in their environment. Their hiding places should be located at cooler sites in the background.

## Illumination

For smaller sized terraria the keeper may want to use fluorescent tubes due to their high light output and low heat generation. The author made positive experiences with True-Lite or Philips TLD 80/86, both of which emit the full spectrum of natural daylight. These were combined with one Blacklight fluo tube (Sylvania F18 BLB) per terrarium as an additional source of UV-A radiation; they also emit a small amount of UV-B. In order to ensure a sufficient supply with UV-B radiation the lizards were once a week exposed to an Osram Ultra-VitaLux lamp from a distance of 75 cm for 20 minutes outside their terraria. Today, fluo tubes are available that emit the full spectrum of natural daylight and have an optimum content of UV-A and UV-B (e.g. Reptisun 5.0 UVB by Zoo Med). If this new generation of lamps keep what their manufacturers promise, they will most certainly replace the traditional fluorescent tubes and sun lamps of the "Ultra VitaLux" type in the terrarium hobby.

One should be aware of the fact that all lamps lose parts of their irradiation intensity over time. They should therefore be replaced after a certain number of hours of operation as is usually suggested by the manufacturer. In general the usability of fluorescent tubes lasts for one, at maximum two, years. In the case of large, high terraria, mercury vapor lamps (HQL) or metal halogen vapor lamps can be employed. Various types of incandescent lamps find use in creating hot spots, i.e. for heating and illuminating the substrate and surrounding air locally. It is of utmost importance that all sources of light and heat are placed in the terrarium eccentrically and that the decoration creates enough structure to permit the animals to escape radiation as they wish.

## Heating

The terraria maintained by the author are heated with heating pads of 30 × 40 cm in size. These heat up the substrate within their range to 35-40°C. Many terrarium keepers prefer a variety of spot lights that emit light and warmth to underfloor heating. As with the sources of light, any heating devices should be placed eccentrically and outside the hiding places so that the animals have the opportunity to thermoregulate in an active manner. In general there is a danger of overheating in small terraria which would turn the inhabitants into prisoners of a sweat box. An oversupply with warmth results in various health problems and failing breeding attempts. This problem can be overcome with appropriate measures of ventilation and aeration.

## Temperature requirements

Every species of lizard has their specific temperature requirements that have to be fulfilled in captivity through various technological means including illumination, heating, ventilation and cooling. In their field studies LICHT et al. (1966) noted a mean rectal temperature of 32.7 ± 2.63 °C in free ranging *T. rugosa,* and 33.8 ± 1.1 °C under laboratory conditions. Similar values were also found by BENNETT & JOHN-ALDER (1986). In order for *T. rugosa* to be able to reach its preferred activity temperature of about 30-35°C, a source area offering 35-40°C must be accessible. Whether this temperature range is created by an underfloor heater or a spotlight is of secondary importance since even the experts cannot seem to agree on the physiology of the thermoregulation in the species of *Tiliqua*. While JONES (1987) considered these lizards as "thigmotherms" (absorbing heat from the surrounding substrate), SPELLERBERG (1972) termed them "posturing heliotherms" which means that the animals would have the body warmed up through solar radiation by assuming a variety of body postures. The author tends to agree with JONES' opinion as the species of *Tiliqua* have a fairly secretive way of life throughout much of the year and thus expose themselves less to solar radiation in the open than, for example, agamid lizards. Although shinglebacks are nevertheless often seen in the open, they are likely to cover their heat requirements from physical contact with their environment. They have actually never been observed basking (HENLE pers. comm. 1999).

SPELLERBERG (1972) established the so-called critical minimum and maximum temperatures for various lizards. The critical temperature is the value at which a lizard loses its ability to righten itself after it has been placed on its back (rightening reflex). In praxis these values must be considered lethal temperatures which the animals must never be exposed to as they would suffer irreversible damage or die. Following SPELLERBERG (1972) the critical minimum temperature for *T. rugosa* is 4.0-5.0°C. BENNETT & JOHN-ALDER (1986) established a critical minimum temperature of 3.5°C and a critical maximum temperature of 43.0°C. The lower value is of importance during the cool overwintering period, while the higher one may become a threat in terraria exposed to direct sunlight.

## Humidity and moisture

*T. r. aspera* is distributed in the arid regions of southeastern Australia where a low relative humidity is prevalent. The mean values of relative humidity at Broken Hill, for example, lie between 24 and 30% in the afternoon during the warmer months of the year and may climb to not more than a maximum of 50% in winter. Depending on the season the values may range between 39 and 72% in the morning (GRÜNEWALD et al. 1982). Based on this information the author kept *T. r. aspera* very dry, with the decoration of the terrarium being misted only sporadically, but by no means daily. Daily misting and the resulting elevated humidity of more than 50% brought about an increased susceptibility to flu. In this context HOSER (1989) also mentioned that captive specimens of *T. rugosa* kept in the more humid regions of Australia, such as Brisbane, Sydney and Melbourne, would be rather delicate. WEIGEL (1989) recommended keeping these lizards exclusively indoors at the east coast of Australia. Following this author the animals should even only be given drinking water every 1-2 weeks in order to avoid raising the humidity through the mere presence of a filled water bowl.

## Keeping rhythms

**Day/night rhythm:** The distribution range of *T. r. aspera* is marked by substantial daily fluctuations in the temperature that may vary by 10-20°C throughout the year. A decrease of the temperature at night should also be emulated in the terrarium which is easily achieved by having the heating devices switch off in the evening.

**Annual cycles:** A precondition for the long term husbandry and successful breeding of *T. r. aspera* is the consequent following of an annual rhythm. Experience has shown that it does not really make a difference whether the animals are kept under the annual cycle of the southern hemisphere (Australia) or the northern hemisphere (Europe, North America). Specimens that are translocated from one hemisphere into the other adjust their biorhythm to their new environment within 1-2 years. It is recommendable, however, to link the annual cycle in the terrarium to the hemisphere in which you live. This brings about the advantage of a synchronized sequential change of temperature and photoperiod in both the terrarium and outdoors. If the skinks are to enjoy temporary stays outdoors or in fresh air, it should be ensured that these periods fit into the annual cycle.

When the author ventured into the unchartered territory of trying to breed *T. r. aspera* he tried to emulate in his terraria the annual cycle of southern Australia. This required an outstanding technical effort in the form of illumination, heating and cooling regimes (HITZ 1983; HITZ unpubl.). Employing similar means GROSS (1989) successfully bred *T. r. rugosa*. On the other hand, WAGNER & RICHARDSON (1988), CARD (1993) and FERGER (pers. comm. 1997) successfully kept and bred shinglebacks in the annual cycle of the northern hemisphere. In accordance with the climatological and ecological circumstances described by BUSTARD (1970) the guidelines presented in Table 1 may be followed (northern hemisphere).

The basis of the daily illumination period is given by the natural photoperiod, i.e. the daily duration of the artificial lighting should be linked to the natural number of daylight hours.

**Table 1** Husbandry calendar (northern hemisphere)

| Months | Season | Climate | Food |
|---|---|---|---|
| January thru March | winter | cool | little to no food |
| April thru June | spring | warm, dry | lots of food |
| July thru September | summer | hot, dry | little food |
| October thru December | autumn | warm, dry | little food |

The longest illumination period is 12 hours, the shortest eight hours. The heating regime of the terraria follows an analogous pattern, with the exception of the cool overwintering period and the transitory phases before and after. The author uses a timer for this purpose on which the on- and off-times are changed every fortnight. **Hibernation:** A cool hibernation period is essential for the successful keeping and breeding of *T. r. aspera*. The calendar winter of the southern hemisphere lasts from June 1, to August 31. According to GRÜNEWALD et al. (1982) the months of May, June, July, August and September are rather cool at Broken Hill, New South Wales, with absolute minima of less than 0°C. The mean daily maxima range from 15.3 to 21.1°C, but very warm days with absolute maxima of more than 30°C may be observed during these months. If the weather permits, the lizards may even leave their hibernation quarters during the day (HENLE pers. comm.) and bask. NIEMANN (1984, pers. comm.) studied hibernation quarters of *T. r. aspera* at Dalmeny, 150 km south of Sydney. During the month of August he took temperatures of between 11 and 17°C inside two different shelters. All this suggests that *T. r. aspera* is in nature subjected to a cool period of at least three months, which may, however, be interrupted by short, warmer intervals. For their keeping in captivity this means that the lizards should be offered a cool phase of 2-3 months duration.

The Switzerland based author kept *T. r. aspera* according to the southern Australian annual cycle (HITZ 1983). Winter was emulated by keeping the lizards in open-air terraria on a west facing balcony during the months of July, August and September. The many times cooler summers in central Europe often correspond nicely with the winters in the natural distribution range of *T. r. aspera*. An important factor to consider is that the animals are kept on the north, east or west side of a house, but not on the sun exposed south side!

This method of keeping was changed in later years. The skinks remained in their indoor terraria for hibernating. During a three week transitory period with decreasing offerings of food and reduced duration of illumination and heating the animals were prepared for a two month period of coolness. This was achieved by means of an air conditioner which brought the temperature down to 9-15°C. At the end of this cool phase the animals were again slowly prepared for the normal terrarium routine. GROSS (1989) successfully applied the same method for the propagation of *T. r. rugosa*. JONES (pers. comm.) hibernated *T. rugosa* in a cool room at 10-16°C for two months, and in the US, WAGNER & RICHARDSON (1988) hibernated their animals at 10-15°C during the months November, December and January. The skinks remained in their terraria which were translocated to an unheated room. CARD (1993) applied a two month long cool period at 13-21°C. FERGER (1997, pers. comm.) has been hibernating his shinglebacks at 12-17°C for two months, plus transitory phases before and after the actual cool period.

**Fig. 1** *Tiliqua rugosa aspera,* pair in the mating season        Photo: O. Daniel

**Fig. 2** *Tiliqua rugosa aspera* near Broken Hill.        Photo: O. Daniel

Fig. 3 *Tiliqua rugosa aspera* near Broken Hill.     Photo: O. Daniel

Fig. 4 *Tiliqua rugosa aspera* female with a one week old juvenile     Photo: O. Daniel

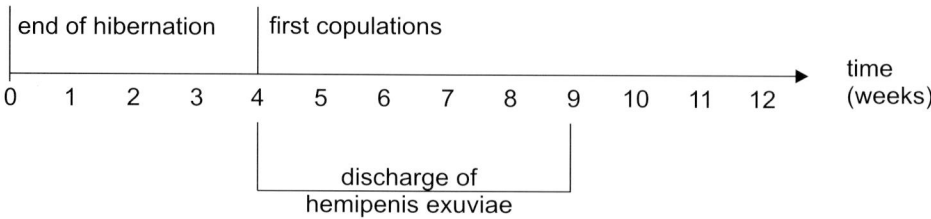

**Fig. 5** Chronological sequence of events during the mating season in a terrarium

Finally it should be mentioned that a cool hibernation of lizards can also be effected, subsequent to a readying phase, in a refrigerator (LASZLO 1977, BANNERT 1993). Preconditions for a success of this method obviously include the regular checking of the temperature and the animals themselves. By means of an aeration pump, as commonly used for aquaria, fresh air from the room can be pumped into the refrigerator intermittently via an automatic timer. In order for this to work properly another small air hose must be fixed in the gasket at the top of the fridge door through which the overpressure may be released.

**Synchronization of the sexes, breeding management**

Given the annual cycle described above, which must include a 2-3 month long cool hibernation period, the reproductive cycles of both sexes are optimally synchronized. Males and females may end their hibernation at the same point of time. Subsequent to every overwintering the author has been subjecting his lizards to a three week transitory period with a gradually increasing intensity of illumination, heating and amounts of food. Corresponding with the conditions in nature, the skinks should then be kept in pairs for 2-3 months. The author observed a commencement of matings 4-6 weeks after the end of their hibernation period (comp. Fig. 5). If this point of time passes without spontaneous copulations, the males can be stimulated with a variety of means. Another

male may, for example, be introduced into the terrarium of the breeding pair which usually results in a fight between the two males. When the "intruder" is then removed after a brief antagonistic encounter, the remaining male will revert to his female with much increased interest. Another way of stimulating the male is to remove it from the common terrarium for a day, or to swap females for a day. Copulations will, however, often take place without a necessity for any manipulation by the eager keeper.

**Feeding**

*T. r. aspera* is an omnivorous lizard (DUBAS & BULL 1991), although the plant content in its diet is so high it could justifiably be regarded a herbivore (HENLE 1990). Its diet in nature includes leaves and flowers of plants, berries and other fruit, terrestrial snails and slugs, insects, mainly in the form of beetles and caterpillars, small vertebrates including small skinks, fledgling birds (DUBAS & BULL 1991) and carrion (HENLE 1990). According to BROWN (1991) the content of plant matter in its diet makes up 93.7%.

Corresponding with these facts the diet of *T. r. aspera* should be composed mainly on the basis of plant matter. Various types of lettuce, bean sprouts, watercress, wheat sprouts, corn leaves, dandelion leaves, clover, dandelion flowers, daisies, various fruit and berries have all proven suitable. Finely cut-up beef heart or fat free fowl meat can be mixed with the plant components. The author advises against the usage of tinned dog or cat food as today's products are tailored to suit the specific vitamin and mineral requirements of dogs and cats, respectively. Live food can be offered in the form of terrestrial snails and slugs, earthworms, grasshoppers, as well as self-bred feeder insects such as crickets, roaches, tenebrionid beetle larvae *(Zophobas),* and pink mice. The food mix should be improved as to its Ca/P ratio by fortifying it with feeder calcium or grated cuttlefish shell. An addition of a multivitamin and trace element preparation is advisable, too. The most important constituent that should be included is vitamin $D_3$. Both vitamins and trace elements should be dosed correctly according to the body mass of the individual animal.

With regard to the feeding regime it is important to know that adult *T. r. aspera* tend to become obese rapidly under terrarium conditions if one is not careful and conservative with their food supply. Feeding twice a week is usually sufficient for adult skinks. The author endeavors to provide every individual animal with the ration of food designated for it. Group feeding usually leads to strong, tame specimens consuming too much whereas not as strong, shyer ones do not receive enough.

The amounts of food are varied over the course of the year according to Table 1. Drinking water in small glass bowls may be available to the skinks at all times if this does not overly raise the humidity in their terraria. If humidity is a problem, the offering of water can be limited to brief periods every two weeks.

## Raising of the juveniles

Although there is a possibility of mother and young forming a social group after the birth of the latter in nature (MAIN & BULL 1996), it is recommendable to keep juveniles and adults separate in captivity. Baby *T. r. aspera* accept no or very little food during their first week of life (HITZ 1983). This is probably due to the fact that newborns consume their placenta and leftover yolk right after their birth which constitutes a very rich meal. After the first week of life the young will readily accept the same food as the adults, and their raising does normally not pose any problems. They can also spend their first winter in hibernation.

## Sheddings

Juvenile *T. r. aspera* shed their skins for the first time in their lives within one to two hours after their birth. They lose their old skin in small pieces, almost scale by scale, and consume most of it themselves. Growing juveniles shed their skins once to three times per year, whereas adults usually shed only once per year. Kept according to the cycle of the Australian seasons these sheddings generally took place in the time between late December and late February with only one shedding recorded for January (pers. data). Another shedding occasionally followed in May or June. Ideally, the old skin will begin to detach on the head, and the lizard will be able to slough its old dress in one piece. Sometimes, however, the skin is also shed in large patches. If a shedding takes an abnormal course, it is advisable to bathe the animal concerned in lukewarm water for about 15 minutes. Thereafter stuck remains of old skin can usually be removed easily with the fingers.

## In closing ...

*T. r. aspera* would be an ideal lizard for the terrarium. Taking into consideration all the information recorded in the herpetological as well as terrarium related literature, these animals can be kept and bred for decades. It is thus very unfortunate that a further distribution of these interesting skinks among terrarium keepers is severely hampered by the restrictive export legislation of Australia. It must therefore be hoped that the specimens existing outside of Australia are bred more successfully in the future. If the present work helps to achieve this goal, an important aim of the author has indeed been achieved.

## Literature

BANNERT, B. (1993): Erfahrungen zur Überwinterung von Eidechsen. – elaphe (N.F.), 1(2): 11–14.

BENNETT, A. F. & H. JOHN-ALDER (1986): Thermal relations of some Australian skinks, Sauria: Scincidae. – Copeia, 1986: 57–64.

BROWN, G.W. (1991): Ecological feeding analysis of south-eastern Australian scincids (Reptilia: Lacertilia). – Aust. J. Zool., 39: 9–29.

BUNDESMINISTERIUM FÜR ERNÄHRUNG, LANDWIRTSCHAFT UND FORSTEN, REFERAT TIERSCHUTZ (1997): Gutachten über Mindestanforderungen an die Haltung von Reptilien, vom 10. Januar 1997. – Unveränderte Sonderausgabe der Deutschen Gesellschaft für Herpetologie und Terrarienkunde (DGHT) e.V., 77 S.

BUSTARD, R. (1970): Australian Lizards. – Sydney, London (William Collins Ltd.), 158 pp.

CARD, W. (1993): Natural history and husbandry of the Shingleback Skink (*Trachydosaurus rugosus*) and the Blotched Blue-tongued Skink (*Tiliqua nigrolutea*). – The Vivarium, Lakeside (Amer. Fed. Herpetoculturists), 6(3): 26–27.

DUBAS, G. & C.M. BULL (1991): Diet choice and food availability in the omnivorous lizard *Trachydosaurus rugosus*. – Wildl. Res., 18(2): 147–155.

GROSS, J. (1989): Pflege, Geschlechtsbestimmung und Zucht der Tannenzapfenechse. – DATZ, 42(10): 612–613.

GRÜNEWALD, G., E. HÖLLER & D. STRANZ (1982): Brockhaus Texte und Tabellen – Länder und Klima – Asien, Australien. – Wiesbaden (F.A. Brockhaus) & Hamburg (Interpress Übersee-Verlag GmbH), 240 S.

HAUSCHILD, A. & P. GAßNER (1995): Skinke im Terrarium. – Hannover (Landbuch-Verlag), 197 S.

HENLE, K. (1990): Notes on the population ecology of the large herbivorous lizard, *Trachydosaurus rugosus*, in arid Australia. – J. Herpetology, 24(1): 100–103.

HITZ, R. (1983): Pflege und Nachzucht von *Trachydosaurus rugosus* GRAY, 1827 im Terrarium. (Sauria: Scincidae). – Salamandra, Bonn, 19(4): 198–210.

HOSER, R.T. (1989): Australian Reptiles & Frogs. – Mosman NSW (Pierson & Co.), 238 pp.

JONES, S. (1987): A report on a reproducible and sustainable system for the captive propagation of the genus *Tiliqua* GRAY, 1825. – Pp. 17–25 in COOTE, J.: Reptiles. – Proceedings of the 1986 U.K. Herpetological Societies Symposium on Captive Breeding. – London (British Herpet. Soc.).

LASZLO, J. (1977): Practical methods of inducing mating in snakes, using extended daylengths and darkness. – Proceedings A.A.Z.P.A. Regional Conferences, 1977.

LICHT, P., W.R. DAWSON, V.H. SHOEMAKER & A.R. MAIN (1966): Observations on the thermal relations of Western Australian lizards. – Copeia, 1966: 97–110.

MAIN, A.R. & C.M. BULL (1996): Mother-offspring recognition in two Australian lizards, *Tiliqua rugosa* and *Egernia stokesii*. – Anim. Behav., 52: 193–200.

NIETZKE, G. (1978): Die Terrarientiere 2. – 2. Aufl., Stuttgart (Eugen Ulmer), 322 S.

SATRAWAHA, R. (1980): Ecology and activity patterns of the lizard *Trachydosaurus rugosus*. – Adelaide (M.Sc. Thesis, The Flinders University of South Australia), 136 pp.

SHEA, G.M. (1992): The systematics and reproduction of bluetongue lizards of the genus *Tiliqua* (Squamata: Scincidae). Vol. 1–4. – Sydney (Ph.D. thesis, University of Sydney).

SPELLERBERG, I.F. (1972): Temperature tolerances of southeast Australian reptiles examined in relation to reptile thermoregulatory behavior and distribution. – Oecologia, 9: 23–46.

STETTLER, P.H. (1978): Handbuch der Terrarienkunde. Terrarientypen, Tiere, Pflanzen, Futter. – Stuttgart (Kosmos. Franckh'sche Verlagshandlung), 228 S.

WAGNER, E. & D. RICHARDSON (1988): Breeding the Shingleback Skink, *Trachydosaurus rugosus*. – The Vivarium, Lakeside (Amer. Fed. Herpetoculturists), 1(2): 40–41.

WEIGEL, J. (1989): Care of Australian Reptiles in Captivity. – Reprint. – Gosford, New South Wales (Reptile Keepers Association), 144 pp.

Author's address
Dr. Robert Hitz
Am Mülibach 8
CH-9425 Thal, Switzerland

# The bobtail, *Tiliqua rugosa rugosa* (Gray, 1825) - Biology, husbandry and breeding

Peter Ferger & Robert Hitz

Key words: Reptilia: Sauria: Scincidae: *Tiliqua: Tiliqua rugosa rugosa,* Australia, description, distribution, biology, ecology, reproduction, husbandry, breeding

## Introduction

*Tiliqua rugosa rugosa* was described as a new species under the name *Trachydosaurus rugosus* by Gray in the year 1825. This description also formed the original description of the genus *Trachydosaurus.* The type specimens had been collected by P.P. King in the King George Sound (Shea 1992).

The genus *Trachydosaurus,* alternatively also spelled *Trachysaurus,* was maintained for a very long time, until immunological (Hutchinson 1980) and anatomical (Mitchell 1950, Shea 1990) studies showed that the representatives of the genus *Trachydosaurus* would actually have to be included in the genus *Tiliqua.* This point of view is, however, not shared by all specialists.

The nominate form of *Tiliqua rugosa* is not the most spectacular subspecies in a number of aspects. For example, it is the subspecies *T. rugosa palarra,* described by Shea as new in the original edition of this book (2000), which was the first shingleback lizard to cross the path of European explorers at Shark Bay, Western Australia, and to find mention in the literature (Dampier 1729). The distribution range of *T. r. rugosa* is furthermore much smaller than that of the eastern subspecies *T. r. aspera,* described by Gray in 1845. It is also the latter which gained much more importance in the scientific literature due to the works published by researchers such as Bourne and Bull and their co-workers.

The common name of *Tiliqua rugosa rugosa* is "bobtail". This term is widely used by the population in its distribution range (Shea pers. com. to the junior author).

Some reviews on the herpetofauna of Australia do not make much mention of the individual subspecies of *T. rugosa* (e.g. Cogger 1992). The books by Wilson & Knowles (1988) and Ehmann (1992) are much more detailed in this respect, and a very comprehensive presentation of the systematics and reproductive biology of *T. r. rugosa* can be found in Shea (1992). As far as the terrarium keeping is concerned, *T. r. rugosa* is equally widespread as *T. r. aspera,* although publications on their successful keeping and breeding are comparatively rare. The first to publish their successes were Wagner & Richardson (1988) in the US and Gross (1989) in Europe. For the past six years (as of 2000) the senior author was able to reproduce *T. r. rugosa* on a regular basis. This shall also be considered in the present work.

## Diagnosis (Shea 1992)

*T. rugosa* differs from all other forms of *Tiliqua* by having large, heavily ossified dorsal scales in combination with a short, blunt tipped tail, and the presence of divided subdigital lamellae. *T. r. rugosa* in turn differs from all other subspecies by having a relatively longer, more slender tail, normally 16 or more subcaudal scales, 22-30 scales at midbody, a relatively more slender head, the presence of a median occipital shield, the separation of the first supraciliary from the frontal, divided nasals, a relatively large ear opening,

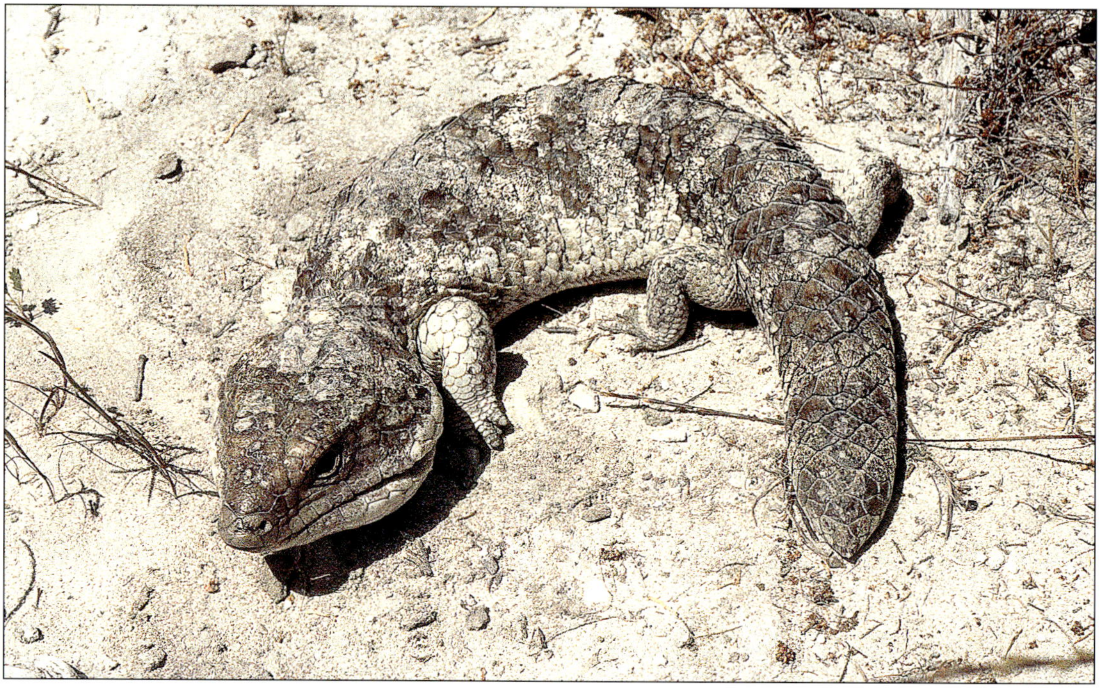

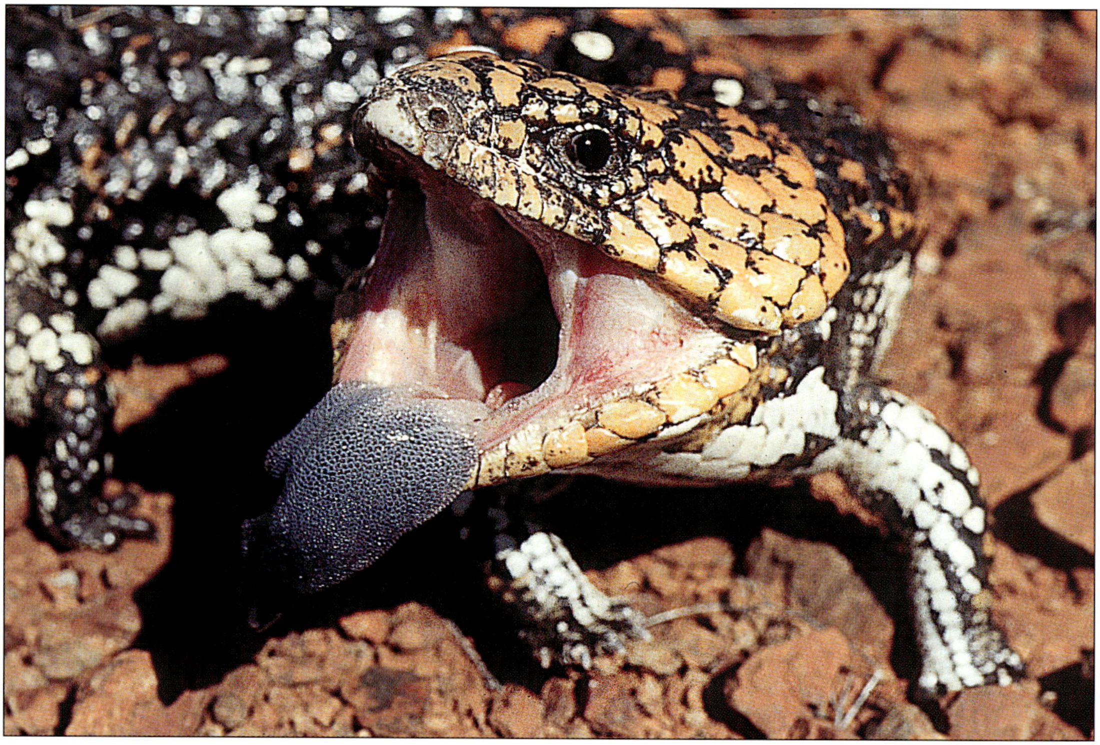

Opposite: *T. r. rugosa*
**Fig. 1** (top) Common, inconspicuous variety
**Fig. 2** Defense display of "red" specimen near Kalgoorlie
Photographs: O. Daniel

*Tiliqua rugosa rugosa*

and by its dorsal coloration which includes a banded pattern.

## Description

A detailed account of the scalation and body proportions can be found in SHEA (1992) and WILSON & KNOWLES (1988). The dorsal scales of *T. r. rugosa* appear less rough surfaced than those of *T. r. aspera*. This gives the western subspecies an altogether smoother, more skink like appearance which is complemented by its rather slender body and the longer, slimmer tail. *T. r. rugosa* grows to a maximum SVL of 30.3 cm, in contrast to the 34.1 cm recorded for *T. r. aspera*. SWITAK (1997) indicated a maximum total length of 40 cm as opposed to 45 cm. The tail of *T. r. rugosa* equals 29% of the SVL on average (20.7-37.2%, n = 269), in contrast to 21.5% (14.5-30.2%, n = 648) in *T. r. aspera* (SHEA 1992).

The ground color of *T. r. rugosa* may vary from light to dark brown or olive brown, or from gray to black. The back and tail show narrow to wide, irregular cross bands that traverse the sides of the body up to the venter. These are cream colored, yellow, orange or pale gray to white. The ventral side is yellow, cream colored, to white or bluish gray, with irregular gray to brown stripes, bands, or spots. In general the head is paler than the rest of the body. Specimens with bright orange heads are particularly stunning. The most obvious geographical variations refer to coloration and tail length.

## Distribution and habitat

The distribution range of *T. r. rugosa* extends from the western margin of the Nullarbor Plain in the south of Western Australia in the region

**Fig. 3** The bright "Christmas tree" forms part of the mistletoe family and as such is a root parasite. Together with the "black boys" it creates a typical biotope of *T. r. rugosa*. Photograph: U. Röhe

of 123° eastern longitude, along the coast line, to the lower Murchison River region (SHEA 1992). Besides on the mainland this subspecies also occurs on various islands, including Garden Island, Mondrain Island, Middle Island, North Twin Peaks Island, and Salisbury Island. *T. r. rugosa* inhabits a variety of arid habitats near the coast marked by open vegetation. These include heath, bush steppe, open *Eucalyptus* forests as well as farm land.

## On the reproductive biology of *Tiliqua r. rugosa*

A number of methods are available to distinguish between the sexes of *T. r. rugosa* (compare the chapter "Sex identification in blue-tongued skinks (Sauria: Scincidae: *Tiliqua*)" in this book). Sub-adult and adult females have shorter heads, longer bodies, wider hips, shorter legs, and shorter and broader tails in proportion to their SVL than males (SHEA 1992). According to the latter author, males mature on reaching a mean SVL of $26.2 \pm 1.7$ cm (22.4-30.3 cm; n = 128), females at $26.0 \pm 1.71$ cm (22.2-28.8 cm, n = 98); by then the animals are two or three years old.

In nature the mating season falls into the months October and November. Not all females will reproduce every year. The young are born after a gestation period of about five months towards the end of March or in early April. A litter may comprise 1-3 babies. Their sizes vary to some extent around a value of 14.5 cm.

## Husbandry and propagation

From 1992, the senior author managed to acquire several adult *T. r. rugosa* of unknown ages from private individuals and through the reptile trade. All specimens were meticulously examined and then subjected to a quarantine of at least three months.

**Housing:** The animals are kept in groups of up to five specimens in indoor terraria of between $160 \times 80 \times 80$ cm (l × w × h) and $165 \times 130$ (l × w, open above) in dimension.

**Decoration:** It is always attempted to make as much surface space available to the skinks as possible. This is achieved by a mainly schematic infrastructure consisting of several platforms that are fixed horizontally, or in a slightly oblique manner, at various levels. These platforms are made of wood and covered above with a well structured natural material, cork for example, so that the animals are able to climb them with ease. Depending on the proximity of these platforms to heating sources, the lizards are so enabled to pursue an active thermoregulation. The bottom parts of the terraria hold several hiding places which can be controlled like drawers. These hiding places are each covered with a piece of natural cork bark with a hole in them through which the animals can descend into their shelters. They are bedded with a variety of substrates including sand, raffia straw, corn stalk fibers, hay, wood wool, or fine branchwork. Some cork tubes, branches, roots, rocks, and a water bowl complete the interior. A granulate of small, smooth-edged pieces of wood (as used for smoking meat) is used as substrate after it has been freed from dust through winnowing and sifting.

**Illumination:** Metal halogen vapor lamps (HQI) of 75 or 150 watts are the preferred sources of artificial light since they provide not only a suitable spectrum of radiation, but also radiant heat. They are complemented with fluorescent tubes of 18 and 36 watts, respectively. In an experimental setting, "black light" fluo tubes of 18 watts are added as an additional source of UV-A radiation for a few hours every day.

**Heating:** Local hot spots of up to 45°C are created mainly by the radiant heat emitted by the lamps. This setting creates a continuous temperature gradient from 45°C right down to 18-25°C in the marginal zones of the terraria. Some cages are additionally equipped with mild underfloor heaters with a maximum temperature output of 30°C.

**Ventilation:** The terraria are ventilated through the rotational forces created by the generation of warmth by the lamps. Fresh air from the room enters the terraria through aeration strips in the lower parts of the cages while heated air escapes through respective openings in the lid of the terraria.

**Humidity:** Since shingleback lizards are very susceptible to infections of the breathing system, the levels of humidity must be given careful attention. Under the lighting and heating management described above daily misting in the early morning proved adequate.

**Feeding:** The *T. r. rugosa* kept by the senior author are fed at irregular intervals, usually twice per week, with equal amounts of plant and animal matter. These include various flowers (dandelion, red clover), herbs, wheat sprouts, berries (red currant, gooseberry, strawberry, raspberry and blackberry), hips, local and exotic fruit, shredded carrots, mushrooms (champignons), fruit juices, crickets, roaches, locusts, grubs, earthworms, snails, mice, fish meat, liver, and chicken eggs. Vitamin, mineral and trace element (Multimusin, Multi VT Min) preparations are added on an occasional basis. Cat food (tinned or pellets) is offered only as an exception. Juveniles receive the same food, but more regularly and in larger amounts. Drinking water is available to the animals from water bowls at all times.

**Keeping cycle:** The *T. r. rugosa* are kept in accordance with the European cycle of seasons. Corresponding to the daylight hours outside, the daily duration of illumination ranges from 8 to 14 hours. The heating regime follows the same pattern, driven by the duration of illumination and influenced by ambient temperatures. Adhering to a cool hibernation period of 6-8 weeks duration is of utmost importance. This time is preceded and followed by adaptation periods of three weeks each during which illumination, heating and feeding are gradually reduced, or increased, respectively. The ani-

**Table 1** Breeding results

| Year | Number of babies | | |
|---|---|---|---|
| | Female 1 (wild caught) | Female 2 (captive bred 1993) | Female 3 (captive bred 1994) |
| 1993 | 3 babies | | |
| 1994 | 2 babies | | |
| 1995 | 2 babies, 1 stillborn | | |
| 1996 | – | – | |
| 1997 | 2 babies | – | 1 baby |
| 1998 | – | 1 baby | 1 baby |

mals spend the actual hibernation phases in plastic containers of $60 \times 40 \times 22$ cm ($l \times w \times h$) in an underground air raid shelter where they are exposed to temperatures of 14-17°C. The containers are furnished with deep layers of newspaper, some substrate from their terrarium, and crumpled-up newspaper. Only healthy specimens in good condition may be hibernated. Those skinks which make themselves noticed by continually scuttling around and through scraping sounds during the initial phase are returned to their terraria. Depending on their further behavior their hibernation may be attempted again at a later stage.

### Behavior

Given the husbandry conditions in well structured terraria described above, *T. r. rugosa* displays a calm behavior even when kept in a group. Harmonizing specimens often spend time together relaxing in close body contact. Occasionally there will be a specimen which prefers solitude and often keeps to himself in a hiding place. In such cases it may be attempted to integrate the "problem animal" into another group. Fights were observed only during the mating season among specimens of the same sex.

The robust appearance of *T. r. rugosa* should not mislead the keeper into ignoring the rather "sensitive mind" of these animals. This fact has to be

97

taken into consideration for all aspects of their keeping.

## Reproduction of *T. r. rugosa* in captivity

Under the husbandry conditions described above, and kept in groups of up to five specimens representing both sexes, mating activities could be witnessed some 4-8 weeks after the end of their hibernation. Interestingly enough only one female (wild caught) and two of her daughters were covered by males and became gravid in six years of keeping. The wild caught female appeared to accept only one particular partner over all those years, which then unfortunately died during the 1997/98 hibernation. Gestation took, as far as could be determined, 3.5-5 months. Litters comprised 1-3 juveniles (see Table 1). It was subsequently particularly pleasing to also obtain babies from two captive bred females. These started breeding for the first time at ages of three and five years, respectively.

In view of the fact that several females and males have not reproduced to date in their groups, the question comes to mind whether these specimens should better be kept in pairs or even singly for much of the year in order to improve breeding results. The juveniles are kept and raised under the same circumstances as the adults.

## Literature

DAMPIER, L. (1729): A voyage to New Holland in the year 1699. – London (J. & J. Knapton).

EHMANN, H. (1992): Encyclopedia of Australian Animals. Reptiles. – The National Photographic Index of Australian Wildlife. (R. STRAHAN, series ed.). – Pymble (Angus & Robertson): 495 pp.

GRAY, J.E. (1825): A synopsis of the genera of reptiles and amphibia, with a discription of some new species. – Annals of Philosophy, (2)10(3): 193–217.

– (1845): Catalogue of the specimens of lizards in the collection of the British Museum. – London (Trustees of the British Museum), 289 pp.

GROSS, J. (1989): Pflege, Geschlechtsbestimmung und Zucht der Tannenzapfenechse. – DATZ, 42(10): 612–613.

HUTCHINSON, M. N.(1980): The systematic relationship of the genera *Egernia* and *Tiliqua* (Lacertilia: Scincidae). A review and immunological reassessment. – Pp. 176–193 in BANKS, C.B. & A.A. MARTIN (edts): Proc. Melb. Herp. Symp., Melbourne.

MITCHELL, F.J. (1950): The scincid genera *Egernia* and *Tiliqua* (Lacertilia). – Records of the South Australian Museum, 9(3): 275–308, + pl. XXIII.

SHEA, G.M. (1990): The genera *Tiliqua* and *Cyclodomorphus* (Lacertilia: Scincidae): Generic diagnoses and systematic relationships. – Memoirs of the Queensland Museum, 29(2): 495–519.

– (1992): The systematics and reproduction of blue-tongue lizards of the genus *Tiliqua* (Squamata: Scincidae). – Ph.D. thesis, University of Sydney, 4 Vols.

–(2000): Die Shark-Bay-Tannenzapfenechse *Tiliqua rugosa palarra* subsp. nov. – S. 108-112 in HAUSCHILD, A., R. HITZ, K. HENLE, G.M. SHEA & H. WERNING (Hrsg.): Blauzungenskinke. Beiträge zu *Tiliqua* und *Cyclodomorphus*. – Münster (Natur und Tier-Verlag), 287 S.

SWITAK, K.H. (1997): Shingle-backed Skinks. – Reptiles, February 1997, 48–69.

WAGNER, E. & D. RICHARDSON (1988): Breeding the Shingleback Skink, *Trachydosaurus rugosus*. – The Vivarium, California (American Federation of Herpetoculturists), 1(2): 40–41.

WILSON, S.K. & D.G. KNOWLES (1988): Australia's Reptiles. A Photographic Reference to the Terrestrial Reptiles of Australia. – Sydney (Collins): 447 pp.

Authors' addresses
Peter Ferger
Winkelweg 17
CH-4435 Niederdorf, Switzerland

Dr. Robert Hitz
Am Mülibach 8
CH-9425 Thal, Switzerland

# Biology, husbandry and reproduction of *Tiliqua rugosa konowi* (Mertens, 1958) - what is the challenge for the successful breeding?

## Heidrun Röhe

Key words: Reptilia: Sauria: Scincidae: *Tiliqua: Tiliqua rugosa konowi*, Australia, Rottnest Island, description, distribution, ecology, reproduction, husbandry, breeding

## Introduction

*Tiliqua rugosa konowi,* the island shingleback lizard, is the smallest of the subspecies of *Tiliqua rugosa.* It occurs only on Rottnest Island, an island at level with the city of Perth, Western Australia. The earliest reports on these animals were authored by Werner (1910) and Glauert (1929). In the course of an expedition to Australia by Mertens and co-workers in 1957, G. Konow and G.A. Philipp collected five of these skinks on Rottnest Island. These specimens then formed the basis of the description of a new subspecies, *Tiliqua rugosa konowi,* by Mertens in 1958.

The island shingleback is very rarely seen in a terrarium. Reports on its keeping and propagation do not exist as yet. For this reason our respective experiences, made over eight years of keeping, will be summarized in the following.

## Diagnosis

*T. r. konowi* is the smallest subspecies of *T. rugosa,* growing to a maximum SVL of 26.0 cm. It has a relatively long, slender tail, 16 or more subcaudals, 24-30 scale rows at midbody, and a relatively slender head (Shea 1992). A median occipital is usually absent, the first supraciliar is in contact with the frontal, and the nasals are divided. The ear opening is fairly large. The dorsal coloration includes dark gray on the head and a fine light speckling on the body and tail. *T. r. konowi* differs from all other subspecies by its finer scalation, a more slender body, a smaller total length, and particularly by its unique coloration (Mertens 1958).

## Description

A detailed account of the scalation and body proportions can be found in Shea (1992). The total length ranges between 28 and 31 cm with a maximum SVL of 26.0 cm. The tail accounts for 28.6% (22.8-37.0%, n = 51) on average of the total length. These proportions thus hardly differ from those of *T. r. rugosa.* Whilst a dorsal pattern of cross bands is hardly recognizable (Shea 1989), such is well defined on the tail where it forms closed rings. The lower side of the body is finely speckled with grayish black or olive black, and so are the limbs. The tongue is of a dark blue color, the head distinct from the neck. The grayish black or medium brown dorsal scales show olive colored vermiculations or dots. Some individuals of this subspecies display this unusual pattern in such an intensity that their bodies appear like spangled with gold.

## Sexual dimorphism

Females sport a longer body in relation to their SVL and slightly wider hips, furthermore shorter legs and a shorter head than males (Shea 1989, 1992). These identification traits are particularly distinct in newborn sibling specimens (pers. obs.).

Tiliqua rugosa konowi

**Fig. 1** Natural habitat of *T. r. konowi*. Dense vegetation provides ample cover and means sufficient food throughout the year. Photograph: U. Röhe

## Distribution

*T. r. konowi* is endemic to Rottnest Island, 20 km off the coast of Western Australia, at about the latitude of the city of Perth.

## Climate

Temperatures are moderate, topping a maximum of 30°C in summer and still climbing to 20°C in winter. The lowest temperatures rarely fall short of 10°C. The annual amount of precipitation ranges around 750 mm and is experienced mainly during the period from May through September (GENTILLI 1971).

## Ecology

Rottnest Island was separated from the mainland some 7000 years ago by a rising sea level. The island is about 11 km long and 5 km wide at its widest point. Its highest elevation is only 45 meters. A number of small salt lakes are scattered over the inland; they are up to eight meters deep and more saline than the surrounding ocean (CHRISTIANE & WICKE 1994). The shore line is dominated by white dunes with usually dense, low vegetation. Originally, the vegetation was the same as that of the coastal strip of the mainland, but the more salty air, a series devastating fires, and the appetite of quokkas (short-tailed kangaroos) have all but almost eradicated it by now. It has been tried for several years to improve the species diversity by planting out other plants species. These also include salt tolerant plants from Africa, for example *Trachyandra divaricata,* a bulbous plant known to stabilize dunes (RIPPEY & MARCHANT n.d.). The forest of stalks is sometimes used by the passionately climbing juveniles of *T. r. konowi* which are then difficult to spot in the semi-shade, but lets them enjoy a good overview of the surrounds.

The perennial thornlily *Acanthocarpus preisii* is an important fodder plant for the shingleback skinks as it is fire resistant, salt tolerant, and shunned by the quokkas. The berries of the thornlily are available to the lizards from October through March (SHEA 1989). An analysis of the stomach contents of 63 specimens performed at the Western Australian Museum at Perth revealed a 70% content of the berries of *A. preisii.* The rest consisted of various monocotyledonous and dicotyledonous herbs and, to a smaller extent, mosses. The main constituent of the animal portion was spotted beetles, snails, and hairy caterpillars.

These skinks find enough food throughout the year so that the fact that they are smaller in total length than *T. r. rugosa* cannot be led back to a lack of nutrition (SHEA 1989). This phenomenon is, however, not too unusual for an island population, although a comprehensive scientific explanation is still wanting.

*T. r. konowi* inhabits the coastal dune strip as well as the flatter hinterland. With some luck you can spot individuals basking in the morning sun on the smaller sandy patches which dot the otherwise dense brush. If they cannot retreat in time, they will assume the defense posture typical for *Tiliqua* and curl up the body to a near perfect ring. They will often gape the mouth and stick out the blue tongue widely in the antagonist's direction. In spring (September through October) you may see pairs lying closely together.

The island has been enjoying the protection of nature conservation already since 1917. Visitors may not use motor vehicles for their excursions, but only bicycles that can also be hired. Nevertheless you will find killed skinks on the roads, and closer inspection will reveal the distinct

**Fig. 2** With some luck you may stumble over a basking *T. r. konowi*     Photograph: O. Daniel

**Fig. 3** A pair of *T. r. konowi* in the Australian spring          Photograph: O. Daniel

tyremark of a bicycle crossing the head or back!

## Husbandry

The terraria are constructed and furnished in the same manner as those for *T. occipitalis* (see the chapter "Husbandry and reproduction of *Tiliqua occipitalis* (PETERS, 1864) - A challenge for the terrarium keeper"), also as far as their dimensions, illumination, interior decoration and substrate are concerned. Two terraria are connected with a tailor made wooden box structure. This two-story wooden box measures 20 × 45 × 15 cm (l × w × h) and allows the skinks free passage between the two terraria. When the box structure is closed off by means of a slider, two separate "chambers" are created that can be used as sleeping quarters. Since both terraria house a male each, this variable construction of passage

and non-passage is very practicable. It is, however, rarely used for sleeping. For this the animals prefer the space beneath the plastic plant or the cork tube where they love to bury themselves in the substrate.

The latter consists of soft wood shavings that are kept dry at all times other than on the days of shedding when it is well dampened in order to support the sloughing process. The lizards then mostly rid themselves of the old skin in one piece. Remains are often left only on the limbs and are then removed by hand. An almost undamaged shedding is also a good indicator of the present state of good health.

## Feeding

Our "konowis" are very active from mid-August through the end of February and, accordingly, very hungry. They will roam their terraria agitatedly and in a tenacious manner beg for food. Even a switching off of the illumination for a couple of hours during the day (simulating "bad weather") will not calm them down. For this reason they are fed almost daily during this time, also because the search for food will provide some variety in the otherwise very unstimulating habitat "terrarium". To prevent the skinks from becoming obese during this period, they receive for the major part cut-up green feedstuffs which are spread widely on a large piece of cork bark. This causes our lizards to occupy themselves for some time with the retrieving of small pieces from the cracks and crevices of the cork. Insects are offered individually.

"Cutting up" the food is of particular importance as, in nature, shinglebacks pluck only very small pieces or leaves off of their feeder plants. A small flower or leaf is torn from the stalk with a deft lateral jerk of the head and then swallowed. Then the next wild herb is targeted and evaluated as to its edibility. The plant is never consumed whole and thus suffers hardly any damage. If the skinks are offered too large pieces of food in the terrarium, they will try to shear off smaller bits by shaking their heads vehemently and rubbing the item in the substrate. This is not only not particularly hygienic, but in the cases of fruit and insects can also lead to an excessive ingestion of sand which may in turn cause a blockage in the intestinal tract.

The green fodder varies with the seasons and is based mainly on dandelion leaves and flowers, white clover leaves and flowers, and rape leaves. The latter are consumed with much gusto. Rape can be harvested on meadows from autumn through spring, and, kept in a fridge after it has been rinsed thoroughly, a portion provides fresh green fodder with a lot of vitamins for a week. Kitchen herbs, such as parsley, tarragon, lemon balm, mint, thyme (exclusive of marjoram) and many others, grown on the window sill, are also readily consumed. During the winter, we do not resort to lettuce grown in greenhouses, but rather use cabbage, all types of which are readily consumed. *T. r. konowi* is furthermore very fond of fruit and meat. The latter should, however, be offered only very occasionally and in small amounts for variety.

## Diseases

Besides the dreaded flu, about which many keepers of shinglebacks have long stories to tell, the keeping of *T. r. konowi* has not as yet revealed any particular susceptibilities. The problem with flu appears to exist also in nature as STEIN (pers. comm.) found an adult male *T. r. rugosa* in the vicinity of Perth which suffered badly from flu as well.

Given the husbandry conditions described above, sporadic cases of flu may occur at any time of the year. Defying all efforts this disease breaks out every year anew right before the mating season. Even gravid females fell sick with it shortly after the mating season. In one case a female in the middle of her gravidity just had to be treated with antibiotics, but fortunately both "mother and child" lived through the procedure well. Two juveniles were also affected despite all measures of care.

Various bacteria and viruses may be responsible. If a case of flu becomes obvious, the climate in the terrarium needs to be checked. Once properly diagnosed by a veterinarian, affected specimens will often be treated with antibiotics of which doxycyclin (vibravenous, Pfizer) produced good results in our cases. Flu may also heal spontaneously. We are fortunate that none of the cases of flu so far led to the loss of an animal.

## "Bluetongue psychology"

Outside the mating season *Tiliqua r. konowi* live in solitude. But because shinglebacks were considered very unaggressive and gregarious by terrarium keepers, we also used to keep them in a group of 3 males, 3 females for three years. Nothing extraordinary was observed, but also no breeding occurred.

In the course of the spring of 1992 we first came to notice a newly matured male for its striking signal colors. Close observations then revealed that it was harassed and at times even attacked by the oldest male of the group. Diving into the loose substrate the young male managed to escape the attacks, and no sign of injuries could be discovered. It was separated from the group, and on the following day it had lost all its signal colors.

The two remaining adult males of the group behaved inconspicuously for another year and were often seen sleeping side by side. But after another period of hibernation fights also broke out between these two and they had to be separated as well.

Our experiences indicated that *T. r. konowi* may well be kept in groups as long as this group includes only one male. The females have always been very compatible, even during the mating season and at times of gravidity.

Towards their keeper the "konowis" are docile. During maintenance work inside the terrarium they will approach, usually with care, and test the fingers as to their possible edibility. If they are picked up, however, they will often respond with releasing large amounts of urine. In general, *T. r. konowi* is somewhat reserved and does not appreciate being touched by the keeper.

## On the reproduction of *T. r. konowi*

**Field observations:** During the mating season pairs and individuals have been found at a ratio of 3 : 1. Outside the mating season more females than males were found; 32 of 55 adult specimens encountered were female. Mating activities may be observed on Rottnest Island during the months of September and October resulting in births in the time from February through March. The size of newborns ranges from 14 to 16 cm (SHEA 1989).

**Terrarium observations:** Mating activities can be noted also during the months of September and October. Whilst babies were born already in late January in 1998, births had during the preceding years been recorded between early and mid-February. This timing corresponds almost with the situation found in nature. Captive born siblings measured 17.5 cm on average and weighed about 65 g. A single baby was 20 cm long and weighed 120 g.

**Conditioning for an "Australian spring":** Our skinks are kept following an annual cycle which largely corresponds with that of the southern hemisphere. The lizards spend the usually cool months of May and June in an outdoor enclosure and are moved for hibernation to an airconditioned room with temperatures of 13-15°C and about 70% relative humidity for about four weeks during the warmer month of July.

In the first or second week of August they are all returned to their outdoor enclosure provided the weather is sunny and warm. This method does obviously not include a transitory phase with a gradually increasing photoperiod and climbing temperatures as such measures have actually proved to be unnecessary. Because the males of *T. r. konowi* (in contrast to *T. occipitalis*) do not shed their skins after completion of their hibernation, they need not be taken out of their overwintering earlier than the females.

At latest towards the end of August the "Australian spring" is "moved" from outdoors into the indoor terraria. These have been cleaned thoroughly and filled with fresh soft wood shavings before, the sources of artificial light (fluorescent tubes and mercury vapor lamps) have been checked for their radiation output and replaced if necessary. Trying to save money here would be inopportune as it would send the animals back into hibernation mood.

**Copulations and births:** It took three years and probably the separation of the males (see above) to eventually experience a breakthrough. In the following we will summarize our observations made over several years.

**1993/94**: Other than an increased activity level in the males hardly anything extraordinary could be noted during the first three weeks after hibernation. In order to eliminate any stress factors, only the oldest male was left with the females. The latter are very hungry and crave insects of all kinds. The first copulation was witnessed in the forenoon hours of the second week of September. It happened with so much calm and harmony as we had expected it to be with shinglebacks. Although the male continued to sniff all females, he always stayed beside his favorite partner. No copulations with other females were noted.

The mated female was left with the group. It was often found lying on the underfloor heater, ate very well, and developed a slightly more laborious breathing. It shed its skin 3.5 months later - labor contractions commenced at the same time. With utmost effort the female subsequently discharged an almost liquid "wax egg" (infertile egg) in a step by step manner from its cloaca, followed by another, solid one in the evening. Although this result was disappointing, the production of "wax eggs" by young bluetongue females in their first breeding season can also be regarded as a promise for the next year to be more successful.

**1994/95:** The oldest male again mated with "his" female in mid-September. To ensure their privacy the connection tunnel between the two terraria was closed off leaving the young male and the two other females on the other side. Soon afterwards the young male courted the larger one of these two females, and about a fortnight later we could for the first time also witness a harmonious copulation here.

The first female was found in labor pains in the morning hours of a day in the first week of February resulting in the birth of a still grayish black baby during the course of the forenoon. It weighed 70 g and measured 18 cm in total length. Its sibling was born one hour later, weighing 60 g and measuring 17 cm in total length. Both births passed without problems, but could not be observed directly as the female had retreated under a plastic plant.

The other female gave birth to a baby of 120 g in mid-February. Measuring 20 cm in total length at birth it equalled about two thirds of its mother.

**1998/99:** The smallest of the three females had never fallen gravid over the eight year period. During each mating season it had either been kept with the older or with the younger male, alternating every year, and always together with another female. Although the slight scratch marks on its scales in the shoulder region had suggested a great interest in it by the respective male and made us hope for babies every year again, the outcome had always been a disappointment. Therefore, we kept this female with the younger male in a terrarium of their own from September 1998 ... resulting in the birth of a strong baby in February 1999. We presume that this particular female had felt disturbed by the presence of a "rival" female before.

In summary we can state that *T. r. konowi* will come into mating mood about six weeks after the end of hibernation. About one week before copulations commence, the male begins to court "his" female by carefully taking her head, shoulder or back in his mouth. The female tolerates this behavior, but it does at this stage not yet lead to a copulation. Although the motivation of the males may be augmented through rival fights, we presume that the trigger for a copulation is provided by the female in the form of olfactory cues (pheromones), and we have been avoiding such confrontation and the stress that comes with it. Like in the natural habitat bonded pairs are most often seen lying side by side. During this time the male will often place his head on the back of his female. It appears that he actively seeks

**Fig. 4** This female only had one baby, but with 20 cm in total length it was a monster baby!

Photograph: H. Röhe

the female's proximity, one reason probably being to be in a position to fend off possible rivals. This behavioral pattern is maintained for at least another month, and is apparently enjoyed by the female.

**Raising the young**

Newborns respond with indifference towards adult specimens, a notion that is returned by the adults towards them. After briefly sniffing each other, each individual will be on their way again. Mothers do not exhibit any signs of aggression towards other adult conspecifics. If the keeper approaches, however, he must expect an attack by the female. In order to protect the juveniles from infections and for better control of their further development they are removed from the group. "Searching" for her babies by the mother is hardly noticeable.

The terrarium for raising the juveniles corresponds almost perfectly with those for the adult as to its technology and furnishing. A mercury vapor lamp HPL-50 watts provides UV-A and UV-B radiation. The substrate beneath the plastic plant is kept slightly moist in the mornings of the first few days.

During their first month of life the small *T. r. konowi* are very shy and skittish. But soon they will have learnt to associate the long pair of forceps with food and then are rather difficult to contain. This then also leads to an increasingly trusting response towards the keeper. Eventually, even the smallest sounds will lure them out of their hiding places.

Juveniles are fed the same diet as the adults, plus a ration of three medium size locusts, crickets or roaches each every other day. The latter are fortified with "ReptiCal" (a mineral preparation for terrarium animals containing a.o. calcium,

**Fig. 5** Juvenile *T. r. konowi*. Two months after its birth the originally grayish black monster baby turned into an olive green beauty.                                                                 Photograph: H. Röhe

phosphorus, sodium, and the vitamins A, E and $D_3$). Intermittently they also receive a piece of "Doko Classic", a dry type of dog food. Fresh drinking water is always accessible. To ensure a sufficient supply with calcium and vitamins we furthermore provide them with half a tablet of "Calcipot $D_3$" (a vitamin $D_3$ preparation on the basis of calcium citrate and calcium phosphate) every three days, alternating with a tablet of "Carfortan" (a strengthening supplement for dogs). Both preparations are eagerly consumed directly from the hand.

Two months after their birth the siblings (1 male, 1 female) had grown to total lengths of 23 and 23.5 cm, and body masses of 135 and 140 g, respectively. At this point of time they also went through their first regular shedding. We were then very much surprised when the inconspicuous, black young turned into more or less olive speckled beauties within the next half hour. The olive color may become more and more intensive as the skinks age making some individuals appear as though peppered with gold dust. In such cases the grayish black ground color will be limited to some spots.

During their first year the juveniles are kept outdoors between June and August with no additional source of heat. This is our attempt to emulate an "Australian winter". During prolonged periods of warm weather they are fed. It is only for the subsequent year that they are subjected to the same hibernation procedure as the adults.

Given these husbandry conditions *T. r. konowi* matures at an age of about three years.

## Reproduction in the terrarium - what are the challenges?

As far as the species of *Tiliqua* are concerned, the successful breeding of shinglebacks is still a highlight, especially in view of the fact that their reproduction rate of one or two babies per female every one to two years is extremely low. The actual challenge for ourselves is, however, neither the seasonal stimulation, nor the for-

mation of pairs, but much rather keeping our animals in perfect health. In order to minimize the risk of losing specimens to flu, we have split our group within an association of experienced keepers of bluetongues. It is our common goal to find out through observation under different husbandry conditions how an outbreak of this disease can be prevented. Only once we have managed to do this we can hope for offspring of the $F_1$ generation.

## Literature

CHRISTIANE, U. & H. WICKE (1994): West-Australien natürlich. – Hürth (Verbe Verlag und Beratung), 431 S.

GENTILLI, J. (1971): Climates of Australia and New Zealand. – World Survey of Climatology, Vol.13, Nedlands W.A. (University of Western Australia), 371 pp.

GLAUERT, L. (1929): Contributions to the fauna of Rottnest Island. No. 1. Introduction and vertebrates. – Journal of the Royal Society of Western Australia, 15: 37–46.

MERTENS, R. (1958): Neue Eidechsen aus Australien. – Senckenb. biol., 39: 51–56.

RIPPEY, E. & N. MARCHANT (ohne Datum): Rottnest Island plants. – Rottnest Island Authority.

SHEA, G.M. (1989): Diet and reproductive biology of the Rottnest Island bobtail, *Tiliqua rugosa konowi* (Lacertilia, Scincidae). – Herpetological Journal, 1: 366–369.

– (1992): The systematics and reproduction of bluetongue lizards of the genus *Tiliqua* (Squamata: Scincidae). – Ph.D. thesis, University of Sydney, 4 Vols.

WERNER, F. (1910): Reptilia (Geckonidae und Scincidae). – S. 451–493 in MICHAELSEN, W. & R. HARTMEYER (Hrsg.): Die Fauna Südwest Australiens. Ergebnisse der Hamburger südwest-australischen Forschungsreise 1905. Volume 2. – Jena (Gustav Fischer), 493 S.

Author's location
Heidrun Röhe
Hamburg, Germany

# The Shark Bay bobtail (*Tiliqua rugosa palarra* SHEA, 2000)

## GLENN M. SHEA

**Key words: Reptilia: Sauria: Scincidae:** *Tiliqua: Tiliqua rugosa palarra*, **description, systematics, Western Australia, reproduction**

The Shark Bay population of *Tiliqua rugosa* was the first population to be seen by Europeans. First noticed and described by DAMPIER (1729), prior to the introduction of bionomial nomenclature, in a description reprinted on a number of occasions (e.g., FLINDERS 1814, RIDE 1962, SERVENTY 1970, WHITLEY 1970, STANBURY & PHIPPS 1980, GREER 1989), it was next collected by François PÉRON, during the Baudin Expedition of 1800-1804. Unfortunately, PÉRON died before completing his treatise of the zoological results of the expedition, and no formal description appeared. However, in the general narrative of the expedition, when describing the period spent at the "Barren Islands" (now known as Bernier and Dorre Islands), PÉRON (1807) provided a name, *Scincus tropisurus,* with the brief annotation: "Les Reptiles ne comptoient qu'une espèce de Scinque (*Scincus tropisurus* N.), l'une des plus grandes de ce genre, et dont la queue très-courte et très-grosse fait paroître, au premier instant, cet animal comme ayant deux têtes...". This comment is sufficient to formally name the species. However, due to the informal nature of the proposal of this new name, it was overlooked by all authors until 1962, when DOUGLAS & RIDE (1962) noted its existence.

PÉRON did not indicate the number of specimens collected. However, the leader of the expedition, Nicolas BAUDIN, noted that two were collected, presumably between June 27, and July 14, 1801, when the expedition visited the Barren Islands (BAUDIN 1974). A specimen in the Nationaal Natuurhistorisch Museum, Leiden, The Netherlands (RMNH 2842), although not previously identified as a type, appears to be one of the specimens collected by PÉRON. The specimen is in spirit, in a permanently sealed jar, which bears two labels. The older label reads "*Scincus pachyurus* Per. *Trachysaurus rugosus* Gray. Voy. Peron. Nouv. Holl.", while the more recent label reads "*Trachysaurus rugosus* (s.n. *Scincus pachyurus,* Pér.) Voyage Péron, Nieuw Holland". While the locality is not precise, the faded specimen is typical of the Shark Bay morph of *T. rugosa,* and PÉRON (1807) did not report collecting specimens of *T. rugosa* anywhere outside of Shark Bay.

Consequently, I consider this specimen to be one of two syntypes of *Scincus tropisurus* PÉRON, 1807. The species name *pachyurus* on the bottle label (which also appears, attributed to PÉRON, in the synononymies of *Tiliqua rugosa* provided by GRAY [1831, 1838, 1841, 1845], and DUMÉRIL & BIBRON [1839]) is probably due to a later decision by PÉRON to formally name the species as such in the publication of the zoological results of the expedition, and emphasizes the informal nature of the names proposed in the narrative.

Further evidence for the identity of the species named comes from a painting by the artist LESUEUR made during the expedition (BONNEMAINS et al. 1988) which is of a typical individual of the Shark Bay population. As noted by DOUGLAS & RIDE (1962), the name *Scincus tropisurus* antedates the name *Trachydosaurus rugosus* GRAY, 1825 by 18 years, and hence to recognize it as the name for the Shark Bay subspecies is impossible without overturning more than 170 years of usage of *rugosa* as the species name. As DOU-

GLAS & RIDE (1962) recommended treating the name as a nomen oblitum during the period when Article 23(b) of the Code of Zoological Nomenclature was in force, it cannot now be used, and hence a new name must be proposed for the Shark Bay bobtail. Consequently, I have (2000) proposed the name *Tiliqua rugosa palarra*. "Palarra" is the Aboriginal name for the bobtail in the Gascoyne River area, where the subspecies occurs (ALEXANDER 1921).

**Holotype:** Australian Museum R 133199, Tamala Station rubbish tip, Western Australia. Collected by A. GREER, R. SADLIER et al., 20 October, 1981 (Fig. 1).

**Paratypes:** Australian Museum R 81388, 6 km N Gascoyne River; R 102710-14, R 112444, R 133197-98, R 133200-01, Tamala homestead; R 105690, 0.7 km E of highway on Gascoyne Junction rd; Nationaal Natuurhistorisch Museum, Leiden 2842, New Holland; South Australian Museum R 4371, R 33403, Carnarvon; R 33404, 2 km S Denham; Western Australian Museum R 13160, R 20496, R 54394-95, R 58815, R 69644-45, R 73127-28, R 73130-31, Bernier I.; R 13460, R 69640, Dorre I.; R 16949, 10 mi E Carnarvon; R 22681, between Denham and Monkey Mia; R 22755-58, Denham; R 22958, 1 mi N Gascoyne River, east of Carnarvon; R 23879, 5 km S Tamala; R 41637, NW corner, Callagiddy Station; R 42375-76, R 59704, Dirk Hartog I.; R 46547-48, White Beach, Dorre I.; R 53795, 45 km S Denham; R 54588, 5 km S Carrarang homestead; R 54607, 12 km S Carrarang homestead; R 54666, 21 km N Biddy Giddy outcamp, Carrarang Stn; R 54757, 4 km S Useless Loop; R 55259, 55 km S Denham; R 55260, 4 km E Denham; R 60609, R 60712-13, 20 km N Nanga; R 62371, 7 km W of NW Coastal Hwy, nr Boolathana homestead; R 64448, 1 km S Tamala homestead; R 67335, 5 km N Gascoyne River on Coastal Hwy; R 71467, Carnarvon; R 80428, 20 km SSE Carnarvon; R 114080-81, Carnarvon airport.

**Diagnosis:** A moderate-sized (maximum SVL 300 mm), robust subspecies of *T. rugosa* with 17-22 subcaudal scales (mean 18.8, n = 42), 26-35 midbody scales (mean 29.3, n = 58), 23-38 paravertebral scales (mean 30.0, n = 51), head relatively narrow (mean head width/head length 94.7%, n = 51), median occipital usually present (98%, n = 52), first supraciliary and frontal usually separated (77%, n = 22), nasal scales usually in contact (68%, n = 59), a small ear aperture (mean ear diameter/head length 6.5%, n = 51), dorsal color pattern consisting of yellow streaks and spots on an olive brown ground color, body venter with a large brown patch medially, and head dark.
**Differs from *T. r. rugosa*** in lacking pale-variegated bands in the dorsal pattern, having a

**Fig. 1** Holotype of *Tiliqua rugosa palarra,* Tamala Station rubbish tip, leg. A. Greer, R. Sadlier et al.
Photograph: G. Shea

Fig. 2 Geographical distribution of *Tiliqua rugosa* and its subspecies

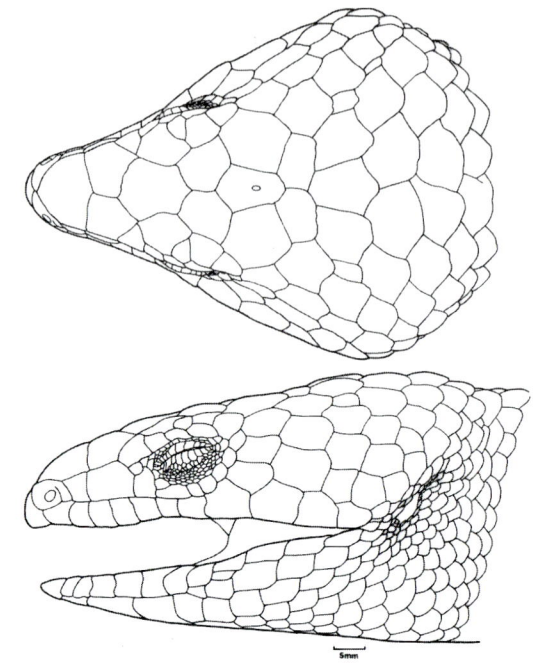

Fig. 3 Holotype of *Tiliqua r. palarra*
Sketch: G. Shea

dark head (vs. usually pale), and body venter with a brown patch (vs. pale with dark streaks, stripes or transverse bars), usual contact of nasal scales (vs. 4% in contact, n = 304), a smaller ear (vs. mean ear diameter/head length 11.4%, n = 262), and greater number of midbody scales (vs. 20-30, mean = 24.4, n = 304) and paravertebral scales (vs. 20-30, mean = 25.1, n = 264).

**Differs from *T. r. aspera*** in having usual contact of nasal scales (vs. 3% in contact, n = 697), a smaller ear (vs. mean ear diameter/head length 12.4%, n = 656), greater number of midbody scales (vs. 19-27, mean = 22.1, n = 704), paravertebral scales (vs. 18-31, mean = 23.6, n = 685) and subcaudal scales (vs. 11-20, mean = 13.8, n = 624), and a narrower head (vs. mean head diameter/head length 103.5%, n = 674).

**Differs from *T. r. konowi*** in lacking the finely variegated coloration of that subspecies, usual presence of a median occipital (vs. 34% present, n = 59), usual separation of first supraciliary and frontal (vs. 29% separate, n = 56), usual contact of nasals (vs. always separated, n = 61), smaller ear (vs. mean ear diameter/head length = 11.5%, n = 55), and fewer midbody scales (vs. 24-30, mean = 26.2, n = 67).

On the mainland, the Shark Bay bobtail occurs in the Carnarvon area (from Boolathana to Callagiddy stations), and on Peron Peninsula and Edel Land, south to the vicinity of Tamala station. It is also present on Bernier, Dorre and Dirk Hartog Islands. Farther south, in the vicinity of the Murchison River, there is a relatively narrow zone of intermediacy (about 70 km) with the common bobtail.

The Shark Bay bobtail occurs mostly in *Acacia* scrub on loose to compacted red to white sandy soils, although it is also found in *Olearia* (daisy-bush) thickets, coastal saltmarshes and claypans (DOUGLAS & RIDE 1962, STORR & HAROLD 1978, SHEA 1992). The population around Carnarvon also occurs in banana plantations (STORR & HAROLD 1984).

In captivity, it seems to require the same housing and diet as other subspecies of *Tiliqua rugosa,* captive animals having lived for up to five

**Fig. 4** *Tiliqua rugosa palarra* from Carnarvon Tip, Western Australia          Photograph: G. Shea

years (pers. obs.). From dissection of museum specimens, litter size is 1-3 (n = 3), with gravid females collected in spring and summer, as with other subspecies. It is probable that this subspecies forms breeding pairs similar to other subspecies, as pairs were often seen on Bernier Island by DOUGLAS & RIDE (1962) in late July.

## Literature

ALEXANDER, W.B. (1921): Aboriginal names of the animals of the Lyons River district. – Journal and Proceedings of the Royal Society of Western Australia 6(1): 37–40.

BAUDIN, N.-T. (1974): The Journal of Post Captain Nicolas Baudin Commander-in-Chief of the Corvettes Géographe and Naturaliste assigned by order of the Government to a voyage of discovery. – Libraries Board of South Australia, Adelaide, xxi + 609 pp.

BONNEMAINS, J., E. FORSYTH & B. SMITH (1988): Baudin in Australian Waters. The Artwork of the French Voyage of Discovery to the Southern Lands 1800–1804. – Oxford University Press, Melbourne, 347 pp.

DAMPIER, L. (1729): A Voyage to New Holland, & c. In the year 1699. – J & J Knapton, London.

DOUGLAS, A.M. & W.D.L. RIDE (1962): Reptiles. – Pp. 113–119 in FRASER, A.J. (ed.): The Results of an Expedition to Bernier and Dorre Islands Shark Bay, Western Australia in July, 1959. – Western Australian Fisheries Department Fauna Bulletin (2): 1–131.

DUMÉRIL, A.M.C. & G. BIBRON (1839): Erpétologie Générale ou Histoire Naturelle Complète des Reptiles. Vol. 5. – Librairie Encyclopédique de Roret, Paris, 854 S.

FLINDERS, M. (1814): A voyage to Terra Australis; undertaken for the purpose of completing the discovery of that vast country, and prosecuted in the years 1801, 1802, and 1803, in His Majesty's Ship The Investigator, and subsequently in the armed vessel Porpoise and Cumberland schooner. With an account of the shipwreck of the Porpoise, arrival of the Cumberland at Mauritius, and imprisonment of the commander during six years and a half in that island. Vol. I. – G. and W. Nicol, London, cciv + 269 pp.

GRAY, J.E. (1825): A synopsis of the genera of Reptiles and Amphibia, with a description of some new species. – Annals of Philosophy (2)10(3): 193–217.

– (1831): A synopsis of the species of the Class Reptilia. – In GRIFFITH, E. & E. PIDGEON: The Animal Kingdom arranged in conformity with its organization, by the Baron Cuvier, member of the Institute of France, &c. &c. &c. with additional descriptions of all the species hitherto named, and of many not before noticed. Vol. 9. The class Reptilia arranged by the Baron Cuvier, with specific descriptions. – Whittaker, Treacher, and Co., London, 481 + 110 pp.

– (1838): Catalogue of the Slender-tongued Saurians, with Descriptions of many new Genera and Species. – Annals and Magazine of Natural History, ser. 2, 2(10): 287–293.

– (1841): A Catalogue of the Species of Reptiles and Amphibia hitherto described as inhabiting Australia, with a description of some New Species from Western Australia, and some remarks on their geographical distribution. – Pp. 422–449 in GREY, G. Journals of two expeditions of discovery in North-west and Western Australia, during the years 1837, 38, and 39, Under the Authority of Her Majesty's Government. Vol. 2. – T. and W. Boone, London, 482 pp.

– (1845): Catalogue of the specimens of lizards in the collection of the British Museum. – Edward Newman, London, xxviii + 289 pp.

GREER, A.E. (1989): The Biology and Evolution of Australian Lizards. – Surrey Beatty & Sons, Chipping Norton, xvi + 264 pp.

PÉRON, F. (1807): Voyage de Découvertes aux Terres Australes, exécuté par ordre de Sa Majesté l'Empereur et Roi, sur les Corvettes le Géographe, le Naturaliste, la Golette et le Casuarina, pendant les Années 1800, 1801, 1802, 1803 et 1804. Vol. I. – Imprimerie Impériale, Paris, 496 S.

RIDE, W.D.L. (1962): Narrative. – Pp. 10–18 in FRASER, A.J. (ed.): The Results of an Expedition to Bernier and Dorre Islands, Shark Bay, Western Australia in July, 1959. – Western Australian Fisheries Department Fauna Bulletin (2): 1–131.

SERVENTY, V. (1970): Dryandra. The story of an Australian forest. – A.H. & A.W. Reed, Sydney, 205 pp.

SHEA, G.M. (1992): The systematics and reproduction of bluetongue lizards of the genus Tiliqua (Squamata: Scincidae). – 4 Vols., Ph. D. thesis, University of Sydney.

– (2000): Die Shark-Bay-Tannenzapfenechse *Tiliqua rugosa palarra* subsp. nov. – S. 108-112 in HAUSCHILD, A., R. HITZ, K. HENLE, G.M. SHEA & H. WERNING (Hrsg.): Blauzungenskinke. Beiträge zu *Tiliqua* und *Cyclodomorphus*. – Münster (Natur und Tier-Verlag), 287 S.

STANBURY, P.J. & G. PHIPPS (1980): Australia's Animals Discovered. – Pergamon Press, Sydney. 120 pp.

STORR, G.M. & G. HAROLD (1978): Herpetofauna of the Shark Bay region, Western Australia. Records of the Western Australian Museum 6(4): 449–467.

– (1984): Herpetofauna of the Lake MacLeod region, Western Australia. – Records of the Western Australian Museum 11(2): 173–189.

WHITLEY, G.P. (1970): Early history of Australian zoology. – Royal Zoological Society of New South Wales, Sydney, 75 pp.

Author's address
Dr. Glenn M. Shea
Faculty of Veterinary Science
University of Sydney
New South Wales 2006
Australia

# The pygmy bluetongue, *Tiliqua adelaidensis* (PETERS, 1863)

MARK HUTCHINSON and TIM MILNE

**Key words:** Reptilia: Sauria: Scincidae: *Tiliqua adelaidensis,* history, distribution, natural history, conservation

In 1863, Wilhelm PETERS, then Curator at the Zoological Museum, Berlin, announced in the pages of the Monthly Proceedings of the Royal Prussian Academy of Science the arrival of a small but interesting collection of herpetofauna from Richard SCHOMBURGK, a German settler with a farm on the outskirsts of the town of Gawler, about 80 km north of Adelaide, South Australia. SCHOMBURGK had a passion for natural history and collected specimens over several years from the surrounding parts of southern South Australia. Although the collection was small, PETERS found it necessary to describe most of the species as new. Over the intervening years, most of these species did indeed prove to be distinct, and many are among the more familiar species of southern Australia

Two of the new species were assigned to the skink genus *Cyclodus* as *C. adelaidensis* and *C. occipitalis. Cyclodus* was the name given by WAGLER (1830) to a group of skinks now placed in the genus *Tiliqua* (BOULENGER 1896, MITCHELL 1950, SHEA 1990), characterized in part by enlarged, obtusely pointed cheek teeth. *Tiliqua occipitalis,* the western bluetongue, is now a familiar species still found in the coastal areas just to the west of Gawler, its range extending over the semiarid to arid landscapes of southern, central and western Australia (COGGER 1992). The other species, *T. adelaidensis,* the pygmy bluetongue, was hardly ever heard of again. The Berlin Museum acquired a total of seven specimens, presumably all via SCHOMBURGK. One specimen was sent by Gerard KREFFT to the British Museum (now the

Natural History Museum, London), and three were donated to the Vienna Museum by the pioneer botanist Ferdinand VON MÜLLER. The Museum of Victoria, Melbourne, acquired a specimen, some time prior to 1900. The South Australian Museum in Adelaide received several specimens during the late 19th Century, the last in 1899.

During the 20th Century, this species became something of a mystery animal. This began with Edgar WAITE, in his "Reptiles and Amphibians of South Australia"', published in 1929. WAITE referred to this species as the "Doubtful Bluetongue". He had no first-hand knowledge of the species and expressed doubts about whether the species was truly part of the South Australian fauna. He also suggested that the name was perhaps based on misidentified juveniles of one of the larger species.

During the late 1940's, two new specimens were received by the South Australian Museum from a schoolteacher who had worked at Burra, about 160 km north of Adelaide. He was unable to provide precise information on the origins or year of collection of these specimens. Then, in October 1959, workmen at a building site in Adelaide's southern outskirts (now the suburb of Mitchell Park), collected two specimens which were handed on to the Reptile Curator at the South Australian Museum, John MITCHELL. MITCHELL was greatly excited and tried to follow up the discovery, but no further specimens were found. One of the two survived as a captive for several months but sickened and was eventually added to the Museum collection in early 1960.

For the next thirty years, *Tiliqua adelaidensis* became a sort of "Holy Grail" to any herpetologist, amateur or professional, living in or visiting the Adelaide area. Considerable efforts were made to find the species but with no success (EHMANN 1983). Searchers were greatly hampered by the lack of information on this species. Its preferred habitat had never been recorded (SCHOMBURGK had recorded only "in sandy, stony terrain") and most specimens had no precise locality data ("South Australia" or "central South Australia"), or if they did, the areas had already been greatly altered by human activities. Its habits were unrecorded. By 1992, it seemed likely to most herpetologists that, like the Holy Grail, *T. adelaidensis* no longer existed (COGGER 1992, EHMANN 1992). It had seemingly achieved the sad distinction of being the first Australian reptile species to be become extinct as a result of European settlement.

On October 14, 1992, Graham ARMSTRONG, a respected amateur herpetologist, was driving towards Burra with fellow naturalist Julian REID. Close to the town GRAHAM examined a specimen of the elapid snake *Pseudonaja textilis,* the eastern brown snake, which had been killed on the road, and noticed the lump of a recent meal. On opening the snake's body he found an almost perfect adult male *T. adelaidensis.* The snake had only recently eaten the lizard, so it was obvious that a population of the species occurred in the immediate vicinity (ARMSTRONG & REID 1993). The find launched a research program which is still in progress today (ARMSTRONG et al. 1993, HUTCHINSON et al. 1994, MILNE & HUTCHINSON 1997). Most of the following information comes directly from this research.

## Description

*Tiliqua adelaidensis* is indeed a pygmy. Adults reach a snout-vent length of 110 mm and a mass of about 18 g. Tail length is about 60% of the snout-vent length, giving a total maximum of about 180 mm. Females grow slightly larger than males, which seldom exceed 100 mm. Thus the maximum size of this species is close to the neonate size of all other living *Tiliqua* species (SHEA 1992).

The habitus of the animal is distinctive. The head is disproportionately large and very heavily armoured due to the thick osteoderms underlying the cephalic scalation. The body, by contrast, is soft and flexible with relatively small scales. The tail is not only short, as in other *Tiliqua,* it is also very thin, narrowing abruptly at the base rather than gradually tapering as in most of the larger species. Fore and hind limbs are similar in length.

Individuals vary in color and pattern. Dorsal color can be light gray, pale to very dark brown, or rust-colored to almost orange. Most specimens have a dorsal pattern of irregular small black spots. The degree of spotting varies from few and poorly contrasting to numerous and tending to coalesce into series, commonly forming an indistinct vertebral stripe and tending to be arranged as vague transverse series dorsolaterally. In at least one population, a large minority of specimens are unpatterned, i.e. plain light brown, orange-brown or dark brown. Neonates may have nu-

**Fig. 1** Female of *Tiliqua adelaidensis*
Photograph: M. Hutchinson

**Fig. 2** Male of *Tiliqua adelaidensis*                                          Photograph: M. Hutchinson

merous off-white spots on the flanks and sometimes the back, but in most individuals these light spots are completely lost as the animals mature. The underside is white to pale gray, usually unmarked, but specimens with a heavily patterned dorsum may also have numerous gray spots on the venter.

Sexual dimorphism is obvious in the relative proportions of the head and body. Males show a strong positive allometry of the head as they mature, so that in large individuals the snout to axilla distance is about one third of the snout-vent length. In females the snout-axilla distance is only one-quarter of the snout-vent length. As well as absolute size, the head of the male is also distinctive in having thicker, more deeply embossed head shields.

**Present and former geographic distribution**

Historical records, as mentioned above, have few precise locality data. Specimens have been found from Adelaide to just south of Peterborough, about 180 km to the north.
All known populations live within a triangular strip which measures approximately 75 kilometres north to south and about 90 km across its base (east to west). All are between about at 250 and 600 m above sea level.

**Ecology and demography**

All known populations of pygmy bluetongue lizards occur in grassland, either completely treeless or, in a few cases, grassland with a

115

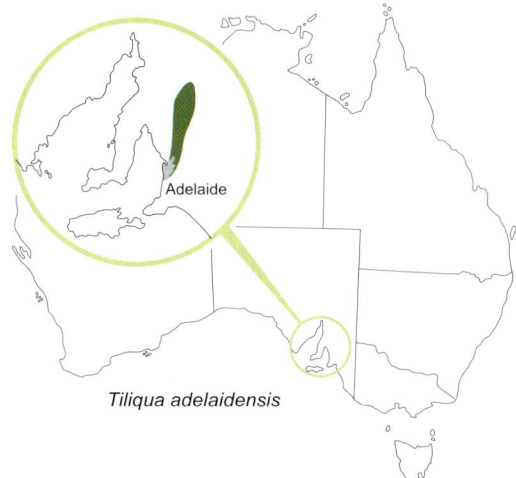

Adelaide

*Tiliqua adelaidensis*

**Fig. 3** Distribution of *Tiliqua adelaidensis*

widely spaced overstory of trees *(Eucalyptus leucoxylon, E. odorata)*. The region of South Australia where the species occurs was formerly dominated by a ground cover of native perennial grasses and an associated suite of herbaceous plants, but very little of this habitat remains today. Clearing for agriculture by European settlers, beginning in the 1830s, converted almost all of this habitat (which extended east into Victoria and southern New South Wales) to cereal crops and cattle and sheep pastures, replacing the perennial native grasses with introduced annual species for grain and hay production. Only 2% of the original 2 million square kilometres of temperate grassland habitat survived throughout the whole of southeastern Australia (SPECHT 1972, HYDE 1995). The surviving pygmy bluetongue lizards are found in small patches that have never been ploughed.

The climate is warm temperate Mediterranean, with moderate rainfall, about 450 to 550 mm annually, mostly falling in winter. Average minimum-maximum temperature range in summer (February) is 14-29°C, with maxima occasionally reaching 40°C, while winter (July) temperatures average 5-15°C, with frequent frosts and occasional brief snow falls on the higher hill tops (over 700 m elevation) (FRENCH et al. 1968).

Within the grassland habitat, pygmy bluetongues are restricted to a specialized microhabitat. Their whole existence centers on a burrow which is used as a retreat from predators and climatic extremes. The burrows are invariably spider holes, with those dug by mygalomorphs (trapdoor spiders) being preferred for their diameter (up to 2 cm) and depth (up to 40 cm). Lycosid wolf spiders are also common, and their burrows are also used, although they are narrower and shallower and probably more valuable to immature lizards than to adults. The soil of the region is very stable, and dries very hard during the warm months of the year. The spider holes are consequently relatively permanent, and their presence means that the otherwise featureless grassy landscape offers many refuges for small animals.

The lizard's unusual appearance is related to this hole-dwelling way of life. The soft, flexible body enables the lizards to move within the cramped spaces of the holes. The lizards normally rest head-up in the hole, the thin flexible tail curling laterally to facilitate movement in reverse. When threatened the lizards retreat to the bottom of the hole. They may try to bite an intruder, but persistent attack elicits a characteristic defensive response. The threatened lizard wedges its head in the burrow, with the snout pressed against one side and the occiput of the skull against the opposite side. The lizard thus presents the predator with the heavy, bony scales of the head, while the preference of the lizards for holes with a diameter close to the head size ensures that the predator cannot get around the head to the more vulnerable body. The lizards will steadfastly resist any attempts to dislodge them, and only complete excavation of the hole will release them. The hard, compact soil makes such excavation difficult or impossible for most animals.

**Fig. 4 u. 5** Grasslands north of Adelaide in spring - the habitat of *Tiliqua adelaidensis* (right)
Photographs: M. Hutchinson

Pygmy bluetongues are strictly diurnal. The emerge to bask on sunny mornings and spend most of their time sitting with perhaps two thirds of the body out of the hole, with the head held high watching out for prey or predators. The slightest disturbance stimulates an instant retreat into the hole. They prey on a variety of insects, both hard-bodied and soft-bodied, including caterpillars, spiders, beetles and grasshoppers (EHMANN 1983, HUTCHINSON et al. 1994). They also take some soft herbage in spring, and have been recorded eating introduced *Medicago* leaves and flowers.

Mating occurs in late October-early November. Both male and female gonad cycles peak at this time, with a testicular maximum at the end of winter and ovulation in November. During the spring mating season males become much more active and will leave their burrows to wander, presumably, in search of a mate. At this time of year males can be trapped in pitfalls, whereas at any other time of the year this method of collection is completely unsuccessful. Females seldom move far from their holes at any time of the year. During this period of increased activity males are more vulnerable to predators. Natural predators include the eastern brown snake, *Pseudonaja textilis,* and small birds of prey (Australian kestrel, *Falco cenchroides,* and, probably, the black-shouldered kite, *Elanus notatus).* Anecdotal evidence (T. MILNE pers. obs.) suggests that pygmy bluetongues may

117

have considerable immunity to the powerfully neurotoxic venom of *Pseudonaja*. One adult male was found in the process of being swallowed by a large *Pseudonaja*. The lizard was regurgitated when the snake was disturbed, and it showed few ill effects (some coagulopathy indicated by leakage of blood from bite marks) and made a complete recovery.

Gestation is about three months, with young being born during a four-week period from the end of January to the end of February. The usual litter size is two or three, with occasionally one or four. Neonate snout-vent length is 40-44 mm, and weight at birth averages 1.5 g. Records of marked individuals indicate that most pygmy bluetongues become sexually mature in their third spring, although a minority of males may become reproductive in their second spring. The smallest reproductive males average about 80 mm snout-vent, while the smallest females with young (at three years of age) are about 90 mm in snout-vent length. Skeletochronology of a small number of specimens produced age estimates up to 8 years.

Although the known populations are very few, pygmy bluetongues can be relatively abundant where they occur. At the best-studied site, a one-hectare plot has had a stable population of 80-100 adult pygmy bluetongues since records were first gathered in 1993. This translates to a biomass of over 1 kg per hectare, comparable with some of the highest lizard population densities recorded for non-island species (BULL 1987, HENLE 1989, 1990). A preliminary estimate of all populations gives an estimation of the wild population at about 5,500.

## Conservation

The continued survival of this species depends on the conservation of its grassland habitat. At our present level of knowledge, it seems most likely that ploughing of the habitat during the last century was the primary cause of the species' present endangered status. Ploughing produces a series of undesirable effects on the soil and biota of the grassland habitat. It would have directly killed many lizards. Those that survived would have found themselves without the spider hole homes they depend on and would have been easy prey. Ploughing permanently alters the soil, increasing its friability so that spider burrows are not likely to last as permanent features of the soil, and the less compacted soil is more easily dug by predators trying to remove the lizards from their holes. In addition, plant diversity plummets as ploughing leads to the replacement of a complex assemblage of mostly perennial native species (with their associated insect fauna) by a low diversity, mostly exotic community of mostly annual species.

So far, attempts by the Adelaide Zoo to breed pygmy bluetongues have not succeeded. The lizards are easily maintained in captivity but show extreme aggression under confined conditions, such that it has been difficult to devise an appropriate density which permits mate choice but discourages potentially lethal fights (T. MORLEY pers. comm.). The species' long-term survival will hinge on the willingness of those landowners whose farms harbor populations of pygmy bluetongues to follow guidelines that are now being developed for the preservation of the lizards' habitat. Sympathy for conservation is generally good in the area, with one of the local schools playing an active part in monitoring the effects of a number of perturbations on land owned by the school and used for agricultural and environmental education. Continued community support such as this will be the best hope for the survival of the pygmy bluetongue.

## Literature

ARMSTRONG, G. & J. REID (1993): The rediscovery of the Adelaide Pygmy Bluetongue, *Tiliqua adelaidensis* (Peters, 1863). – Herpetofauna 22: 3–6.

ARMSTRONG, G., J. REID & M. N. HUTCHINSON (1993): Discovery of a population of the rare scincid lizard, *Tiliqua adelaidensis* (Peters). – Records of the South Australian Museum 26: 153–155.

BULL, C.M. (1987): A population study of the viviparous Australian lizard, *Trachydosaurus rugosus* (Scincidae). – Copeia 1987: 749–757.

COGGER, H.G. (1992): Reptiles and Amphibians of Australia. – 5th edt. (A.H. & A.W. Reed, Sydney), 775 pp.

EHMANN, H. (1983): The natural history and conservation status of the Adelaide Pygmy Bluetongue Lizard, *Tiliqua adelaidensis*. – Herpetofauna (Sydney) 14: 61–76.

– (1992): Encyclopaedia of Australian Wildlife. Reptiles – Angus & Robertson, with the National Photographic Index of Australian Wildlife, Sydney.

FRENCH, R. J., W.E. MATHESON & A. L. CLARKE (1968): Soils and agriculture of the northern and Yorke Peninsula regions of South Australia. – Special Bulletin No. 1.68, Dept. of Agriculture, South Australia (Government Printer, Adelaide).

HENLE, K. (1989): Population ecology and life history of the diurnal skink *Morethia boulengeri* in arid Australia. – Oecologia 78: 521–532.

– (1990): Notes on the population ecology of the large herbivorous lizard *Trachydosaurus rugosus* in arid Australia. – Journal of Herpetology 24: 100–103.

HUTCHINSON, M.N., T. MILNE & T. CROFT (1994): Redescription and ecological notes on the Adelaide Pygmy Bluetongue, *Tiliqua adelaidensis* (Squamata: Scincidae). – Transactions of the Royal Society of South Australia 118: 216–227.

HYDE, M. (1995): The temperate grasslands of South Australia: their composition and conservation status. – World Wide Fund for Nature, Sydney.

MILNE, T.I. & M.N. HUTCHINSON (1997): Draft Recovery Plan for the Adelaide Pygmy Bluetongue Lizard (*Tiliqua adelaidensis*). – Environment Australia, Canberra: 1–27.

MITCHELL, F. J. (1950): The scincid genera *Egernia*

and *Tiliqua* (Lacertilia). – Records of the South Australian Museum 9: 275–308.

PETERS, W. (1863): Eine Übersicht der von Hrn. Richard Schomburgk an das zoologische Museum eingesandten Amphibien, aus Buchsfelde bei Adelaide in Südaustralien. – Monatsberichte der Preussichen Naturwissenschaften 1864[sic]: 228–236.

SHEA, G.M. (1990): The genera *Tiliqua* and *Cyclodomorphus*; generic diagnoses and systematic relationships. – Memoirs of the Queensland Museum 29: 495–520.

– (1992): The systematics and reproduction of bluetongue lizards of the genus *Tiliqua* (Squamata: Scincidae). – Unpub. PhD thesis, Dept of Veterinary Anatomy, University of Sydney.

SPECHT, R.L. (1972): The vegetation of South Australia. – Government Printer, Adelaide, 328 pp.

WAITE, E.R. (1929): The Reptiles and Amphibians of South Australia. – Adelaide (Government Printer), 270 pp.

Authors' addresses
Dr. Mark Hutchinson
South Australian Museum
North Terrace,
Adelaide 5000, Australia

Dr. Tim Milne
Nature Conservation Society of South Australia
5 Fitzgerald Road,
Pasadena 5042, Australia

# Lungata, the banded blue-tongued skink *Tiliqua multifasciata* Sᴛᴇʀɴꜰᴇʟᴅ, 1919

Aɴᴅʀᴇᴇ Hᴀᴜꜱᴄʜɪʟᴅ

**Key words: Reptilia: Sauria: Scincidae: *Tiliqua multifasciata*, Australia, distribution, ecology, reproduction**

## Description

*Tiliqua multifasciata* is a relatively large species of skink growing to an SVL of nearly 25 cm. The tail equals only about 40% of the SVL in length, and none of the specimens seen by me exceeded a total length of 40 cm. The scales on the head are large, those on the body very small, numbering 37-46 around midbody. The head is wedge shaped, its coloration pale gray or brown. A small black iris forms the center of the orange colored eye. The fair rosy mucous membrane of the oral cavity produces a stark contrast in conjunction with the cobalt blue, long and broad tongue. The latter tapers towards a tip with a small median notch. Both ear apertures are obvious, relatively large and covered with five scales.

**Fig. 1** *Tiliqua multifasciata* from Shay Gap, Western Australia                    Photograph: R. Hoser

The dorsal side of the skink displays a brown ground color with several wide, yellow to orange colored bands on the nape of the neck, the body, and on the anterior third of the tail. These bands are wider than their interspaces, and widest on the flanks, narrowing vertebrally. A broad black temporal stripe begins at the eye and ends at the ear opening. The throat region is light, sometimes speckled with dark. The venter is cream colored or white, with the ventral scales sometimes being bordered pale or dark in alternating fashion. The legs are tinted black on their outsides, with weakly pronounced, yellow to orange colored cross bands on the thighs.

## Sexual dimorphism

A first glance will not reveal any obvious differences between males and females. On closer inspection of a larger number of specimens one will find that females grow slightly larger than males. A significant sex indicative trait is found in the tail lengths of adult specimens, with females having shorter tails than males (SHEA 1992).

## Differentiating from other species of *Tiliqua*

Some degree of similarity exists at most with *T. occipitalis* which also sports a lively banded pattern. However, *T. occipitalis* never have orange or orange yellow bands on their backs, but much rather dark brown to black bands. A major point of distinction is the presence of a weakly developed, narrow, dark streak in the center of the head of *T. multifasciata*. This streak begins at the level of the eyes and ends at the level of the ear openings. Such marking is absent in *T. occipitalis*. The latter species also grows slightly larger and has larger ear openings (SHEA 1992). The small number of unpaired subdigital lamellae under the fourth toe (5-8) is a trait which distinguishes *Tiliqua multifasciata* from all other species of *Tiliqua* (SHEA 1992).

## Distribution

*Tiliqua multifasciata* occupies a vast range on the Australian continent. It is known there as the "centralian blue-tongued lizard", and named lungata, lungkata, langkute, loongardi, lulga, culamee, jidna or looma by the Aborigines.

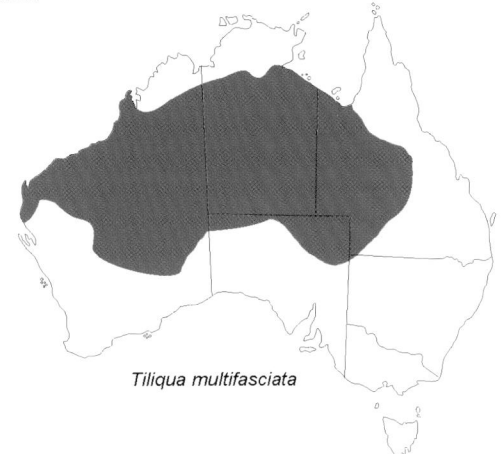

*Tiliqua multifasciata*

The center of its distribution lies in the northern half of Australia, covering the northern half of Western Australia, the southern half of Northern Territory, and a southwestern portion of Queensland. In South Australia, *Tiliqua multifasciata* occurs in the Sturt Stony Desert, in New South Wales it is present in the far northwestern corner of the state (COGGER 1992).
In his publication "Skinks of the Northern Territory" HORNER (1991) described with great precision all skinks and their distribution ranges in Northern Territory. According to this author *Tiliqua multifasciata* can be found in the following biogeographic regions: Kimberleys, Barkly Tableland, Tanami Desert, and Mac Donnell Ranges.

## Sympatry with other species of *Tiliqua*

*Tiliqua multifasciata* was previously regarded as a subspecies of *Tiliqua occipitalis*. COGGER (1979) then justified its elevation to species level with its distinctive color pattern, morphology, habitat preferences, and genetic as well as geographic isolation. The latter reasoning was subsequently corrected by SHEA & PETERSON (1981) who found both species living sympatrically near Laverton in Western Australia. Together with Norbert SCHUSTER (Rossdorf, Germany) I was able to confirm this observation during field studies undertaken in 1985 when two specimens of each species were seen on the route from Leonora to Laverton. The *T. occipitalis* we found perched next to high grass between *Eucalyptus* and *Casuarina* trees. While driving we spotted two specimens of *T. multifasciata* in front of us on the gravel track which disappeared in a flash into spiky *Triodia* grass. I would not be aware of any bastards found in nature or produced in a terrarium. FYFE (1983) reported on another transitory zone in which *Tiliqua multifasciata* and *T. oc-*

*cipitalis* encounter each other, i.e. the Ayers Rock region (Curting Springs, Armstrong Creek and Mt. Conner). FYFE had learnt from Aboriginals that both bluetongue species would be present in this area and his subsequent search confirmed this observation.

## Biology and ecology

**Natural habitat:** Names such as spiny grass, spinifex grass, kangaroo grass, porcupine grass, Australian hummock grass all refer to *Triodia* in among which *Tiliqua multifasciata* feels at home. It is a plant that thrives in extreme aridity. Spinifex grass forms large, round tussocks of very hard, gaunt and pointed blades. By growing fresh blades in between old withered ones these tussocks expand constantly. It is a durable plant with a low nutritional value for farm animals, but is of great importance for

**Fig. 2** Female *T. multifasciata* in the vicinity of Alice Springs          Photograph: O. Daniel

native wild animals. Kangaroos feed on the blades, parrakeets consume the seeds, the night parrot *Geopsittacus occidentalis* builds its nest among the spikes, and smaller animals, including the lungata, find protection in spinifex grass (PETTIT 1985).

Most descriptions of localities where banded blue-tongued skinks were found mention next to the location of the observation the presence of *Triodia* grass, usually as the hiding place of the lizard. In places where no *Triodia* grows, e.g. on the coast, *T. multifasciata* inhabits similar types of vegetation, such as *Zygochloa paradoxa* (GIBSON & COLE 1988). Other than these, the skinks also inhabit the margins of deserts and other arid or semi-arid regions where mulga and mallee scrub dominate, these being characteristic shrub and tree formations that offer the skink suitable habitats. The leading species here are representatives of the *Acacia, Eucalyptus* and *Casuarina* families.

The color of the ground and soil varies from the classic red of central Australia, through the yellow of loam and gray sand, to the black soils of the moderately moist zones of Queensland. The diurnal lizard is a ground dweller which seems to live in rather inhospitable environments where rains may stay away for years on end. But however hostile these arid areas may appear, they are in fact home to a wealth of animal life which has adapted to the circumstances. Spinifex grass, holes in the ground, deserted burrows, and piles of rocks all offer the skink protection from both predators and heat.

**Diet:** All large skinks of Australia are omnivores that feed on arthropods, small vertebrates, and tender greens, flowers and fruit. Following HORNER (1991) the food spectrum of *Tiliqua multifasciata* includes beetles, locusts, roaches and plant material. Examining the teeth of large blue-tongued skinks one will find that they all have very large molars which suggests that their diets include hard-shelled prey such as beetles and snails, whose armors are cracked with ease (HUTCHINSON 1993).

**Activity and annual cycle:** The reason for many animals being nocturnal is to avoid the greatest heat of the day. During spring N. SCHUSTER and the author found several *Tiliqua multifasciata* on the sides of roads or while crossing roads in the north of Western Australia. Our records show that sightings always occurred around noon or in the afternoon, never in the morning and never towards the evening. Nocturnal activity was not observed, but SWANSON (1976) and SCHMIDA (1985) mentioned di- and nocturnal *Tiliqua multifasciata*. This appears to be possible considering that diurnal reptiles may shift their activities to the night hours if the day temperatures are too high and provided that all other conditions are suitable. HOSER (1996) found numerous *T. multifasciata* on the roads crossing the Pilbara of Western Australia during several nights, and he considered nocturnal activity of blue-tongued skinks as normal in hot weather. The behavioral pattern of *Tiliqua multifasciata* varies distinctly from season to season (CHRISTIAN 1977). From May through August, i.e. in the Australian winter, the skinks are relatively inactive and spend most of this period sleeping. If they are disturbed at this stage, they are so defenseless that they do not even manage to display their normal defense repertoire. During this period they are hardly ever seen outside their shelters. The subsequent season lasts from August through late September and has the blue-tongued skinks at their greatest activity. This is little surprising as it is also their mating season. The lizards are now very often spotted basking in the sun on roads. In the early morning and late afternoon hours they can be found in their shelters. If they are disturbed in their hiding places or approached while lying on the road, they show little inclination to flee. The third phase, from end of September through April, sees a change of their behavior in so far as they seem to slow down and shift many activities into the night. If the months of summer are very hot, the bluetongues limit their activity to the coolness of the nights which is when they can also encounter their prey that has made the same change from day to night. This change of habits lasts until about the beginning of January. Now begins the time when the females give birth to their young. CHRISTIAN (1977) reported of the very first births taking place two days before Christmas and the latest towards the end of January. During the hottest time of the year the adult bluetongues have become more wary and more careful. Spotting an approaching car from afar will already cause them to move off the road with lightning speed in order to seek cover. In doing so they can reach speeds equal to that of a small monitor (CHRISTIAN 1977).

With the temperatures decreasing the bluetongues return to their normal diurnal activity pattern. Some time in May the winter period begins and the cycle starts anew.

**Offspring:** An average litter consists of four youngs. The author noted that the sizes of siblings in a litter may vary substantially with large babies being four to five times heavier than their siblings. Newborns are practically identical in their appearances to their parents save for the head proportions which are larger in relation to the body.

BARNETT (1977) reported about captive bred juveniles which he and Trevor CHRISTIAN obtained from several females in 1976 and 1977. The following table gives an overview:

**Table 1** Terrarium bred T. multifasciata in relation to litter size, length, and mass (Barnett 1977)

| Born on | Number | Min. mass | Max. mass | Min. length | Max. length |
|---------|--------|-----------|-----------|-------------|-------------|
| 25.12.76 | 5 | 12 g | 23 g | 10 cm | 11 cm |
| 04.01.77 | 3 | 16 g | 21,5 g | 12 cm | 13 cm |
| 06.01.77 | 5 | 25 g | 29,5 g | 14 cm | 14 cm |
| 10.01.77 | 3 | 5 g | 6,5 g | 9 cm | 9 cm |
| 16.01.77 | 6 | 22.5 g | 26 g | 14 cm | 14 cm |

**Predators and defense behavior:** Motor vehicles are responsible for a death toll of about 10,000 *Tiliqua multifasciata* every year. These victims of traffic are often instantly "removed" by birds. FYFE (1981) reported of two species of falcons that were particularly involved in this: *Falco berigora* and *Falco cenchroides*. The author also observed the birds of preys not only attacking freshly killed, but also live blue-tongued skinks. Other than that, Aborigines (see below), dingos, wedge-tailed eagles, large snakes and monitors are likely to predate on bluetongues, plus the "keepsakes" brought along by the new settlers, i.e. dogs, cats, foxes and wild boars.

The defense behavior displayed by *Tiliqua multifasciata* follows the pattern employed by most blue-tongued skinks. If the animal feels threatened, it will rise on all four legs and inflate its body with air in order to appear larger. If the antagonist comes closer, the skink will bend its body to assume a horseshoe shaped posture with the tension of a loaded spring readying to attack. All the while it has the mouth opened wide with the cobalt blue tongue moving in and out, comparable with a flag that is rolled in and out. The entire display is underlined with noisy, threatening hissing. Careless fingers that want to grasp a *Tiliqua multifasciata* ready to fight for its life will experience the impressive power of jaws that are otherwise used to cracking the shell of terrestrial snails (SWITAK 1986).

### Aboriginals and lizards

For the nomad Aboriginals of central Australia *Tiliqua multifasciata* represents an important source of protein. Blue-tongued skinks are traditionally a type of game for them. Armed with sticks, they find the lizards by following their tracks in the sand, flushing them out of their hiding places, and beating them to death. The quarry is then fried, baked or steamed.

### Keeping in a terrarium

**Terrarium:** Where respective legislation ex-

ists, prescribed minimum keeping requirements must be fulfilled. In Germany, for example, the following dimensions are prescribed for the keeping of one or two blue-tongued skinks of about 25 cm in total length:
length: 6 × 25 cm = 150 cm
width: 4 × 25 cm = 100 cm
height: 3 × 25 cm = 75 cm
Although the author does not necessarily agree with all the minimum dimensions prescribed by the relevant regulations, these measurements of a terrarium are fairly adequate.

**Substrate:** Coarse sand or fine gravel without sharp edges.

**Decoration:** Numerous tubes, pieces of cork bark, and a shallow hiding place made of well anchored rock plates satisfy the basic needs. A second level in the terrarium is readily accepted. The water bowl must be sturdy.

**Heating:** An underfloor heater of not more than 25 watts output, covering two thirds of the ground space has proved beneficial.

**Illumination:** Very intense, HQI lamps, one spot light.

**Temperature:** Soil 25°C, air 30°C, local hot spot 40°C.

**Humidity:** All experiments with misting so far had negative consequences (flu, pneumonia) so that I have come to keeping my specimens entirely dry with best results.

**Diet:** Other than in the case of sweet fruit, vegetarian food finds little acceptance, maybe with the exception of ice lettuce and Chinese cole slaw, but with other keepers some skinks have been accepting finely grated carrots. Large roaches, locusts and pink mice are favorite prey items, and snails are also very popular.

**Breeding:** Following numerous failed attempts in the keeping of *T. multifasciata,* field studies and the collection of environmental data revealed light intensities and temperatures that are now regarded as vital for the animal and which are also confirmed in the scientific literature (LICHT et al. 1966). The terrarium must therefore offer an area that permits the skinks to heat themselves to a temperature of 37.5°C. At this spot the sub-

**Fig. 3** Terrarium room for skinks, including *T. multifasciata* Photograph: A. Hauschild

strate should offer a temperature of 37.5 to 40°C. The substrate and air temperatures inside the hiding places, and most of the terrarium in general, should otherwise not exceed 25°C. Only such a temperature structure enables the animals to thermoregulate in an active manner (LICHT et al. 1966) and saves them from becoming prisoners of a sweat box. I can only advise every keeper of *T. multifasciata* to install a weak underfloor heater which may, however, only be switched on during the day. The granules of the substrate must always be round, never sharp edged, as the ventral side of *T. multifasciata* is very susceptible to scratch wounds. Even small lacerations will become inflamed if exposed to moisture (water bowl, excrements) resulting in infections. A lack of general hygiene appears to render this species particularly susceptible to diseases, similar to the situation described by HAUSCHILD & GASSNER (1995) for *T. occipitalis.* Even a moderate supply with moisture resulted in flu with subsequent pneumonia, and fungal or bacterial, purulent infections beneath the scales. These health problems were only eliminated once the keeping conditions were changed to "entirely dry".

Limiting the population of a terrarium to just one pair is of advantage. Communal keeping with other lizards also produces a lot of stress and should therefore not be undertaken. And as a remark on the side - these bluetongues will never become really tame, maintaining their shy to reserved attitude towards the keeper. A mature pair can be easily converted to the annual cycle of the northern hemisphere.

An individual hibernation period of about six weeks duration at 18°C in a dark room is recommendable. Upon completion of the overwintering the male is placed with the "willing" female, and, at the latest, ten days thereafter one may expect to see them copulating. The latter follows the same pattern as with other species of *Tiliqua,* but is much more gentle and not nearly as savage as in *Tiliqua nigrolutea* or *T. scincoides.* In the case of *T. multifasciata* it is important to remove the male soon after the mating season in order to protect the female from stress. In nature the pairs also separate immediately after they have stopped copulating. Approximately three and a half months later the baby bluetongues are born. They number between three and six, measure about 14 cm in total length and weigh about 25 g, and thus are relatively large. They should be raised separated from the parents in order to have better control of their development. Daily exposure to UV radiation is crucial. They can receive the same food as the adults, i.e. roaches, locusts, crickets, fruit and "skink pudding", just in smaller formats. Feeding must be supervised as it may become necessary to intervene in fights that break out over food. These may lead to injuries which take a long time to heal.

## Literature

BARNETT, B. (1977): Additional Notes on New-born Centralian Bluetongues (*Tiliqua mulitfasciata*). – Newsletter Vict. Herp. Soc., 1: 10.

BUNDESMINISTERIUM FÜR ERNÄHRUNG, LANDWIRTSCHAFT UND FORSTEN (1997): Gutachten über Mindestanforderungen an die Haltung von Reptilien vom 10. Januar 1997. – Sonderausgabe der DGHT, Rheinbach, 80 S.

COGGER, H. G. (1979): Reptiles and Amphibians of Australia. – Revised edition 1979. Ralph Curtis Books, Hollywood, USA, 608 pp.

FYFE, G. (1981): Predation on reptiles by the brown falcon (*Falco berigora*). – Herpetofauna, Sydney, 13(1): 31.

– (1983): Some Notes on the Sympatry between *Tiliqua occipitalis* and *Tiliqua multifasciata* in the Ayers Rock Region and their Associations with Aboriginal People of the Area. – Herpetofauna, Sydney, 15(1): 18–19.

GIBSON, D. B. & J. R. Cole (1988): A biological survey of the northern Simpson Desert. – C.C.N.T.T.R. 40: 1–205.

HAUSCHILD, A. & P. GAßNER (1995): Skinke im Terrarium. – Landbuch-Verlag, Hannover, 197 S.

HORNER, P. (1991): Skinks of the Northern Territory. – NT Museum Handbook Series No.2., Darwin, 174 pp.

HOSER, R. (1996): Reptiles encountered collecting in the Pilbara-Australia. – Reptilian, 4(2): 25–35.

HUTCHINSON, M. (1993): Family Scincidae. – In: GLASBY, C.J., G.J.B. ROSS & P.L. BEESLEY (eds) (1993): Fauna of Australia, Vol. 2A Amphibia & Reptilia. – Australian Government Publishing Service, Canberra, 439 pp.

LIGHT, P., W. R. DAWSON, H. SHOEMAKER & A. R. MAIN (1966): Observations on the thermal relations on Western Australian lizards. – Copeia, Washington, 1: 97–110.

PETTIT, R. (1985): Australien. Tier- und Pflanzenwelt. – Landbuch-Verlag, Hannover, 176 S.

SCHMIDA, G. (1985): The Cold-Blooded Australians. A unique photographic study of Australia's reptiles, amphibians and freshwater fish. – Doubleday Australia Pty Limited, Lane Cove, NSW, 208 pp.

SHEA, G. M. & M. PETERSON (1981): Observations on Sympatry of the Social Lizards *Tiliqua multifasciata* STERNFELD and *T. occipitals* (PETERS). – Aust. J. Herp., 1(1): 27–28.

SHEA, G. M. (1992): The systematics and reproduction of bluetongue lizards of the genus *Tiliqua* (Squamata: Scincidae). – Ph. D. thesis, University of Sydney, 4 Vols.

SWANSON, S. (1976): Lizards of Australia. – Angus & Robertson Publishers, 142 pp.

SWITAK, K.H. (1986): Zwei Echsen aus Australien: Tannenzapfen- und Blauzungenskink. Verhalten und Pflegeansprüche. – Das Aquarienmagazin, Stuttgart, 20 (7): 296–299.

TREVOR, C. (1977): Notes on Centralian Bluetongues (*Tiliqua multifasciata*). – Newsletter Vict. Herp. Soc., 1: 8–9.

Author's address
Andree Hauschild
Narzissenweg 7
D-41516 Grevenbroich, Germany

# On the biology, husbandry and breeding of *Tiliqua nigrolutea* (Quoy & Gaimard, 1824)

Robert Hitz

Key words: Reptilia: Sauria: Scincidae: *Tiliqua: Tiliqua nigrolutea,* Australia, description, distribution, ecology, taxonomic history, reproduction, husbandry, breeding

## Introduction

*Tiliqua nigrolutea* is mentioned in all encyclopedic works by Australian herpetologists, examples being WORRELL (1963), BUSTARD (1970), WILSON & KNOWLES (1988) and COGGER (1992). Unfortunately though, the chapters on *T. nigrolutea* usually contain only brief descriptions and distribution data. In his comprehensive study SHEA (1992) also dealt with *T. nigrolutea* in great detail. SHEA consulted all the existing literature up to 1992 summarizing its contents, examined some 360 museum specimens with modern herpetological methods as to their morphology, and analyzed and presented the results statistically. It is most unfortunate that this work is very difficult to obtain and can be purchased only in the form of microfiches. As far as the keeping and breeding of *T. nigrolutea* under terrarium conditions is concerned, the literature is rather sparse though. Besides some smaller articles the work by JONES (1987) offers some good start off points. The most detailed and up to date portrayal stems from HAUSCHILD & GASSNER (1995).

For the purpose of the present contribution the author has undertaken to combine in a synop-

**Fig. 1** *T. nigrolutea,* subadult male of the highland morph, in a terrarium    Photograph: R. Hitz

sis the results presented by SHEA and other Australian herpetologists, as well as the information contained in amateur papers, with his own experiences with these lizards.

## Etymology and synonyms

The species name is derived from Latin *niger* = black, and *luteus* = yellow, *Tiliqua nigrolutea* = the black and yellow blue-tongued skink. In English it is commonly referred to as the blotched or southern blue-tongued lizard or skink, or in abbreviated form as southern blue-tongue or blotched bluetongue, but its scientific name is also widespread, at least in terrarium keeper circles.

A detailed list of synonyms was presented by SHEA (1992):

*Lacerta tarda* ANDERSON (discovered in 1777, published only in 1967)
*Scincus nigro-luteus* QUOY & GAIMARD, 1824
*Cyclodus nigro-luteus* WAGLER 1830
*Tiliqua nigrolutea* GRAY 1831
*Tiliqua milleri* WELLS & WELLINGTON, 1985

## Diagnosis (SHEA 1992)

A large to very large species of the genus *Tiliqua,* with a maximum snout-vent length (SVL) of 368 mm, differing from all other species of *Tiliqua* by its unique dorsal color pattern dominated by broad, dark cross bands, light spots that are arranged in longitudinal series. A continuous dark temporal streak is absent. Venter with dark markings; primary temporals present, in pairs; normally four supraoculars, the first two of which in contact with the frontal; 41-57 paravertebrals; 32 or fewer scale rows at midbody (COGGER 1992).

## Description (COGGER 1992, SHEA 1992, WILSON & KNOWLES 1988)

A highland and a lowland form are distinguished, differing mainly as to their coloration and size (SHEA 1992, WORRELL 1963). SHEA

(1992) drew the borderline between the distribution ranges of the two forms along the 500 m isohype.

**Body shape:** *T. nigrolutea* is a species of *Tiliqua* with a short, wide, massive head, an elongated, robust body, a relatively short, conically tapering tail, and powerful, relatively short limbs.

**Scalation:** *T. nigrolutea* has small, relatively smooth scales. Together with *T. rugosa, T. nigrolutea* has, however, the roughest scales within the genus *Tiliqua.* SHEA (1992) compiled the pholidotic traits with acribic precision and analyzed them statistically. He presented a detailed description of the pholidosis with additional information on asymmetries, sexual dimorphism, and geographic variation.

**Coloration:** The color pattern consists of a light and a dark color element. SHEA (1992) considered the light constituent as the ground color, whereas all other authors, including COGGER (1992), EHMANN (1992) and WILSON & KNOWLES (1988), regarded the dark element as the basic color. The present author follows the majority of Australian herpetologists here. The ground color of the dorsal side is dark brown (lowland morph) to black (highland morph), embedded in which are small to large, elongate blotches that may be arranged in transverse or longitudinal series. The coloration of these blotches is highly variable, ranging from light brown, gray, bluish gray, whitish, light yellow, bluish yellow (lowland morph), to brownish yellow, yellow, salmon red, or dark red (highland morph). The spotted pattern is usually continued in the form of cross bands on the dorsal side of the tail. The individual blotches may fuse to form more expansive markings on the nape of the neck and on the shoulders. The spots and blotches are paler on the flanks than on the back, forming reticulated patterns in conjunction with the dark ground color. The upper side of the head is brownish gray (lowland morph) to black (highland morph), with a yellow or greenish pattern in the latter. A very pretty color variety native to the Blue Moun-

**Table 1** SVL of adult *T. nigrolutea*, grouped according to origin (highland / lowland) and sex (SHEA 1992). SVL = snout-vent length, TL = total length

| Origin | Sex | SVL | Mean SVL | Mean SVL projected to TL |
|--------|-----|-----|----------|--------------------------|
| Lowland | male | 227–300 mm | 260,2 mm | 377,6 mm |
| Lowland | female | 239–328 mm | 269,5 mm | 391,1 mm |
| Highland | male | 242–368 mm | 296,6 mm | 430,4 mm |
| Highland | female | 280–368 mm | 313,1 mm | 454,3 mm |

tains sports red parietal shields. The sides of the head inclusive of the lips are grayish brown in the lowland morph, and light green or yellow in the highland morph. The eyes consist of a reddish brown iris and a black pupil. The ear apertures are protected by two or three large auricular scales (pers. obs.). The gular region, venter, and the ventral side of the tail are grayish blue, bluish yellow (lowland morph), to yellow (highland morph). The throat may be spotted with black. The ventral side of the body sports a black pattern of various types ranging from fine banding to fine striation, reticulation or a marbled pattern. The legs are dark in color, with fine speckles, in the same manner as the flanks. The palmar granules and subdigital lamellae are dark brown to black.

Juveniles show the same color pattern as adult specimens. The light blotched and spotted pattern is more intense, even bright in some cases, in young animals, fades as the specimens age reducing the initial contrast. The arrangement and shape of the markings is, however, constant (pers. obs., SHEA 1992).

**Body length, snout-vent length** (SHEA 1992): The body length, and the snout-vent length for that matter, of adult *T. nigrolutea* differs between the sexes as well as between the lowland and the highland morphs (see Table 1). The tail length is given by SHEA (1992) as 29.3-55.1% (mean 45.1%, n = 322) of the SVL, the length of the hind limbs as 14.3-27.4% (mean 18.1%, n = 353) of the SVL. The maximum SVL noted by SHEA is 368 mm in both male and female highland specimens. Based on an average tail length of 45.1% of the SVL this adds up to a maximum total length of 534 mm. HOSER (1989) stated a maximum total length of 600 mm which appears slightly exaggerated considering the results quoted by SHEA.

**Body proportion:** In both the highland and the lowland forms the females have longer bodies in proportion to their SVL and shorter heads and tails than the males.

**Body mass** (pers. obs.): Two adult wild caught specimens of the lowland morph had masses of 320 and 390 g, respectively, while wild caught highland specimens weighed 360-590 g. Old specimens representing the highland morph may reach 600-700 g in human care.

**Geographic variation** (SHEA 1992)

SHEA assigned the available material to 25 different populations and compared pholidotic, SVL and coloration traits. Extreme differences showed only with regard to the body sizes of lowland and highland populations. The differences in coloration between the populations are of a rather gradual nature, ranging from the poorly contrasting, little variable coloration of Tasmanian specimens to the highly contrasting, bright, highly variable color pattern of specimens from the highest altitudes. SHEA concluded that the current state of knowledge does not permit a definition of subspecies within the species *T. nigrolutea*.

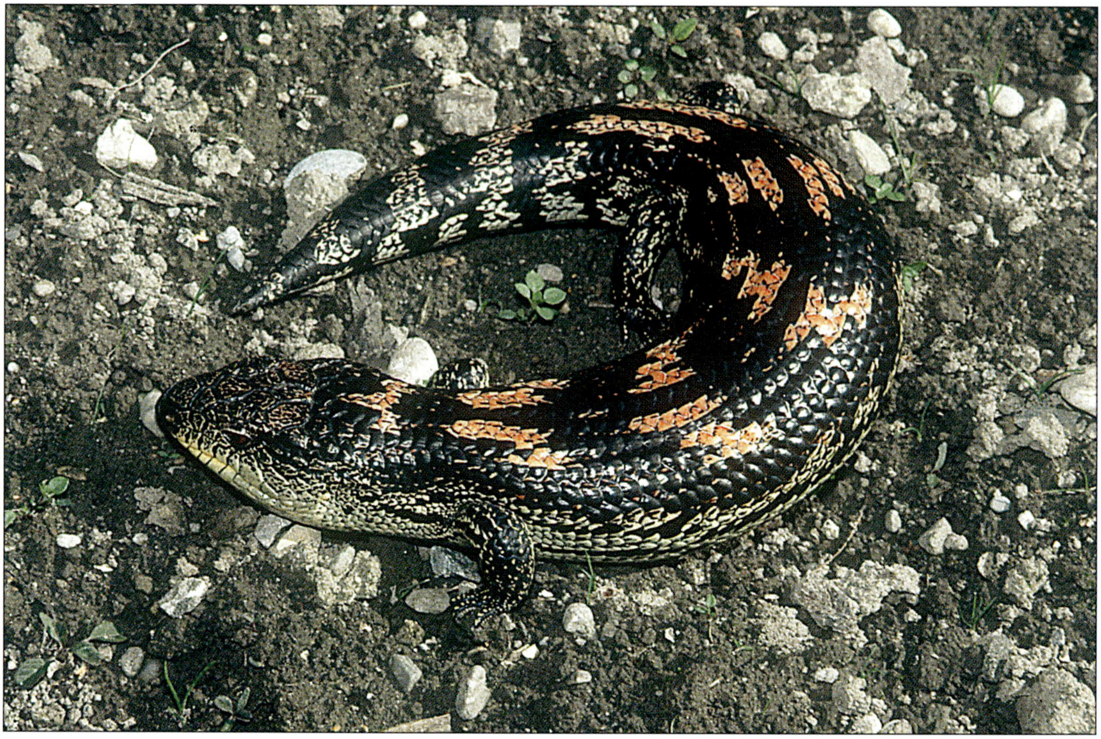

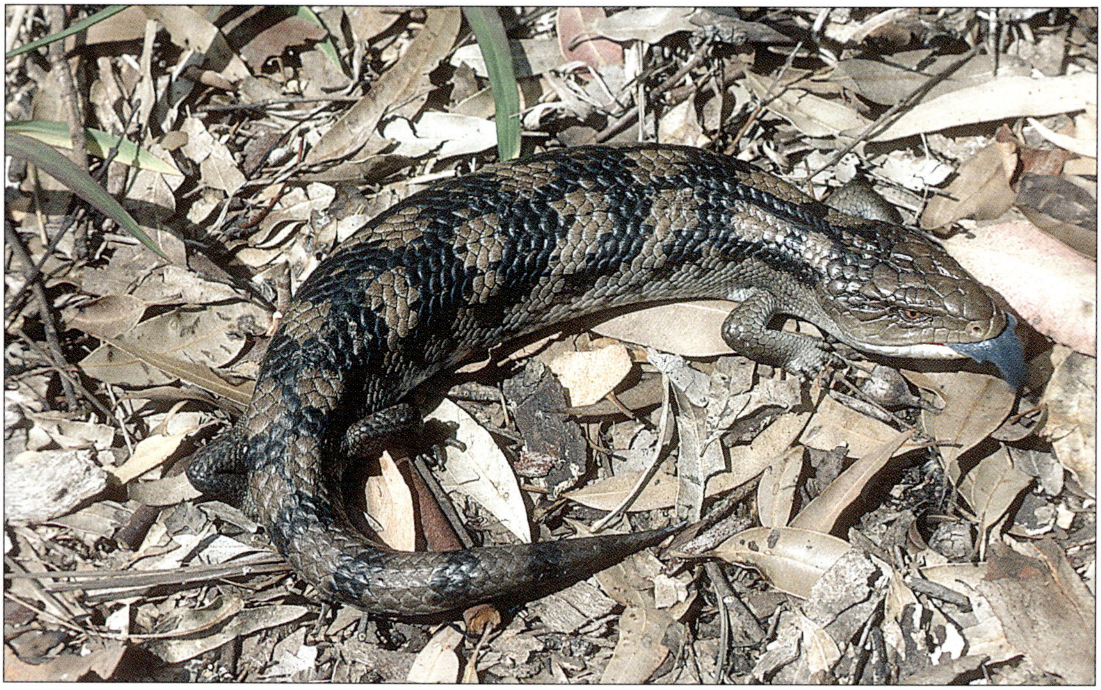

Opposite from above
**Fig. 2** *Tiliqua nigrolutea,* semiadult specimen of the highland morph, in the author's garden
Photograph: R. Hitz

**Fig. 3** *T. nigrolutea,* lowland morph, in the field
Photograph: K. Griffiths

## Differentiation of *Tiliqua nigrolutea* from other species of *Tiliqua* (SHEA 1992)

*T. nigrolutea* is easily distinguished from all other species of *Tiliqua* by its color pattern. Solely some specimens of the lowland morph in which the lateral blotches are fused to form bands may show a resemblance of *T. s. scincoides.* However, *T. nigrolutea* is readily distinguished from *T. s. scincoides* by the following traits: a dark ventral pattern, a yellow throat, fewer paravertebral scales (41-57), fewer scale rows at midbody (26-35), fewer supralabials (6-9), and no dark temporal streak in *T. nigrolutea.*

## Chromosomes

DONNELLAN (1991) published the caryotypes of Australian skinks of the *Egernia* group (genera *Egernia, Corucia* and *Tiliqua*). In all species examined, including *T. nigrolutea,* he had found diploid sets of chromosomes numbering 2n = 32. No heteromorphous sex chromosomes could be detected.

## Distribution (SHEA 1992, WILSON & KNOWLES 1988)

The distribution range of *T. nigrolutea* lies in southeastern Australia. On the mainland it extends from the southeast of South Australia through the south of Victoria and through the highlands of southern and central New South Wales, to the Blue Mountains. Whilst the species is widely distributed at lower and higher elevations in the south of this area, it is limited to higher elevations (above 500 m) in the north. Finally the species

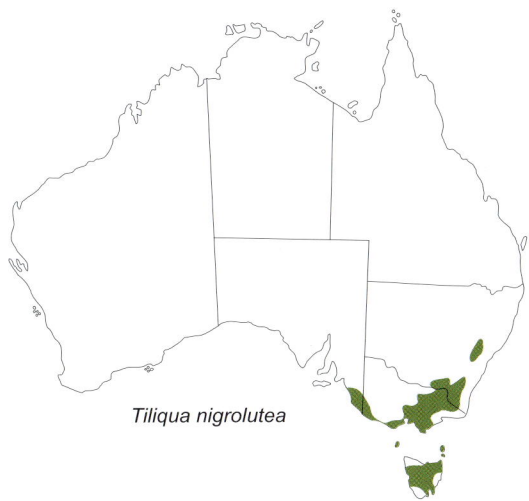

*Tiliqua nigrolutea*

also inhabits large parts of Tasmania and the western and eastern islands of the Bass Strait. It has also been recorded from three islands in the Westernport Bay, i.e. Philipp, French and Quail Islands. The Blue Mountain population is possibly isolated from all other populations in New South Wales. The altitudinal distribution extends from sea level to about 1600 m in the Snowy Mountains. In general it can be stated that the range of *T. nigrolutea* is correlated to the cooler regions of southeastern Australia. In his treatise SHEA (1992) listed every single specimen examined with its collection number and locality data. He assigned the studied specimens to 25 populations. Their areas of origin are listed in the following in order to illustrate the entire distribution range in more detail: south Tasmania / northeast Tasmania / northwest Tasmania / Swan Island / Clarkes I. / Cape Barren I. / Flinders I. / Babel I. / East Sister I. / West Sister I. / Deal I. / Hogan I. / Hunter I. / King I. / southeast of South Australia and southwest of Victoria / Otway Ranges and hinterland, Victoria / Melbourne District, Victoria / Westernport Bay Islands / south of Gippsland, Victoria / Omeo District, Victoria / Victorian Highlands / Snowy Mountains, New South Wales (NSW) / Monaro Tablelands, NSW / South-West Slopes, NSW / Blue Mountains region, NSW.

**Fig. 4** Wentworth Falls, Blue Mountains, New South Wales.         Photograph: K. Griffiths

## Ecology

Australia can be divided in four zoogeographical regions, i.e. the tropical Torresian region, the central (eremic) Eyrian region, the Southwest Australian region, and the southern Bassian region (BAEHR 1976). The distribution range of *T. nigrolutea* falls, according to the same author, entirely into the Bassian region. The latter itself is divided in a warm temperate, a cool temperate, and a cold temperate subregion. The higher mountains in the east of Victoria and in New South Wales, as well as large parts of Tasmania, that is a considerable portion of the distribution range of *T. nigrolutea,* thus belong to the cold temperate subregion.

HANCOCK & THOMPSON (1997) conducted a computer aided analysis of climatic data pertaining to collection sites of *T. nigrolutea* in New South Wales. The result, a so-called climate profile, reveals in 16 parameters, that refer to the temperatures and amounts of precipitation, the requirements *T. nigrolutea* (in the case being the highland morph) poses to its habitat (see Table 2). The analysis showed, not entirely unexpected, that this species is very sensitive to high temperatures. Its occurrence is thus bound to areas with relatively low temperatures. These temperature requirements lie at significantly lower levels than those posed by *T. s. scincoides* and *T. rugosa aspera* established in the same study. The required minimum amount of precipitation for *T. nigrolutea,* on the other hand, is twice as high as that for *T. s. scincoides.* The available distribution range for *T. nigrolutea* is therefore not only limited by the species' temperature requirements, but also by its moisture requirements, to regions with higher precipitation levels, and these are

**Table 2** Climate profile for *Tiliqua nigrolutea* within New South Wales (n = 90, all temperatures in degr. C, all precipitation quantities in mm). From: HANCOCK & THOMPSON 1997

| Climate Parameter | Minimum | 5% | 95% | Maximum |
|---|---|---|---|---|
| 1. Annual mean temperature | 6,0* | 8,9 | 14,8 | 25,4* |
| 2. Minimum temperature coolest month | -3,2 | -2,5 | 5,4 | 5,4 |
| 3. Maximum temperature warmest month | 18,5 | 21,5 | 28,7 | 31,1 |
| 4. Annual temperature range (max.-min.) | 18,5 | 20,2 | 27,6 | 29,8 |
| 5. Mean temperature coolest quarter | 0,3** | 3 | 9,7 | 10,9 |
| 6. Mean temperature warmest quarter | 11,9 | 14,7 | 20,9 | 21,9 |
| 7. Mean temperature wettest quarter | 0,7** | 4,7 | 19,7 | 21,2 |
| 8. Mean temperature driest quarter | 4,7* | 5 | 19,6 | 21,6 |
| 9. Annual mean precipitation | 599 | 663 | 1446 | 1883 |
| 10. Precipitation wettest month | 65 | 69 | 171 | 204 |
| 11. Precipitation driest month | 29 | 36 | 77 | 106 |
| 12. Coeff. variation monthly precipitation | 8,7 | 9 | 35,2 | 41,7 |
| 13. Precipitation wettest quarter | 178 | 194 | 480 | 592 |
| 14. Precipitation driest quarter | 99 | 117 | 256 | 331 |
| 15. Precipitation coolest quarter | 124 | 144 | 480 | 559 |
| 16. Precipitation warmest quarter | 99 | 118 | 336 | 373 |

* Significant difference (>30 %) between the minimum and the five percentile values or the 95 percentile and maximum values. ** Difference > 80 %.

the higher elevations. Unfortunately no such study is available for the lowland morph of *T. nigrolutea*. However, because the latter also occurs in warmer subregions than the highland form in New South Wales, it may be presumed that it shows a different climate profile with a preference for higher temperatures.

The ground dwelling *T. nigrolutea* is little choosy with regard to its biotope; an overview of the relevant literature was provided by SHEA (1992). Within its distribution range this species of *Tiliqua* is found in all types of forests, including savannah woodland (open plains forest), dry sclerophyll forest (dry *Eucalyptus* forest), wet sclerophyll forest (moist *Eucalyptus* forest, a component of montane forests), temperate rain forest (rain forest of temperate latitudes), and a variety of other montane forests. Preferred sites are the margins of forests and

clearings where opportunities for basking exist. Other than these, the species also inhabits a wide variety of grasslands and even the margins of swamps.

In its mainland biotopes *T. nigrolutea* finds shelter in the leaf litter stratum on forest floors, in cavities beneath wood, rocks, tussocks of grass, as well as in caves and burrows abandoned by other animals. In contrast it may hide in more than half a meter deep tunnels in the ground or among rocks on the island of Tasmania (BAEHR 1976).

*T. nigrolutea* is a diurnal lizard with a solitary disposition. According to EHMANN (1992) it feeds on terrestrial snails and slugs, insects (mainly beetles, cicadas and caterpillars), spiders, but also plant matter such as leaves, flowers, and fruit. BUSTARD (1970) suggested that plant materials account for a large portion of their food during most seasons of the year. The same author also listed small vertebrates, including other small skinks, that would expand the food spectrum. In their studies of stomach contents of freshly road killed specimens WEBB & SIMPSON (1985) also found, besides of the already mentioned food components, mushrooms, pieces of grass, and plant seeds.

As to the conservation status of *T. nigrolutea* EHMANN (1992) considered it "secure", and evaluated its occurrence as rare to common while SMITH & SMITH (1990) considered its occurrence in the Blue Mountains as moderately common. Another indication of the considerable regional commonness of this species was given by HAUSCHILD & GASSNER (1995) by quoting JAKOB who had counted not fewer than 95 specimens killed on the road between Bega and Cooma in New South Wales on three days during the mating season. This observation corresponds well with what other visitors to the distribution range were faced with. It is generally said that the species can only be found without effort during its mating season. Outside this period, and especially during the warmer phases of the year, the animals have a very secretive way of life.

### Sympatry and hybridization of *T. nigrolutea* with other species of *Tiliqua*

*T. nigrolutea* / *T. s. scincoides:* Both species have their distribution ranges in southeastern Australia. In general, *T. nigrolutea* is restricted here to cooler, more elevated, or more southerly regions. This attribute also corresponds with the climate profiles established for both species by HANCOCK & THOMPSON (1997). Nevertheless, there are many areas where they occur sympatrically, an overview of which was provided by SHEA (1992). This concerns both the highland and the lowland forms. Accordingly, known areas of sympatry include the southeast of South Australia, numerous locations in Victoria, but also the Blue Mountains and the western slopes of the Great Dividing Range in New South Wales. SHEA (1992) compared sympatric populations of both species, involving the lowland as well as the highland morphs, according to a selection of pholidotic traits. The result was a complete separation of both species based on the absence of phenotypically intermediary specimens in nature which would have suggested a hybridization in the wild.

That a hybridization is possible notwithstanding, was reported by LONGLEY (1939, 1941). Repeatedly, he mated a female *T. s. scincoides* with a male *T. nigrolutea* representing the highland morph. Live young were born, but whether these could be raised and whether they were fertile cannot be deduced from his reports. SHEA himself also bred one litter of hybrids from a female *T. nigrolutea* from Bombala and a male *T. s. scincoides* from St. Ives, both localities being situated in New South Wales. The resulting seven young were small, frail, and with the exception of one specimen all suffered from substantial deformations. Three specimens perished shortly after their birth. The hybrids produced by SHEA resembled *T. s. scincoides* in their general appearance. WORRELL (1963) reported that he (and LONGLEY) had produced captive bred offspring from hybrid matings. Their colors varied from the normal color patterns of either species to intermediary traits. These hybrid animals were fertile and continued to breed over several generations. This indicates that *T. nigrolutea* and *T. s. scincoides* are obviously not fully incompatible genetically. It would be most interesting to find out which mechanisms are in place that prevent hybridization at localities where both occur sympatrically in nature.

***T. nigrolutea* / *T. rugosa aspera:*** According to SHEA (1992) the distribution ranges of both species overlap only in small areas in the extreme southeast of South Australia, for example at Cape Jaffa, and in adjacent parts of Victoria. Animals from the region of sympatry are readily identified on the basis of external traits. SHEA compared various pholidotic traits of specimens of both species and found that both taxa are entirely separated. A single museum specimen, however, proves that hybridization is possible, although very rare. It is a normally formed, subadult female from a zone of sympatry that shows an intermediary phenotype.

## On the taxonomic history of *T. nigrolutea*

A very detailed chapter on this subject can again be found in SHEA (1992).
William ANDERSON, a surgeon participating in a journey of James COOK during the years 1776-1780, discovered a 37.5 cm long, black and yellow colored lizard near Adventure Bay on Tasmania on January 30, 1777, which he named *Lacerta tarda* (Latin *tardus* = slow, sluggish) (ANDERSON, in BEAGLEHOLE 1967). What happened to this specimen subsequently is unknown. Due to the fact that this description was published only 143 years after the name *nigrolutea* was introduced, *tarda* cannot be used to replace *nigrolutea* according to the rules of nomenclature.
A French expedition commanded by L. DE FREYCINET during the years 1817-1820 provided the naturalists QUOY and GAIMARD with an opportunity to discover two specimens of a beautiful lizard on a tedious march into the Blue Mountains (QUOY & GAIMARD 1824). On the sail back to Europe their ship was wrecked in the South Pacific, but fortunately one of the specimens from the Blue Mountains, contained in the zoological collection, was saved. In 1824, QUOY and GAIMARD described this species as *Scincus nigro-luteus* in DE FREYCINET's report of the expedition. This original description, in French language, first makes mention of how this animal was obtained. Then follows a detailed description of its external anatomy and its coloration. An excellent color plate eventually portrays the holotype and leaves no doubt of it pertaining to the highland form. This holotype is very likely extant in the Muséum national d'Histoire naturelle in Paris (MNHP) with the catalogue number 7134.

WAGLER (1830) then transferred *Scincus nigroluteus* to the genus *Cyclodus,* and GRAY (1831) finally assigned the taxon to the genus *Tiliqua.* It was not before 1963 that a publication hinted to the existence of a highland and a lowland morph within the species *T. nigrolutea:* WORRELL distinguished both forms on the basis of their different colorations and the difference in size. WELLS & WELLINGTON (1985) then attempted a partial solution to the highland/lowland concept by assigning the animals from the southeast of South Australia to their new taxon *Tiliqua milleri.* SHEA (1992) examined the designated type of *T. milleri,* but neither granted it species, nor subspecies status.

## Reproductive biology

Detailed data on the reproductive biology of *T. nigrolutea* are contained in SHEA (1992), and smaller contributions were published by LONGLEY (1941), BARTLETT (1984), GIDDINGS (1984), JONES (1987), and CARD (1993). Over the past ten years the author was able to collect a lot of data from the keeping of a group of this species of lizard, which could be verified and even expanded through a continuous correspondence with A. HAUSCHILD and H. RÖHE, both Germany.
**Sexual dimorphism:** With regard to external differences between males and females, *T. nigrolutea* must be termed an almost monomorphous species of lizard. Distinguishing the sexes is therefore often an arduous task, in particular if the subjects are juveniles or subadults. Various techniques are available, a description of which can be found in the chapter "Sex identification in blue-tongued skinks (Sauria: Scincidae: *Tiliqua*)" of this book.
**The male sexual cycle:** In the course of his studies SHEA (1992) noted that the testes of *T. nigrolutea* showed varying lengths and turgor (state of tissue tension) at different seasons, although it must be said that no data is available for the time from May to mid-September, i.e. the cooler months. The length of the testes

and their turgor increase in spring reaching their maxima in late October and November. Beginning in late spring and throughout the summer the length of the testes and their turgor decrease again (see Table 4). These data prove that the male reproductive cycle of *T. nigrolutea* reaches its peak in spring, i.e. in the mating season. *T. nigrolutea* thus displays the testicular activity Type III of LICHT (1972).

In captivity this peak will be noted by the discharge of hemipenis exuviae during a 5-7 week period in the mating season. This time is also marked by the outbreak of vicious fights among the males, which cannot only be observed in a terrarium (pers. obs., SHEA 1992), but also in nature (SHEA 1992).

SHEA (1993) described another, lower peak in the testicular cycle for *T. s. scincoides* in autumn (March). This phenomenon corresponds with the discharge of hemipenis exuviae by captive *T. nigrolutea* in autumn, before the cool hibernation phase (pers. obs.). It occurs equally in European and Australian seasonal cycles.

**The female sexual cycle:** SHEA (1992) noted the same annual pattern of variation of the follicle diameter in both the lowland and the highland morph of *T. nigrolutea* (see Table 4). No data are available for the time between May and July. The follicles grow continually from late winter to spring reaching their greatest diameter at the end of November and in December. This is also the time when yolk is produced and deposited in the follicles. Between after the first third of November through the end of December the follicles are ovulated. In females which have not been covered a regression of the follicles takes place, or they may be ovulating as well. In the latter case the unused yolk masses are usually discharged after the normal gestation period. Some females also show only a minor follicle growth in spring which indicates that they will not reproduce during this particular year.

**Synchronization of the sexes:** As *Tiliqua nigrolutea* originates from regions marked by cool winters it is very likely that it is this cool phase that has a governing effect on the reproductive cycle of both sexes and their synchronization (DUVALL et al. 1982, HITZ pers. obs.).

As far as the breeding under terrarium conditions is concerned, the author's personal experiences are limited to observations made with the highland form. It showed that a synchronization of the sexes can only be achieved in a perfect manner if the females end their hibernation a few weeks after the males. The males may shed shortly before they begin to hibernate in autumn, but usually do so only in the subsequent spring. They will only be ready to mate once this spring shedding has been completed. If the females are taken out of their hibernation together with the males, they will often be receptive before or during the shedding phase of the males for which reason no mating will take place. The same observations were also made by other terrarium keepers (EBBERT pers. comm., RÖHE pers. comm.).

Following the schedule suggested in Table 3 is therefore recommended, whereby it should be noted that the transitory phase from the end of hibernation to the normal functioning of the terraria takes three weeks for the males, but only one week for the females.

The chronological course of events usually follows this pattern: four to five weeks after the end of hibernation the males shed and then remain ready to mate for about four weeks. Once signs of an impending shedding are noted in the form of the pale appearance of the reddish yellow blotches, the females should be taken out of their hibernation. They will be receptive for five days about two weeks later. This phase now falls well within the period in which the males are also ready to mate. The latter will indicate this by discharging hemipenis exuviae over a period of two to nine weeks after the end of their hibernation.

An asynchronous completion of hibernation by the sexes is well documented in the herpetological literature for various reptiles. BANNERT (1993) described observations for lizards of the genera *Gallotia, Lacerta* and *Podarcis* that are nearly identical with the observations the author made in the case of highland *T. nigrolutea*. An early leaving of the hibernation quarters by the males is also known to occur in nature in the case of, e.g., species of *Podarcis* (BÖHME 1986), and *Anolis carolinensis* (CREWS 1975), and probably serves the establishment of territories. VERON (1969) noted that more males than females of *Sphenomorphus quoyii* are present in the biotope at the beginning of the mating season. This could also point to an asynchronous reappearing from hibernation.

Whether the observations made by the author and other terrarium keepers with the highland morph of *T. nigrolutea* regarding the synchronization of the sexes correspond with the situation in nature or not was questionable, until EDWARDS & JONES (2001) published investigation results dealing with the lowland morph of *Tiliqua nigrolutea* of Tasmania. They found that also in the wild males emerge from hibernation about four weeks earlier than females.

**Mating season and copulations:** The mating season of *T. nigrolutea* falls into the southern Australian spring in the months of October and November (see Table 4). This is the time when free ranging males can be seen chasing each other around and fighting (CLUTTERBUCK cit. fide SHEA 1992).

Under terrarium conditions it is advisable to keep the sexes separately. A female can be placed in the terrarium of a male every two or three days. The male will then approach the female with robot-like movements and with his head lowered and the throat slightly inflated. If the female is ready to mate, it will tolerate the advances of the male, moving only little, in a jerking manner, and with snaking movements of the tail. The male will then take hold of the female with a bite to its lateral skin of the neck, followed by a copulation that does not differ from other lizards. A copulation may take from half a minute to several minutes before the animals separate at their cloacal regions. The male may, however, hold on to the female for up to an hour. After they have separated the animals wipe their cloacae on the substrate. Copulations may sometimes be observed several times per day.

Females not ready to mate respond with trying to escape the approaching male, often resulting in wild chases through the terrarium and

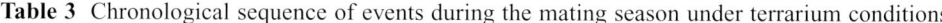

**Table 3** Chronological sequence of events during the mating season under terrarium conditions

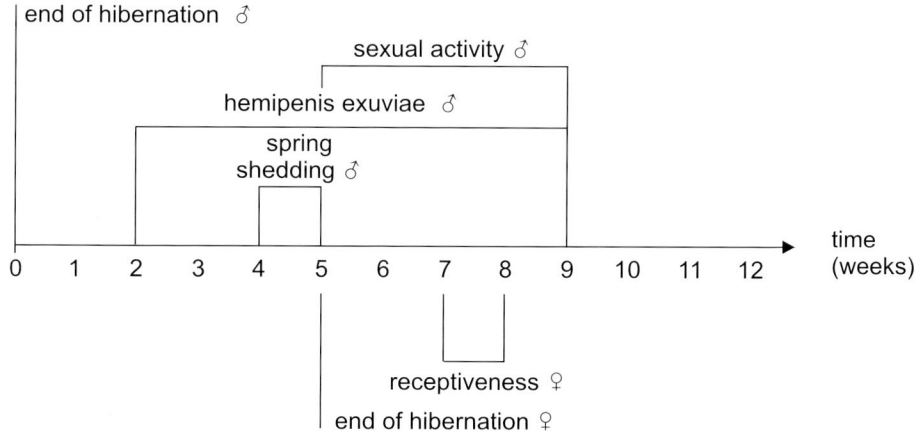

**Fig. 5** *T. nigrolutea,* highland morph, copulating in a terrarium                    Photograph: R. Hitz

bitings. If the animals are not separated quickly in such a case, the females occasionally suffer large, bleeding wounds in the neck and chest areas. The female remain receptive for one to five days. Thereafter they will again fend off an approaching male by fleeing and biting.

About one week after mating the female may be seen lying in a peculiar zigzag-like, tensed-up body posture. This phenomenon might be an expression of ovulation pains and was also noted by RÖHE (pers. comm.).

**Pregnancy:** Like all representatives of the genus *Tiliqua, T. nigrolutea* is a livebearing species. Placentation takes place in the form of an allanto-placentation (FLYNN 1923, WEEKES 1935), or in more recent nomenclature, chorioallantois-placentation (STEWART & BLACKBURN 1988). Gravidity takes 4-4.5 months in nature (SHEA 1992), from November through March or April. The babies are thus born in late summer or early autumn (see Table 4).

Under the conditions of a terrarium a full term is usually 3.5 months. Gravid females spend most of their days at the warmest sites of their terrarium. They feed voraciously. With the advancing of the pregnancy they become increasingly massive and a more labored breathing is noted. Gravid females will only stop feeding a few days before giving birth.

**Birth:** Giving birth usually takes place during the day when the mother skink has warmed up (pers. obs.). The events were recorded by GIDDINGS (1984): if the egg membranes do not tear open while the baby is expulsed and release it, the mother will bite into the envelope until the juvenile is freed. A few minutes after their birth the babies will start moving, still connected to the egg membrane by the umbilical cord. With her mouth the mother skink will

**Table 4** Chronological course of the reproductive cycle of *T. nigrolutea* (after SHEA 1992)

| Jan. | Feb. | Mar. | Apr. | May | June | July | Aug. | Sept. | Oct. | Nov. | Dec. |
|------|------|------|------|-----|------|------|------|-------|------|------|------|
| Summer | | I | | Autum | | I | | Winter | | I | Spring | | | I |
| – – – – – – – | | | | | | (no data available) | | | ++++++++++++++ – – – – | | |
| length and turgor of testes (+ increase, high level in the last phase / - decrease) | | | | | | | | | | | |
| ——————————— | | | | | (no data) | | _ +++++++++++++++++++++++++++++++++++ | | | | |
| diameter of follicles (+ increase, high level in the last phase) | | | | | | | | | | | |
| vitellogenesis (yolk production) | | | | | | | | I————————————I | | | |
| ovulation | | | | | | | | | I————————I | | |
| ————————————————I | | | | | eggs / embryos in oviducts | | | | I—————————I | | |
| I——————————I | | | births | | | | | | | | |
| mating season | | | | | | | | I————————I | | |
| Jan. | Feb. | Mar. | Apr. | May | June | July | Aug. | Sept. | Oct. | Nov. | Dec. |

actively help the young to rid themselves of the umbilical cord and the pieces of placenta. GIDDINGS furthermore observed how the babies subsequently ingested the pieces of placenta and leftover yolk. The yolk of an infertile egg was consumed by the mother. The pieces of placenta, remains of yolk, and infertile eggs are likely to serve as energy reserves for the juveniles, as was described for *T. r. aspera* by BULL et al. (1993). During and after birth the mother skinks are fairly aggressive and protective of their offspring.

**Complications during pregnancy and birth:** Complications during pregnancy and birth are unfortunately quite common in captive kept *T. nigrolutea* of the highland morph (pers. obs., RÖHE pers. comm.); no personal experiences could be made with the lowland form and relevant literature seems to be non-existent. Complications include malformed juveniles, stillborn babies after full term, and abnormally large yolk masses blocking the oviducts (more on this subject can be found in the chapter "Complications observed during pregnancy and birth in blue-tongued skinks" in this book).

**Litter size:** According to SHEA (1992) an average litter contains 6.1 ± 1.6 babies (3-10, n = 46), i.e. in the lowland morph an average of 6.4 ± 1.55 (n = 27), and in the highland form 5.8 ± 1.64 (n = 9). No correlation could be found to exist between motherly SVL and litter size.

As far as the keeping in a terrarium is concerned the author can only record data for the highland form. The averages are low, only 2.62 ± 1.63 babies per litter (1-5, n = 16). This low average of litters in captivity is probably based on husbandry related problems in connection with the reproductive cycle. The primary cause is likely to be an average temperature that is simply too high.

## Newly born juveniles

SHEA (1992) mentioned that the sizes of the juveniles at birth are subjected only to a small amount of geographic and individual variation. He gave an average of 95.8 ± 5.8 mm SVL (89.5-103 mm, n = 6). Converted to total length measurements (based on tail length, TL = 45.1% SVL) this produces an average value of 139 mm (130-150 mm). Under terrarium conditions the average total length is 164.7 ± 8.4 mm (152-175 mm, n = 9 normally developed newborns; deformed ones not taken into consideration). Juveniles born in captivity are thus larger than those born in nature. Their body masses average 46.1 ± 6.98 g (40-60 g, n = 9, deformed babies not included, after consumption of parts of placenta and yolk).

Newborn juveniles are very shy and spend most of their time in hiding. They also present themselves as hesitant feeders. This phenomenon is probably based on the fact that they are born in the Australian autumn and have to start hibernating a short time after their birth. A similar observation was described by SHEA (1992) for *T. rugosa*.

## Onset of maturity

The onset of maturity is correlated to a minimum body length and a minimum body mass (JONES 1987, SHEA 1992). SHEA found respective differences between males and females as well as between the highland and the lowland forms (see Table 5).

In nature it probably takes *T. nigrolutea* 3-4 years to mature, whereas in a terrarium one group kept by the author required only 19 months. At this stage the animals measured 402-418 mm in total lengths and had body masses of 390-470 g.

## Life expectancy

*T. nigrolutea* is a lizard species with a life expectancy of decades. SHEA (1992) mentioned a female that was acquired as an adult and lived for another 25 years in a terrarium. There are, however, no indications in the literature as to how old these animals may become in

**Table 5** Total length (TotL) on reaching maturity, minimum values from SHEA (1992), SVL projected to TotL (tail length, TL = 45.1% of SVL)

| Geographical morph | Sex | Minimum total length |
|---|---|---|
| Lowland | male | 329,4 mm |
| Lowland | female | 346,8 mm |
| Highland | male | 351,1 mm |
| Highland | female | 406,3 mm |

nature or up to which age they are able to reproduce.

## Sex ratio

The sex ratio of the material examined by SHEA (1992) was nearly 1 : 1. In the highland morph as well as in the lowland form more males than females were collected in November and more females in March to April. These seasonal differences are likely to be correlated to reproduction related activity. During spring the males display an increased level of activity in search for females. In contrast, more gravid females are found basking in late summer and autumn. These ratios correspond with the observations made in *T. r. aspera* (BULL et al. 1991).

## Frequency of reproduction

In a collection of 50 females, which were caught in the period between mid-December and mid-March, SHEA (1992) could only deduce reproductive activity from the inner organs of 24 specimens. Similarly, not all males showed signs of increased testicular activity between October and November. SHEA concluded from these findings that *T. nigrolutea* does not reproduce according to an annual rhythm, but rather at a multiennial, presumably mainly a bi-ennial, cycle. This is probably based on the fact that females which give birth to their young late in autumn have no sufficient

time span during the cool winter to build up enough reserves for the next spring's matings. Under the conditions of an indoor keeping an annual reproduction cycle is often observed, but a biennial rhythm does also occur (pers. obs., CLUTTERBUCK cit. fide SHEA 1992, RÖHE pers. comm.).

## Keeping and breeding

Literature information on the husbandry and breeding of *T. nigrolutea* is sparse and has become available only recently. The publications by JONES (1987), CARD (1993), and the book "Skinke im Terrarium" by HAUSCHILD & GASSNER (1995) are particularly useful.

### Individual vs. group keeping

Adult *Tiliqua nigrolutea* are highly incompatible when kept according to their needs. JONES (1987) therefore recommended keeping them individually. No information is available on the population structure of this species of skink in nature. It may, however, be presumed that the individuals of *T. nigrolutea* live solitarily in very large home ranges, as is the case, for example, with *T. rugosa aspera*. The author keeps his animals individually throughout the year, with encounters being facilitated only during the mating season. Other terrarium keepers (FERGER pers. comm., RÖHE pers. comm.) assert that this species can also be kept in groups. This may, however, carry the risk that the animals become dull psychologically and as a result discontinue displaying their specific behavioral repertoire. Other dangers include damaging fights between adult males and males inflicting injuries on females in the mating season.

**Housing:** In Europe and North America *T. nigrolutea* is usually kept in indoor terraria. This basic type of keeping is often expanded by including temporary stays in open air terraria or outdoor enclosures between late spring and early autumn. In regions where the climate corresponds with that of the natural distribution range the animals can also be kept outdoors all year round.

**Terrarium:** With *T. nigrolutea* being a ground dwelling lizard, its terrarium should offer as much ground space as possible whereas the height of the cage is of secondary importance. Some countries have laws in effect that regulate the captive keeping of wild animals and these may also include minimum sizes for a terrarium. In Germany, for example, dimensions of 220 × 150 × 110 cm would be recommended (l × w × h; based on 6 × 4 × 3 cm SVL with a maximum SVL of 36.8 cm [SHEA 1992]) for adult individuals of one pair. JONES (1987) kept his specimens in terraria of 60 × 60 × 30 cm (l × w × h), and the author uses terraria measuring 120 × 60 × 50 cm (l × w × h). Where relevant legislation exists, the keeper should adhere to it.

**Illumination:** The author uses Philips fluorescent tubes of the type TLD 80/86 18 watts, and Sylvania F18 BLB of the same wattage as a source of UV-A radiation. The transformers of these fluo tubes are installed outside the terrarium in a service tube. Once every week the skinks are placed in plastic boxes outside their terraria and exposed to the radiation of an Osram Ulta VitaLux lamp at 75 cm distance for 20 minutes. This ensures that their UV-B requirements are satisfied. Further information on lighting can be found in the chapter "On the husbandry and breeding of *Tiliqua rugosa aspera* (GRAY, 1845)".

**Heating:** The author's terraria are heated by eccentrically arranged underfloor heating mats of 30 × 40 cm which heat up the substrate in their ranges to 35-40°C.

## Temperature requirements

No information exists on the body temperature of *T. nigrolutea* in their natural habitats. Using a specialized laboratory setting RAWLINSON (1974) established a preferred body temperature of 31.9-37.7°C, on average 34.8°C, during the lizards' active period. In order to enable the animals to reach this activity temperature, their terrarium must offer an area of 35-40°C. These high values seem to contradict the fact that the natural distribution range of *T. nigrolutea* is restricted to the cooler and more elevated regions of southeastern Australia. According to the climate profile established by HANCOCK & THOMPSON (1997), *T. nigrolutea* inhabits parts of New South Wales where the mean annual minimum temperature is 6.0°C and the mean annual maximum temperature lies at 25.4°C. It must be borne in mind, though, that the temperatures affecting microhabitats are often higher than those recorded for meteorological purposes. Nevertheless do these facts indicate that *T. nigrolutea* is suitable for the keeping in an indoor terrarium only with reservations. Whilst, on the one hand, there must be a spot that offers enough heat to enable the animals to reach their activity temperature, the temperature in large parts of the terrarium, and therefore also in the room where the latter is set up, must be relatively low. This is indeed a technological challenge that is difficult to overcome. For their existence in nature all this means that *T. nigrolutea* spend large parts of the year, i.e. the warmer periods and of course the cold season, in one or another type of cover.

SPELLERBERG (1972) established a critical minimum temperature of 4.7-5.8°C, on average 5.2°C, for *T. nigrolutea,* and a critical maximum temperature of 41.0-43.0°C, on average 42.5°C. He classified *T. nigrolutea* as being "posturing heliotherm". The low temperature range must be taken into consideration when the skinks are kept in outdoor enclosures and during hibernation, the high values in the case of terraria that are exposed to direct sunlight. More information on this subject can be found in respective paragraph of the chapter on *T. rugosa aspera.*

**Decoration of the terrarium:** In the area affected by the underfloor heating mats, substrates consisting of quartz sand with a granulation of 2-3 mm, other types of sand, or fine gravel have proved beneficial. The unheated areas can be covered with an up to 10 cm deep layer of wood shavings, bark mulch, or cannabis bedding may be used. Some spots may be kept slightly moist. The skinks love to bury themselves in these materials. They are available from pet shops and/or nurseries.

Arched pieces of bark, ridging tiles, or a cavity under some artfully arranged larger rock flakes all create acceptable hiding places. Much more important than their looks is that these shelters are located at cooler sites in the background of the terrarium. Rocks and pieces of bark can be used for other decoration purposes. Robust live plants, or plastic plants, are suitable for "greening" the terrarium. The skinks often use the latter to hide in when they feel disturbed.

**Humidity and moisture:** Days with precipitation may occur at any time of the year in the natural distribution range of *T. nigrolutea*. Accordingly, the relative humidity varies between 45 and 85% depending on the time of day and season. Under terrarium conditions a nightly misting of parts of the substrate two to three times per week has proved adequate. However, *T. nigrolutea* has shown itself to be rather ignorant of the humidity.

When an animal shows signs of an impending shedding it is of advantage to moisten the substrate in its shelter. Sheddings that are assisted like that proceed with much more ease than those in a dry environment. Instead of moistening the substrate, a moist piece of cloth placed inside the shelter does the same trick.

## Keeping rhythms

**Day/night rhythm:** The distribution range of *T. nigrolutea* is marked by substantial changes in the temperature, i.e. it may vary by as much as 15°C throughout the year. The decrease of the temperature at night should also be emulated in the terrarium.

**Annual cycles:** A precondition for the long term husbandry and successful breeding of *T. nigrolutea* is the consequent following of an annual rhythm. More details on this subject can be found in the relevant paragraph of the chapter dealing with *T. rugosa aspera*. If the skinks are to enjoy temporary stays outdoors or in fresh air, it should be ensured that these periods fit into the annual cycle. If this is not the case, the synchronization of the sexes for their mating period will fail.

The *T. nigrolutea* of the author are kept according to the European seasonal cycle. The basis of the daily illumination period is provided by the natural photoperiod, i.e. the daily duration of the artificial lighting is linked to the natural number of daylight hours. The longest illumination period is 12 hours, the shortest eight hours. The heating regime of the terraria follows an analogous pattern. Starting in November, the animals are subjected to a three week preparation period leading up to their cool hibernation. During this time feeding is halted, and the heating of the terrarium is gradually reduced. The cold hibernation then takes 2.5 months, until about mid-February. Its end is marked by another three week transitory phase in their terraria where lighting intensity and heating are again gradually increased, and eventually also feeding is resumed. Between May and October the animals spend the days of fine weather in open air terraria outdoors. They are, however, always brought back inside for the night in order to prevent the excessive cooling down from interfering negatively with the annual rhythm.

**Hibernation:** A cool hibernation period is essential. The lizard's natural distribution range is marked by frosty winters. The author's animals are therefore individually placed in plastic boxes (with a lid) measuring 40 × 30 × 13 cm (l × w × h) which are furnished with 2 cm deep layer of quartz sand and a 5 cm deep layer of wood shavings. In order to ensure a raised level of humidity a small plastic container with a wet sponge in it is placed inside. For the in-

**Fig. 6** *T. nigrolutea* in a hibernation box
Photograph: R. Hitz

tended hibernation period of 2.5 months the boxes are then kept in a cellar that receives fresh air and daylight through a ventilation shaft. During phases of extreme winter weather the temperature is checked daily. The latter should range between 8 and 10°C, but in praxis usually varies from 8 to 12°C. At temperatures of 10°C or less the animals are in deep sleep, above 10°C especially the males show some activity during the day. The temperature must never sink to, or even below of, the critical minimum values established by SPELLERBERG (1972) of 4.7-5.8°C, mean 5.2 °C. Specimens in less than perfect health condition must not be hibernated. This also applies to specimens which are nearing a shedding.

**Feeding**

*T. nigrolutea* is an omnivorous skink. Its food spectrum in nature is described in the paragraph on its ecology. Following the suggestions by JONES (1987) the author supplies his *T. nigrolutea* with a mixed food consisting of 25% meat, 25% fruit, and 50% vegetable. The meat portion is made up of finely cut-up beef heart or lean chicken or turkey hen. The fruit content may make use of the entire range of local fruit and berries as well as exotic fruit. In this

connection kiwi is particularly valuable due to its high calcium content. The vegetable portion is composed of diverse lettuces, bean sprouts, water cress, wheat sprouts, dandelion leaves, clover as well as flowers of dandelion and daisies. The three constituents are cut up with a knife and mixed. The author advises against the usage of dog or cat food because their vitamin and mineral contents are not dosed to suit the requirements of reptiles. Live food may consist of terrestrial snails, earthworms, locusts, and self-bred feeder insects such as crickets, roaches, tenebrionid beetle larvae (giant mealworms) as well as pink mice. The food mix should be improved as to its Ca/P ratio by fortifying it with feeder calcium or grated cuttlefish shell. A supplementation with a multivitamin and trace element preparation is advisable, too. The most important constituent that should be included here is vitamin $D_3$. Both vitamins and trace elements should be dosed correctly according to the body mass of the individual animal.

Adult specimens should be fed conservatively as they tend to become obese quickly under terrarium conditions. Feeding them twice per week is sufficient. The author endeavors to provide every individual animal with the ration of food designated for it in order to prevent squabbles over food and stronger specimens feeding at the cost of weaker ones. Drinking water in small glass bowls may be available to the skinks at all times.

Before and after the cool hibernation phase it is recommendable to limit the food mix to some easily digested fruit, such as banana, peach or apple, for a few feedings. In the first case this prevents that hard-to-digest plant fibers and animal proteins remain in the digestive tract of the animals that may start rotting and kill them during their overwintering. After completion of their hibernation the metabolism first has to adjust to renewed activity so that easily digested food helps to avoid disturbances of the digestion and thus possibly severe consequences (STETTLER 1953).

In closing of this paragraph it should be mentioned that the offering of the mixed food described above leads to a very good texture of the feces. The skinks usually produce compact, elongate droppings that dry up quickly resulting in an improved hygiene in their terrarium. These droppings are also easily removed from the substrate - in contrast to the mushy or liquid deposits that may result from a sole feeding with fruit or meat. The described feeding regime of the author even led to a spontaneous disappearance of an infection with cocciids and *Entamoeba invadens* his animals had been infested. Other measures for the improvement of hygiene include the regular boiling of food and water bowls as well as the feeder forceps following each clean-up. This also eliminates otherwise highly resistant amoeba cysts.

### Raising of the young

It is of advantage to place baby skinks in individual terraria. This enables the keeper to feed them according to their individual needs and keep control of each individual's acceptance of the food. It also eliminates the risks of fights over food and possible injuries as a result. The first meal of the newborns consists of parts of the placenta and left over yolk. Thereafter they may receive the same diet as the adults.

During their first weeks of life newly born *T. nigrolutea* are very shy and tend to hide in the substrate or in shelters. They will accept food only with hesitation. This may have to do with the fact that they are born in late summer or autumn in nature and that they would soon have to start hibernating.

Feeding them well leads to a rapid growth with up to 2 cm added to their total lengths and body masses increasing by 20-40 g every month. The juveniles can be hibernated in the same manner as the adults already in their first winter.

### Sheddings

Newborns shed their skin within hours after their birth (pers. obs.). The fine skin is lost in small bits, as is the case with *T. rugosa aspera* (pers. obs.) and *T. scincoides scincoides* (TURNER 1996). Juvenile specimens of the highland morph show only a faded version of the colorful blotched pattern during their first weeks of life, with the bright yellow or red colors (which one obviously depends on the origin of their parents) appearing not before after their second shedding. Under terrarium conditions the juveniles shed their skin three or four times in their first year. Adults shed two to four times a year, with the first shedding of male specimens being observed four to five weeks after the completion of hibernation and that of the females some time later in spring. The skin is then lost in large flakes, ideally even in one piece. With a shedding coming up, it is recommendable to make an area available in the terrarium where the substrate offers an increased level of moisture. If a shedding does not proceed to its completion, the animals can be bathed in lukewarm water for 15 minutes and then freed of remaining old skin manually.

### Note

*T. nigrolutea* is rarely kept in terraria. This can certainly be attributed to the fact that, on the one hand, hardly any wild caught specimens from Australia find a way into the pet market and, on the other, that very few juveniles are produced from the few specimens kept outside of Australia. The price tag for these lizards is therefore rather high. The colorful highland form is particularly sought after, although the lowland form with its unpretentious robe also has a lot of charm. *T. nigrolutea* is not really well suited for the terrarium. Owing to their natural incompatibility specimens have to be kept separately for most of the year, and they will show themselves outside their shelters only for a few hours every day from early summer through autumn. A hibernation period of several months is an essential precondition - not necessarily for a high life expectancy, but for their breeding. The requirements suggested by their climate profile, marked by low average temperatures, are extremely difficult to fulfil in an indoor terrarium. In the light of all these considerations the keeping of *T. nigrolutea* can only be recommended to the really interested keeper. He, however, will experience a lot of joy and satisfaction from the husbandry of these interesting animals.

## Literature

ANDERSON, W. (1967): Appendix 1 – A journal of voyage in his majestys sloop resolution. – Pp. 723–986 in BEAGLEHOLE, J.C. (ed.): The journals of captain James Cook on his voyages of Discovery. Vol. III: The voyage of the Resolution and Discovery 1776–1780. Part Two. – Cambridge (Cambridge University Press & Hakluyt Society), 1647 pp.

BAEHR, M. (1976): Beiträge zur Verbreitung und Ökologie tasmanischer Reptilien. – Stuttgarter Beitr. Naturk. Ser. A (Biologie), Stuttgart, (292), 1–24.

BANNERT, B. (1993): Erfahrungen zur Überwinterung von Eidechsen. – elaphe (N.F.), 1(2): 11–14.

BARTLETT, R.D. ( 1984 ): Notes on the captive reproduction of the Australian skink, *Tiliqua nigrolutea*. – British Herpetological Society Bulletin, 10: 34–35.

BÖHME, W. (1986): Handbuch der Reptilien und Amphibien Europas. Band 2/II: Echsen III (*Podarcis*). – Aula, Wiesbaden, 434 S.

BULL, C.M., A. MC NALLY & G. DUBAS (1991): Asynchronous seasonal activity of male and female Sleepy Lizards, *Tiliqua rugosa*. – Journal of Herpetology, 25(4): 436–441.

BULL, C.M., Y. PAMULA & L. SCHULZE (1993): Parturition in the Sleepy Lizard, *Tiliqua rugosa*. – Journal of Herpetology, 27: 489–492.

BUNDESMINISTERIUMFÜR ERNÄHRUNG, LANDWIRTSCHAFT UND FORSTEN, REFERAT TIERSCHUTZ (1997): Gutachten über Mindestanforderungen an die Haltung von Reptilien vom 10. Januar 1997. – Unveränderte Sonderausgabe der Deutschen Gesellschaft für Herpetologie und Terrarienkunde (DGHT) e.V., 77 S.

BUSTARD, R. (1970): Australian Lizards. – Sydney, London (William Collins Ltd.), 158 pp.

CARD, W. (1993): Natural history and husbandry of the Shingleback Skink (*Trachydosaurus rugosus*) and the Blotched Blue–tongued Skink (*Tiliqua nigrolutea*). – The Vivarium, Lakeside, Amerikan Federation of Herpetoculturists, 6(3): 26–27.

COGGER, H.G. (1992): Reptiles and Amphibians of Australia. 5th edition. – Ithaca, New York (Cornell University Press), 775 pp.

CREWS, D.P. (1975): Psychobiology of reptilian reproduction. – Science, 189: 1059–1065.

DONNELLAN, S.C. (1991): Chromosomes of Australian lygosomine skinks. – Genetica, 83(3): 207–222.

DUVALL, D., L.J. GUILLETTE JR. & R.E. JONES (1982): Environmental control of reptilian breeding cycles. – Pp. 201–231 in GANS, C. & B. HUE (edts): Biology of the reptilia. – Vol. 13.

EDWARDS, A. & S.M. JONES (2001): Changes in plasma testosterone, estrogen, and progesterone concentrations throughout the annual reproductive cycle in male viviparous blue-tongued skinks, *Tiliqua nigrolutea*, in Tasmania. - Journal of Herpetology, 35(2): 293-299.

EHMANN, H. (1992): Encyclopedia of Australian Animals. Reptiles. The National Photographic Index of Australian Wildlife. (R. Strahan, series ed.). – Pymble (Angus & Robertson), 495 pp.

FLYNN, T.T. (1923): On the occurrence of a true allantoplacenta of the conjoint type in an Australian lizard. – Records of the Australian Museum, 14(1): 72–77.

GIDDINGS, S. (1984): An observation of parturition of a Blotched-Bluetongue. (*Tiliqua nigrolutea*). – South Aust. Herp. Group Newsletter, May: 4.

GRAY, J.E. (1831): A synopsis of the species of the class Reptilia. – Pp. 483–600 in GRIFFITH, E. & E. PIDGEON: The animal kingdom arranged in conformity with its organization, by Baron Cuvier, member of the Institute of France, & c. with additional descriptions of all the species hitherto named, and of many not before noticed. Volume 9. The class Reptilia arranged by the Baron Cuvier, with specific descriptions. – London (Whittaker, Treacher & Co.).

– (1845): Catalogue of the specimens of lizards in the collection of the British Museum. – London (Trustees of the British Museum), 289 pp.

HANCOCK, L.J. & M.B. THOMPSON (1997): Distributional limits of Eastern Blue-tongue Lizards *Tiliqua scincoides*, Blotched Blue-tongue Lizards *T. nigro-*

*lutea* and Shingleback Lizards *T. rugosa* (GRAY) in New South Wales. – Australian Zoologist, 30(3): 340–345.

HAUSCHILD, A. & P. GAßNER (1995): Skinke im Terrarium. – Hannover (Landbuch-Verlag), 197 S.

HOSER, R.T. (1989): Australian Reptiles & Frogs. – Mosman NSW (Pierson & Co.), 238 pp.

JONES, S. (1987): A report on a reproducible and sustainable system for the captive propagation of the genus *Tiliqua* GRAY 1825. – Pp. 17–25 in COOTE, J. (ed.): Reptiles. – Proceedings of the 1986 U.K. Herpet. Societies Symposium on Captive Breeding. – London (British Herpet. Soc.).

LICHT, P. (1972): Environmental physiology of reptilian breeding cycles: Role of temperature. – General and Comparative Endocrinology, Supplement 3: 477–488.

LONGLEY, G. (1939): The Blue-tongued Lizard (*Tiliqua scincoides*). – Proceedings of the Royal Zoological Society of New South Wales, 1938/39: 39–42.

– (1941): Notes on some Australian lizards. – Proceedings of the Royal Zoological Society of New South Wales, 1940–1941: 30–35.

QUOY, J.R.C. & P. GAIMARD (1824): Zoologie. – Pp. 176–178, pl. 41 in DE FREYCINET, L.: Voyage autour du monde, entrepris par ordre du Roi, sous le ministère et conformément aux instructions de s. exc. m. le vicomte du Bouchage, secrétaire d'état au Département de la Marine, éxécuté sur les corvettes de S. M. l'Uranie et la Physicienne, pendant les années 1817, 1818, 1819 et 1820. – Paris (Pillet Aîné, Imprimeur-Libraire, de l'Imprimerie Royale), 712 pp.

RAWLINSON, P.A. (1974): Biogeography and ecology of the reptiles of Tasmania and the Bass Strait Area. – Pp. 291–338 in WILLIAMS, W.D. (ed.): Biogeography and ecology in Tasmania. – Monographiae Biologicae (25). The Hague (W. Junk), 498 pp.

SHEA, G.M. (1992): The systematics and reproduction of bluetongue lizards of the genus *Tiliqua* (Squamata: Scincidae). – Ph.D. thesis, University of Sydney, 4 Vols.

– (1993): The male reproductive cycle of the Eastern Blue-tongued Lizard *Tiliqua scincoides scincoides* (Squamata: Scincidae). – Pp. 397–403 in LUNNEY, D. & D. AYERS (eds): Herpetology in Australia. – Sydney (Royal Zoological Society of New South Wales), 414 pp.

SMITH, J. & P. SMITH (1990): Fauna of the Blue Mountains. – Kenthurst NSW (Kangaroo Press Pty Ltd), 95 pp.

SPELLERBERG, I.F. (1972): Temperature tolerances of southeast Australian reptiles examined in relation to reptile thermoregulatory behavior and distribution. – Oecologia, Berlin, 9: 23–46.

STETTLER, P.H. (1953): Die kalte Überwinterung südaustralischer Großechsen. – Aquarien- und Terrar. Zeitschr., Stuttgart, 6(12): 321–324.

STEWART, J.R. & D.G. BLACKBURN (1988): Reptilian placentation: Structural diversity and terminology. – Copeia, 4: 839–852.

TURNER, G. (1996): Some litters of the Eastern Blue-tongued Skink *Tiliqua scincoides scincoides* (Scincidae). – Herpetofauna, Sydney, 26(2): 39–47.

VERON, J.E.N. (1969): The reproductive cycle of the Water Skink, *Sphenomorphus quoyii*. – J. Herpetol., 3: 55–63.

WAGLER, J. (1830): Natürliches System der Amphibien, mit vorangehender Classifikation der Säugthiere und Vögel. – S. 162–163. München, Stuttgart und Tübingen (J.G. Cotta), 354 S.

WEBB, G.A. & J.A. SIMPSON (1985): Some unusual food items for the Southern Blotched Blue-tongue Lizard *Tiliqua nigrolutea* (QUOY & GAIMARD) at Bombala, New South Wales. – Herpetofauna, 16(2): 44–45.

WEEKES, H.C. (1935): A review of placentation among reptiles with particular regard to the function and evolution of the placenta. – Proceedings of the Zoological Society of London., 2: 625–645.

WELLS, R.W. & C. R. WELLINGTON (1985): A classification of the Amphibia and Reptilia of Australia. – Australian Journal of Herpetology, Supplementary Series (1): 1–61.

WILSON, S.K. & D.G. KNOWLES (1988): Australia's Reptiles. A Photographic Reference to the Terrestrial Reptiles of Australia. – Sydney (Collins), 447 pp.

WORRELL, E. (1963): Reptiles of Australia. – Sydney (Angus & Robertson), 207 pp.

Author's address
Dr. Robert Hitz
Am Mülibach 8
CH-9425 Thal, Switzerland

# Husbandry and reproduction of *Tiliqua occipitalis* (PETERS, 1864) - A challenge for the terrarium keeper

HEIDRUN RÖHE

**Key words:** Reptilia: Sauria: Scincidae: *Tiliqua: Tiliqua occipitalis,* Australia, description, distribution, ecology, husbandry, breeding

## Description

*Tiliqua occipitalis* is a moderately large, short-legged blue-tongued skink of about 40 cm in total length, of which the tail accounts for some 12 cm. Its maximum body mass may reach 500 g. Specimens originating from coastal areas (western form) often show a light gray to beige ground color. The dorsal side is marked with three to five, about 3 cm wide, very conspicuous dark brown cross bands on the body plus four to six bands on the tail. The first band is always situated on the neck, and the last covers the tip of the tail. These dark brown bands are often split by double series of very fine, light gray dots across the body. The head is uniform light brown and distinctly set off from the neck. A conspicuous trait is the presence of a brownish black temporal streak of up to 2 cm in width. It begins behind the eye and ends above the ear aperture. It appears that the temporal streak and the dorsal bands also play a role in individual recognition (pers. obs.). The tongue is dark blue, the ventral side uniform white, and only the tail is circled by the almost black cross bands.

Specimens from the inland (eastern morph) sport a brownish yellow ground color (brownish specimens are also found at the coast and vice versa). This causes the temporal streak and dorsal bands to be less conspicuous, making some specimens appear rather dusky. The relatively large distribution range is inhabited only by color varieties, but there is no evidence of subspecies (COGGER 1992).

## Sexual dimorphism

There are significant differences distinguishing the sexes. Females have a longer body, wider hips, a shorter tail, shorter legs, a shorter head, and distinctly larger eyes in proportion to their SVL than males (SHEA 1992). These traits are particularly obvious in newly born juveniles and help to distinguish the sexes. Adult males are marked by bulging hemipenis pockets to the left and right at the base of the tail behind the cloaca which becomes particularly notable in the mating season. Males as young as one year of age can furthermore be enticed through bathing in handwarm water to not only defecate, but also evert their hemipenes.

## Distribution

*T. occipitalis* occupies a large distribution range. The species inhabits the more arid regions of

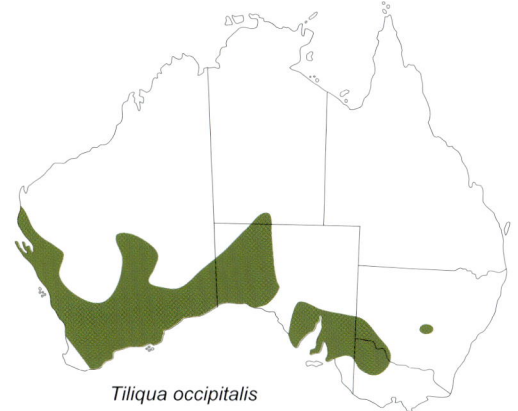

*Tiliqua occipitalis*

147

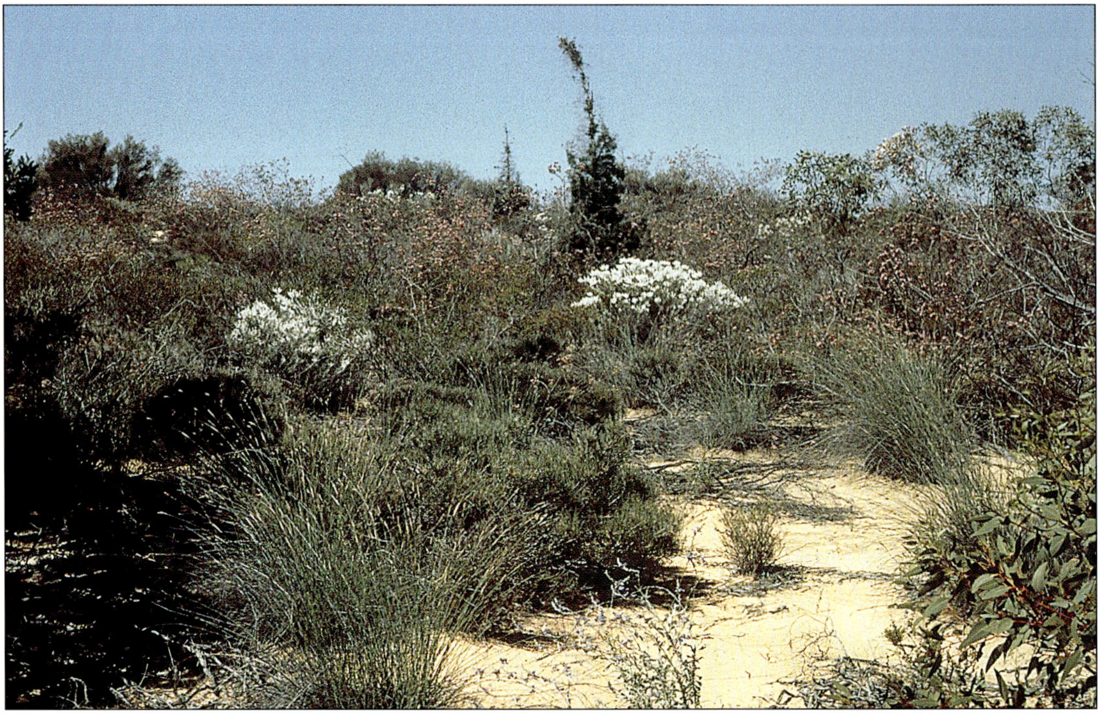

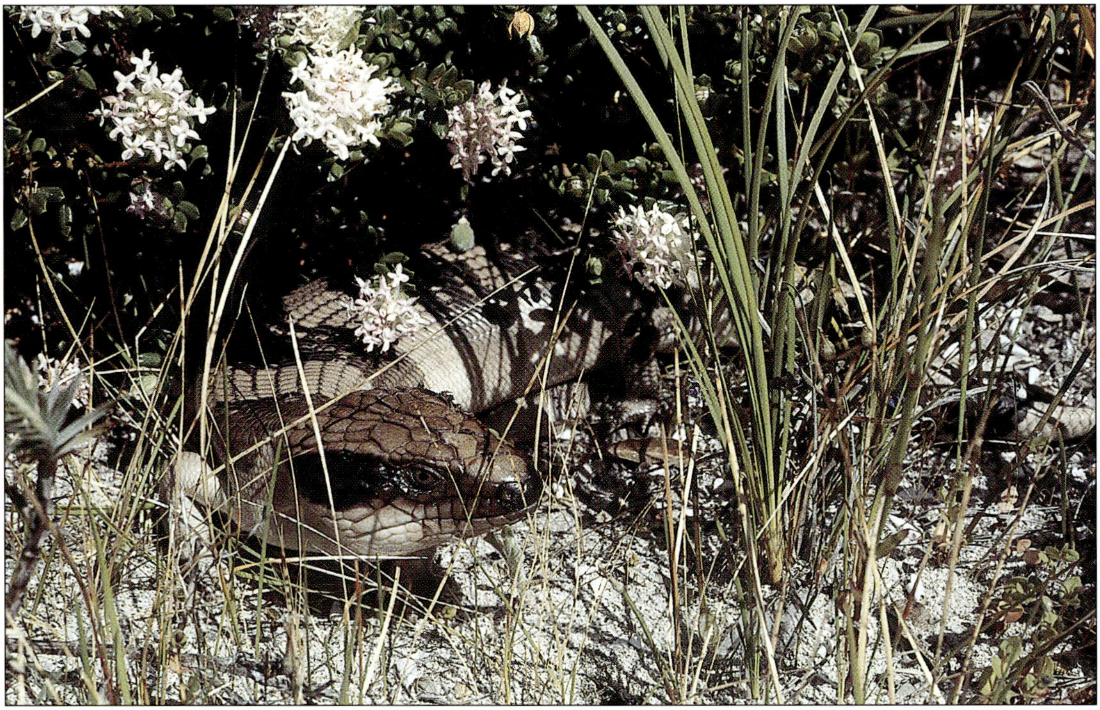

Opposite from above

**Fig. 1** Blooming wild flowers in the natural habitat of *T. occipitalis* in Western Australia

**Fig. 2** *T. occipitalis* keeps to dense vegetation and will quickly retreat into it in a case of danger

Photographs: O. Daniel

the state of South Australia, the south of Western Australia to the latitude of Carnarvon, southern Northern Territory, the west of New South Wales, and northwestern Victoria (COGGER 1992).

## Ecology

*T. occipitalis* prefers flat, open habitats with sandy or sandy-loamy soil. It also lives on dunes in the coastal strip of Western Australia (WILSON & KNOWLES 1988). Although these biotopes are richly vegetated, the plants are usually low, hardly exceeding 2 m in height, and often form thickets consisting of *Acacia, Banksia, Mimosa,* and spinifex species. When threatened *T. occipitalis* will escape into holes and rodent burrows in the ground which also provide protection from the frequent bush fires. With some luck an animal can be found basking in the sun at the margin of a thicket during the morning hours. If it then disappears in the light underbrush it will become almost invisible, and it is difficult to spot the lizard even in a decrepit tussock of spinifex. *T. occipitalis* appears to have come to like the proximity of tar roads which it either crosses swiftly or, usually in the evening hours, where it lies down on the margin of the tarmac for some time. The latter will then still be warm from the day's heat and this heating from below is obviously much enjoyed. This field observation we have taken into account by installing an underfloor heater into their terrarium (see below).

### Sympatry with other species of *Tiliqua*

*Tiliqua multifasciata* was previously treated as a subspecies of *Tiliqua occipitalis,* for example,

by BUSTARD (1970). COGGER (1979) then justified its elevation to species level with its distinct color pattern, morphology, habitat preferences, and genetic isolation. At Laverton, Western Australia, however, *Tiliqua multifasciata* and *Tiliqua occipitalis* occur in the same habitat (SHEA & PETERSON 1981).

## Husbandry

Our terraria are basically open above, covered only partially by the casings of the lamps. They are decorated with halved tubes of cork bark, ground covering plastic plants, and a flat artificial rock. The water bowl sits snug in a cork tube, but can be removed from above, so that it cannot be soiled or toppled. The substrate consists of soft wood shavings.

A terrarium measuring $180 \times 60 \times 40$ cm (l × w × h) is illuminated with two fluorescent tubes of 56 watts each (Philips TLD 56/84) that provide the required light intensity. In addition, a small section is lit by a 40 watt reflector lamp which heats the ground in its range to about 50°C. The transformers of the fluorescent tubes are mounted on an aluminium sheet measuring $40 \times 20 \times 0.2$ cm that is used as an underfloor heater (equivalent to 20 watts output). This structure is encased in an artificial rock modelled out of plaster of Paris and thus cannot be accessed by the lizards. Heating up to about 40°C this "rock" is situated outside the area affected by the heating lamp. Temperatures outside the areas directly heated range around 27°C during the day. This lizard show a preference for the heating lamp in the morning, but later shifts to the underfloor heater. A particularly popular spot is the one beneath a plastic plant that partly covers the "hot rock". As a general rule the terrarium should be furnished in a way that does not include hard, rough surfaces and sharp edges as *T. occipitalis* very easily injures its claws and scales. The substrate contributes a lot to the wellbeing of the skinks. After various experiments with materials such as sand, gravel, shredded beech wood, bark mulch, our skinks now live comfortably on and in soft wood shavings which are available in every pet shop at little costs. This substrate brings about a number of advantages:

– It is of a light color and starts dusting only after several weeks (the skinks always look shiny and clean).
– Feces dry up quickly, and urine is absorbed.
– Ingesting shavings that are stuck to dropped pieces of food does not cause harm.
– The substrate weighs little so that exchanging it three times or more per year is light work.
– Blue-tongue skinks love to bury themselves in the substrate. Given a five centimeter deep layer they manage to do so with ease.
– Irritation of the eyes does not occur.

Two disadvantages should also be mentioned:
– There is no natural wear on the claws.
– It has no similarity with the situation in nature.

Our lizards are kept very dry. It is only for the day of a shedding that the substrate is thoroughly moistened in order to ensure that the old skin comes off the sensitive toes in particular. Each foot is then carefully examined since even small remains stuck to the base of a claw may subsequently cause it to die off. Stubborn remains of the old skin are then removed manually following a bath in lukewarm water.

## Feeding

Our *T. occipitalis* receive food in the form of mainly insects, a little fruit, and even less meat, every two days. Meat is offered only about three times per month for which we use pieces of Doko (a type of dry dog food); it results in an increased need for water. Cabbage, carrots and yellow flowers are accepted only with hesitation, green feedstuffs are largely ignored. Suitable diets were discussed in detail by HAUSCHILD & GASSNER (1995) (see also the chapter "A contribution to the feeding of blue-tongued skinks").

## Diseases

In general *T. occipitalis* is not susceptible to diseases, also not to flu. Merely two problems should find mention here: a purulent infection of the skin that manifests itself in raised scales, and foul smelling diarrhea, the latter being the result of a cocciid infection. Both syndromes are usually caused by stress and will alleviate themselves without medical attention once the stress factors are eliminated. The cocciids are of course not destroyed by this, but the animals can live with the parasites if their environment is right.

## "Bluetongue psychology"

The following contribution is based exclusively on observations and experiences made over many years of keeping and breeding our livebearing skinks. By no means is it our intention to claim that this is "the only way"! We have to look back on set backs, but also on successes. And we are still learning. It is our objective to help future keepers of *Tiliqua occipitalis* in the form of this contribution to avoid a repetition of the mistakes we - and our lizards - had to go through. The often underrated "psyche" of our "sensitive livebearers" is possibly the reason why the breeding of this species by other terrarium keepers does as yet not stand on a secure enough basis.

An individual housing is best, simply because one would be hard pressed to find any two *T. occipitalis* in close proximity in nature. Our females attack each other instantly, given the chance, and any male will also be attacked. Inferior individuals mostly evade a fight by hiding away. Because no injuries are obvious, the stress the animals are exposed to will only be noted very late or never. By this time the inferior specimen may be severely diseased already, or, even worse, lie dead in its hiding place.

In the case of a large and well structured terrarium one may consider a communal keeping with other species of *Tiliqua*. The power of perception of these animals must not be underestimated. They recognize each other by scent, and apparently also visually, and will behave accordingly. There are individuals that will never be compatible, and "old buddies" which nothing can turn into "enemies". For many years we have thus been keeping together without any stress, *T. occipitalis, T. nigrolutea,* and *T. rugosa rugosa,* irrespective of their individual sexes. Two older *T. occipitalis* males have been getting along well with each other for ten years, even during mating seasons. The major point is here that one has to know every lizard individually, and that one does not, other than for very good reasons, change the composition of a harmonious group. In this sense we want to close by quoting Wilhelm KLINGELHÖFER who, as early as in 1957, said in Volume 3 of his "Terrarienkunde": "... larger reptiles have quite some personality, and their character may show so substantial, individual differences, that a generalization would lead to gross misconclusions."

## Reproduction

**Field observations:** SHEA (1992) established that during the Australian summer (in January and February) only 60% of the adult females were gravid. He concluded that their reproduction would not follow an annual pattern, that is they would not become gravid every year. There are also no evidence that would prove that *T. occipitalis* give birth to young more than once a year. In spring, i.e. during the mating period, the males are more active than the females as they are the ones searching for a partner. On the other hand are the females more active in summer (increased need for food due to gravidity). SHEA furthermore reported that there is no correlation between the size of a female and the number of babies in her litter. This means that a small female may have a larger litter than a big one. In nature the litter size ranges from three to five. Newborns measure 11 cm on average, with a minimum of 8.5 cm. Melbourne Zoo saw the birth of a litter containing seven *T. oc-*

*cipitalis* in 1974 (report of the Zoological Society of London, 1976, cited by SHEA 1992). HORNER (1991) stated that a litter may comprise as many as ten young per litter.

**Terrarium observations:** Our group consists of three males and three females of the light colored form from the coast of Western Australia. One male and one female of these already represent an $F_1$ generation.

So far we have been able to witness copulations every year. Our well fed females gave birth to three babies on average for two subsequent years without any problems. The young measured about 16 cm and weighed about 40 g and thus were clearly larger and heavier than juveniles born in the wild. Both females paused in the third year and commenced again in the fourth. Our gravid females showed a greater need for respite and were less active in comparison to the females observed in the wild by SHEA (1992), the reason probably being that the latter have to hunt for their food.

Breeding of *T. occipitalis* is, however, not a very easy feat. Four preconditions should be given:

– a harmonizing pair,
– a stress free environment,
– stimulation, and
– synchronization.

**Conditioning for the "Australian spring":** After a switch to the European annual cycle did not lead to the desired breeding success for two subsequent years, the lizards have since 1989 been kept according to an "Australian climate", which means they are moved to an outdoor enclosure in the German spring month of May (about corresponding with the Australian autumn). This time is marked by still cool nights, and direct sunlight reaches our lizards only in the afternoon. The latter is then very obviously greatly enjoyed. As temperatures usually rise excessively in July, the lizards spend this time, at maximum 4.5 weeks (shortened Australian winter) in a airconditioned, dark room at about 13-15°C and about 70% relative humidity.

Each specimen is placed in a low cardboard box that is furnished with aeration holes and slightly crumpled newspaper. Feeding ceases a few days before the start of their hibernation to ensure their stomachs will be empty. Unlike in the case of chelonians it appears to be unimportant whether the intestine is empty or not, though, since the first defecation after their hibernation never caused any problems.

Sending the lizards into hibernation is always a risk, in particular if the keeper is ignorant or makes avoidable mistakes. The excuse of a "natural selection" for losses we do not accept! By checking on the animals daily in the early stages of hibernation, a restless specimen must be obvious to everybody. It is a clear indication that it is not yet ready for hibernation and must be placed back in its terrarium for further observation. Sunk-in eyes may suggest a very deep sleep, but if the tail appears emaciated at the same time, all is not right. If there is the slightest doubt as to the general condition of a skink, its overwintering should be given a short break. It is no problem whatsoever to let a healthy bluetongue resume its hibernation two days later. To the contrary, a brief break with an opportunity to drink is only positive. An excessively long hibernation period is not only senseless, but also dangerous (compare GENTILLI 1971), and a three month long overwintering can only be justified with reservations for the highland form of *T. nigrolutea*. Acting according to the maxim "lots helps a lot", that is a very long and very cold hibernation does not lead to particularly numerous babies, but much rather to cases of death.

During the second week of August, the males are the first to be returned to their outdoor enclosures. Temperatures are usually warm to hot at this time, but in the north of Germany the weather is changeable and therefore may pass for an "Australian spring".

The head start of the males is important in order to enable them to shed before they encounter receptive females. Not one of our bluetongued skinks approaching a shedding has ever copulated. In contrast to the females our *T. occipitalis* males shed in general about two weeks after completion of their hibernation. Unfortunately, it took us two years to realize this correlation. The females usually remain receptive only for a few days so that the timing (synchronization) must be precise. If, however, a male has shed its skin shortly before the start of its hibernation, such "head start" is unnecessary.

**Mating and mating behavior:** As soon as the males have rid themselves of their old skins they are ready to mate and in a restless manner cruise around in search of a female. The animals should be permitted to live out this increased need for movement and should therefore be left outdoors (the decreasing length of daylight hours never had any dampening effect on their stimulation). The females are awakened from their hibernation about ten days after the males and placed back into their prepared and functional terraria. The best time for this is the evening. A transitory phase with a gradually increasing photoperiod is not necessary.

As early as one and a half weeks later a designated male is placed with a female. Those not yet ready to mate are particularly aggressive now, and if such a female goes for the male with the mouth wide agape, the test is terminated immediately. In order to hit the right point of time, we repeat these brief encounters every day from now (they may also take place in the evening hours). Over the course of a few days the level of aggression subsides, and the female will start running away rather than attack. This running-away stimulates the male to pursue the female. But usually it is then still discouraged to take it any further by the female turning around briskly and showing short, jerky movements with the mouth agape. If the male nevertheless takes hold of the female, a biting fight may ensue. In one case we just managed to save the male from having an already everted hemipenis bitten off!

**Fig. 3** This copulation turned out to be a success          Photograph: H. Röhe

On the next day, the second male is given his first chance. It will approach the female unprejudiced and still very carefully. This may now lead to a success, especially if one found out from the previous years that this male is favored by the female (harmonizing pair). Since the females usually come in heat at different points of time, the male that was rejected until now may still successfully copulate with another female. To-date only the two older, more experienced males were accepted as mating partners, whereas the four year old $F_1$ male is always and immediately attacked.

Following the brief, about one minute long copulation the female often discharges excess sperm from its cloaca. It then tries to wriggle out of the male's grip, underlining her intentions by impatiently waving her tail and soft hissing. The male will, however, usually hold on to it for another copulation which may occur up to an hour later. So far we observed up to three successive copulations in one day. Then the jaw muscles of the male appear to tire, and the female eventually manages to escape. The next day may see some more copulations, but often the male is just under attack again. It is not unusual that individual females will allow one mating only. Nevertheless the keeper can confidently hope for offspring. What follows next is a thrilling, some three and half to four month long period of waiting. Pregnant - Yes or No? Babies or "wax eggs"?

**Pregnancy and birth:** In the following we will describe our observations made during four cases of gravid females.

**Case 1:** The female has a terrarium all for herself (an absolute must). She is very calm. Her frequent lying on the underfloor heater is a good sign. Her diet now includes more protein, and particular attention is paid to her proper supply with calcium, other minerals and vitamins. The continually progressing, slight increase in the body mass does not mean much, simply because the skink now receives more food. But hopes are increasing. As early as six weeks later the breathing may appear somewhat more labored, with the female "sighing" often. The breathing becomes even heavier over the subsequent weeks. And then it happens - the female's breathing gradually becomes normal again, three or four weeks

**Fig. 4** The first of four baby bluetongues *(T. occipitalis)* was born after a gestation period of three and a half months.
Photograph: H. Röhe

before the expected birth, she becomes slimmer, and nothing whatsoever happens. X-rays reveal no embryos in the body cavity. Probably unfertilized eggs, commonly known as "wax eggs", resorbed.

**Case 2:** It starts off with just as many hopes as described before. Our female breathes with increased difficulty, and begins to ignore food a few days before the expected birth. A couple of days later labor contractions are noted. But instead of the expected babies, only those detested, yellow, shiny "wax eggs" are deposited. Fortunately though, this happen without complications. These masses of yolk may also become stuck in the oviducts and will lead to certain death if no emergency surgery is performed. The female rewards herself for the effort and consumes some of the "wax eggs".

**Case 3:** Our female does not behave any differently from normal. She even does not eat as well as she used to and as a result appears fairly slim. As always she enjoys the warmth emit-

ted by the underfloor heater, but not more often than usual. A more labored breathing is hardly noticeable. Notwithstanding, a most beautiful, yellow and dark brown banded baby suddenly lies next to its mother some four months later. A second one may still follow.

**Case 4:** Hopes are just as high as in case 1, but the labored breathing continues right through full term. Labor contractions set in during the afternoon, and two babies are born in the evening about one hour apart. The mother drinks eagerly from the water offered between the two births. Nothing happens on the next day, but the female is extremely agitated. In the afternoon of the following day, labor contractions resume, the third baby is born, with a fourth following later in the evening.

With these long intervals between the individual births being an exception until now, case 4 may otherwise represent a normal course of events with juveniles being born on one day between half an hour and about two hours apart.

## Remarks on the births

Being enabled to witness the births is certainly not only a highlight for us breeders of *Tiliqua,* but for terrarium keepers in general. Some additional observations may therefore be of interest:

The release of amniotic fluid during a birth indicates that a baby will be born and no "wax egg". The birth of a baby takes less than one minute. The miniature bluetongue consumes the placenta immediately and would eagerly accept any other food at this point of time. This being unnatural, we refrain from making use of the opportunity. A distribution of births over two days was observed in 20% of the cases (as compared with about 50% in *Egernia stokesii*). Unfortunately, complications may occur. Three cases should be mentioned here:

**Case 1:** The embryos have died during their development in the oviducts, reasons unknown. If you are lucky, the perished embryos are discharged in time through a premature birth. If not, they will start decomposing and, even if removed surgically, may result in the mother to die.

**Case 2:** One baby is born without any problems. Despite ongoing, heavy labor contractions nothing further happens. Having X-rays taken reveals that another baby lies across the birth canal blocking it solidly; two more embryos are recognizable. Emergency surgery saves the mother and the two well developed babies. The embryo blocking the cloaca is freshly dead.

**Case 3:** Caused by an unnecessary administration of oxytocin and the heavy labor contractions in the oviduct provoked thus, one embryo is pressed through the oviduct's wall and ends up in the body cavity. Since the umbilical cord has remained intact, emergency surgery saves everybody: mother and all juveniles.

## Raising the juveniles

Although the babies could be left in the company of their mother, they are kept in a group raising terrarium of their own for reasons of im-

**Fig. 5** Newly born baby *T. occipitalis* consuming its placenta                     Photograph: H. Röhe

proved hygiene and monitoring. The technological equipment of this terrarium is about the same as that for the adult skinks, but it is furnished with lots of newspaper as a substrate. It

**Fig. 6** The vet was the best bet: a freshly deceased juvenile made a normal birth impossible. The mother and the two other babies survived the surgery well.

Photograph: U. Röhe

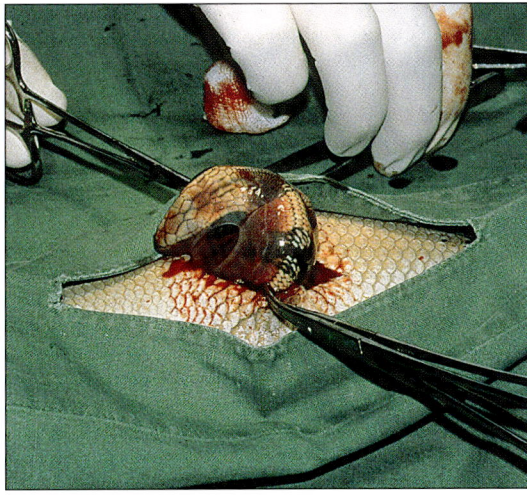

**Fig. 7** A three year old $F_1$ female with her first litter - a hopeful future for the conservation of the species in human hands                    Photograph: H. Röhe

is kept slightly moist for the first few weeks. A mercury vapor lamp, HPL 50 watts, provides the juveniles with UV-A and UV-B radiation.

The small bluetongues are fed with insects daily. They receive half a Calcipot $D_3$ (a vitamin $D_3$ preparation containing calcium citrate and calcium phosphate) tablet each every three days. It is crushed and hidden in a very small amount of tinned cat food initially. Another three days later half a tablet of Carfortan (a supplementary strengthening preparation for dogs) is added. Both preparations are subsequently readily consumed directly from the hand. Crushed cuttlefish shell or calcium grit for birds is available to the babies at designated spots in the terrarium. As a chasing of live insects may culminate in a frenzy which then poses a risk to the tails and limbs of siblings, the juveniles should preferably be fed separately. This also lets the keeper fully enjoy the small *T. occipitalis* when they manage for the first time to catch a locust all by themselves.

The juveniles are at once adjusted to the "Australian annual cycle" and spend their first season of rest from June through August in an outdoor enclosure. They receive food only during periods of warmer weather. The next year they are subjected to the same hibernation procedure as the adults. Our juveniles grow very fast, reaching almost full length after about half a year, although they still appear more fragile than the adults. Males usually mature in their second year of life, females in their third. Then one may begin to hope for offspring of the $F_1$ or $F_2$ generation. The way to there is a long one and a great challenge for the keeper.

## Literature

BUSTARD, R. (1970): Australian Lizards. – Sydney (Collins), 162 pp.

COGGER, H.G. (1992): Reptiles and Amphibians of Australia. 5th edition. – Ithaca, New York (Cornell University Press), 775 pp.

GENTILLI, J. (1971): Climates of Australia and New Zealand. – World Survey of Climatology, Vol.13. – Nedlands, W. A. (University of Western Australia), 371 pp.

HAUSCHILD, A. & P. GAßNER (1995): Skinke im Terrarium. – Hannover (Landbuch-Verlag), 197 S.

HORNER, P. (1991): Skinks of the Northern Territory. – Northern Territory Museum Handbook Series No. 2, Darwin, 174 pp.

KLINGELHÖFFER, W. (1957): Terrarienkunde. 3.Teil. Echsen. – CHRISTOPH SCHERPNER, 2. vollständig neubearbeitete Auflage. Stuttgart (Alfred Kernen Verlag), 264 S.

PETERS, W. (1864): Übersicht der von Hrn. RICHARD SCHOMBURGK an das zoologische Museum eingesandten Amphibien, aus Buchsfelde bei Adelaide in Südaustralien. – Monatsberi. – Königl. Preussi. Akad. Wiss. Berlin, 1863: 228–236.

SHEA, G. M. & M. PETERSON (1981): Observations on sympatry of the social lizards *Tiliqua multifasciata* STERNFELD and *T. occipitals* (PETERS). – Aust. J. Herp., 1(1): 27–28.

SHEA, G.M.(1992): The systematics and reproduction of bluetongue lizards of the genus *Tiliqua* (Squamata: Scincidae). – Ph.D. thesis, University of Sydney, 4 Vols.

WILSON, S.K. & D.G. KNOWLES (1988): Australia's Reptiles. A Photographic Reference to the Terrestrial Reptiles of Australia. – Sydney (Collins Publishers), 447 pp.

Author's location
Heidrun Röhe
Hamburg, Germany

# The Sunda bluetongue
# (*Tiliqua scincoides chimaerea* SHEA, 2000)

GLENN M. SHEA

**Key words: Reptilia: Sauria: Scincidae:** *Tiliqua: Tiliqua scincoides chimaerea*, **description, systematics, Indonesia**

Until recently, all non-Australian bluetongue populations were considered to belong to the species *Tiliqua gigas* (sometimes considered a subspecies of *T. scincoides*). Populations occurring in the Baber and Tanimbar Island groups at the eastern extremity of the Lesser Sunda Islands of Indonesia were no exception. The existence of these populations was first noted by KOPSTEIN (1926) from the Tanimbar Islands, and BRONGERSMA (1933) from the Baber Islands. Both authors identified these populations as *T. g. keyensis,* a subspecies described from the Kei Islands. Recent studies by SHEA (1992), however, clearly identified the Lesser Sunda populations as distinct from that subspecies, although geographically closest to it, and more similar in most respects to *T. scincoides,* previously regarded as confined to Australia. However, several differences from Australian populations were apparent in this study, in some cases reflecting a similarity with *T. gigas.* Because of the distinctiveness of Tanimbar and Baber Is-

land *Tiliqua,* they were named *Tiliqua scincoides chimaerea* (SHEA 2000). The subspecies name is from the Latin adjective chimaereus, after the Chimaera of Greek mythology, offspring of Echidna and Typhon, a creature with a mixture of lion, goat and dragon characters. The name alludes to the combination in this subspecies of characters of both *T. scincoides* and *T. gigas.*

**Holotype:** Nationaal Natuurhistorisch Museum, Leiden (RMNH) 5198a (snout-vent length 250 mm; the only one of four specimens under this number with a complete original tail; Fig. 1). An adult female from Samlaki, Tanimbar Islands, collected by F. KOPSTEIN in May 1924.

**Paratypes:** RMNH 5198b-d, same data as holotype; RMNH 5707a-c, 7229, Baber Islands; RMNH 24050, Naturhistorisches Museum, Wien 10691, 10708-09, Tanimbar Islands.

**Fig. 1** Holotype of *Tiliqua scincoides chimaerea,* Samlaki (Tanimbar Islands), leg. F. Kopstein

Photograph: G. Shea

**Diagnosis:** A small, insular subspecies of *Tiliqua scincoides* (maximum SVL 269 mm), distinguished from all other *Tiliqua* by the combination of primary temporals absent (replaced by anterior extensions of secondary temporals), first two supraoculars in contact with the frontal, supralabials modally eight (8-9, mean 8.2, n = 24), free edge of dorsal body scales rounded, midbody scales 31-33 (mean 31.6, n = 12), paravertebral scales 53-59 (mean 55.7, n = 12), subcaudal scales 45-50 (mean 47.5, n = 6), body dorsum light brown to grayish brown with darker brown bands, lateral pattern concordant with dorsal pattern, head without dark margins to head shields dorsally, nape with several equally-developed narrow brown stripes, venter pale and im-

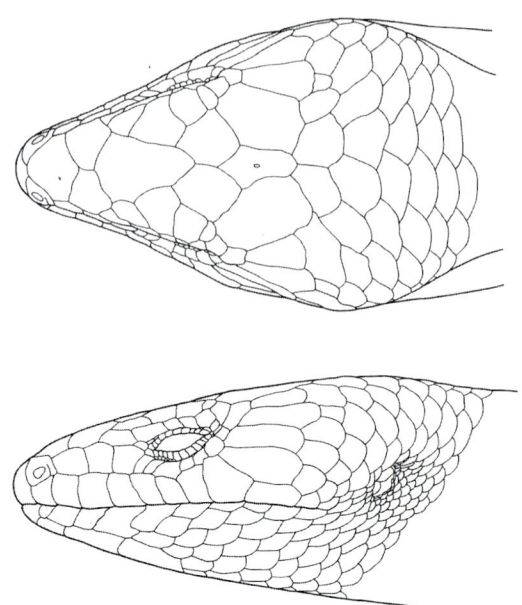

**Fig. 3** Holotype of *Tiliqua scincoides chimaerea*
Sketch: G. Shea

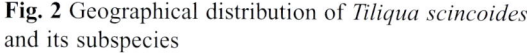

**Fig. 2** Geographical distribution of *Tiliqua scincoides* and its subspecies

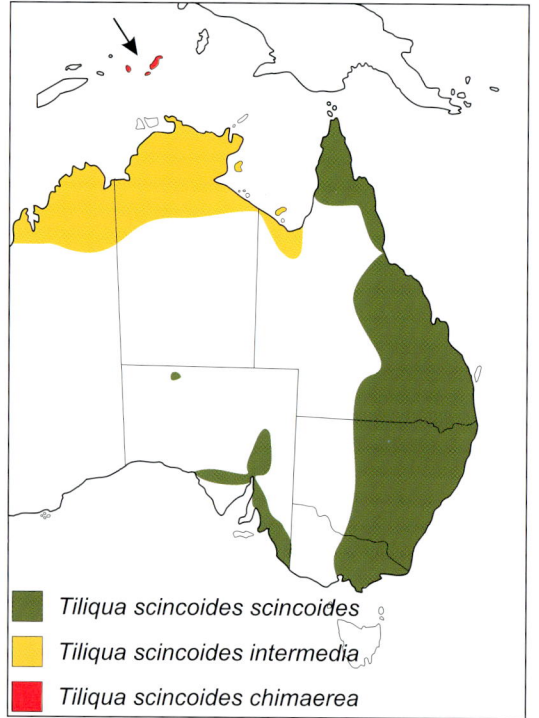

Tiliqua scincoides scincoides

Tiliqua scincoides intermedia

Tiliqua scincoides chimaerea

maculate, and forelimbs usually pale and unpatterned above (one individual with brown variegations).

**Differentiation from *T. s. scincoides*:** Differs from *T. s. scincoides* in having fewer supralabials (vs. 7-11, mode nine, mean 9.0, n = 1163), lesser adult size (geographically variable in *T. s. scincoides,* but smallest in the south and largest in the north, Queensland material having maximum SVLs of 371 mm, mature males 258-302 mm, mean 311.3 mm, n = 23; mature females 277-359 mm, mean 312.5 mm, n = 17), tail variegated (vs. usually strongly banded), and body venter immaculate (vs. usually patterned with weak to bold, fine to coarse, light to dark brown bands, variegations or stripes). Most southern Australian populations of *T. s. scincoides,* which are more similar in adult size to *T. s. chimaerea,* differ in having a dark stripe over the temporal region, and forelimbs dorsally dark.

**Differentiation from *T. s. intermedia:*** Differs from *T. s. intermedia,* to which it is geographically closer, and with which it shares the same modal number of supralabials and an unpatterned venter, in having fewer paravertebral scales (vs. 57-75, mean 65.9, n = 175), dorsal dark bands continuous with lateral pattern (vs. alternation of dark markings dorsally and laterally), and lesser adult size (vs. maximum SVL 371 mm, mature males in the east 296-361 mm, mean 320.3 mm, n = 34, in the west 269-341 mm, mean 294.0 mm, n = 23; mature eastern females 297-362 mm, mean 324.1 mm, n = 27; western 264-325 mm, mean 299.1 mm, n = 18).

**Differentiation from *T. gigas:*** Although the Sunda bluetongue is similar to *Tiliqua gigas* in having a low number of paravertebral scales, it can be distinguished from all subspecies of *Tiliqua gigas* by having forelimbs pale and usually unpatterned dorsally (vs. usually brown to black, often with pale spots), nape with several equally developed dark stripes (vs. median vertebral stripe much broader than others), venter pale and immaculate (vs. usually dark patterned), dorsal scales smooth with rounded margins (vs. angulate to unicarinate, especially posteriorly on body), and fewer subcaudals (vs. 47 or more, usually greater than 50). It is furthermore distinguished from *T. gigas gigas* by the brown (vs. black) dorsal bands, lack of any reduction or loss of the elongate secondary temporals, and variegated (vs. banded) tail, and from the other two subspecies of *T. gigas* in its

**Fig. 4** *Tiliqua scincoides chimaerea,* Tanimbar Islands                    Photograph:  F.B. Yuwono

much smaller adult size (maximum SVL 343 mm for *T. g. evanescens,* 336 mm for *T. g. keyensis*). The difference in the number of subcaudal scales is most pronounced in *T. g. keyensis,* which has 58-65 subcaudals (mean 59.8, n = 11), despite being the geographically closest subspecies of *T. gigas.*

The occurrence of an otherwise Australian species in the Lesser Sunda Islands is not unique. Although the Lesser Sunda Islands lie on the edge of the Sunda Shelf, and are separated from the Australian continental plate by the Timor Trough (FAIRBRIDGE 1953, JONGSMA 1970, 1974), the fauna of the Lesser Sunda Islands includes other species with Australian affinities, including among reptiles the *Glaphyromorphus isolepis* species group of skinks (GREER 1990), the varanid lizard subgenus *Odatria* and the agamid lizard *Amphibolurus temporalis* (DE ROOIJ 1915), the chelid tortoise genus *Chelodina* (RHODIN 1994), and among snakes the *Ramphotyphlops polygrammicus* complex of typhlopids and the python genus *Liasis* (DE ROOIJ 1917).

Nothing is known about the habitat preferences and ecology of this subspecies, although it has recently appeared in the commercial pet trade initiated by Indonesian dealers due to the ban in trade of the more widely distributed *Tiliqua gigas* by the Indonesian government. Among the type series are four apparently mature females (ovaries with follicles greater than 3 mm, oviducts in the largest two convoluted) with SVLs of 240-269 mm, and one immature female (ovaries with follicles less than 2 mm, oviduct not convoluted) with a SVL of 231 mm. Of the three males, the largest (SVL 261 mm) is mature, with enlarged turgid testes, while the others (SVL 181-201 mm) are apparently immature, with small flattened testes. The smallest specimen in the type series has a SVL of 86.5 mm, and appears to be either a newborn or a late embryo.

## Literature

BRONGERSMA, L.D. (1933): Herpetological notes IX. Contribution to the herpetology of the Babber Islands. – Zoologische Mededeelingen 16(1–2): 27–29.

DE ROOIJ, N. (1915): The Reptiles of the Indo-Australian Archipelago I: Lacertilia, Chelonia, Emydosauria. – Leiden (E.J. Brill), 384 pp.

– (1917): The Reptiles of the Indo-Australian Archipelago II: Ophidia. – Leiden (E.J. Brill), xiv + 314 pp.

FAIRBRIDGE, R.W. (1953): The Sahul Shelf, northern Australia; its structure and geological relationships. – Journal of the Royal Society of Western Australia 37: 1–33.

GREER, A.E. (1990): The *Glaphyromorphus isolepis* species group (Lacertilia: Scincidae): diagnosis of the taxon and description of a new species from Timor. – Journal of Herpetology 24: 372–377.

JONGSMA, D. (1970): Eustatic sea level changes in the Arafura Sea. – Nature 228: 150–151.

– (1974): Marine geology of the Arafura Sea. – Commonwealth of Australia Department of Minerals and Energy, Bureau of Mineral Resources, Geology and Geophysics Bulletin (157): 1–73.

KOPSTEIN, P.F. (1926): Reptilien von den Molukken und den benachbarten Inseln. Zoologische Mededeelingen 9(2–3): 71–112.

RHODIN, A.G.J. (1994): Chelid turtles of the Australasian Archipelago II: A new species of *Chelodina* from Roti Island, Indonesia. – Breviora (498): 1–31.

SHEA, G.M. (1992): The systematics and reproduction of bluetongue lizards of the genus *Tiliqua* (Squamata: Scincidae). 4 Vols. – Ph. D. thesis, University of Sydney.

– (2000): Der Sunda-Blauzungenskink *Tiliqua scincoides chimaerea* subsp. nov. – S. 157-160 in HAUSCHILD, A., R. HITZ, K. HENLE, G.M. SHEA & H. WERNING (Hrsg.): Blauzungenskinke. Beiträge zu *Tiliqua* und *Cyclodomorphus*. – Münster (Natur und Tier-Verlag), 287 S.

Author's address
Dr. Glenn M. Shea
Faculty of Veterinary Science
University of Sydney
New South Wales 2006
Australia

# The northern blue-tongued skink,
# *Tiliqua scincoides intermedia* MITCHELL, 1955

PAUL HORNER

Key words: Reptilia: Sauria: Scincidae: *Tiliqua scincoides intermedia,* Australia, distribution, natural history, reproduction

## Introduction

The northern blue-tongued skink, *Tiliqua scincoides intermedia* MITCHELL, 1955 is one of the best known and most conspicuous elements of the northern Australian herpetofauna. It is a docile skink, hardy, and is therefore a popular terrarium animal within Australia as well as in other countries. This popularity has resulted in considerable information about its requirements in captivity (e.g. HAUSCHILD & GASSNER 1995, WALLIS 1996), but we still know very little about its biology and ecology in its natural habitat in the north of Australia. Although ecological information is wanting for much of the Australian fauna, it is still unusual that so well known an animal has not yet been studied more closely. I therefore hope that this contribution will help to close the gap in our knowledge about the largest skink of Australia, and probably the largest skink of the world.

The common bluetongue, *Tiliqua scincoides* (WHITE, 1790) was not only among the first Australian animals ever described, but the first scientifically described species of Australian reptile (SHEA 1993). The northern bluetongue, on the other hand, was first identified during an American-Australian expedition to Arnhem Land, a virtually unexplored part of the Northern Territory, when specimens were collected in 1948. Some of the reptile material collected by the expedition was subsequently studied at the South Australian Museum by the then curator F.J. MITCHELL who concluded that these unusually large bluetongues from Arnhem Land were different from the typical eastern form. Based on information gathered from the six specimens available, he described the new subspecies in 1955, his findings being published in Volume 11 of the Records of the South Australian Museum.

As points of distinction between *T. s. intermedia* and the eastern subspecies *T. s. scincoides* MITCHELL emphasized the differences in color pattern and the larger size of adult specimens. The six specimens examined by him all originated from the extreme northeastern region of Arnhem Land, four from the coastal mainland at Yirrkalla, and two from Groote Eylandt, a large continental island in the western part of the Gulf of Carpentaria.

## Description

*T. s. intermedia* is a large, stout bodied skink with a large, wedge-shaped head that is distinct from the neck. The relatively short, cylindrical tail tapers to a point. The legs are short and inconspicuous, with each foot having five short toes that terminate in stout, curved claws. Body and tail are covered with small, smoothly rounded, glossy scales, 30-38 rows of which are counted at midbody (SHEA 1992). The skink has large, distinct head scales, and up to four prominent lobule-like scales in each ear opening. Free ranging specimens often show damaged feet and toes usually caused by the lizard crawling through hot coals, or burning grass,

**Fig. 1** Blue-tongued skinks survive the frequent bushfires in subterranean holes, but often burn their toes and feet when racing for cover.                                                    Photograph: U. Röhe

when trapped by the annual bush fires that occur over much of their woodland habitat.

The largest skink of northern Australia differs from its eastern relative *T. s. scincoides* by the following traits: a characteristic combination of body coloration and pattern (in particular the wide, yellowish brown to orange colored zones on the flanks), the number of supralabial scales (normally eight versus normally nine; Shea 1992), and geographic distribution (northern versus eastern Australia).

In body coloration and pattern northern bluetongues exhibit a substantial degree of individual and geographic variation. A typical specimen from the Northern Territory shows a light brown to light gray ground color with a pattern of 5-12 indistinct to sharply demarcated, irregular cross bands. Dorsally these cross bands are usually grayish with black

margins and contain numerous black dashes. Most specimens have the cross bands interrupted in the vertebral region, sometimes so much so that some bands may be shifted out of line. The bands become darker and increase in width on the flanks where they are separated from each other by yellowish brown to orange interspaces. The lower portion of each flank is normally cream colored with irregular brown

Opposite from above
**Fig. 2** Typical adult northern bluetongue *(Tiliqua scincoides intermedia)* from Sleisbeck (Northern Territory)
**Fig. 3** Adult northern bluetongue *(Tiliqua scincoides intermedia)* from Kununurra (Western Australia) showing the dark dorsal pattern typical for the western population                                    Photographs: P. Horner

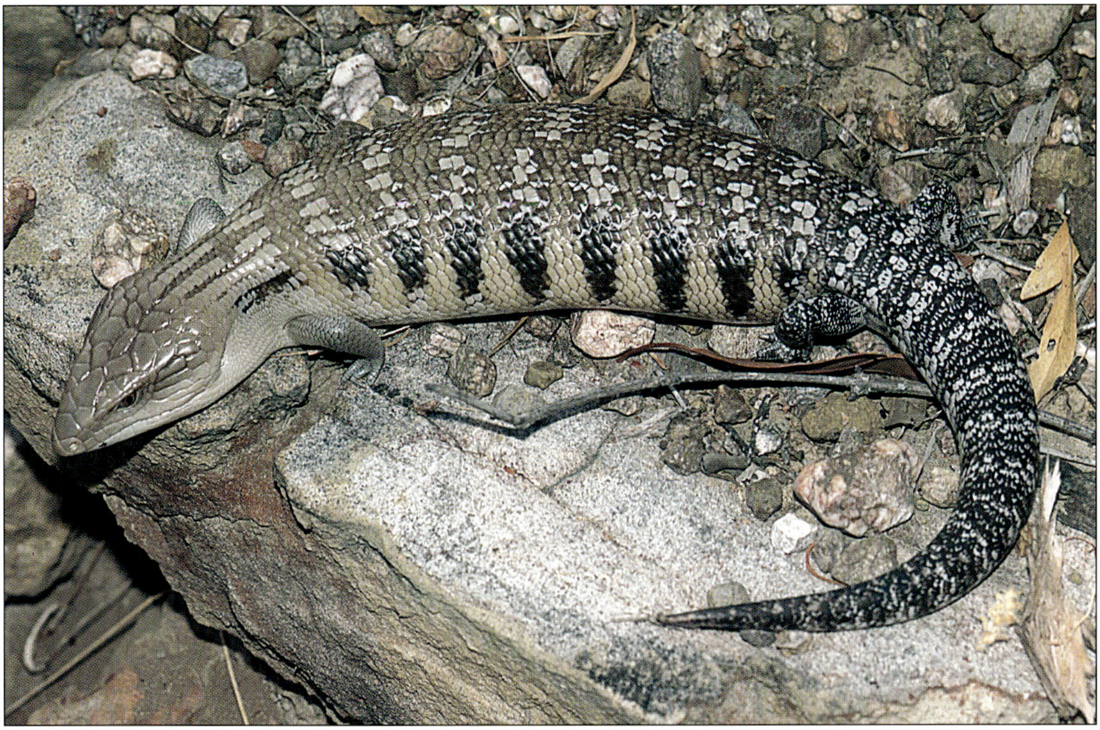

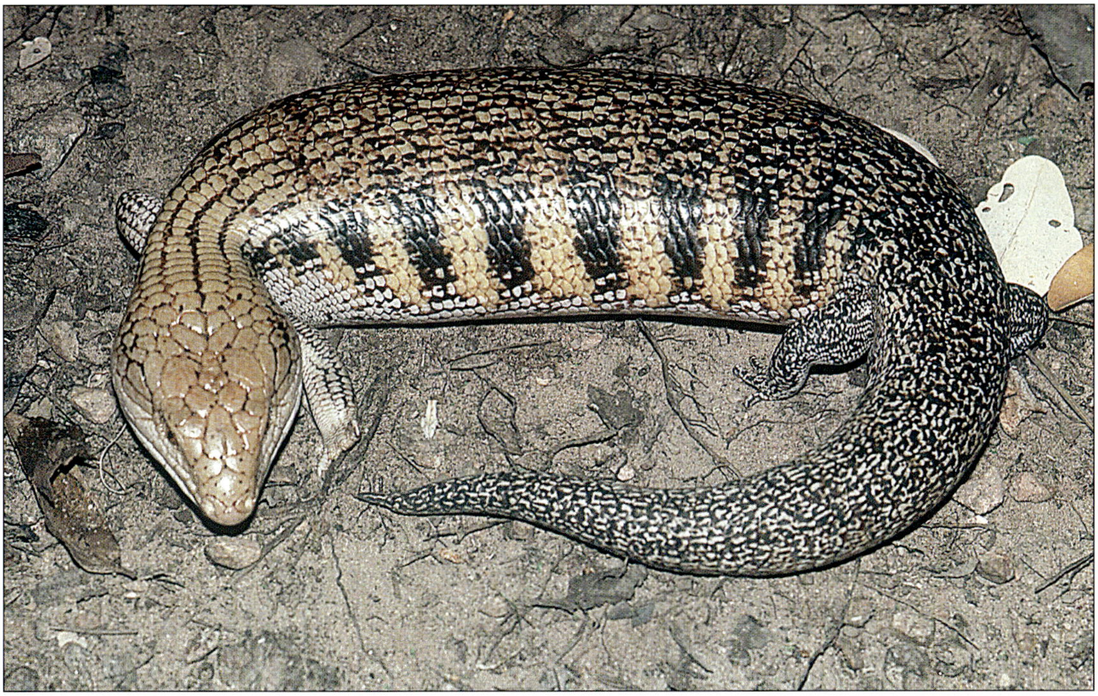

than adults, having a matt rather than glossy sheen to their scales. The glossy sheen and bright adult colors only develop at about 8-9 months of age.

Although the colors and patterning of adult northern bluetongues appear bright and conspicuous, they in fact have a cryptic function enabling the skinks to blend in with their natural environment. Both color and pattern have a dissolving effect on the body contours when the skinks are in leaf litter, grass or other ground debris and therefore give excellent camouflage.

**Fig. 4** Adult *Tiliqua s. intermedia* from Keep River (Northern Territory) with the dark speckling and marbling of the head and front limbs typical for the western population    Photograph: P. Horner

**Size**

spots and dashes. The upper neck area usually shows a distinct pattern consisting of several conspicuous, narrow, dark longitudinal lines which are formed by the dark lateral margins of the neck scales. The head is light brown to light gray and usually unpatterned, although the temporal region may have an indistinct, brown stripe extending from the eye to the ear opening. This temporal stripe is, however, never as prominent as in the eastern bluetongue. The tail is brown to grayish and densely patterned with indistinct dark cross bands and dark flecks. The limbs are brownish in color. Usually the front legs do not show any markings, while the hind legs have a distinct, blackish brown spotted pattern. In most specimens the ventral surfaces are immaculate cream, but may be patterned with brown spots and cross streaks in subadult, and occasionaladult, animals. Some individuals may have a pink or yellow tinge to  the cream ventral surface.

Color and pattern of the northern bluetongue are subject to ontogenetic changes. Newly born juveniles are less intensely patterned and duller

The northern bluetongue is the largest blue-tongued skink and probably also the largest living skink on earth (SHEA 1998). Many measurements given in the literature are based on total lengths, , and may lead to misunderstanding if the specimens measured actually had damaged or autotomized (regenerated) tails. In order to minimise errors, lizards should routinely be measured from the tip of the snout to the anterior margin of the cloaca (= snout-vent length, SVL) as a standard measurement.

MITCHELL (1955) recorded a specimen measuring 334 mm SVL, with a total length of 447 mm including its (incomplete) tail. Other documented SVLs are 370 mm (HORNER 1991, STORR et al. 1981), 300 mm (COGGER 1992), 320 mm (WILSON & KNOWLES 1988), and 371 mm (SHEA 1992). With the tail being, on average, 60% of the SVL (SHEA 1992), the largest of the mentioned measurements suggests that this species may reach about 594 mm in total length.

Whilst no relevant data is available from nature, representatives of this skink lived to an age of 12 and 10 years, in captivity (SHEA

1992) indicating northern bluetongues are extremely long lived skinks.

## Variability

In his analysis of *T. s. intermedia* SHEA (1992) found that populations living in the eastern part of the distribution range (Northern Territory and Queensland) grow substantially larger than those inhabiting the western portion (Kimberley) (mean value 322 versus 296 mm). The western populations also differ in some traits of body patterning with most specimens having prominent finely scattered black speckles and marbled markings. This trait is most distinct on the head which is normally unpatterned in eastern specimens, but often densely peppered and spotted in those from western populations.

SHEA (1992) also detected a certain degree of sexual dimorphism. He established that adult females are slightly larger than adult males, although the difference was not statistically significant. He also found, although the difference is small, that males differ from females by having a shorter body, but longer tails, legs and heads.

## Distribution

The northern bluetongue is widely distributed in the monsoon regions of northern Australia.

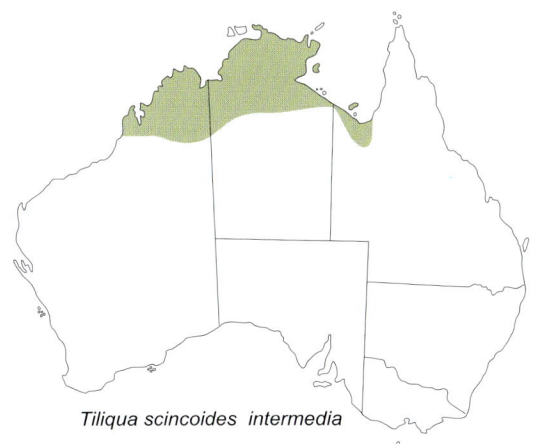

*Tiliqua scincoides  intermedia*

In Western Australia they are present in the Kimberley region south to about Broome and Wolf Creek. In the Northern Territory they inhabit the "Top End" south to about Wave Hill in the Victoria River District and Helen Springs in the Barkly Tablelands. In Queensland the skinks appear to be restricted to the extreme northwest where they have been recorded from Gregory Downs and Cloncurry (SHEA 1992). It appears that their distribution is limited by the increasing aridity of the central and western Australian deserts. Where *T. s. intermedia* occurs in semi-arid areas, it is not uncommon to find striped blue-tongues *T. multifasciata in the same area as T. s. intermedia.*

## Preferred habitats

Northern blue-tongued skinks are most common in *Eucalyptus* woodlands, but are actually not bound to any specific habitat. They are also found in a number of other important habitat types, including open forests and shrublands. Within these they inhabit numerous microhabitats, but tend to avoid wet and humid situations. In *Eucalyptus* woodland they are most com-

**Fig. 5** Rock massif of the Mitchell Plateau (Western Australia) with crevices and flat boulders occasionally used by northern bluetongues as shelters

Photograph:  P. Horner

165

**Fig. 6** Natural habitat of the northern bluetongue *(Tiliqua scincoides intermedia)* in an open forest flanking a stream in central Arnheimland (Northern Territory)                    Photograph: P. Horner

monly found in places offering a deep layer of leaf litter, dense grass tussocks and accumulations of other litter such as fallen trees or piled up debris. Other preferred localities are boulder strewn areas or rock outcrops where the animals find suitable shelter in deep crevices or in cavities beneath flat pieces of rock. Although they do not excavate burrows themselves the skinks are occasionally found occupying the burrows of other animals. The northern bluetongue appears to have developed a particular liking for sites where building rubble or other solid rubbish has been dumped and left undisturbed for long periods of time.

## Reproduction

Northern blue-tongued skinks are live bearing, but detailed reproductive data is scanty. In his study of the genus *Tiliqua, Dr Glenn* SHEA (1992) recorded the following information from preserved museum material: males mature at a SVL of between 269 and 321 mm, females at 264-362 mm. The testes of males increase distinctly in size and turgidity between August and mid-September, while females reach the climax of their follicle development at the middle of the dry season in July/August. These data suggest that mating takes place when the female and male reproductive cycles coincide at some point of time in September. Gestation takes about 3-4 months so that young are born at the beginning of the wet monsoon season (about December/January). The number of juveniles per litter is correlated to the size of the female, and up 14 young have been documented (SHEA 1992). The presence of distinct bite marks on the flanks of females during the mating season indicate that copulation has taken place; these are inflicted by the males attempting to hold their partners in position for mating.

The following data is based on a birth observed under terrarium conditions; the parent specimens originate from the Keep River region in the extreme northwest of the Northern Territory. The female measured 343 mm in SVL and gave birth to 11 young on January 26, 1997. The juveniles measured 116. mm on average (range 113-123 mm) and had an average mass of 26.4 g (range 22.2 to 31.0 g). Three of these were raised in a terrarium and had grown to an average SVL of 280.6 mm (275-292 mm), a total length of 468.7 (458-485 mm), and a weight of 459 g (381-563 g) after 12 months. The same female gave birth to another litter of five on January 5, 1998. Interestingly enough the specimens comprising the first litter attained virtually mature adult size after one year.

## Diet

Northern bluetongues are omnivores whose diet includes both animal and plant material. They are particularly fond of large insects including locusts and roaches, but they will practically consume any type of arthropod crossing their path. They also prey upon the young of ground nesting bird species and raid the nests of rodents and other small mammals in order to consume the young and, probably, the odd adult not swift enough to make an escape. As to what extent plant material is consumed in nature is unknown, but it may be presumed that it constitutes an important part of the diet. GREER (1989) noted that larger bluetongue species also feed on carrion.

## Behavior

The behavior of this subspecies does not differ substantially from that of other large bluetongues. Although it is a ground dwelling lizard that is not particularly agile, it is nevertheless able to overcome obstacles (such as heaps of rocks) which require certain climbing skills. Northern bluetongues can move with surprising speed and quickly disappear in dense vegetation. If obstacles or dense grass hinder their progress, the skinks simply adpress their limbs to the body and move forward with snake-like movements. The animals are normally diurnal, but will avoid the hottest hours of the tropical day being most active in the early morning and late afternoon. They may be active in the late evening, often being encountered on tarred roads enjoying the radiant warmth stored by the substrate during the day.

Northern bluetongues are common in both urban and rural areas. Where towns and suburbs have replaced the original bushlands, they have adapted to the changed environmental conditions and now inhabit gardens and parks. In some cases these changes have even brought about improved living conditions, and suitable refuges - such as a richly vegetated and regularly watered garden - may offer a number of skinks a good home for many years. Obviously these artificial habitats also present some new dangers to which the lizards have not developed defense strategies. Predation by free ranging dogs and cats accounts for many losses, and so does road traffic which kills numbers of lizards when they wander from one place to another.

Being equipped with strong jaws and short, blunt teeth, northern bluetongues are able to inflict painful bites. Biting is, however, a last resort as the lizards have evolved an impressive threat display which they use to bluff and discourage potential aggressors. If they feel threatened, they flatten the body, lift it off the ground, and present it to the aggressor in an arched manner. This posture enhances the bright colors and makes the specimen appear larger than it actually is. As long as the threat persists the body is kept turned towards the attacker which often requires the lizard to spin around quickly. This warning display is accompanied by loud hissing. If the attacker comes too close, the skink will open its mouth wide and display the wide, vividly blue tongue. This display has had the unexpected result that many older Australians believe that these harmless lizards are highly venomous, probably based on the similarities of this display with that of Australian death adders, *Acanthophis* spp.

Being large, bulky lizards with an intimidating threat display, adult northern bluetongues face few natural enemies. The most important predators presumably are large snakes, such as the black-headed python, *Aspidites melanocephalus* and the elapid snake *Pseudechis australis, and* large predatory birds, such as the kookaburra and falcons, but dingos and stray domestic cats and dogs are also known to predate on these lizards. Juveniles and subadults may become victims of a multitude of predatory reptiles, mammals and birds. The greater number of dangers faced by young specimens is probably the reason why juveniles are shyer and more secretive than adults.

Like most other skinks northern bluetongues are able to voluntarily detach all or part of their tail. This behavior helps to escape predators, in that the detached, wriggling tail will hopefully distract the latter, giving the lizard a chance to escape. However, they will not part with their tails as readily as many smaller skink species, and it usually requires some seriously rough handling to provoke this behavior. Specimens that have lost their tails are able to regenerate it, but the replacement will never look original, having a different scalation and a different type of internal support structure (cartilage instead of caudal vertebrae). A regenerated tail is readily recognized as such by its shorter length and imperfect proportions.

## Literature

COGGER, H.G. (1992): Reptiles and Amphibians of Australia. Fifth Edition. – Reed Books, Chatswood.

GREER, A.E. (1989): The biology and evolution of Australian lizards. – Surrey Beatty and Sons, Chipping Norton.

HORNER, P. (1992): Skinks of the Northern Territory. Handbook Series No.2. – Northern Territory Museum of Arts and Sciences, Darwin.

HAUSCHILD, A. & P. GAßNER (1995): Skinke im Terrarium. – Landbuch-Verlag, Hannover.

MITCHELL, F.J. (1955): Preliminary account of the Reptilia and Amphibia collected by the National Geographic Society - Commonwealth Government - Smithsonian Expedition to Arnhem Land (April to November, 1948) – In: Records of the South Australian Museum 11: 373–408.

SHEA, G.M. (1992): The systematics and reproduction of Bluetongue lizards of the genus *Tiliqua* (Squamata: Scincidae). – Ph.D. Thesis, University of Sydney.

– (1993): The anatomist John Hunter (1728–1793), the Eastern Bluetongue Skink *Tiliqua scincoides* (Squamata: Scincidae) and the discovery of herbivory in skinks. – In: Archives of Natural History 20(3): 303–306.

– (1997): Reptiles, Lizards / Skinks, Blue-tongued Skinks. – S. 339 in: Encyclopedia of Australian Wildlife, Reader's Digest (Australia), Surrey Hills.

STORR, G.M., L.A. SMITH & R.E. JOHNSTONE (1981): Lizards of Western Australia. 1. Skinks. – University of Western Australia Press and Western Australian Museum, Perth.

WALLIS, J.G. (1996): Blue-tongued skinks: keeping and breeding them in captivity. – T.F.H. Publications, Neptune City (U.S.A.)

WILSON, S.K. & D.G. KNOWLES (1988): Australia's reptiles. A photographic reference to the terrestrial reptiles of Australia. – William Collins Pty. Ltd., Sydney.

Author's address
Paul Horner
Northern Territory Museum
G.P.O. Box 4646
Darwin, NT 0801, Australia

# The continuous keeping and breeding of
# *Tiliqua scincoides scincoides* (HUNTER, 1790) in the terrarium

THOMAS UNVERZAGT

**Key words: Reptilia: Sauria: Scincidae:** *Tiliqua scincoides scincoides,* **Australia, natural history, husbandry, reproduction**

## Introduction

Despite the common blue-tongued skink *Tiliqua scincoides scincoides* being a more frequently kept large skink, there are only a few articles in the literature dealing with its husbandry and propagation in captivity (JONES 1987, SCHOLDERMAN 1994, TURNER 1996). As a result of the strict ban of exports by the Australian legislative, the establishment of new, or a supplementation of existing, groups with wild caught specimens has become almost impossible. Given this background it appears even more crucial to intensify its keeping and breeding in order to preserve a beautiful and impressive species for the terrarium hobby.

**Fig. 1** Distribution of *Tiliqua scincoides scincoides*

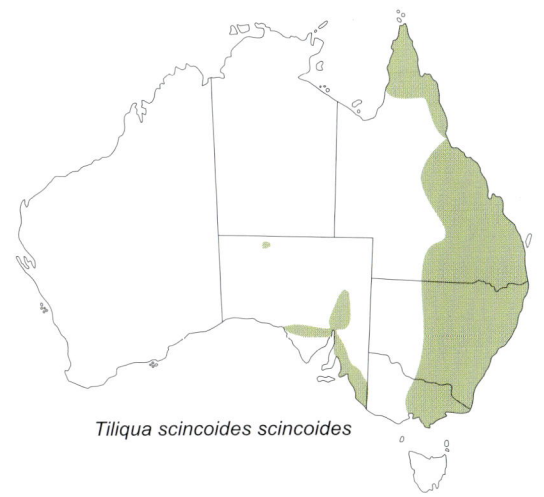

*Tiliqua scincoides scincoides*

## Distribution

*Tiliqua scincoides* is present in all states of mainland Australia (COGGER 1979, HOSER 1989, EHMANN 1992). The distribution range extends in an arched, at maximum 700 km wide coastal strip from the northeast of Western Australia through the northern sections of Northern Territory, the northeastern part of Queensland, eastern New South Wales, and Victoria, to the southeastern portion of South Australia. The central parts of the Australian mainland as well as Tasmania are excluded from the distribution range. In this vast geographical area subspecies have evolved next to the nominate form. These are *Tiliqua s. intermedia* which inhabits the north of Western Australia, Northern Territory and Queensland, and *T. s. chimaerea* on Babber and Tanimbar Islands (SHEA 2000, this book).

## Description

*Tiliqua s. scincoides* is a muscular skink with a compact build that may grow to a total length of 45-50 cm, of which the SVL makes up about two thirds. The head is distinct from the body by a short, slender neck, and appears triangular when viewed from above. The lower jaw is well developed and equipped with a strong musculature. A look into the open mouth will reveal a thick meaty, blue tongue. The jaws carry small teeth, dominated by imposing, wide, flat molars on the sides. The eyes are situated on the sides of the head and are well developed; the lower eyelid is movable. Some populations are marked by having a dark streak which may extend from the eye to the

**Fig. 2** *Tiliqua s. scincoides* from Adelaide / SA.                    Photograph: R. Hoser

shoulder region (BUSTARD 1970, JENKINS & BARTELL 1980, SWANSON 1987, SWAN 1990, WORRELL 1963). The exterior ear opening is distinct, and has a partial cover in the form of three small scales anteriorly. The body has a cylindrical, elongated shape with an oval cross section. Four elongated, conspicuously large scales cover the temporal region. The smooth scales are arranged in an imbricate manner. Depending on the geographic origin of a specimen gray and yellowish brown colors often dominate. The shoulder region is marked with narrow, black streaks in longitudinal direction. Eight to ten black bands cross the back and flanks and may include yellow or cream colored spots on the sides. The venter is often uniform, gray, without any markings. Specimens from the southern parts of the distribution range are generally more dusky (pers. obs.). The legs are short and muscular, with each of the feet having five short toes with small claws. Both the front and hind legs are often speckled with

black in a reticulated fashion. The tail is round to horizontally oval, stout, and tapering to a point (COGGER 1979, STORR 1981, HOSER 1989, HORNER 1991, SHEA 1992). The fully grown specimens kept by myself have body masses between 370 and 410 g. Distinguishing between the sexes on the basis of external traits is not possible with certainty.

**Ecology**

Within its gigantic distribution range *Tiliqua s. scincoides* has only spared the tropical rainforest and cool montane regions from colonization, all other types of habitats have been conquered (HAUSCHILD & GASSNER 1995). This also includes public parks and private gardens of the suburbs where the skinks are usually considered welcomed guests which keep snails at bay. These blue-tongued skinks are mainly diurnal ground dwellers which spend the night inside their shelters. The latter may be rodent burrows, cavities beneath rocks, logs, rock crevices, or leaf litter (EHMANN 1992). Despite their plump appearance these skinks show surprising skill when the need for climbing arises. As far as their food is concerned they are little choosy. Besides their much favored snails they appear to consume just about anything they are able to overcome, including carrion. Plant material constitutes a substantial component in their diet.

In their natural habitat these blue-tongued skinks live solitarily and will meet with other individuals only during the mating season in the Australian spring. A study done by SHEA (1993) showed that the males also have a pronounced annual gonad cycle, with the testes being largest, and the epithels of the sperm ducts being most differentiated, in the months from September through November. Once the mating season is over, these organs regress again. The females give birth to their offspring in summer with litters comprising 10 to 25 young (COGGER 1979, JENKINS & BARTELL 1980). The latter are independent immediately and consume the attached placenta right after birth.

Within its distribution range this blue-tongued skink is considered common and "secure" in its conservation status (EHMANN 1992). Due to their size adult specimens have few natural enemies, these being limited to dingos, large birds of prey, pythons, and large monitors. If the skinks feel threatened, they will put up an impressive defense display. They will bend the body into horseshoe shape, gape the mouth wide and extrude the flattened blue tongue widely. All this is accompanied by loud hissing, and if it is still not enough discouragement, they will bite fiercely. Little is known about their life expectancy, but more than 17 years in a terrarium have been documented by FLOWER (in GREER 1989).

**Fig. 3** *Tiliqua s. scincoides* from St. Claire / NSW.   Photograph: R. Hoser

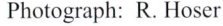

## Acquisition

Due to the strict export ban imposed by Australia it is impossible to legally acquire wild caught specimens. The terrarium keeper with a keen interest therefore has to resort to acquiring captive bred material and is best advised to secure himself several specimens if and when the opportunity arises. Swapping or acquiring suitable specimens at a later stage might turn out to be an arduous undertaking.

## Terrarium

The author's animals are housed individually in terraria measuring 200 × 50 × 100 cm (l × w × h). These are placed in a shelving system made of zinc-coated iron. The rear and side walls as well as the upper and front panels of the cages are made of twinwall sheets cut to size. Where the sheets touch they are sealed with silicone. The front panels carry glued-on sliding profiles for the glass sliding "doors". The bottom panel is isolated and protected from corrosion by a thin underlying layer of styrofoam and a thin plastic sheet. Ventilation is ensured by two aeration surfaces in the side walls.

**Decoration:** Round-edged, light-colored gravel with a granulation of 2-4 mm has proved to be beneficial as substrate in the terraria. Whilst it facilitates a natural degree of wear on the claws, it does not stick to the animals, is easy to keep clean, and can be recycled. Trials with various types of bark mulch and sifted orchid soil were unsatisfactory over longer periods of time and were eventually abandoned. Positive experiences in the raising of young were made with cat litter. Being an absorbent substrate based on mineral compounds, exchange intervals were prolonged and the development of bad odors was reduced

**Fig. 4** Bluetongues kept in terraria in Germany                Photograph: A. Hauschild

substantially. No negative effects from inadvertently swallowed particles could be noted in the animals. Hiding places are made available, according to the sizes of the individuals, in the form of piled-up sandstone flakes or tubular pieces of cork bark. It showed clearly that those shelters were preferred that provided the most amount of body contact. The terraria are vegetated with *Scindapsus* sp. that are kept in hydroculture in hanging pots so that they are protected from being dug up all the time. They, however, do not appear to contribute substantially to the well being of the animals.

**Illumination:** The array of terraria faces a large window front towards the northeast. No provision has been made to cover these windows so that the natural annual changes in the daylight hours can affect the keeping of the animals. The terraria are in addition illuminated by fluorescent tubes of the type Osram Lumilux Daylight or Radium Spectralux Daylight, of the spectral types 11, with an output of 116 watts/m5 at a distance of 40-70 cm, unfiltered for 12 hours/day. By using respective reflectors the light yield is maximized and directed downwards. In order to prevent any overheating, the transformers of the fluorescent tubes are mounted outside the terraria. The fluo tubes are exchanged routinely every one and a half years in order to ensure a constant quality and intensity. Additional light and heat is generated in each terrarium by one or two spot lamps with an output of 60 watts mounted above designated basking sites parallel to the fluo tubes. The entire illumination equipment is run by electronic timers and dimmers.

**Heating:** Given the shelf-like arrangement of the terraria, the ground and air temperatures oscillate between 22 and 28°C. An additional heating of the substrate is therefore unnecessary. The temperatures at the basking sites may rise up to about 43°C. During the night the values decrease to between 17 and 20°C. The spot lights are left off if very warm summer days raise the ambient temperatures to levels at which doing so might lead to overheating.

## Feeding

Feeding these skinks is anything but difficult. They will basically eat everything they can overpower. Snails are the favorite food, but all types of insects, worms, and small mammals are also readily consumed. Ripe fruit, berries, vegetables and mushrooms complete their menu. Canned cat and dog food is also willingly accepted. In order to ensure a balanced diet in the terrarium, the diet should be varied with the seasons of the year. With the animals having a tendency to become obese their calorie supply should be limited, and every individual's weight should be monitored by means of regular weighing. An ideal supplement to fruit porridge or tinned cat food was found to be oat bran. Fully grown specimens are fed twice per week, juveniles every day. Gravid females receive as much food as they want to consume in one session three or four times per week. Once every week vitamins and minerals are supplied, for which purpose I have been using Korvimin ZVT or Multimulsin in conjunction with Osspulvit.

## Behavior

After a short period of adjustment the blue-tongued skink presents itself as a calm terrarium

**Fig. 5** *Tiliqua scincoides* has separated the shell from the rest of a snail. If necessary, snails may also be consumed with their shells.  Photograph: U. Röhe

animal that loses its shyness quickly and also observes events outside its confines with eager interest. Already KLINGELHÖFER (1957) observed, "... that captive kept skinks are a picture of greatest tameness and most harmless benevolence ...". The blue-tongued skink will routinely roam its terrarium in search of food. Attempts to socialize conspecifics, no matter of which sex, or other, even larger skinks, always resulted in biting fights and continuous pursuits, so that I have come to suppose some degree of territoriality, at least under the confines of a terrarium. Other keepers (HAUSCHILD, BÜSTRIN pers. comms.) were more successful with the communal keeping of groups. After some time, many blue-tongued skinks become very docile, will come to the opened door of the terrarium and pick their food right off the keeper's hand. They can be picked up, and maintenance work can be done in their cages without them losing their calm and collectedness; wild biting around or even threatening behavior was never observed.

## Annual cycle and synchronization of the sexes

Corresponding with their geographical origin the animals are exposed to a periodic change

**Fig. 6** *Tiliqua s. scincoides* in a hibernation box
Photograph: A. Hauschild

of the seasons with the respective varying of the climatic factors involved. This annual rhythm appears to be vitally important for a successful long term husbandry and breeding in a terrarium, no matter whether it follows the pattern of seasons of the southern or the northern hemisphere. Under the given circumstances it is necessary to emulate a suitable annual cycle with the aid of timers and dimmers. Once a successful pattern has been established, it should be followed without further changes since the animals are then difficult to "re-program" within a short period of time. I have made the best experiences with the following set-up: around mid-January all feeding is stopped, but water remains available. The illumination is reduced by one hour per day, until only the natural daylight from the window is left at the end of January. The animals become increasingly inactive during this time and leave their shelters only sporadically. Following a thorough health check only those skinks in perfect condition are translocated into specially prepared, stackable plastic containers. These boxes measure 50 × 40 × 30 cm and are filled for about one third with fine, dry beechwood shavings. A tubular piece of cork bark forms a shelter in every container. I keep on making water available in a small water bowl. An exchange of air is facilitated by mesh-covered openings of 10 × 5 cm in the side and back walls of the container. Two days later these boxes are brought into a cellar with temperatures of between 13 and 16°C. Every box is checked two or three times per week. Skinks that have not buried themselves in the substrate or hide in their shelter after one week are brought back into their terraria. Another attempt then follows one week later, but if the specimen then still does not calm down, I abandon the thought of it hibernating and continue with the annual rhythm without hibernation.

## Reproduction

The males rest for about five weeks and then move back into illuminated terraria. The females complete their hibernation ten to fourteen days later.

One week later, once daylight hours and temperatures have been gradually raised to normal levels, males and females are allowed their first encounters.

Right after their hibernation the males are particularly agile and cruise their terraria with intense tongue flicking. If a female is then placed into a male's terrarium, it is immediately tested with the tongue and pursued. If the female is ready to mate, it will slowly walk in front of the male for some time. The latter will then try from the side to place a mating bite in the nape region of the female. If he succeeds in doing so, he will bend his body into a horseshoe shape and push it from the opposite side under that of the female in order to connect their cloacae. The hind leg facing the female is then always placed on her base of the tail and the hemipenis of the same side inserted. This position is subsequently held motionlessly for several minutes. I have observed a maximum of two copulations per day, but a preference for a mating from any particular side was never apparent. Following a mating the partners do not display any of the aggression quite normally exhibited when specimens encounter one another outside the mating season. Just to the contrary I have often seen the animals basking right next to each other. Some days later the calm and rather passive behavior of the female subsides and the male is chased away with bites. This is the time to separate the animals again and return to their individual keeping. I have as yet been unable to note a true bonding of a pair or a preference for a particular female. Another female willing to mate was tested by means of tongue flicking and accepted right thereafter.

## Pregnancy

A successful mating leads to a slight change in the female's subsequent behavior. She will now spend more time under the spot lamp and have an increased appetite. I respond to this by feeding these females three or four times a week ad libitum. With the gravidity progressing the females will appear increasingly roundish, starting anterior to the hind legs, and the subsequent space requirements within the body cavity leads to a more labored working of the breathing musculature in the shoulder girdle and rib cage. Gravid females now have to breathe with outright pumping motions, and walking and chasing food is obviously much harder now. During this period the females may actually double their body mass, with one fully grown female weighing 783 g shortly before giving birth to her ten babies.

## Birth

The approaching end of pregnancy makes itself known by a decreasing appetite and an increasing restlessness. Females nearing full term roam their terraria and ingest large amounts of substrate until such is excremented with nearly no fecal components. The actual birth is then initiated by S-shaped writhing movements of the body with the tail being lifted off the ground slightly, whilst the hind legs are extended forward and do not touch the ground. Then the cloaca opens and a small amount of fluid is released, followed by the baby, head first. One labor contraction produces the baby up to about midbody, another then completes the birth inclusive of the attached placenta. The baby is independent right from its birth and will consume the attached placenta; thereafter it will hide somewhere in the terrarium. Within the next 2.5 hours more babies are born. Their heads appear disproportionately large, their bodies elongated, and the tails thin and short. The juveniles are 15.4 cm long on average and weigh 16.4 g. Their color pattern corresponds fully with that of their parents. In one case I was able to leave them with their mother for three weeks without the latter pursuing her offspring.

## Raising

A few hours after their birth the small blue-tongued skinks will have shed their skins. They are usually raised in a separate terrarium which offers the same conditions as those of the parental specimens. Food, in the form of crickets or fruit porridge, is accepted on the second or third day for the first time. During feeding a pronounced jealousy over food may surface with the small skinks biting each other. As this has led to damaged tails in the past they are now fed individually. This ensures perfect control and a purposeful supply with vitamins and minerals, but, on the other hand, it is rather time consuming. Provided with sufficient amounts of a balanced diet the young grow very rapidly. From month three through six their changing of the teeth can be witnessed. Following a brief swelling of the lower jaw region the large molar will fall out, and a new one will appear within the next few weeks. With the completion of their first year of life the young measure about 38 cm in total length and weigh 300 g on average. I know of three juveniles which developed rickets-based alterations to the vertebral column during their growth. Whether these were caused by inappropriate husbandry conditions of the parents or mistakes made in the raising of the young could not be clarified.

My young blue-tongued skinks are not hibernated in their first winter. This certainly lead to a more rapid growth, but whether it also causes the animals to mature earlier, I cannot as yet say.

## Literature

BARTLETT, R. D. (1984): Notes on the captive reproduction of the Australian skink, *Tiliqua nigrolutea*. – British Herpetological Society Bulletin, 10: 34–35.

BUSTARD, R. (1970): Australian Lizards. – Sydney, London (William Collins Ltd.), 158 pp.

COGGER, H. G. (1979): Reptiles and Amphibiens of Australia. – Reed, Sydney, 608 pp.

– (1983): Zoological Catalogue of Australia, Vol. 1: Amphibia and Reptilia. – Netley, South Australia (Griffin Press Ltd.)

EHMANN, H. (1992): Encyclopedia of Australian Animals : Reptiles. – Angus & Robertson Publishers Pty Limited, NSW, North Ryde, 495 pp.

GREER, A. E. (1989): The biology and evolution of Australian lizards. – Surey Beatty & Sons PTY Limited, NSW, Chipping Norton, 264 pp.

HAUSCHILD, A. & P. GASSNER (1995): Skinke im Terrarium. – Landbuch-Verlag, Hannover, 197 S.

HORNER, P. (1991): Skinks of the Northern Territory. – NT Museum Handbook Series, 2, Darwin, 174 pp.

HOSER, R.T. (1989): Australian Reptiles & Frogs. – Pierson & Co., NSW, Mosman, 238 pp.

JENKINS, R. & R. BARTELL (1980): A Field Guide to Reptiles of the Australian High Country. – Inkata Press, Melbourne, 278 pp.

JONES, S. (1987): A report on a reproducible and sustainable system for the captive propagation of the genus *Tiliqua* GRAY, 1825. – British Herpetological Society Symposium Proceedings: 17–25.

KLINGELHÖFFER, W. (1957): Terrarienkunde. Bd. III, Echsen. – Alfred Kernen Verlag, Stuttgart, 264 S.

SCHOOLDERMAN, G. (1994): Verzorging en voortplanting van de Australische Blauwtongskink (*Tiliqua scincoides intermedia*). – Lacerta, 52(4): 91–94.

SHEA, G. M. (1992): The systematics and reproduction of bluetongued lizards of the genus *Tiliqua* (Squamata: Scincidae). – Department of Veterinary Anatomy, University of Sydney, 4 Vols.

– (1993): The male reproductive cycle of the Eastern Blue-tongued Lizard *Tiliqua scincoides scincoides* ( Squamata: Scincidae). – Pp. 397–403 in LUNNEY, D. & D. AYERS (edts): Herpetology in Australia. A diverse discipline. – Transactions of the Royal Zoological Society of New South Wales, 414 pp.

STORR, G. M., L. A. SMITH & R. E. JONSTONE (1981): Lizards of Western Australia, Vol. I: Skinks. – University of Western Australia Press, Nedlands, 200 pp.

SWAN, G. (1990): A Field Guide to the Snakes and Lizards of New South Wales. – Three Sisters Productions, NSW, Winmalee, 224 pp.

SWANSON, S. (1976): Lizards of Australia. – Angus & Robertson Book, NSW, North Ryde, 80 pp.

TURNER, G. (1996): Some litters of the Blue-tongued skink *Tiliqua scincoides scincoides* (Scincidae). – Herpetofauna, Sydney, 26(2): 39–47.

WAITE, E. R. (1929): The Reptiles and Amphibians of South Australia. – North Terrace, Adelaide (Harrsion Weir, Government Printer).

WORRELL, E. (1963): Reptiles of Australia. - Sydney (Angus & Robertson), 207 pp.

Author's address
Dr. med. Thomas Unverzagt
Dammstr. 23
47119 Duisburg, Germany

# The New Guinea bluetongue, *Tiliqua gigas* (Schneider, 1801): Ecology and review of the subspecies, with the description of the subspecies *Tiliqua gigas evanesces* Shea, 2000

Glenn M. Shea

**Key words: Reptilia: Sauria: Scincidae: *Tiliqua gigas: T. g. gigas, T. g. keyensis, T. g. evanescens,* systematics, Indonesia, New Guinea, reproduction**

The New Guinea bluetongue, *Tiliqua gigas,* inhabits a vast distribution range that is considerably fragmented by islands and mountain ranges, and extends over more than 1600 km from the east of Indonesia to eastern Papua New Guinea. It is therefore little surprising that this species is fairly variable as to its color pattern and size. This has led to the recognition of two subspecies, described long ago, viz. the nominate subspecies *Tiliqua gigas gigas* and *T. g. keyensis.* It was, however, not until the publication of the original version of this book (2000) that a third subspecies, the southern New Guinea bluetongue, *Tiliqua gigas evanescens,* was defined by SHEA. This necessitated the compilation of a catalogue of reference specimens which some readers may want to pass by, but which is of substantial value for the expert. With New Guinea bluetongues being distributed exclusively outside of the "traditional" distribution range of the genus *Tiliqua,* they received hardly any attention from the otherwise lively research of the Australian herpetological community. This has resulted in *Tiliqua gigas* usually being only mentioned in collection lists, and few publications exist that provide detailed information on the exact geographical distribution and the ecology of this species. As far as possible, the existing data has been taken into consideration for the following paragraphs.

**Fig. 1** Neotype of *Scincus gigas* Schneider, 1801, collected by Felix Kopstein on Ambon in 1923

Photograph: G. Shea

**Fig. 2** *Tiliqua g. gigas* from Seram.                                   Photograph: F. B. Yuwono

## 1. The northern New Guinea bluetongue, *Tiliqua gigas gigas*

The northern New Guinea bluetongue is a relatively small, dark subspecies occurring in the Maluka Islands (formerly the Moluccas), west of New Guinea, and along the north coast and adjacent islands of New Guinea from the Vogelkop east to Huon Peninsula. In the Maluka Islands, it has been recorded from Ambon, Saparau, Seram (formerly Ceram), Misool, Ternate, Halmaheira and Morotai Islands. Along the north coast of New Guinea, it has been found on Doom, Japen (formerly Jobi), Biak, Seleo and Karkar Islands. On mainland New Guinea, it is known from sea level up to an altitude of about 500 m, and up to 40 km inland. Little is known of the habitat preferences of this subspecies. On Karkar Island, it has been found in secondary forests, plantations and scattered rainforest patches, sheltering in piles of coconut husks (SHEA 1982, 1992, O'SHEA 1991, 1994). One museum specimen from mainland New Guinea was found in a eucalypt planta-

tion with dense grass ground cover, while one from Halmaheira was collected in primary rainforest (SHEA 1992).

Mature males of this subspecies have snout-vent lengths of 212-288 mm (mean 244.4 mm, n = 34), while mature females are slightly larger, with SVLs of 217-295 mm (mean 256.6 mm, n = 35). Possibly related to its distribution over a number of islands, there is much geographic variation in this subspecies (SHEA 1992). Among the more obvious variations are the following: Populations from the northern Maluka islands (Ternate, Halmaheira, Misool) tend to attain larger sizes than other populations, with 9 of 20 specimens seen from these islands having a SVL greater than 270 mm, but only 14 of 154 lizards from other parts of the range having SVLs in excess of 257 mm. Halmaheira lizards frequently have a striped belly pattern (4 of 7 lizards examined), a feature otherwise only seen on the adjacent Vogelkop (5 of 34 lizards). Paired posterior loreals were present in 5 of 7 Halmaheira lizards, but elsewhere only in 5 of 203. The ten individuals examined from Ter-

**Fig. 3** Habitat of *Tiliqua g. gigas* at Wardo Falls on Biak Island    Photo: C. Langner

**Fig. 4** *Tiliqua g. gigas* at Wardo Falls on Biak Island    Photo: C. Langner

nate had fewer presubocular, postsubocular and supralabial scales, but more subocular scales than other populations.

Lizards from the southern Maluka islands show other pecularities. Those from Ambon, Saparau, Seram and Misool commonly have the parietals divided into an anterior and posterior scale (25 of 36 specimens), a feature otherwise only seen at low frequencies on the adjacent mainland. Numbers of paravertebral and subcaudal scales are also relatively high in these islands, and Ambon and Seram lizards are often very dark, with the pale areas obscured by dark clouding. There are also differences between adjacent islands. Ambon lizards generally have fewer supralabial scales and dark bands than those from neighboring Seram.

At the eastern end of the distribution, lizards from Karkar Island and the adjacent mainland show a reduction in size of the anterior supraciliaries, together with fusion to other scales.

Despite this extensive variation, all populations have a generally similar intensity and form of color pattern and body proportions. Dorsal ground color is olive brown to golden brown with 6-10 narrow, dark, transverse bands on the body and 11-18 dark bands on the tail. On the nape is a prominent dark vertebral streak up to three-quarters of a scale wide. The head shields are usually dark spotted or marbled, especially along the margins of the scales. Both fore- and hindlimbs are black above, with or without a few small yellow spots.

The earliest formal naming of this subspecies was by SCHNEIDER (1801), who considered that three earlier mentions, by BODDAERT (1783), GEVERS (1787) and HOUTTUYN (1787), referred to the one species, which he named *Scincus gigas* (all skinks known at the time were placed in the genus *Scincus*). In fact, the description by BODDAERT (1783) refers to a large skink from Ambon, that by GEVERS (1787) to a banded skink from Ambon, and that by HOUTTUYN (1787) to a large, banded skink. The specimens on which these three earlier accounts are based are not traceable today (the collections of GEVERS and HOUTTUYN were dispersed by auction in 1787, and searches of the major modern museum collections in Europe have not located these bluetongues). In the absence of specimen material, it is not possible to confirm that the three very brief accounts describe the same species. In order to stabilize the application of the name, I designated (SHEA 2000) as neotype for *Scincus gigas* SCHNEIDER, 1801, the specimen 5197a, in the Nationaal Natuurhistorisch Museum, Leiden. This is the larger of two specimens under this number. This specimen (Fig. 1), a female with an SVL of 241 mm, collected by Felix KOPSTEIN on January 18, 1923, on Ambon, is typical of the species and subspecies to which the name has been applied by previous authors.

Although New Guinea bluetongues have frequently been kept and bred in captivity, much of the literature does not indicate the original sources of the lizards, and hence it is not possible to identify the subspecies to which most accounts refer. It is probable, though, that most refer to the northern subspecies, which has been more common in the pet trade. Based on the dissection of museum specimens, litter size in this subspecies is from 2 to 14 (mean 7.1, n = 18). Litter sizes from captive animals have ranged from 1 to 12 (BARTLETT 1984, SCHMIDT 1979, RICHES 1988, SHEA 1992 and references therein). Small females generally have small litters, although both large and small litters were found in large females (SHEA 1992). Newborn young usually measure between 81 and 96 mm SVL (SHEA 1992), although they may be as small as 76 mm (RICHES 1988). Although RICHES (1988) considered his breeding pair to be unusually small, they are of similar size to wild caught sexually mature lizards.

Museum specimens do not give an indication of a fixed reproductive season. Enlarged ovarian follicles were seen in lizards collected in June (n = 1) and October (n = 1), and developing oviductal embryos in females collected in

**Fig. 5** *Tiliqua gigas keyensis*, specimen No. 5467 in the Museum of National History, Basel, Switzerland
Photograph: G. Shea

January (n = 1), May (n = 2), August (n = 2) and October (n = 4). One wild caught gravid female gave birth in October (SHEA 1982). However, as all of the eight adult females collected between June and October were either vitellogenic or gravid, while six of nine mature females collected at other times of the year were not reproductive, there is a suggestion that reproduction may occur mostly in the dry season. Captive animals in Europe have been observed mating in between March and June and in October, while litters have been born in March, August, November and December (SCHMIDT 1979, RICHES 1988).

## 2. The Kei Islands bluetongue *(Tiliqua gigas keyensis)*

The existence of bluetongues on the Aru and Kei Islands, off the south coast of Irian Jaya, was first noted by DORIA (1874) and BOULENGER (1887), who reported on material collected in those island groups by the Italian explorer Odoardo BECCARI and the "Challenger" Oceanographic Expedition, respectively. However, it was not until 1894 that the population on the Kei Islands was described as taxonomically distinct, by OUDEMANS (1894), who examined two individuals collected by the Wertheim Expedition of 1888, at least one of which was kept alive for some time at Amsterdam Zoo. Further specimens from the Kei Islands were described by ROUX (1910), who altered the subspecies name to *keiensis,* based on the spelling of the island group name most common at the time. However, as the spelling Key Islands was in use at the time of the original description, the spelling *keyensis* must be maintained (SHEA 1992). Bluetongues from the Aru Islands were identified as this subspecies by SHEA (1992).

The Kei Islands bluetongue is most similar in size and scalation to the southern New Guinea bluetongue *(Tiliqua gigas evanescens),* but has a distinctive adult coloration (Fig. 5). Its dorsal color is pale gray to yellowish brown, with the individual scales often having brown bases and darker brown spots at the free posterior edges. Darker bands are present on most individuals, at least on the body, but are usually obscured by fine pale marbling, which may be confined to the edges of dark markings, or may completely cover the dorsal surface. The ventral sides of body and tail are usually mottled or streaked with brown, the throat either immaculate or with a few brown streaks.

Little is known about this subspecies. The Kei and Aru Islands have been described as covered by dense rainforest (HARTERT 1901, MERTON 1910, BARBOUR 1912, SCHODDE & MATHEWS 1977), and the Aru Islands are mostly composed of limestone (FAIRBRIDGE 1953). It is presumed that the Kei Islands bluetongue has a similar ecology to other subspecies of *Tiliqua gigas.* Among the few museum specimens of this subspecies are two gravid females, one (SVL 285 mm) with ten enlarged ovarian follicles, the other (SVL 271 mm) with seven developing embryos (SHEA 1992). Unfortunately, the date of collection of these two lizards is not recorded.

## 3. The southern New Guinea bluetongue *(Tiliqua gigas evanescens* Shea, 2000)

The distribution of the northern New Guinea bluetongue *(Tiliqua gigas gigas)* in New Guinea extends east to the northwestern side of the Huon Peninsula. On the southeastern side of it (Lae, Finschhafen), the bluetongues are noticeably different in size, coloration and scalation. This form occurs in the lowlands and adjacent foothills of eastern and southern New Guinea in the form of three, probably discontinuous, populations: from Huon Peninsula to the vicinity of Popondetta and Mt. Lamington along the northeast coast; between Kubuna and Hula in the southeast, and in the Western Province and adjacent areas of Irian Jaya. It is also present on several islands off the northeast and east coast: Los Negros, Lou and Manus Is. in the Admiralty Is.; Goodenough, Fergusson and Normanby Is. in the D'Entrecasteaux Group; Tanpora I., and possibly the Trobriand Islands. It occurs up to 235 km inland at Derongo, and altitudinally from sea level up to at least 700 m at Haveri, but apparently does not occur above 1000 m (PERNETTA 1983).

Because of the abrupt nature of the morphological discontinuity between the northern New Guinea bluetongue and the southeastern form at Huon Peninsula, the latter form is treated as taxonomically distinct. However, the populations in the northern part of the Western Province, although geographically continuous with the typical southeastern form in the lower Fly River area, and geographically separated from the northern New Guinea bluetongue by the central cordillera, do show some resemblance to the northern New Guinea bluetongue in coloration. Because of the apparent intermediacy of this population, the southeastern taxon was described as a new subspecies, *Tiliqua gigas evanescens* Shea, 2000, the southern New Guinea bluetongue:

**Holotype:** Australian Museum R 116664, Port Moresby, Papua New Guinea. An adult female, collected by John PERNETTA (Fig. 6).

**Paratypes** (unless otherwise stated, all localities are in Papua New Guinea)**:** Australian Museum, Sydney: R 9873, R 9875, Imanaturi, Mt. Lamington; R 9962, R 9976, Mt. Lamington; R 10435, Salamaua; R 10470, Trobriand Is.; R 11412, New Guinea; R 14430, 2 mi. S Tau Ck., Era R.; R 19307, Pisik, Lou I.; R 21188, Balimo; R 21189, Pt. Moresby; R 21401, Konedobu; R 24287, R 93219, Lake Murray; R 40709, Morehead; R 93216, R 93220-23, Wipim; R 97572-73, Los Negros I.; R 122490, R 122688, Waro; American Museum of Natural History, New York: R 41627, Fergusson I.; R 42372, Goodenough I.; R 57532, probably

**Fig. 6** Holotype of *Tiliqua gigas evanescens* from Port Moresby, Papua New Guinea    Photograph: G. Shea

upper Fly River; R 57896-97, Dogwa, nr. Daru; R 58405, Tarara; R 59183, Kubana; R 59936-37, Lake Daviumbo; R 59940, Sturt I., Fly River; R 74337, Peria Ck. crossing, Kwagira R.; R 82551-52, Laloki Stn.; R 82553-54, R 82672, Pt. Moresby; R 92349, Oomsis Ck.; R 95879, Lae; R 103624, Itikinumu Plantation; R 103974, Lake Murray; R 103975-76, R 105865, Wipim; R 107238, Maka, Lake Murray; R 111745, Morehead; Natural History Museum, London: 95.4.26.17, Fergusson I.; 97.12.10.20, Hula; 97.12.10.21, Haveri, 2300 ft.; 1904.3.17.6, Dinawa, Owen Stanley Ranges; 1935.5.10.29, Kokoda, 1200 ft; 1980.521, nr. Buso; 1987.894, Pt. Moresby; Bernice P. Bishop Museum, Honolulu: 3471-72, Singauwa R., vicinity of Lae; 3797, Soputa Swamp, Popondetta; 3855, Jumbora Plantation; Field Museum of Natural History, Chicago: 42586, Manus I.; Museum of Comparative Zoology, Harvard: 49242, Finschafen; 65211, Mabudawan; 65213, Madiri; 65214, Pt. Moresby; 65222, 156445, Konedobu; 101334, Sogeri, 2000 ft.; 101335-36, Uraru; 101523, Sapphire Ck., Sogeri Rd.; 101987, 2 mi. E Ruana Falls, Sogeri Rd.; 121532-33, Maka, Lake Murray; 124455, Derongo; 124456, Abam, Oriomo R.; 124457-60, 124464, 137286, Wipim; 124463, 130348, Lake Murray; 124465-66, Bobos I., Lake Murray; 137262, Zim; 137549, Emeti; Museum of Victoria, Melbourne: D2970, no locality; D 5942, Bora Bada; D 14411-12, Wipim; D 49990, Mt. Bosavi; Naturhistorisches Museum, Wien: 10694, Pt. Moresby; Queensland Museum, Brisbane: J 1289, no locality; J 14055, St. Joseph's R.; J 32967, Moitaka, Pt. Moresby; Nationaal Natuurhistorisch Museum, Leiden: 24317, 24339-40, Koerik, Irian Jaya; 24350-51, Tanah Merah, Irian Jaya; South Australian Museum, Adelaide: R 1639, Tanpora I.; R 11419, R 11447, R 13582, Wipim; United States National Museum, Washington: 119487, Gusika; 121264, Manus I.; 195732, Balimo;

195733, Abam, Oriomo R.; 195734, Emeti; 213389, Konedobu; 213390, Makapa Village, Aramia R.; 213391, Ali Village, Aramia R.; Zoologisches Museum, Berlin, 14192, Haveri; 18865, New Guinea; 22280-81, German New Guinea; 27995a-b, Sattelberg.

**Diagnosis:** A large subspecies of *Tiliqua gigas,* differing from all other *Tiliqua* in the combination of primary temporals absent; last supralabial and lower secondary temporal paired, resulting in five scales between lip and parietal; two supraoculars in contact with the frontal; supralabials modally eight; free edge of dorsal body scales angulate; midbody scales 27-36 (mean 31.5, n = 121); paravertebral scales from parietal to last scale anterior to level of anterior margin of hindlimbs 49-63 (mean 55.0, n = 120); subcaudal scales 47-64 (mean 57.2, n = 89); forelimbs relatively long (mean forelimb length/snout-vent length 22.8%, n = 116); tail long (mean tail length/snout-vent length 69.3%, n = 86); dorsal pattern strongly banded in juveniles, but tending to disappear with age in most populations; dark margins to head shields, when present, largely restricted to margins of more median shields; body venter usually uniformly pale or with variably expressed brown variegations, and throat usually immaculate.

This subspecies differs from *Tiliqua g. gigas* in attaining a larger size (SVL up to 343 mm, vs. 315 mm, rarely above 270 mm except in extreme west of distribution), usually possessing four elongate temporal scales between supralabials and parietal (95.0% bilaterally, n = 120) (vs. usually fewer due to variable fusion of some scales in this series: 30.3%, n = 195, with four scales in series bilaterally; 60.5%

**Fig. 7** Differences in the pholidosis of the neotype of *Tiliqua g. gigas* (left) and the holotype of *T. g. evanescens* (right)
Drawing: G. Shea

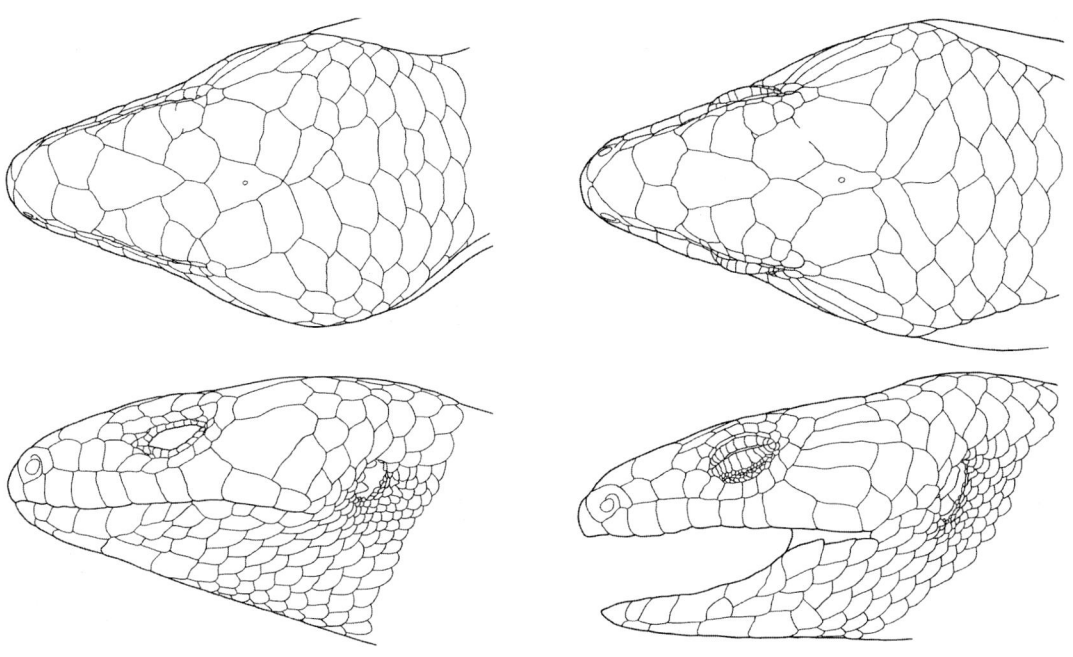

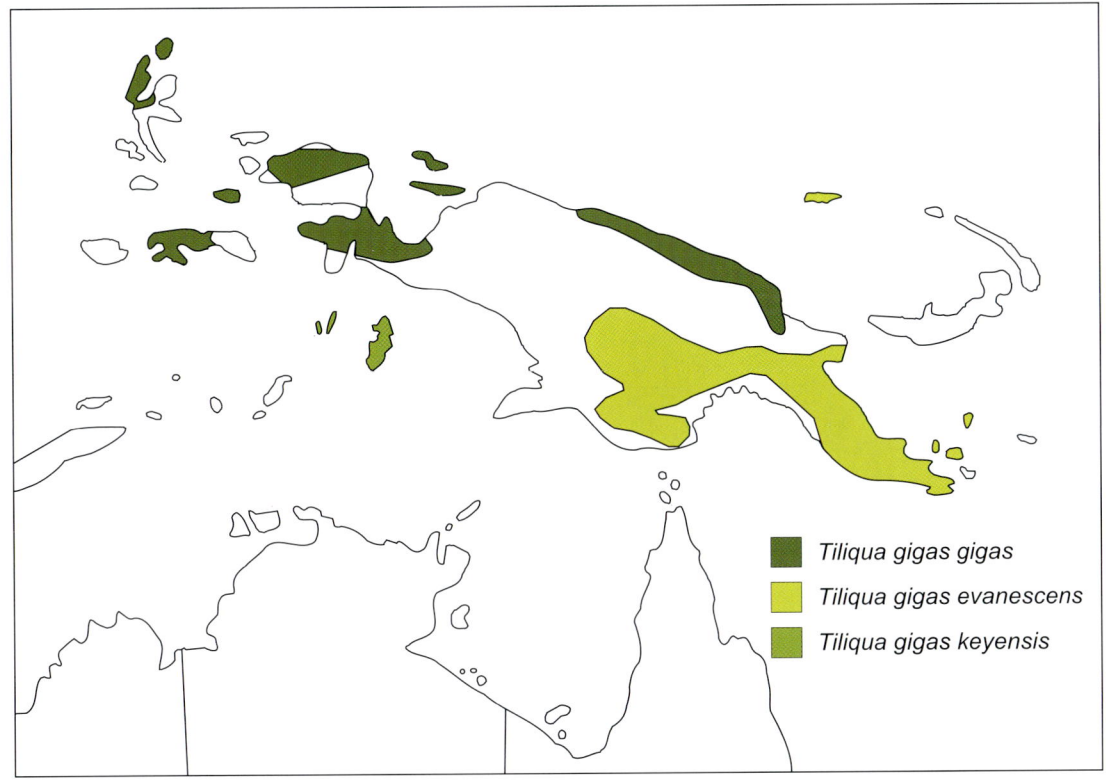

**Fig. 8**   Geographical distribution of *Tiliqua gigas* and its subspecies

with three or fewer bilaterally), and dark elements of colour pattern less distinct in adults (head shields not or narrowly edged with black, vs. usually strongly variegated black margins, dark markings often so extensive that head shields are completely dark and light variegated; body venter usually either immaculate pale or with variably expressed light brown variegations vs. usually with extensive dark brown to black markings; throat usually immaculate, sometimes with a few dark spots or flecks vs. usually with brown to black spots; forelimb dorsum usually pale with darker variegations, vs. dark brown to black, either immaculate or with a few pale spots).

*Tiliqua g. evanescens* is similar to *T. g. keyensis* in adult size and the number of temporal scales, but differs in not showing the extensive pale mottling of the latter subspecies, and in having more strongly angulated free margins to the dorsal body scales. The tail is a little shorter, the forelimbs are longer and the head is narrower and shallower than in *T. g. keyensis* at all body sizes, although growth is strongly allometric, preventing simple comparisons (SHEA 1992).

**Etymology:** The subspecies name is from the Latin evanescere, meaning loss of colors, alluding to the reduction in color pattern in adults of most populations.

The southern New Guinea bluetongue is known from a number of habitats, from grassy flats adjacent to a coral cliff, areas cleared and planted with native crops, and open grassland and savanna, through to dense rainforest (LOVERIDGE 1948, O'SHEA 1991, F. PARKER pers. comm.; data associated with specimens in Bernice P. Bishop Museum). In other respects, it seems to be similar in behavior to *Tiliqua scincoides,* being secretive, usually found under and in decaying logs, piles of vegetation and under sheets of iron, or occasionally seen basking in the early morning (F. PARKER pers. comm.).

Mature males have SVLs of 245-323 mm (mean 290.2 mm, n = 26), with the minimum size at maturity possibly a little smaller, while mature females have SVLs of 237-343 mm (mean 292.4 mm, n = 34). From the size of testes in museum specimens, the male reproductive cycle peaks in the dry season (July-August), with a decrease in testis size in September-October. Females also appear to ovulate in the dry season, about August, with females collected be-

Opposite from above
**Fig. 10**  Lowland forest on Normanby Island, habitat of *T. g. evanescens*
**Fig. 11**  *Tiliqua g. evanescens,* juvenile, from Normanby Island          Photographs: P. German

tween mid-November and June having small ovarian follicles, those collected in July and early August having larger ones, and most of those collected between mid-August and early November carrying embryos (SHEA 1992). Fully developed young were found in a dead-on-road female on September 25, (ROOM 1974), while F. PARKER (pers. comm.) observed litters being born between October and February. As seven of nine mature females collected in September and October were gravid, reproduc-

**Fig. 9**  *Tiliqua g. evanescens* from Port Moresby, Papua New Guinea          Photograph: G. Shea

tion is probably annual in the wild. The interval between the inferred time of mating and the usual time of birth is about three months, i.e. similar to other bluetongue species.

Although the original sources of most captive animals are not reported, making it impossible to determine the identity of most captive breeding records of *T. gigas,* two reports (JONES 1987, LAPTHORNE & LAPTHORNE 1987) are based on Papuan animals, which must be of this subspecies. The timing of mating and birth in these captives is not synchronous with that of wild populations, and gestation is also reported to be much longer.

Litter size of wild populations is 4-13 (mean 7.6, n = 17; SHEA 1992), with reports from captive animals of similarly sized litters (JONES 1987, LAPTHORNE & LAPTHORNE 1987). The size of young at birth is about 100-120 mm SVL.

## Literature

BARBOUR, T. (1912): A contribution to the zoögeography of the East Indian islands. – Memoirs of the Museum of Comparative Zoölogy 44(1): 1–203 + 8 pls.

BARTLETT, R.D. (1984): Notes on the captive reproduction of the Australian skink, *Tiliqua nigrolutea.* – British Herpetological Society Bulletin (10): 34–35.

BODDAERT, P. (1783): Specimen Novae Methodi distinguendi Serpentia. – Nova Acta Physico-Medica Academiae Caesareae Leopoldino Carolinae Naturae Curiosorum 7: 12–16.

BOULENGER, G.A. (1887): Catalogue of Lizards in the British Museum (Natural History). Vol. III. Lacertidae, Gerrhosauridae, Scincidae, Anelytropidae, Dibamidae, Chamaeleontidae. – Trustees of the British Museum, London, 575 pp. + XL pls.

DORIA, G. (1874): Enumerazione dei rettili raccolti Dal Dott. O. Beccari in Amboina, alle isole Aru ed alle isole Kei durante gli anni 1872–73. – Annali del Museo Civico di Storia Naturale di Genova 6: 325–357 + Taf. X–XI.

FAIRBRIDGE, R.W. (1953): The Sahul Shelf, northern Australia; its structure and geological relationships. – Journal of the Royal Society of Western Australia 37: 1–33.

GEVERS, A. (1787): Museum Geversianum sive index rerum naturalium continens instructissimam copiam pretiosissimorum omnis generis ex tribus regnis naturae objectorum quam dum in vivis erat magna diligentia multaque cura comparavit vir amplissimus. – P. & J. Holsteyn, Rotterdam, IV + 659 S.

GORSEMAN, P.D. (1998) *Tiliqua gigas*, de Nieuw-Guinea-blauwtongskink. – Lacerta 57(2): 54–63.

GRÜNEWALD, G., E. HÖLLER & D. STRANZ (1982): Länder und Klima: Asien / Australien. – In Brockhaus Texte und Tabellen. Verlag Brockhaus, Wiesbaden, 240 S.

HARTERT, E. (1901): On the birds of the Key and South-East Islands, and of Ceram-Laut. – Novitates Zoologicae 8(1): 1–5.

HOUTTUYN, M. (1787): Catalogus Van eene uitmuntende Verzameling van allerley Sorrt van Dieren en Dierlyke Zaaken, Tot opheldering der Natuurlyke Historie In meer dan dertig jaaren vergaderd en, volgens het Samenstel van den wydberoemden Linnaeus, in orde geschikt. – Amsterdam, VIII + 170 S.

JONES, S. (1987): A report on a reproducible and sustainable system for the captive propagation of the genus *Tiliqua* Gray 1825. – Pp. 17–25 in COOTE, J. (Hg.). Reptiles: proceeding of the 1986 U.K. Herpetological Societies symposium on captive breeding. – British Herpetological Society, London, 97 pp.

KOPSTEIN, F. (1926): Reptilien von den Molukken und den benachbarten Inseln. – Zoologische Mededeelingen, Leiden, 9(2/3): 71–112.

LAPTHORNE, T.A. & A.A. LAPTHORNE (1987): Some notes on the captive reproduction of the New Guinea blue-tongued skink. – SWHS [South Western Herpetological Society, U.K.] Journal 1(1): 32–33.

LOVERIDGE, A. (1948): New Guinean reptiles and amphibians in the Museum of Comparative Zoölogy and United States National Museum. – Bulletin of the Museum of Comparative Zoölogy 101(2): 305–430.

MERTON, H. (1910): Forschungsreise in den

südöstlichen Molukken. – Abhandlungen herausgegeben von der Senckenbergischen Naturforschenden Gesellschaft 33(1–2): 1–208.

O'SHEA, M. (1991): The reptiles of Papua New Guinea. – British Herpetological Society Bulletin (37): 15–32.

– (1994): The herpetofauna of coconut husk piles on Kar Kar Island, Madang Province, Papua New Guinea. – ASRA (Association for the Study of Reptilia and Amphibia) Journal 1994: 51–72.

OUDEMANS, J.T. (1894): Eidechsen und Schildkröten. – S. 127–146 in SEMON, R. (Hg.): Zoologische Forschungsreisen in Australien und dem Malayischen Archipel. Band 5. – Denkschriften der Medizinisch-Naturwissenschaftlichen Gesellschaft zu Jena. Band 8., 778 S. + LXVII Taf..

PERNETTA, J.C. (1983): The wildlife of the Purari catchment. – S. 253–268 in PETR, T. (Hg.): The Purari – tropical environment of a high rainfall river basin. – Monographiae Biologicae (51). W. Junk, The Hague, 624 pp.

RICHES, B. (1988): Unplanned breeding of bluetongue skinks. – The Herptile 13(2): 52–54.

ROOM, P.M. (1974): Lizards and snakes from the Northern district of Papua, New Guinea. – British Journal of Herpetology 5(3): 438–446.

ROUX, J. (1910): Reptilien und Amphibien der Aru- und Kei-Inseln. – Abhandlungen herausgegeben von der Senckenbergischen Naturforschenden Gesellschaft 33(3): 211–247 + Taf. XIII–XIV.

SCHMIDT, A. (1979): Opdraet af *Tiliqua gigas*. Nordisk Herpetologisk Forening 22(10): 238–245.

SCHNEIDER, J.G. (1801): Historiae Amphibiorum naturalis et literariae. Fasciculus Secundus continens Crocodilos, Scincos, Chamaesauras, Boas, Pseudoboas, Elapes, Angues, Amphisbaenas et Caecilias. – F. Frommann, Jena, 364 S.

SCHODDE, R. & S.J. MATHEWS (1977): Contributions to Papuasian Ornithology V. Survey of the birds of Taam Island, Kai Group. – CSIRO Division of Wildlife Research Technical Paper (33): 1–29.

SHEA, G.M. (1992): The systematics and reproduction of bluetongue lizards of the genus *Tiliqua* (Squamata: Scincidae). – 4 Vols. Ph.D. thesis, University of Sydney.

– (1982): Insular range extensions for the New Guinea bluetongue, *Tiliqua gigas* (BODDAERT)(Lacertilia: Scincidae). – Herpetofauna 13(2): 7–12.

– (2000): Die Neuguinea-Blauzunge, *Tiliqua gigas* (SCHNEIDER, 1801): Ökologie und Übersicht über die Unterarten nebst Beschreibung einer neuen Unterart, *Tiliqua gigas evanescens* subsp. nov. – S. 177-189 in HAUSCHILD, A., R. HITZ, K. HENLE, G.M. SHEA & H. WERNING (Hrsg.): Blauzungenskinke. Beiträge zu *Tiliqua* und *Cyclodomorphus*. – Münster (Natur und Tier-Verlag), 287 S.

WOLTER, W. (1980): Unternehmen Kopfjäger. – Pietsch Verlag, Stuttgart, 189 S.

Author's address
Dr. Glenn M. Shea
Faculty of Veterinary Science
University of Sydney
New South Wales 2006
Australia

# Husbandry and reproduction of *Tiliqua gigas* (SCHNEIDER, 1801) in the terrarium

PAUL GASSNER

**Key words: Reptilia: Sauria: Scincidae: *Tiliqua gigas,* husbandry, reproduction**

With *Tiliqua gigas* not being affected by the Australian export ban, they are relatively easy to obtain. This has made them a rather unspectacular species whose popularity level among terrarium keepers fluctuates substantially. The periodically reduced demand is certainly a blessing for the populations in the wild. The keeper who, on the other hand, wants to inform himself about the specific husbandry conditions of the New Guinea bluetongue, will soon find out that there are also very few reports on this subject. Even in the more recent literature one finds, time and again, photographs of *Tiliqua gigas gigas* captioned "*Tiliqua scincoides*", although the nominate form of the New Guinea bluetongue is readily and with certainty identified by just two traits: a) the nape of the neck is marked with a relatively wide, black vertebral streak, and b) the ground color of the legs is very dark, usually black. As was mentioned before, *Tiliqua gigas gigas* is the most often available bluetongue for which reason the information contained in the following paragraphs refers mainly to the nominate subspecies.

## Housing

**Terrarium size:** Some countries have laws in effect that regulate the captive keeping of wild animals and these may also include minimum sizes for a terrarium. In Germany, for example, dimensions of $160 \times 100 \times 70$ cm ($l \times w \times h$) are prescribed for the keeping of one adult pair. Emphasis thus clearly lays on the ground space, although *T. gigas* climb well and their terrarium should not be lacking some low structures.

**Substrate:** Compared with other species of *Tiliqua, T. gigas* requires a slightly moister environment. However, with these animals inhabiting a wide variety of habitats and the point of origin being usually unknown, one cannot necessarily suppose a need for a moist substrate. To be on the safe side, one should therefore keep only one section of the ground slightly (!) moist and make available dry shelters as well as one with a raised moisture level among which the animals can choose for themselves. In general round-edged gravel for the aquarium (granulation 2-5 mm) is suitable for a substrate. Sharp-edged crushed gravel should never be used as it leads (with all bluetongues) to injuries of the soles of the feet which heal only with difficulty and often result in the loss of toes. Aquarium gravel has, however, a number of disadvantages: it is expensive, heavy, not easily disposed, and hardly absorbent. A more manageable substrate is therefore bark mulch which should contain only a minimum of fine, dust producing components. This is an inexpensive material that stores moisture well. The possibly most ideal substrate may turn out to be beechwood shavings which are easily obtained from pet shops or suppliers for butcheries. They are almost dust free, light, deodorizing, absorbent, relatively resistant to decomposition, but still compostable.

**Decoration:** Whole or halved tubes of cork bark are readily accepted as shelters, and so are earthenware ridging tiles which also have a semicircular cross section and by their massiveness provide the animals with a sense of safety. Each specimen should at least have one hiding place

190

available. Larger rocks or firmly secured rock build-ups serve as basking sites and assist with shedding, and also ensure that the claws are worn to a sufficient extent. Furthermore, some rough-barked, thick branches or roots can be installed as these are readily used for climbing. If you do not want to do without life plants, these should be placed where the animals cannot reach them, as otherwise they will be destroyed in no time by the skinks just climbing over them. A robust water bowl must not be wanting.

**Heating:** A mild, locally restricted underfloor heater (e.g. Thermolux 30 W) is recommendable. It is installed in a manner so that it covers part of the basking site and is switched on only during the day.

**Illumination:** As the terrarium is not all that high, a large number of types of lamps are suitable for its illumination. These include HQL lamps or fluorescent tubes with a spectral composition similar to daylight. A spot light furnished with a reflector serves for the heating of the basking site. Halogen flood lights have proved beneficial when it comes to very large terraria. These are available from DIY and hardware stores, and even those with a relatively low energy output of 150 W provide a good combination of heating and illumination effects.

**Temperatures:** The ground should offer a temperature of about 24°C while the air should be heated to between 24 and 30°C. The basking site may be up to 35°C warm, but must be locally restricted in order to allow the animals to escape the heat. At night the temperatures should decrease to 20-22°C.

**Humidity:** The natural habitats of the animals are marked by a mean relative humidity of more than 70% in the afternoon (GRÜNEWALD et al. 1982). This degree of constant humidity is not easy to maintain in large terraria and is usually achieved only by reducing the ventilation. As, however, *Tiliqua gigas* also does well at lower humidity levels, it may be an acceptable compromise to maintain only a humidity above 40% during the day, and mist the terrarium thoroughly in the morning before, and in the evening after,

the heaters and lights are switched on and off, respectively. This causes the humidity to rise to 70-80% at night and decrease again in the course of the day. GORSEMAN (1998) also noted that the animals appear to feel well at nightly humidity levels of up to 100%. If diseases of the breathing system are noted, the humidity must be raised also during the day.

**Diet:** "In the wild" large insects, small vertebrates, snails, worms, eggs, and sweet fruit make up the menu for the New Guinea bluetongue (LOVERIDGE 1946). This also forms the guideline for their alimentation in captivity. They will eagerly consume locusts, roaches, shrimps (soaked in tap water for a few hours to desalinate them), and pink mice are some examples. The absolute favorite food of *T. gigas* are June bugs (NIEDERMAIR pers. comm.) and snails which are cracked with a passion. The skinks also have a taste for sweet fruit, "skink pudding" (HAUSCHILD & GASSNER 1995), and mashed beef heart. Due to its high protein and low fiber contents the latter is mixed at a ratio of 1 : 1 with various types of vegetables, wild herbs and dog flakes. *T. gigas* also readily accepts mussels (KÜHN verbal comm.), but these should also be desalinated by soaking them in freshwater (one day, in the fridge, change water several times). Pure vegetable food is usually not accepted by *T. gigas*.

Adult New Guinea bluetongues are fed about twice per week. Juveniles of this species grow at a rapid rate and therefore require large amounts of food. They should receive food daily over their first few months, changing over to a rhythm of every other day later.

## Propagation under terrarium conditions

**Sexual dimorphism:** The best method of identifying the sexes of adult New Guinea bluetongues without the need to employ surgical means is to examine the base of the tail. In females the taper of the tail begins right behind the cloacal slit, whereas in males - due to the hemipenis pockets - the tail initially maintains its thickness, or even appears swollen, before it begins to taper a few centimeters farther back. A wider head, on the other hand, is no typical sign of a male in this species. For other methods of identifying the sexes refer to the relevant chapter in this book.

**Group composition:** New Guinea blue-tongued skinks are best kept in pairs throughout the year. A group comprising one male and two females will also live together in harmony in most cases, but it may happen that a weaker specimen is suppressed, does hardly venture out to bask, and also does not dare to try and secure itself some food. Such suppressed specimens must then be kept separated or matched with a new partner. Males are highly incompatible among each other, with signs of intermale aggression becoming apparent already at an age of just a few months. Fights are aimed at injuring the opponent.

**Initiating mating behavior:** *Tiliqua gigas* are native to geographical regions near the equator. It would therefore be unnatural to expose them to an annual cycle marked by distinct fluctuations in the number of daylight hours. Instead, the duration of daily illumination should be kept at 12 hours. Roughly described, the major portion of the distribution range of the New Guinea bluetongue has a permamoist rain forest climate without distinct dry seasons. Only the southern parts of New Guinea are marked by a several months long dry season during which also the temperatures decrease slightly. Accordingly, mating activities are induced by subjecting the lizards to a 4-6 week long period of rest at room temperature: illumination and heating are gradually reduced in the course of two weeks, and feeding is suspended. Heating and illumination remain switched off for the duration of the resting phase, and the moisture level is reduced. The animals may remain in their terraria, but should always have access to drinking water. With the supply of fresh feedstuffs that can be collected from the wild coming to a near hold in the European winter, it makes sense to let the resting period coincide with this time of the year. By

gradually returning to the normal husbandry conditions the period of rest is ended.

NIEDERMAIR (pers. comm.) experimentally inserted two resting periods in one year and so obtained two reproductive seasons, but admitted that this results in excessive wear on the female's part.

**Mating, pregnancy and birth:** About a fortnight after the completion of the resting period the first matings may be expected to occur. A mating can take from a few minutes (NIEDERMAIR pers. comm.) to one hour and a half (JONES 1987). Repeated mating ensures the fertilization of the matured egg cells of the female. The mating season is over after a maximum of two weeks. The gestation period is about 125 days (pers. obs.), NIEDERMAIR (pers. comm.) noted 120-140 days, and JONES (1987) even recorded 127-257 days, with the latter most certainly being an exception. Births appear to always take place in the early afternoon hours and may unfold over several hours. The number of babies born varies from three to seventeen, their lengths may range between 13 and 18 cm, and their body masses are about 16 g on average (JONES 1987, pers.

**Fig. 1** *Tiliqua gigas* mating in an terrarium
Photograph: A. Niedermair

**Fig. 2** *Tiliqua gigas* giving birth in a terrarium Photograph: A. Niedermair

**Fig. 3** *Tiliqua gigas* female with baby Photograph: A. Niedermair

obs., HAUSCHILD pers. comm.,
NIEDERMAIR pers. comm.).

**Raising of the young and maturity:** The young can be raised
under the conditions described
for the adults above. Their optimum husbandry, however, necessitates them to be separated from
their parents. Owing to their rapid
growth young *Tiliqua gigas* require sufficiently large amounts
of varying food (see above) and a
regular supply of minerals and vitamins in order to prevent deficiencies. Exposure to UV-radiation on a regular basis is a must,
otherwise rickets will rear its ugly
face!

One of my female skinks gave
birth to a litter of eight for the
first time at an age of only 13 months so that it
must have become mature at about nine months
of age. LAPTHORNE & LAPTHORNE (1987) even
indicated that *T. gigas* would mature as early
as on reaching six months of age. According
to JONES (1987) the reaching of maturity depends on the body size much rather than age
of a juvenile. He estimated an age of about 18
months for *T. gigas* living in the wild. Attempts
to regulate the growth by means of limiting the
food supply results in the juveniles to become
stunted which suggests that the high food requirements and rapid growth rate is a normal
feature of this species. Nevertheless should the
young skinks not be exposed to the strains
brought on by breeding earlier than at an age
of 18-24 months.

**Fig. 4** Juveniles of *Tiliqua gigas* in a terrarium  Photograph: A. Niedermair

## Literature

BUNDESMINISTERIUM FÜR ERNÄHRUNG, LANDWIRT-
SCHAFT UND FORSTEN (1997): Gutachten über die
Mindestanforderungen an die Haltung von
Reptilien vom 10. Januar 1997. – Inhaltlich
unveränderte Sonderausgabe der Deutschen
Gesellschaft für Herpetologie und Terrarienkunde
(DGHT) e.V., Rheinbach, 78 S.

GORSEMAN, P.D. (1998): *Tiliqua gigas*, de Nieuw-
Guinea-blauwtongskink. – Lacerta 57(2):54-63.

GRÜNEWALD, G., E. HÖLLER & D. STRANZ (1982):
Länder und Klima: Asien/Australien. – In
Brockhaus Texte und Tabellen. – Verlag Brockhaus, Wiesbaden. 240 S.

HAUSCHILD, A. & P. GAßNER (1995): Skinke im Terrarium. – Landbuch-Verlag, Hannover, 197 S.

JONES, S. (1987): A report on a reproducible and
sustainable system for the captive propagation of
the genus *Tiliqua* GRAY, 1825. – Pp. 17–25 in
COOTE, J. (Hg.). Reptiles: proceeding of the 1986
U.K. Herpetological Societies symposium on captive breeding. – British Herpetological Society,
London, 97 pp.

LAPTHORNE, T.A. & A.A. LAPTHORNE (1987): Some
notes on the captive reproduction of the New Guinea
blue-tongued skink. – SWHS [South Western Herpetological Society, U.K.] Journal 1(1): 32–33.

LOVERIDGE, A. (1946): Reptiles of the Pacific World.
– Museum of Comparative Zoology, Cambridge,
Mass., 259 pp.

Author's address
Dr. Paul Gassner
Universitätsstrasse 38
D-93053 Regensburg, Germany

# "New" blue-tongued skinks from Indonesia

ROBERT HITZ and ANDREE HAUSCHILD

**Key words: Reptilia: Sauria: Scincidae: *Tiliqua: Tiliqua gigas evanescens, Tiliqua scincoides chimaerea*, Irian Jaya, Merauke, Tanimbar Islands, Babar Islands, husbandry, breeding**

## Introduction

Other than on the Australian continent blue-tongued skinks of the genus *Tiliqua* are found only on New Guinea and surrounding islands, as well as on the easternmost islands of Indonesia. Until a few years ago all bluetongues from this region were undiscriminatingly assigned to the species *Tiliqua gigas*. In his studies of the systematics and reproduction of blue-tongued skinks, SHEA (1992) eventually realized that the populations native to the Tanimbar and Babar Islands were in fact a separate subspecies and described them as *Tiliqua scincoides chimaerea* in the original edition of this book (2000a).

It is quite obvious that in the light of the expansive distribution range occupied by *Tiliqua gigas gigas* and *Tiliqua gigas evanescens*, also described by SHEA in the original edition of this book (2000b), the amount of geographic variation must be vast. This explains that in the past blue-tongued skinks were time and again imported into Europe and the US from Papua New Guinea and Indonesia that were notable for their conspicuous color traits. Unfortunately, their exact points of origin usually remained a mystery. Owing to the very small numbers of specimens imported, all these enigmatic morphs subsequently became extinct again among terrarium keepers.

As a result of ever more strictly enforced laws of species preservation, the particularly popular Australian species of *Tiliqua* disappeared from the pet trade. In order to satisfy a still existing demand for blue-tongued skinks, imports from Indonesia, mainly into the US, but also occasionally into Europe, were used to try and fill the gap during the nineties. Especially the imports into the US came to include with some regularity and in more substantial numbers representatives of blue-tongued skinks originating from the Tanimbar Islands and specimens that were similar to *Tiliqua scincoides* from the southeast of Irian Jaya. Occasionally it is tried to label these animals as Australian bluetongues in order to justify higher prices.

The point of collection of animals imported via the international trade in animals is known only in very few cases. If the collection locality is known, the skinks can usually be assigned to one of the four subspecies dealt with below. If the origin is unknown or the information obtained not credible, the respective specimens have to be examined closely. An important aid in this task is the chapter "Identification aids for the lizard genus *Tiliqua* GRAY, 1825" by HAUSCHILD and HITZ in the present book. Sometimes, however, even an identification key will only reliably guide you to species level with some specimens (*T. gigas* or *T. scincoides*). The specimen at hand may in this case exemplify the normal variation within a subspecies, but there is also a chance for it to represent a hitherto unknown and undescribed subspecies. It should also always be borne in mind that some profit orientated breeder may have fooled you with a crossbreed. That the last mentioned alternative is not as far fetched as one would like to believe is shown by an observation relayed by PHILIPPEN (pers. comm. to the junior author) who found a larger number of gravid bluetongue females of various species in the collection of a

Jakarta based reptile dealer that were kept for breeding purposes and were not for sale.

This contribution is limited to information on the blue-tongued skinks of the Tanimbar and Babar Islands and the *T. scincoides*-like animals from the southeast of Irian Jaya. Hardly anything has been published on these lizards, and it was only as recently as in 1996 that WALLS provided some clues and a few photographs in his book on blue-tongued skinks. At present (2000) several homepages exist on the Internet which give some information on these lizards. It is therefore the goal of the authors to compile the existing data for the enthusiast and also provide basic information on their successful husbandry.

### *Tiliqua gigas evanescens*

Papua New Guinea:

Mainland: southeastern side of the Huon Peninsula (Finschhafen, Lae) along the northeast coast to Popondetta and Mt. Lamington. In the southeast between Kubuna and Hula (Port Moresby). In the south of the Western Province (Morehead).

Islands off the northeast and east coast: Admiralty Islands - Los Negros Island, Lou Island, Manu Island; D'Entrecastaux Islands, - Goodenough Is-

**Fig. 1** Distribution ranges of the subspecies of *Tiliqua gigas* and *Tiliqua scincoides* in Indonesia and Papua New Guinea as concluded from the data published by SHEA (1992)

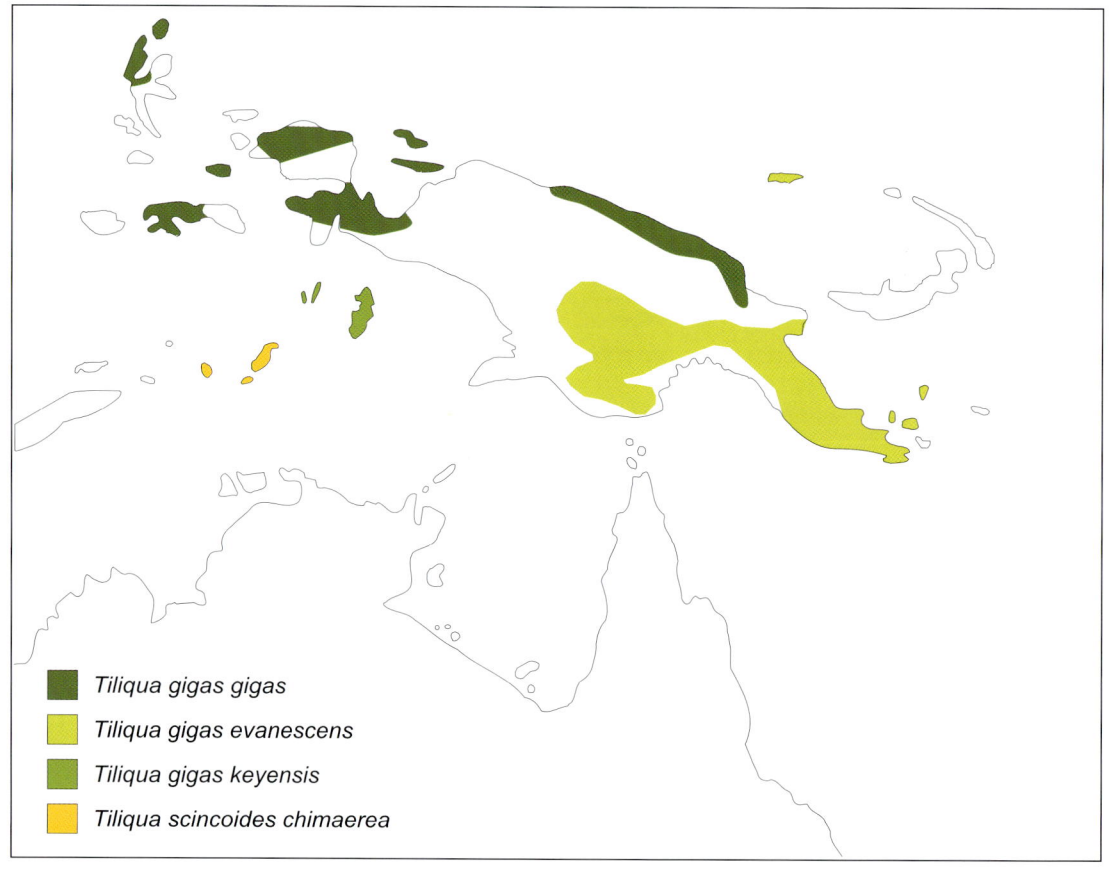

- ■ *Tiliqua gigas gigas*
- ■ *Tiliqua gigas evanescens*
- ■ *Tiliqua gigas keyensis*
- ■ *Tiliqua scincoides chimaerea*

**Fig. 2 and 3**  Variability of *T. g. evanescens* from the vicinity of Merauke

Photographs:  F.B. Yuwono

land, Ferguson Island, Normanby Island; possibly also Trobriand Island.
Irian Jaya (Indonesia):
In the southeast, in the border region with Papua New Guinea (Merauke).

### *Tiliqua gigas gigas*

Papua New Guinea:
Mainland: north coast of Papua New Guinea (Vanimo, Wewak, Madang) to the northwestern side of the Huon Peninsula, to the latitude of Dumpu.
Islands: Karkar Island.
Irian Jaya (Indonesia):
Mainland: from the Doberai Peninsula (= Vogelkop) along the north coast to the border with Papua New Guinea (Jayapura).

**Fig. 4** Typical *Tiliqua gigas gigas* from Halmahera          Photograph: F.B. Yuwono

Adjacent islands to the north: Doom, Yapen, Biak, Seleo.

Maluku (Indonesia) - Moluccas: Ambon, Halmahera, Misool, Morotai Islands, Saparua, Seram, Ternate.

### *Tiliqua gigas keyensis*
Maluku (Indonesia):
Kei Islands, Aru Islands.

### *Tiliqua scincoides chimaerea*
Maluku (Indonesia): Babar Islands, Tanimbar Islands.

As was mentioned before, the blue-tongued skinks of the Tanimbar and Babar Islands have been de-scribed by SHEA (2000a) as a subspecies of *Tiliqua scincoides,* i.e. as *Tiliqua scincoides chimaerea.* The denomination *"chimaerea"* was chosen by SHEA because these animals exhibited traits of both *Tiliqua scincoides* and *Tiliqua gigas.* It is by comparison a rather small form of *T. scincoides* growing to a maximum SVL of 26.9 cm. The coloration of the body is light brown to grayish brown, with 6-7 wide, dark brown bands on the back. The dorsal side of the head is dark brown, without any pattern. A more detailed description and diagnostic characters to distinguish it from other species and subspecies of *Tiliqua* can be found in the respective chapter authored by SHEA in this book. Information on its ecology, husbandry and propagation are as yet unavailable.

**Fig. 5** *Tiliqua scincoides chimaerea* from Tanimbar                    Photograph: F.B. Yuwono

## Blue-tongued skinks from southeastern Irian Jaya similar to *Tiliqua scincoides*

Besides *T. gigas gigas* and *T. gigas evanescens* Irian Jaya also appears home to blue-tongued skinks that differ substantially in their appearance from typical specimens of both mentioned subspecies. This animal is portrayed here.

At a first glance the general appearance points towards the *Tiliqua scincoides* group. These are large blue-tongued skinks with a maximum total length of 56 cm. The ground coloration of the head, body and tail ranges from whitish, through yellowish, cream colored, light brown, to light gray. The nape of the neck is adorned with three fine, longitudinal, dark streaks. The back and flanks are marked with 6-10, the tail with 8-10, distinct cross bands of brown to reddish brown color that may extend onto the ventral side. These dark bands may be bordered with an irregular, fine, white or/and black spotted pattern. A black spot of variable size is located at the side of the neck, above the insertion of the front leg, from which fine black lines may radiate downwards. The legs appear feeble in proportion to the massive body. They are black above, speckled with fine round spots in the ground color or white (comp. Fig. 6). The tail is long and massive.

Based on their appearance both keepers and dealers identify these skinks as a subspecies of *T. scincoides* (WALLS 1996, WEIS 1998, YUWONO 1998). In his dissertation SHEA (1992) also examined some of these specimens. Based on scalation traits he opted in favor of their inclusion in the subsequently described taxon *T. g. evanescens* although he had recognized their intermediary character between *T. gigas* and *T.*

*scincoides* (pers. comm. to the senior author 1998). The present authors tend to support SHEA's point of view. Besides scalation traits, the formation of the cross bands and the coloration of the legs point towards *T. g. evanescens*. The distribution range of the blue-tongued skinks described above lies near the southeastern coast of Irian Jaya centring around the town of Merauke (SHEA 1992, SHEA pers. comm. 1998, YUWONO 1998). SHEA (1992) presented an interesting hypothesis of how this intermediary morph from the coastal region along the Torres Strait came into being: in the course of the geological history of the region the population of the common ancestor of *T. scincoides* and *T. gigas* was split by the opening up of the Torres Strait giving rise to the evolution of the species *T. gigas* north of the water barrier. Various evidence suggests that the Torres Strait opened and closed several times.

Subsequent studies will have to show the real extent of the distribution range of these blue-tongued skinks and whether or not they represent a separate taxon.

**Fig. 6** A typical blue-tongued skink resembling *Tiliqua scincoides* from the Merauke region, Irian Jaya
Photograph: B. Kenney, courtesy of P. Weis

**Fig. 7** As this picture proves the large "Merauke bluetongue" may become quite tame in human care

Photograph: R. Neefs

Until further studies become available, these skinks are to be referred to as *Tiliqua gigas evanescens*. In English speaking countries, and in the US in particular, it is commonly known as the "Irian Jaya bluetongue" which is a rather unprecise denomination. It would be far better for a common understanding to speak of *T. g. evanescens* as the "southern New Guinea bluetongue" or, in the light of their regionally limited distribution range, as the "Merauke bluetongue".

The southeastern part of Irian Jaya includes comparatively dry areas with a tropical savanna climate. Provided that conclusions can be drawn in general from *T. g. evanescens,* the skinks described here prefer habitats in the steppe-like lowlands, open grass lands and savannas, and deforested stretches that are used for agriculture, but possibly also more dense rain forests.

First successful breeding results were mentioned by WALLS (1996) and WEIS (1998). According to these authors, litters comprise 5-15 large, massive babies which grow extraordinarily rapidly. The juveniles have a more contrasting color pattern than the adults.

In closing it should be mentioned that, besides the Merauke bluetongue, numerous other morphs can be found in the pet trade. Whether these specimens also originate from the Merauke region is unknown at this stage. Some specimens could be examined by the junior author and were allocatable to the *T. gigas* species group (Figs. 8 and 9).

**Some recommendations for the husbandry of blue-tongued skinks from Indonesia**

**General:** blue-tongued skinks originating from the Tanimbar and Babar Islands as well as those from the southeast of Irian Jaya may, in principle, be kept like any other large species of blue-

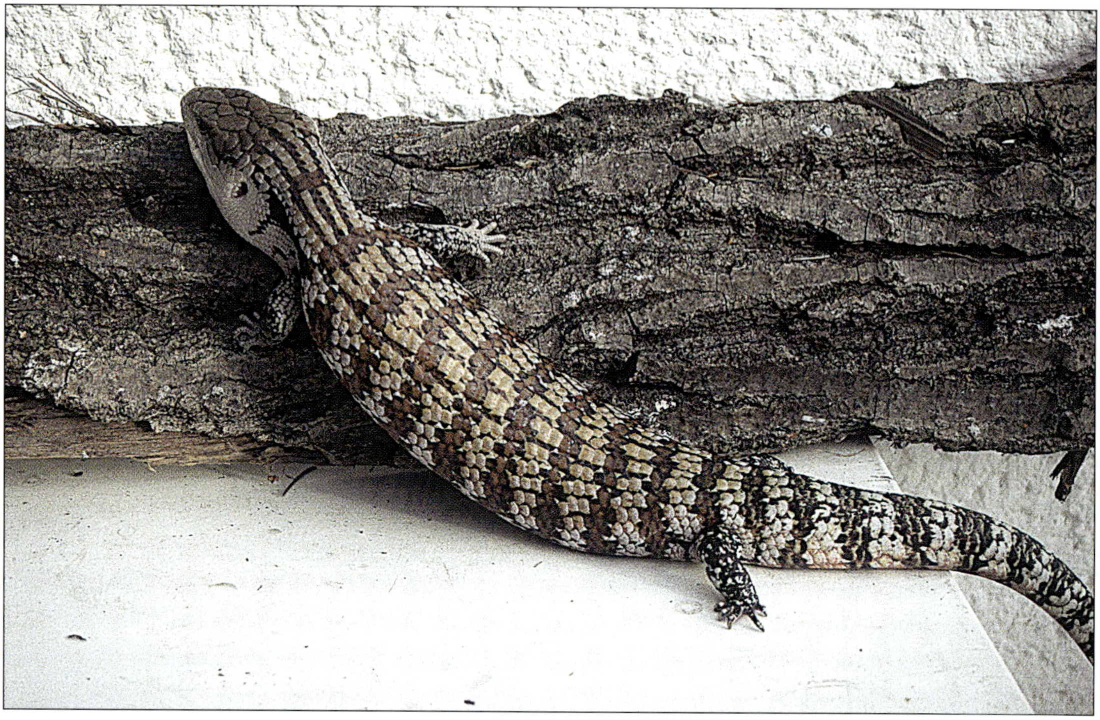

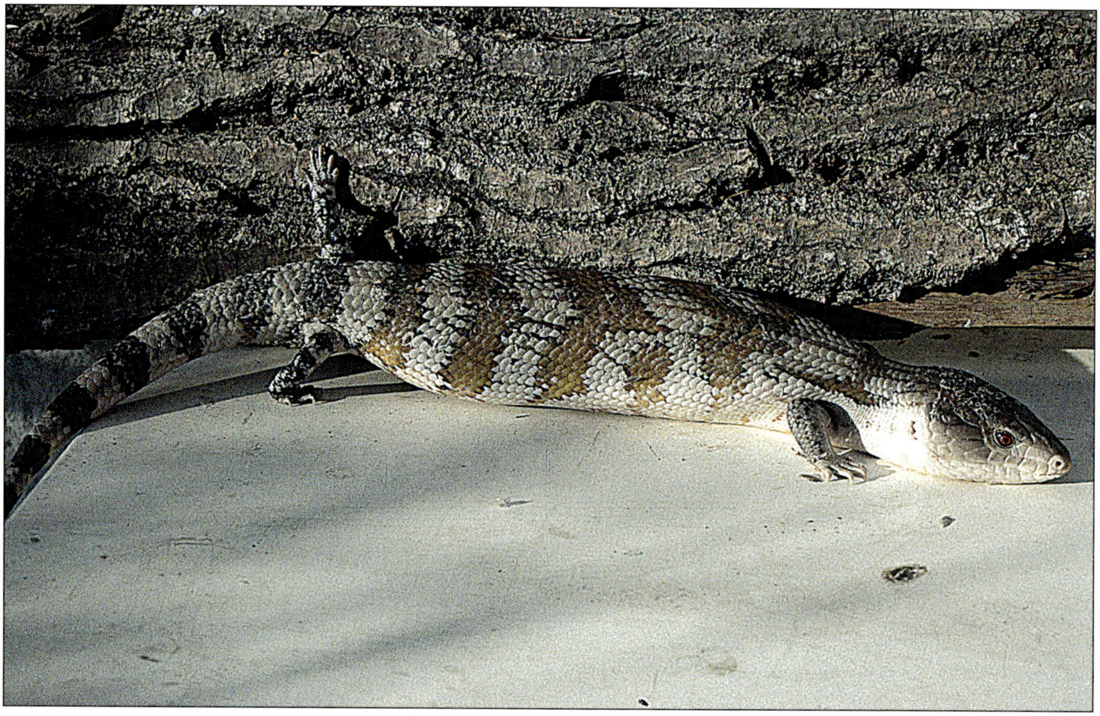

Opposite from above
**Fig. 8** A representative of the genus *Tiliqua* from Indonesia without locality data which was assigned by the junior author to the species *T. gigas* on the basis of pholidotic traits
**Fig. 9** The origin of this blue-tongued skink is also unknown. It might be an intermediary specimen from the Merauke region.    Photographs: A. Hauschild

Fig. 10  Possibly another intermediary form between *T. gigas* and *T. scincoides* from the surrounds of Merauke    Photograph: F.B. Yuwono

tongue. It is recommendable to consult the chapters on *Tiliqua gigas* and *T. scincoides* for details.

**Annual seasonal cycles in nature:** The distribution range lies in Southeast Asia south of the equator covering a strip between 4 and 9° southern latitude and between 129 and 141° longitude, i.e. in the Tropics of the southern hemisphere.

These latitudes near the equator are marked by little annual variation in the number of daylight hours, oscillating only between 12 and 12.5 hours. The shortest days are experienced in the month of June, the longest in December (BARTHOLOMEW & SON 1968). The climate here is moist and warm, i.e. tropical. In permamoist regions it is termed tropical rainy climate, in areas where seasonal dry periods occur it is called tropical savanna climate (ZAHN et al. 1984). The blue-tongued skinks described here primarily live in regions with a tropical savanna climate. This climate pattern is significantly influenced during the course of a year by monsoon winds.

There are two marked seasons, that is a dry and a rainy season. With some geographical variation the dry season lasts from about June through November, the rainy season from December through May. The transitions from one season to the other are usually not abrupt. Many localities within this zone also experience precipitation in the dry season (KÖPPEN & GEIGER 1931, SUKANTO 1969). Temperatures are fairly balanced throughout the year, with the mean daily maxima and minima oscillating only in a narrow range of a few degrees. The cooler period coincides with the dry season, the warmer with the rainy season. Depending on the locality the daily absolute maxima range from 30 to 35°C, the absolute minima from 18 to 21°C (GRÜNEWALD et al. 1982).

Relative humidity is high with the mean daily humidity level varying with the exact locality and the season between 70 and 95% in the morning and 50 to 75% in the afternoon.

**Annual seasonal cycle and husbandry routine in captivity:** Based on the information above the following husbandry routine can be suggested.

As far as the temperature requirements of these skinks are concerned they are predestined for being kept in indoor terraria. Although they originate from the southern hemisphere, photoperiod and temperature fluctuation are ideally adapted to the conditions of the northern hemisphere if they are kept in Europe or the US. It is furthermore recommended to only shift the annual cycle by three months, and not by six. Thus, the six month long dry season with its "short days" of 12 hours daylight at minimum, reduced humidity levels and lower temperatures would coincide with the period from September through February, the rainy season with its "longer days" of 12.5 hours of daylight, high humidity levels and higher temperatures with the time between

March and August, accordingly. The coolest phase, during which the animals are little active and hardly consume any food, may be not longer than one to two months (December through January). During this time the day temperatures may reach 22°C, decreasing to a value of 18°C at night (WEIS 1998). Following this "cold" period of rest mating activities will commence that may soon lead to successful reproduction.

The management described above corresponds with the findings of SHEA (2000b) for *Tiliqua gigas evanescens* in nature with mating being observed during the course of the dry, and births in the rainy season. This pattern ensures that juveniles are born into a time of lush vegetation and a bounty of invertebrates that will enable them to grow rapidly and so overcome the dangerous juvenile stage quickly.

**In closing ...**

It is to be expected that blue-tongued skinks as yet unknown to science will make an appearance from the vast, in parts sparsely populated regions of Indonesia for some time to come. Enthusiasts and scientists alike can be anxious to eventually find out what nature has managed to conceal until now. It is possible that these animals will gradually replace the Australian species of *Tiliqua* at present still kept in terraria, but which are no longer supported by fresh material from that country. At the same time it must be hoped that the Indonesian efforts to secure a long-term utilization of natural resources by man whilst conserving them simultaneously will be successful (ERDELEN 1998, YUWONO 1998) so that blue-tongued skinks from Indonesia can be exported legally to the enthusiasts all over the world in future as well.

**Literature**

BARTHOLOMEW, J. & SON (1971): The Times Atlas of the World. – Zürich (Ex Libris).

BRAAK, C. (1931): Klimakunde von Hinterindien und Insulinde. – Band IV, Teil R in KÖPPEN, W. & R. GEIGER (Hrsg.): Handbuch der Klimatologie in fünf Bänden. – Berlin (Kraus).

GRÜNEWALD, G., E. HÖLLER & D. STRANZ (1982): Brockhaus Texte und Tabellen – Länder und Klima – Asien, Australien. – Wiesbaden (F.A. Brockhaus) & Hamburg (Interpress Übersee-Verlag), 240 S.

ERDELEN, W. (1998): Conservation, Trade and Sustainable Use of Lizards and Snakes in Indonesia. – Mertensiella, Rheinbach, 9: 1–144.

SHEA, G.M. (1992): The systematics and reproduction of blue-tongue lizards of the genus *Tiliqua* (Squamata: Scincidae). – Ph.D. thesis, University of Sydney, 4 Vols.

– (2000a): Der Sunda-Blauzungenskink *Tiliqua scincoides chimaerea* subsp. nov. – S. 157-160 in HAUSCHILD, A., R. HITZ, K. HENLE, G. SHEA & H. WERNING (Hrsg.): Blauzungenskinke. – Münster (Natur und Tier - Verlag).

– (2000b): Die Neuguinea-Blauzunge, *Tiliqua gigas* (SCHNEIDER, 1801): Ökologie und Übersicht über die Unterarten nebst Beschreibung einer neuen Unterart, *Tiliqua gigas evanescens* subsp. nov. – S. 177-189 in HAUSCHILD, A., R. HITZ, K. HENLE, G.M. SHEA & H. WERNING (Hrsg.): Blauzungenskinke. – Münster (Natur und Tier - Verlag).

SUKANTO, M. (1969): Chapter 4: Climate of Indonesia. – Pp. 215–229 in ARAKAWA, H. (ed.): Climates of Northern and Eastern Asia. – In: World Survey of Climatology, Vol. IIX. – Amsterdam, London, New York (Elsevier).

WALLS, J. G. (1996): Blue-tongued Skinks: Keeping and Breeding them in Captivity. – Neptune City, U.S.A. (T.F.H. Publications), 64 pp.

WEIS, P. (1998): Care Sheets – Blue-Tongued Skinks. – Internet, 1998, www.herp.com/care/wr_bts.html

YUWONO, F.B. (1998): The trade of live reptiles in Indonesia. – Pp. 9–15 in ERDELEN, W. (ed.): Conservation, Trade and Sustainable Use of Lizards and Snakes in Indonesia. – Mertensiella, Rheinbach, Nr. 9: 1–144.

ZAHN, U. (1984): Diercke-Universalatlas. – Braunschweig (Georg Westermann Verlag), 447 S.

Authors' addresses
Dr. Robert Hitz
Am Mülibach 8
CH-9425 Thal, Switzerland

Andree Hauschild
Narzissenweg 7
D-41516 Grevenbroich, Germany

# Identification guide to the lizard genus *Tiliqua* GRAY, 1825

ANDREE HAUSCHILD and ROBERT HITZ

with graphics by P. Gassner from drafts by G.M. Shea

**Key words: Reptilia: Sauria: Scincidae: Lygosominae: *Tiliqua*, identification key**

## Introduction

In the daily praxis a blue-tongued skink is readily identified as such. Why these skinks are called thus is pretty obvious: their intensely blue colored tongue has lend them their name. However, identifying the species and subspecies reliably is often a very difficult chore, particularly when it comes to specimens originating from outside of Australia.

The *Tiliqua* lineage comprises two groups: the bluetongues of the genus *Tiliqua* on the one, and the representatives of the genus *Cyclodomorphus* on the other hand. Both genera are easily distinguished on the basis of their appearance. While species of *Cyclodomorphus* are small and slender, those of *Tiliqua* are large and massive by comparison (with the exception of *Tiliqua adelaidensis*). Identifying the species of *Cyclodomorphus* poses hardly any problems so that the reader is here referred to the relevant chapters by SHEA and LÖHR in this book.

With the present contribution the authors have attempted to offer a practically useful aid for the identification of the true blue-tongued skinks. The identification key is mainly meant for use by herpetologists and enthusiasts experienced in taxonomy, whereas the summarized, ID card like characterization of the 14 species and subspecies of *Tiliqua* may help the enthusiast with little or no experience in taxonomy and the pet shop owner.

The matrix for the identification key has been borrowed from COGGER (1992) whereas the

major share of the data used and supplied in this contribution has been extracted from the dissertation by SHEA (1992).

When using the identification aids it should be borne in mind that single individuals of the known species, and subspecies in particular, may exhibit scalation and color traits that render it impossible to assign them to a taxon without leaving doubts. In such cases the examination of a series of specimens from the same locality may lead to a conclusion. In the case of bluetongues acquired via the pet trade the possibility of these being captive bred hybrids must also be taken into consideration. It is also quite probable that the taxonomy of bluetongues from Indonesia and Papua New Guinea has as yet not been fully uncovered, meaning that new taxa may still be awaiting their discovery.

The lizard genus *Tiliqua* comprises a group of moderately large to large skinks (with *T. adelaidensis* again being the exception) in seven species (of which three are split in altogether ten subspecies). They are diagnosed to share the following traits: relatively short legs with five-toed feet; head above with large, regularly shaped and normally symmetrically arranged scales (exception: *Tiliqua rugosa,* head scales split up and only vaguely symmetrical); anterior auricular scales normally present; dorsal scales smooth to rough; lower eyelid with scales and movable; parietals separated behind the interparietal; third and fourth toes nearly of the same length, or third toe slightly longer than fourth.

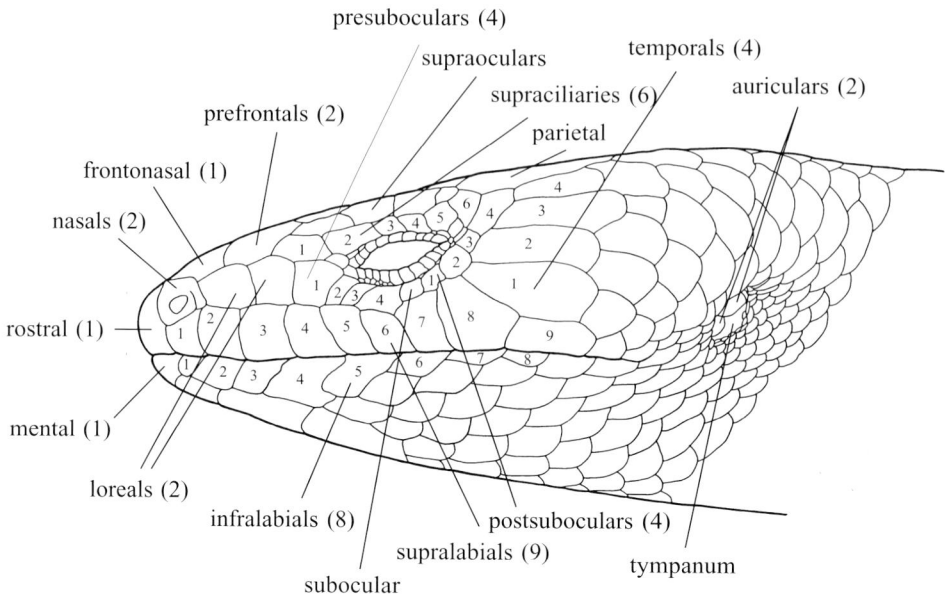

presuboculars (4)

supraoculars

supraciliaries (6)

temporals (4)

auriculars (2)

prefrontals (2)

parietal

frontonasal (1)

nasals (2)

rostral (1)

mental (1)

loreals (2)

infralabials (8)

supralabials (9)

postsuboculars (4)

tympanum

subocular

**Head scales of a blue-tongued skink**

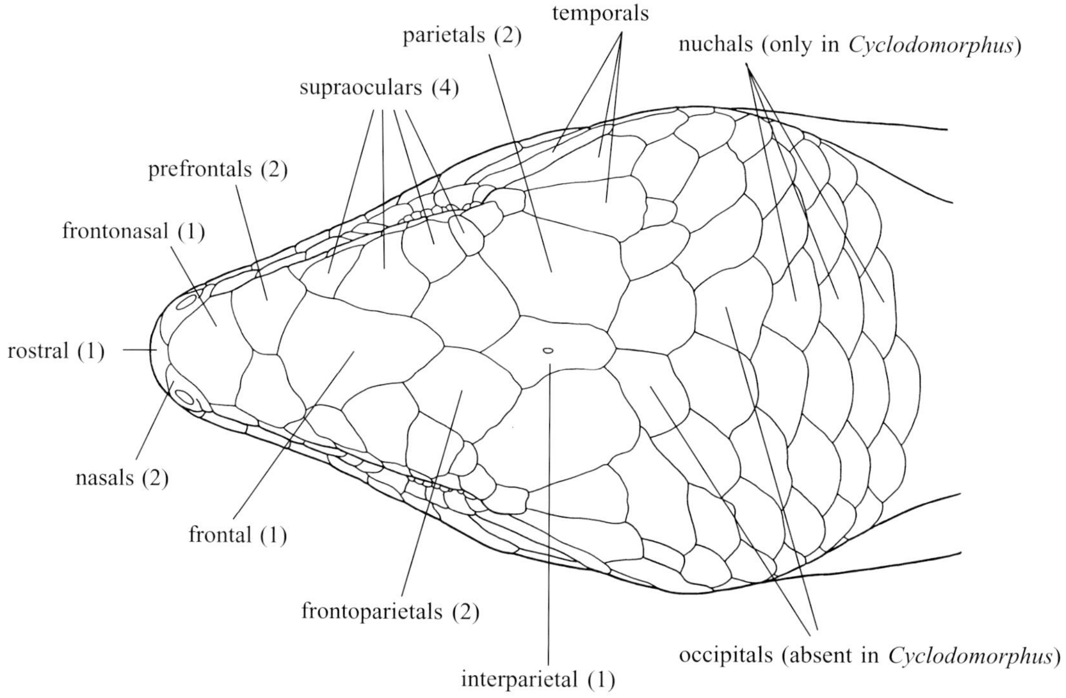

temporals

parietals (2)

nuchals (only in *Cyclodomorphus*)

supraoculars (4)

prefrontals (2)

frontonasal (1)

rostral (1)

nasals (2)

frontal (1)

frontoparietals (2)

interparietal (1)

occipitals (absent in *Cyclodomorphus*)

# Identification key to the species and subspecies of the genus *Tiliqua*

**1** Tail broad, short, tip blunt, not breaking off easily, 14.5-37% of SVL (snout-vent length); max. 25 subcaudals; subdigital lamellae divided, at least basally ......................................................... **4**

• Tail conical, tapering to a point, breaks off easily or not, 30-95.5% of SVL; min. 26 subcaudals; subdigital lamellae entire ..................................... **2**

**2** Anterior temporals (second scale row behind the eye) more or less equal in shape and size to the posterior temporals, not much longer than wide .. ............................................................................... **7**

• Anterior temporals much larger than posterior temporals, much longer than wide ..................... **3**

**3** Scales on dorsum and upper side of tail smooth, free margin rounded; subcaudals/paravertebrals quotient < 0.90; tongue entirely blue ............... **11**

• Scales on dorsum (in particular those in the posterior portion) and on upper side of tail usually with angulated free margins, sometimes slightly keeled; subcaudals/paravertebrals quotient > 0.95; tip of tongue blue, base of tongue pink ..................... **13**

**4** Tail very short, wide, 14.5-30% of SVL; 11-16 subcaudals; 19-25 scale rows at midbody; conspicuously large scales on body; max. SVL 341 mm ................................................................. ......................................... ***Tiliqua rugosa aspera***

• Tail relatively long, 20.6-37% of SVL; number of subcaudals normally > 16 .................................... **5**

**5** Median occipital usually present; first supraciliary and frontal separated; dorsal color pattern normally consisting of pale, colorful bands; 22-30 scale rows at midbody; max. SVL 303 mm ......... ......................................... ***Tiliqua rugosa rugosa***

• Median occipital usually absent; first supraciliary and frontal in contact at least on one side; dorsum with diffuse pattern on dark ground color, or narrow pale streaks and spots on a brown ground .. **6**

**6** Nasals separate; dorsum with diffuse pattern (fine, pale vermiculation) on dark gray ground color; ventter with diffuse, grayish green clouding; 24-30 scale rows at midbody; max. SVL 260 mm ......... ......................................... ***Tiliqua rugosa konowi***

• Nasals normally in contact; brown ground color with yellow streakes and spots; 26-35 scale rows at midbody; max. SVL 300 mm ........................... ......................................... ***Tiliqua rugosa palarra***

**7** 34 or more scale rows at midbody ..................... **9**

• fewer than 34 scale rows at midbody ................ **8**

**8** Dorsum black with yellow to brick red spots; max. SVL 368 mm .......................................................... .................... ***Tiliqua nigrolutea*** (highland morph)

• Dorsum blackish brown with brown spots; max. SVL 328 mm .......................................................... ..................... ***Tiliqua nigrolutea*** (lowland morph)

**9** Body with distinct cross bands; 2-4 rows of enlarged, hexagonal scales (occipitals) between the interparietal and the smaller body scales on the nape of the neck (see sketch) ........................... **10**

• Body without cross bands; at maximum a single row of enlarged, hexagonal scales (occipitals) between interparietal and the smaller body scales on the nape of the neck; small, max. SVL 112 mm .. ............................................... ***Tiliqua adelaidensis***

**10** 8 or fewer, wide, dark cross bands on body ......... ................................................... ***Tiliqua occipitalis***

• 9-15 narrow, irregular cross bands on body ......... ............................................... ***Tiliqua multifasciata***

**11** Supralabials usually 9; a dark temporal streak present in some populations; dorsum gray to grayish brown or olive green to greenish yellow with 4-10 cross bands; banded pattern of back continued on flanks; tail normally strongly patterned with 5-16 cross bands; venter patterned; max. SVL 371 mm ........................................................................
.............................. ***Tiliqua scincoides scincoides***

• Supralabials usually 8; dark temporal streak absent ................................................................ **12**

**12** Tail strongly patterned with 9-22 cross bands; dorsum yellowish brown to fawn, with 5-12, darkmargined cross bands; banded pattern of dorsum and flanks slightly to distinctly out of alignment; venter normally unpatterned or with weakly pronounced brown bands; general appearance of coloration often colorful (yellow to orange sections); max. SVL 371 mm ................................................
.............................. ***Tiliqua scincoides intermedia***

• Tail indistinctly patterned with 7-11 interlinked, brown cross bands; dorsum light brown to grayish brown, with 5-8 brown cross bands; banded pattern of back continued on flanks; venter pale, with no spots; general appearance of color pattern drab, brownish; max. SVL 269 mm ..............................
.............................. ***Tiliqua scincoides chimaerea***

**13** Usually fewer than 5 scales between upper lip and parietal in the second scale row behind the eye (anterior temporals plus basal supralabial; see sketch); legs black, with no or weak spotted pattern; whole body in general with dark appearance; head scales framed with dark; throat with black spots; dorsum grayish green, olive green to dark yellow, with 6-10 black cross bands; venter with distinct black markings; max. SVL 270 mm, rarely up to 315 mm ................................................ ***Tiliqua gigas gigas***

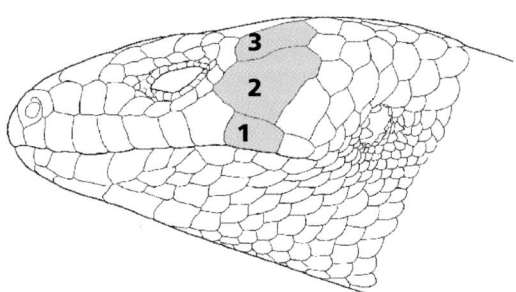

• Five scales between upper lip and parietal in the second scale row behind the eye (anterior temporals plus basal supralabial; see sketch); legs with pattern, often intensely spotted dorsally ............... **14**

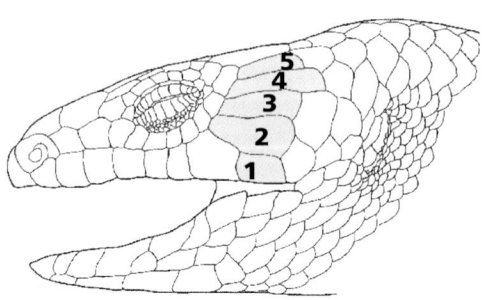

**14** General appearance often colorful; throat normally without spots; dorsum white, cream colored, yellow, olive green, light gray or light brown, with 5-10 cross bands in black, brown or red color; venter light, uniform or with light brown pattern of varying intensity; max. SVL 343 mm ........................
.................................... ***Tiliqua gigas evanescens***

• Free margin of dorsal scales less distinctly angulated; throat without pattern or with few brown streaks; broad vertebral streak on nape of neck, bordered cream or white; dorsum pale gray to yellowish brown, with 6-9 cross bands; dorsal banded pattern in adults diffuse due to fine, pale mottling; venter and lower side of tail spotted or streaked with brown; max. SVL 336 mm ...........................
.......................................... ***Tiliqua gigas keyensis***

# Summary of diagnostic characters of the 14 species of *Tiliqua*

## Tiliqua adelaidensis

**Head:** overproportional, heavily armored, only three supraocular scales
**Nape:** ocellated pattern
**Dorsal scales:** small and soft
**Dorsal pattern:** irregularly scattered black dots indicate an indistinct vertebral stripe which is disrupted by dorsolateral cross lines
**Tail:** long, thin, up to 74.1% of SVL
**Throat:** yellowish
**Venter:** white to grayish beige
**Limbs:** front legs greenish gray to yellow, unpatterned
**SVL:** up to 112 mm

## Tiliqua gigas gigas

**Head:** fewer than five scales between upper lip and parietal; head scales bordered with dark, spotted with dark or marbled
**Nape:** with a distinct longitudinal streak
**Dorsal scales:** keeled; the free margins of the scales are angulated
**Dorsal pattern:** 6-10 black cross bands
**Tail:** long, up to 94.8% of SVL; with 11-18 black bands
**Throat:** with black spots
**Venter:** with distinct black marbled pattern
**Limbs:** black above, without spots, or with a few light spots
**SVL:** at maximum 270 mm; up to 315 mm only in the far west (Ambon and Seram)

## Tiliqua gigas evanescens

**Head:** five scales between upper lip and parietal
**Nape:** with a brown or black longitudinal streak
**Dorsal scales:** keeled; the free margins of the scales angulated
**Dorsal pattern:** 5-10 dark cross bands
**Tail:** long, up to 89.6% of SVL; with 10-16 dark, wide bands
**Throat:** usually without spots
**Venter:** light, uniform, or with varying degree of light brown pattern
**Limbs:** patterned dorsally; often with intense spotted pattern especially on the hind legs
**SVL:** at maximum 343 mm

## Tiliqua gigas keyensis

**Head:** five scales between upper lip and parietal; head scales framed with dark, with few dark brown spots
**Nape:** a wide longitudinal streak, bordered with white or cream, extending to the first dorsal band
**Dorsal scales:** keeled, conspicuously speckled on their margins
**Dorsal pattern:** 6-9 dense, brown bands that are very indistinctly set off from each other
**Tail:** long, up to 95.5% of SVL; 14-15 bands; lower side peppered with brown
**Throat:** without spots, or with a few brown stripes
**Venter:** peppered or streaked with brown
**Limbs:** dark brown above, with yellow or brown spots
**SVL:** at maximum 336 mm

## Tiliqua multifasciata

**Head:** a wide, black temporal streak from the eye to the conspicuously large ear opening; only one of the two supraoculars in contact with the frontal
**Nape:** without particular traits
**Dorsal scales:** very small, smooth
**Dorsal pattern:** 9-15 yellow to orange cross bands on a gray to brown ground color
**Tail:** rather short, up to 55.7% of SVL
**Throat:** gray, sometimes spotted with dark
**Venter:** cream colored or white
**Limbs:** dark to black on the outer sides; thighs slightly banded with yellow or orange
**SVL:** at maximum 289 mm

## Tiliqua nigrolutea

**Head:** temporal streak absent
**Nape:** patterned with large blotches
**Dorsal scales:** small, smooth
**Dorsal pattern:** highland morph: black, with yellow to brick red spots; lowland morph: blackish brown, with brown spots
**Tail:** relatively short, up to 55.1% of SVL
**Throat:** highland morph: yellow, occasionally with black spots; lowland morph: grayish blue to bluish yellow, occasionally with black spots

**Venter:** highland morph: yellow, with black pattern; lowland morph: grayish blue to bluish yellow, occasionally with black spots
**Limbs:** highland morph: black, with fine yellow pattern; lowland morph: brownish gray to black
**SVL:** highland morph: at maximum 368 mm lowland morph: at maximum 328 mm

## *Tiliqua occipitalis*

**Head:** a wide, dark brown to black temporal streak from the eye to the ear opening; conspicuously large occipitals
**Nape:** marked with the first dorsal band
**Dorsal scales:** small, soft
**Dorsal pattern:** dorsum and flanks light gray to beige or yellowish, with at maximum eight wide, dark cross bands
**Tail:** at maximum 55.6% of SVL; bands forming rings
**Throat:** yellowish
**Venter:** cream colored to white
**Limbs:** front limbs light gray to yellowish; hind legs dark brown to black on their outer sides
**SVL:** at maximum 320 mm

## *Tiliqua rugosa rugosa*

**Head:** narrow when compared with the other subspecies
**Nape:** without particular traits
**Dorsal scales:** much smoother than those of *T. rugosa aspera*
**Dorsal pattern:** light to dark brown or black ground color; narrow to wide, irregularly shaped cross bands on back and tail in white, gray, yellow, or orange to red color
**Tail:** relatively long, up to 37.2% of SVL
**Throat:** spotted with dark, occasionally streaked
**Venter:** yellow to bluish gray
**Limbs:** yellowish to bluish gray, sometimes streaked with dark
**SVL:** at maximum 303 mm

## *Tiliqua rugosa aspera*

**Head:** wide, triangular in outline
**Nape:** without particular traits
**Dorsal scales:** large and rough

**Dorsal pattern:** ground color uniform gray, brown, black or multicolored; no cross bands
**Tail:** very short, wide, at maximum 30% of SVL; its shape resembles the head
**Throat:** with light spotting
**Venter:** cream colored to yellow, usually with brown bars in longitudinal and cross direction
**Limbs:** yellowish to dark brown; black in melanistic specimens
**SVL:** at maximum 341 mm

## *Tiliqua rugosa konowi*

**Head:** narrow
**Nape:** without particular traits
**Dorsal scales:** back and flanks with fine scales
**Dorsal pattern:** gray to olive green ground color; fine pale vermiculated pattern
**Tail:** relatively long and slim, up to 37% of SVL; weak banded pattern
**Throat:** in ground color
**Venter:** in ground color
**Limbs:** in ground color
**SVL:** at maximum 260 mm

## *Tiliqua rugosa palarra*

**Head:** relatively narrow; ear opening small; very dark in color
**Nape:** a narrow, brown streak along the vertebral line flanked by light streaks
**Dorsal scales:** much smoother than those of *T. rugosa aspera*
**Dorsal pattern:** ground color olive green to brown; dorsum and flanks with irregularly shaped, white and yellowish streaks (5-6 scales in length) or spots
**Tail:** up to 31.0% of SVL
**Throat:** with a moderate to high content of brown
**Venter:** yellow with a distinct brown pattern
**Limbs:** front and hind legs predominantly brown on the outer surfaces, predominantly yellow on the inner sides; thighs of the hind legs with a white streak (two scales in width)
**SVL:** at maximum 300 mm

## *Tiliqua scincoides scincoides*

**Head:** often with a black temporal streak running from the posterior angle of the eye to the ear opening, continued by a black, wide, lateral streak on the neck; five scales between upper lip and parietal

**Nape:** with several thin, equally formed, densely arranged, dark streaks

**Dorsal scales:** smooth, visible margins rounded

**Dorsal pattern:** 4-10 wide, clearly defined, dark brown to black cross bands

**Tail:** with 5-16 densely arranged cross bands

**Throat:** yellow to light brown, uniform, or spotted with black

**Venter:** yellow or bluish gray, sometimes also pink or red

**Limbs:** front legs without spots on the outer sides

**SVL:** at maximum 371 mm

## Tiliqua scincoides chimaerea

**Head:** fewer than five scales between upper lip and parietal in the second row behind the eye

**Nape:** with several narrow streaks

**Dorsal scales:** smooth, visible margins rounded

**Dorsal pattern:** light brown to grayish brown; with 5-8 brown cross bands

**Tail:** with 7-11, indistinctly defined, confluent, brown cross bands

**Throat:** with a few or no brown spots

**Venter:** yellow, with pattern

**Limbs:** front legs without pattern, also on the outer sides

**SVL:** at maximum 269 mm

## Tiliqua scincoides intermedia

**Head:** black temporal streak from the angle of the eye to the ear opening absent, or limited to a faint indication; five scales between upper lip and parietal

**Nape:** with several yellow or brown, densely arranged longitudinal streaks

**Dorsal scales:** smooth, visible margins rounded

**Dorsal pattern:** 5-12 dark brown cross bands which extend onto the flanks (where they are continued, out of alignment, with yellow or orange margins)

**Tail:** with 9-22 cross bands

**Throat:** yellow to whitish, occasionally with a few brown spots

**Venter:** yellow to whitish, occasionally with a weakly pronounced, brown banded pattern

**Limbs:** front legs light gray to grayish brown, sometimes with dark bars; hind legs with a fine brown speckled pattern

**SVL:** at maximum 371 mm

## Glossary

**hexagonal** - with six angles

**SVL** - snout-vent length; the distance taken on the lower side of the stretched-out animal from the tip of the snout to the posterior margin of the preanal scale

melanistic - black in color

**upper lip** - site of transition from the inner to the outer side of the mouth on the upper jaw

**paravertebrals** - scales along the longitudinal midline of the back, counted from the posterior margin of the parietal / interparietal to the last scale anterior to the line formed by the anterior edge of the hind legs when these are positioned at a right angle to the longitudinal axis of the body

**postsuboculars** - first scale row behind the eye

subcaudals - scales covering the lower side of the tail, counted from the posterior margin of the preanal scale up to the tail tip

**subdigital lamellae** - lamella-like scales covering the lower side of the toe; evaluated on the lower side of the fourth toe

## Literature

COGGER, H.G. (1992): Reptiles and Amphibians of Australia. 5th edition. – Chatswood (Reed International Books), Ithaca, New York (Cornell University Press), 775 pp.

SHEA, G.M. (1992): The systematics and reproduction of bluetongue lizards of the genus *Tiliqua* (Squamata: Scincidae). – 4 Vols. – Ph.D. thesis, University of Sydney.

Authors' addresses
Andree Hauschild
Narzissenweg 7
D-41516 Grevenbroich, Germany
Dr. Robert Hitz
Am Mülibach 8
CH-9425 Thal, Switzerland

# The pink-tongued skink, *Cyclodomorphus gerrardii* (Gray, 1845)

Beate Löhr

**Key words: Reptilia: Sauria: Scincidae:** *Cyclodomorphus gerrardii,* **systematics, husbandry, reproduction**

## Description

*Cyclodomorphus gerrardii* may grow to a maximum total length of 47 cm (Peters 1967), about half of which is made up by the slender tail. Adult specimens can weigh in at up to 150 g (Hauschild & Gassner 1995).

The scales of this skink are shiny and smooth, and are arranged in 30-33 rows at midbody (Peters 1967). The body is cylindrical in cross section and elongated. The limbs are well developed although a tendency for reduction is apparent. The toes are equipped with sharp claws that enable the animals to climb skilfully. During climbing the tail is used like a fifth limb.

The teeth of the pink-tongued skink are noted for their peculiar morphology. The rows of teeth in the upper and lower jaws each end with an enlarged molar. Some individuals may, however, have another one or two smaller teeth behind it (Hauschild & Gassner 1995).

The color pattern is unique in every single specimen and possibly influenced by the natural habitat a population lives in. The ground color ranges

**Fig. 1** *Cyclodomorphus gerrardii* from Springwood, NSW, with a contrasting color pattern    Photograph: R. Hoser

**Fig. 2**  *Cyclodomorphus gerrardii,* juvenile from Springwood, NSW
Photograph: R. Hoser

from beige, through grayish brown, to gray, with more or less distinct, brown cross bands on the body and tail. A specimen figured by HOSER (1989) even has a dark brown ground color with a pattern of light beige lines and a light beige head. According to PETERS (1967) there are also uniform light gray colored specimens with scattered black dots and fine dashes. MATZ & VANDER-HAEGE (1980) mentioned mauve and violet colored animals. Specimens sporting wide, light brown cross lines that are bordered with dark brown,

**Fig. 3**  *Cyclodomorphus gerrardii* with a minimized color pattern          Photograph:  R. Hoser

**Fig. 4** *Cyclodomorphus gerrardii* with a distinct color pattern          Photograph: R. Hoser

have also been portrayed. Some old specimens may be almost uniform grayish white (MUDRACK 1974). The lower side is gray, flesh colored or orange, sometimes with brown streaks on the throat. Unlike *Tiliqua* (exception: *T. adelaidensis*), adult *Cyclodomorphus gerrardii* have a pink colored tongue to which the skink's vernacular name refers. In contrast, the oral mucous membranes are blue.

Juvenile *Cyclodomorphus gerrardii* exhibit a distinctive juvenile color pattern. The ground color may vary between light brown and reddish, with an almost black banded pattern. Juveniles with a yellowish ground color are occasionally found (HAUSCHILD 1988). On reaching an age of four months the previously clearly demarcated cross lines begin to fade and become more indistinct. Juvenile specimens have a cobalt blue inside of the mouth and a dark blue tongue; the tongue then

gradually turns pink at an age of one to two years (EHMANN 1992).

PETERS (1967) reported on an unusually colored juvenile with a ground color described as light gray and a pattern of wide, white-bordered, black bands. At an age of nine months, on having grown to 23 cm in total length, the black cross bands were superseded by indistinct brown bands that were only partially framed with white. The tongue of this specimen was black and assumed its rosy color at the same time.

## Sexual dimorphism

Like with most skinks distinguishing the sexes is difficult. Females usually have narrower heads than male specimens. Viewed from below the base of the tail of a female tapers right from behind the cloaca, whereas weakly pronounced hemipenis pockets may be recognizable in a male (HAUSCHILD 1988). To obtain some degree of certainty in this task, several specimens are required for direct comparison. Still, there may be individuals left which cannot be sexed on the basis of the above mentioned slight differences.

## Taxonomy

A detailed treatise of this subject is included in the dissertation by SHEA (1992), and a more summarized version can also be found in the chapter "History and systematics" by the same author in this book.

The pink-tongued skink was described as *Hinulia gerrardii* by GRAY in 1845. This original description was accompanied by a very beautiful lithograph. It should be mentioned that both the text and the plate have become available again in a more recent publication (GRAY & GÜNTHER 1995).

Based on the peculiar dental morphology PETERS founded his new genus *Hemisphaeriodon* in 1867 to accommodate the species *gerrardii*. After no name changes for the subsequent 83 years, MITCHELL eventually transferred the pink-tongued skink to the genus *Tiliqua* (MITCHELL 1950) so that it would now be known as *Tiliqua gerrardii*. Most scientists followed MITCHELL in this view over many years. Although serum immunological studies eventually showed that the antiserum of this species differed substantially from that of *Tiliqua rugosa,* even HUTCHINSON (1981) left *T. gerrardii* in the genus *Tiliqua*.

WELLS & WELLINGTON (1984, 1985) and COGGER (1989) then resurrected the genus *Hemisphaeriodon* for the species *gerrardii,* while CZECHURA (1986) transferred it to the genus *Cyclodomorphus*. The argumentation by CZECHURA was picked up by WILSON & KNOWLES (1988). SHEA (1990) eventually synonymized *Hemisphaeriodon* with *Cyclodomorphus* arguing that the pink-tongued skink would best fit the diagnosis of the genus *Cyclodomorphus*. This point of view is not shared by all Australian herpetologists rendering the generic allocation of the species *gerrardii* at present as one of the unresolved problems in the systematics of blue-tongued skinks.

## Distribution

The species *C. gerrardii* is native to the east coast of Australia. Its distribution range extends from Sydney in the south of New South Wales to the Cape York Peninsula in the north of Queensland (COGGER 1992).

The distribution range of this species comprises three climate zones (MÜLLER 1987). These are

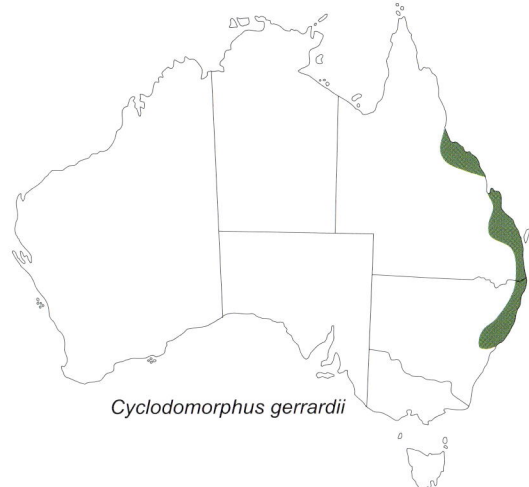

*Cyclodomorphus gerrardii*

the coastal strip, between about latitudes 22 and 35°, where the climate is constantly moist with hot summers. From about latitude 20°, south of Rockhampton, to latitude 14°, north of Townsville, the climate is characterized as tropical, summer humid, and moist. To the south and north of Coen a tropical climate with varying degrees of moisture is encountered (MÜLLER 1987).

## Biology, ecology

*C. gerrardii* is a very agile and active skink. It lives mainly in rain forests, but can also be found in moist and dry sclerophyll forests (COGGER 1992). These lizards are occasionally also encountered in the vicinity of human settlements and gardens (SMITH & SMITH 1990).

The pink-tongued skink has semi-arboreal habits, climbing in shrubs and low trees, but also spends much of its time on the ground. When moving about on the ground it usually employs only its front limbs whereas the hind legs are stretched back. Overnight shelters are found beneath pieces of wood, bark or under rocks.
*Cyclodomorphus gerrardii* is a predominantly crepuscular to nocturnal species which is most often found active during warm, rainy nights. The skinks are, however, occasionally also seen browsing for food in bright daylight (PETERS 1986), and can then even be found basking on large rocks. When startled they flee into their hiding places and will reappear only after some time has lapsed. If their shelters are uncovered, they usually remain motionless. Their defense behavior consists of raising the anterior portion of the body and flicking the tongue, a behavior that has been interpreted as snake mimicry (WILSON & KNOWLES 1988). I have observed a splendid warning and threatening display that is employed especially during feeding, that is when two specimens are interested in the same snail. With the mouth wide agape and well audible hissing sounds produced by the release of breathing air, the opponents attempt to intimidate each other.

The tail can be autotomized in parts or in its entirety which is an effective method to fool and escape predators. For this purpose some vertebrae of the central tail section are equipped with non-ossified separation planes across the longitudinal axis (HAUSCHILD & GASSNER 1995). The lost piece of the original tail is subsequently regenerated. It usually has a different coloration and is shorter than the original tail (ZWINENBERG 1976).

Also known as the snail-eating skink, the pink-tongued skink is specialized in feeding on molluscs in the form of both snails and slugs. Prey is mainly located by the sense of smell. This sense is well developed and permits the skink to not only register visibly moving prey, but also immobile and hidden food (HAUSCHILD & GASSNER 1995). Once a prey item has been discovered the skink approaches it in a direct line while olfactory cues are sampled via a frequent flicking of the tongue. The snail or slug is then grasped with the strong jaws and carried, with the head held high, to a place of safety where it is consumed undisturbed (ZIMMERMANN 1983). Snails are cracked between the jaws, sometimes aided by a hard object which is pressed against the shell. Then the mollusc meat is skilfully separated from the shards of the shell. Even very small pieces of the shell that are inadvertently taken into the mouth are subsequently pushed out of the mouth with the tongue. Slugs are detached from the substrate they stick to by grasping them and rotating the entire body; they are then swallowed whole.

Females of *Cyclodomorphus gerrardii* are viviparous, which means they give birth to live young. Their entire embryonic development is completed in the body of the mother. HOSER (1989) stated litter sizes to be 12-25 young, and OBST et al. (1984) and WEIGEL (1989) even gave maximum litter sizes of 30. Reports on litters of 53, or even 67 (GREER 1989 in HAUSCHILD & GASSNER 1995), on the other hand, seem rather questionable.

## Husbandry

Considering the habitats and habits of *Cyclodomorphus gerrardii* a semi-moist, moderately warm terrarium is recommendable. In countries where laws exist that decree minimum dimensions for a terrarium these have to be adhered to. In Germany, for example, dimensions of 80 × 60 × 120 cm (l × w × h) are prescribed for the keeping of one adult pair. In order to ensure the necessary ventilation, mesh-covered aeration openings must be included in the front and/or sides as well as in the lid.

For a suitable substrate fertilizer-free potting soil can be mixed with coarse sand at a ratio of 4 : 1 and filled in to a depth of 1-15 cm. HAUSCHILD & GASSNER (1995) suggested using a mix of bark mulch, sand and peat at a ratio of 3 : 2 : 1.

The side and rear walls of the terrarium should be covered with cork tiles in order to increase the usable surface space for the animals. Treefern sheets are also usable for this purpose (HAUSCHILD & GASSNER 1995). Thick branches with rough bark, positioned at slight angles, provide the skinks with opportunities to climb and are also used as resting spots, and so do platforms made of thick cork mounted in the rear corners. Hiding places may consist of low tubes of cork bark or adequately structured roots. A water and bathing bowl, maybe in the form of a low earthenware undertray for flower pots, should not be wanting. Although pink-tongued skinks are agile, they are also rather gentle inhabitants of a terrarium so that some robust live plants may be incorporated in the decoration. Suitable plants are, for example, wax flower (*Hoya* sp.), devil's ivy (*Rhaphidophora* aurea), or some dwarf philodendrons such as the climbing philodendron (*Philodendron scandens*).

The terrarium may be illuminated with fluorescent tubes. A low-wattage spot light serves as a local source of heat and is readily frequented by the skinks for basking. The lamp should be installed in a way that it cannot possibly be directly accessed by the pink-tongued skinks. All electrical installations must comply with the regulations for a usage in moist environments. Temperatures should fluctuate between 20 and 30°C, with the lower value representing the night and the higher one the day temperatures.

The number of daylight hours should be 12 hours during the northern hemisphere winter (Australian summer), gradually decreasing to about 8 hours towards the middle of the year. During the northern hemisphere summer (Australian winter) only the fluorescent tubes are still in use. From then on the number of daylight hours is again gradually increased. These measures ensure an adequate emulation of the temperature and daylight hour effects according to the natural annual cycles. Another way to induce a period of rest is to keep the skinks in outdoor terraria during our summer months. Suitable cages can be made from fine metal mesh. These are buried some 20-30 ~~cm~~ cm deep into the ground with the excavated soil being used to fill them up to ground level on the inside. They may be decorated in a manner similar to the indoor terraria.

The substrate in the indoor terrarium should offer areas with varying moisture levels so that the animals can freely choose the spots that suit them best at a time. It is therefore also recommendable to also make available a number of hiding places. Relative humidity levels around 70% are ideal, but can usually be achieved only for brief periods right after misting. I found that it suffices to mist only once a day in the evening. I have come to insert an additional misting right before a feeding session, and the skinks have very quickly learnt to associate these extra "rains" with the imminent arrival of food, causing them to leave their shelters instantly. Following HAUSCHILD & GASSNER (1995), they do not respond negatively to drier periods of several months.

In contrast to most blue-tongued skinks pink-tongued skinks become fully active only at dusk and at night. It is therefore advisable to offer food preferably in the afternoon or evening. Adult *Cyclodomorphus gerrardii* are fed, in accordance with the prevalent season, two or three times a week. A ration should be large enough for every specimen to eat as much as it likes. This means that, depending on the size of the feeder animals, up to 15 snails may be consumed by one specimen in a sitting. Suitable feeder animals are snails and slugs of all kinds, obviously of sizes that are in a sensible ratio to their consumers. The skinks should be fed exclusively with live snails and slugs from spring through autumn. These can be found in large numbers, especially on stinging nettle, after warm summer rains. Common land snails *(Cepaea nemoralis)* and garden snails *(C. hortensis)* are particularly popular with the skinks; they are possibly most similar to the snails encountered in the natural habitats. Only

**Fig. 7** *Cyclodomorphus gerrardii* feeding on a snail
*(Cepaea hortensis)*          Photograph: A. Hauschild

if there is no other alternative should the keeper resort to substitute feedstuffs such as beef heart mixed with snail meat. Some specimens will accept this type of food with visible revulsion and only if they are really starved. Any other type of substitute food was persistently rejected by my specimens. It is therefore urgently advised to build up an appropriately large reserve of frozen snails and slugs for the winter months. When projecting the amounts needed you should not forget to include possible offspring and store small snails and slugs separately. The *Cyclodomorphus gerrardii* kept by myself always gave birth to their young in February or March, that is at a time when free ranging snails are nowhere to be found. Feeding snails and slugs to the skinks throughout the year makes an additional supply with vitamins, calcium and other minerals unnecessary. HAUSCHILD (1988) did not collect a winter supply and adjusted his animals to a diet of beef heart mixed with dog flakes or boiled buckwheat, with the whole mix being fortified with calcium, vitamins and trace elements. BAUER (1980) also suggested a substitute food mix of snail meat, beef heart and banana, minced in a food processor, and kept frozen in rations. Before this was offered to the animals it was mixed with raw or boiled egg yolk.

Different authors evaluate the intraspecific compatibility of *Cyclodomorphus gerrardii* differently. HAUSCHILD & GASSNER (1995) described the species as unaggressive, whereas ZIMMERMANN (1983) reported about frequent squabbles even among specimens of the same sex. The pink-tongued skinks kept by myself also proved to be not particularly amicable among each other. In 1988 I received three juveniles which were subsequently raised together without experiencing any problems. It was apparent, though, that partly aggressive skirmishes ensued during feeding. In order to prevent potentially dangerous injuries from biting, the individuals should be kept at safe distances from each other during feeding. Even after these three skinks had matured, everything went well initially. They had turned out to be a female, a male, and a specimen whose sex I could not possibly identify. Some five years later the latter specimen, which had behaved neutrally all the time, was suddenly attacked with such ferocity that it died from its severe injuries. During the following year the male lost his tail in a fight with the female. It is indeed only towards the keeper that the animals are placid and very tame.

### Breeding

The mating period begins in October or November and continues for 3-4 weeks. The male now begins to chase the female around, intensely probing the female with the tongue and attacking it with bites into her flanks and base of her tail. Initially the female responds with running away or fighting back, but her resistance wears down after some time, and the male eventually succeeds in placing a mating bite on the flank. This is now followed by the male stroking the female's back with his front feet and showing waving, twitching movements of his tail. This stimulation causes the defensive actions of the female to subside, eventually she lifts her tail and so facilitates a copulation. The latter takes about four minutes (ABRAHAM 1980).

Following a gestation period of about five months, baby *Cyclodomorphus gerrardii* are born. The newborn pink-tongued skinks free themselves from their egg membranes without help and then consume these. Sometimes the keeper may note an individual having problems tearing the egg membrane open so that a helping hand may be required (HAUSCHILD & GASSNER 1995). A litter comprises 7 to 25 babies that measure about 6 to 10 cm in total length and weigh 1.5-3 g. According to MATZ (1973) they will have grown to 20.5 cm on average after five months. On reaching an age of nine months the skinks measure around 26.5 cm, and 31.5 cm after one year.

The newborns are initially safe from any aggression by the adults. It is nevertheless recommendable to raise them separated from their parents. A terrarium measuring 60 × 30 × 30 cm is, for the beginning, large enough to house about eight babies. If their number is greater, they should be split up in correspondingly small groups. The babies are first kept on kitchen paper in order to prevent infections of the still not fully closed navel. Once the latter has properly healed the paper is replaced with a mixture of coarse wood shavings and peat. This mix offers the advantage of keeping moisture without becoming sticky. The decoration may consist of some flat pieces of bark or cork tubes for the small skinks to hide under, a few climbing branches, and a water bowl. The terrarium may be illuminated with a fluorescent tube.

MUDRACK (1974) left the newborns with the adults. It became apparent that there is a bite inhibition since the small skinks were left alone even during feeding. This mechanism appears to fall away only on reaching an age of four months when the young have grown to 15-16 cm, and they are from now on attacked during feeding.

Some juveniles accept food already on the first day, whereas in others the hunger will be great enough to overcome the initial shyness only after a week. They feed on small snails and slugs, or cut up snail meat. The ability to crush snails is present right from the beginning. Cat food with very finely crushed snails is also accepted (STEIN pers. comm.). It is advisable to feed them on a daily basis for the first four weeks of life, thereafter one may offer food only every other day. The amounts depend wholly on the appetite of the young: they are fed until all of them are satiated.

The young snail eaters prove to be very jealous of food for which reason the aggressive little rascals should be monitored closely when food is present. If two of them try to secure the same feeder snail, the keeper has to interfere immediately and separate them, because once they have both sunk their teeth into the prey, none will let go. This may result in severe injuries to the jaws, or even the entire head, and usually ends with death. If individual specimens show a stunted growth, it may be an indication of stress. The only remedy is to split up the group again and form new groups with fewer members. Other than that raising young *Cyclodomorphus gerrardii* is easy. They will double their size and mass within four months, and will be fully grown after a year. They mature at two years of age although MATZ & VANDERHAEGE (1980) indicated that maturity would set in only in their third year of life.

## Literature

ABRAHAM, G. (1980): Kopulationsbeobachtungen bei *Tiliqua gerrardii*. – Sauria, Berlin, 2(2): 34.

BUNDESMINISTERIUM FÜR ERNÄHRUNG, LANDWIRTSCHAFT UND FORSTEN (1997): Gutachten über Mindestanforderungen an die Haltung von Reptilien vom 10. Januar 1997. – Sonderausgabe der DGHT, Rheinbach: 77 S.

COGGER, H.G. (1989): Australian Reptiles in Colour. – Port Melbourne (Treasure Press), 112 pp.

– (1992): Reptiles & Amphibians of Australia. – Reed International Books, Chatswood, 775 pp.

CZECHURA, G.V. (1986): Distant exiles: frogs and reptiles recorded from Kroombit Tops, southeastern Queensland. – Queensland Naturalist, 27(1–4): 61–67.

EHMANN, H. (1992): Encyclopedia of Australian Animals. Reptiles. – The National Photographic Index of Australian Wildlife. Strahan, R. & Ehmann, H. Collins, Angus & Robertson Publishers Pty Limited., 495 PP.

GRAY, J.E. (1845): Reptiles. - Pp. 1–8 in: RICHARDSON, J. & J.E. GRAY (eds.) (1844–1875): The Zoology of the Voyage of H.M.S. Erebus and Terror, under the Command of Captain Sire James Clark Ross, R.N., F.R.S., during the Years 1839 to 1843. – Volume 2. – London (E. W. Janson).

GRAY, J.E. & A. GÜNTHER (1995): The Lizards of Australia and New Zealand. With an introduction by GLENN M. SHEA. – St. Louis (Society for the Study of Amphibians and Reptiles.), 29 pp.

HAUSCHILD, A. (1988): Bemerkungen zu Haltung und Zucht des Schneckenskinkes *Tiliqua gerrardii* (GRAY, 1845). – Salamandra, 24 (4): 248–257.

HAUSCHILD, A. & P. GAßNER (1995): Skinke im Terrarium. – Landbuch Verlag, Hannover, 197 S.

HUTCHINSON, M.N. (1981): The systematic relationships of the genera *Egernia* and *Tiliqua* (Lacertilia: Scincidae). A review and immunological reassessment. – Pp. 176–193 in: BANKS, C.B. & A.A. MARTIN (eds.): Proceeedings of the Melbourne Herpetological Symposium. – Melbourne (Zoological Board of Victoria).

HOSER, R. T. (1989): Australian Reptiles & Frogs. – Pierson & Co, Sydney Australia, 238 pp.

MATZ, G. (1973): Biologie et reproduction de *Tiliqua gerrardii*. – Bull. Soc. Zool. de France, 98(4): 5900.

MATZ, G. & M. VANDERHAEGE (1980): BLV Terrarienführer. – BLV Verlagsgesellschaft, München Wien Zürich, 360 S.

MITCHELL, F.J. (1950): The scincid genera *Egernia* and *Tiliqua* (Lacertilia). – Rec. S. Aust. Mus., 9(3): 275–308 + pl. xxiii.

MUDRACK, W. (1974): Der Rosazungenskink, eine terraristische Kostbarkeit. – Das Aquarienmagazin, 8(10): 407–411.

MÜLLER, M.J. (1987): Handbuch ausgewählter Klimastationen der Erde. – Forschungsstelle Bodenerosion, Univ. Trier, 346 S.

OBST, F. J., K. RICHTER & U. JACOB (1984): Lexikon der Terraristik. – Landbuch-Verlag, Hannover, 465 S.

PETERS W. (1867): Herpetologische Notizen. – Monatsber. Königl. Preuss. Akad. Wiss. Berlin, 24: 13–37.

PETERS, U. (1967): *Tiliqua gerrardii* und *Tiliqua casuarinae*, zwei wenig bekannte Echsen – AT, Jena/Leipzig/Berlin, 3: 94–96.

PETERS, U. (1986): Australische Skinke – Das Aquarium, 20(206): 436–440.

SHEA, G.M. (1990): The genera *Tiliqua* and *Cyclodomorphus* (Lacertilia: Scincidae): Generic diagnoses and systematic relationships. – Mem. Queensland Museum 29: 495–519.

– (1992): The Systematics and Reproduction of Bluetongue Lizards of the Genus *Tiliqua* (Squamata: Scincidae) (4 Vols.) – Sydney (Unpubl. Ph.D. thesis, University of Sydney).

SMITH, J. & P. SMITH (1990): Fauna of the Blue Mountains – Kangaroo Press, Kenthurst, 95 pp.

WELLS, R.W. & C.R. WELLINGTON (1984): A synopsis of the class Reptilia in Australia. - Aust. J. Herpetol., 1(3-4): 73–129.

WELLS, R.W. & C.R. WELLINGTON (1985): A classification of the Amphibia and Reptilia of Australia. – Aust. J. Herpetol., Suppl. Ser., 1: 1–61.

WEIGEL, J. (1989): Care of Australian Reptiles in Captivity. – Reprint. Reptile Keepers Association, Gosford, New South Wales, 144 pp.

WILSON, S. K. & D. G. KNOWLES (1988): Australia's Reptiles, A Photographic Reference to the Terrestrial Reptiles of Australia – Collins Publishers, Sydney, 447 pp.

ZWINENBERG, A. J. (1976): Der Schneckenskink *Tiliqua gerrardii* (GRAY). – Aquaria, St. Gallen, 23(8): 123–126.

ZIMMERMANN, E. (1983): Das Züchten von Terrarientieren: Pflege, Verhalten, Fortpflanzung – Franckh'sche Verlagshandlung, Stuttgart, 238 S.

Author's address
Beate Löhr
Kaiserslauterer Str. 37
D-67098 Bad Dürkheim, Germany

# The *Cyclodomorphus branchialis* complex

GLENN M. SHEA

**Key words: Reptilia: Sauria: Scincidae:** *Cyclodomorphus branchialis, C. celatus, C. melanops melanops, C. m. elongatus, C. m. siticulosus, C. maximus, C. venustus,* **systematics, distribution, natural history, reproduction**

The slender bluetongues of the *Cyclodomorphus branchialis* complex are elongate, slender, short-limbed species, superficially similar to the sheoak skinks in body form. However, they differ in having the nasal scales in contact (vs. usually separated), the prefrontal scales separated (vs. in contact), and the pair of scale rows along the centre of the back (paravertebral scales) noticeably broader than those more laterally (vs. the same width or only slightly broader). The snout is also much more pointed than with the sheoak skinks, and the sexual dimorphism in adult body size is much less pronounced, with females only slightly larger than, or equal in size to, males.

The systematics of the *Cyclodomorphus branchialis* complex have confused generations of herpetologists, and have only been resolved recently, with the availability of much more extensive collections. Although a number of species were described between 1867 and 1923, these were described from small samples (between one and three individuals) from widely separated locations, and were gradually synonymized by later authors (LOVERIDGE 1934, MITCHELL 1950, STORR 1976). A new, much larger species from the north Kimberley, *Cyclodomorphus maximus,* was described by STORR (1976), but material from the rest of Australia, from desert to west coast, was regarded as one variable species, *Cyclodomorphus branchialis.* However, analyses of patterns of geographic variation and habitat preferences throughout the extensive distribution of this

"species" eventually resulted in the recognition of four species, one with three subspecies (SHEA & MILLER 1995). Each of these species and subspecies is geographically distinct from all others, with almost no contact between the species. As a result of this study, the name *Cyclodomorphus branchialis* was changed in application from a single widespread species occurring in a variety of habitats, to a species of high conservation significance, with a very restricted distribution in Western Australia that is subject to extensive habitat modification by agriculture.

Two species of gill-necked skink are recognized, the western *(C. branchialis)* and eastern *(C. venustus).* Both differ from the other members of the *C. branchialis* complex in having three or more dark oval blotches on the side of the neck, between ear opening and forelimb. The western and eastern gill-necked skinks differ from one another in scale counts: there are fewer paravertebrals and subcaudal scales in the eastern species. The western gill-necked skink is found in *Acacia* scrub from the Murchison River in the north, to the Irwin River in the south, and inland up to 220 km from the coast. It shelters in earth cracks and leaf litter. The eastern gill-necked skink is most common around the Port Pirie area in South Australia, where it shelters in burrows in coastal sandy soils in chenopod heaths, but also occurs farther inland at several localities in central and eastern South Australia. Populations of gill-necked skinks also occur in cracking alluvial

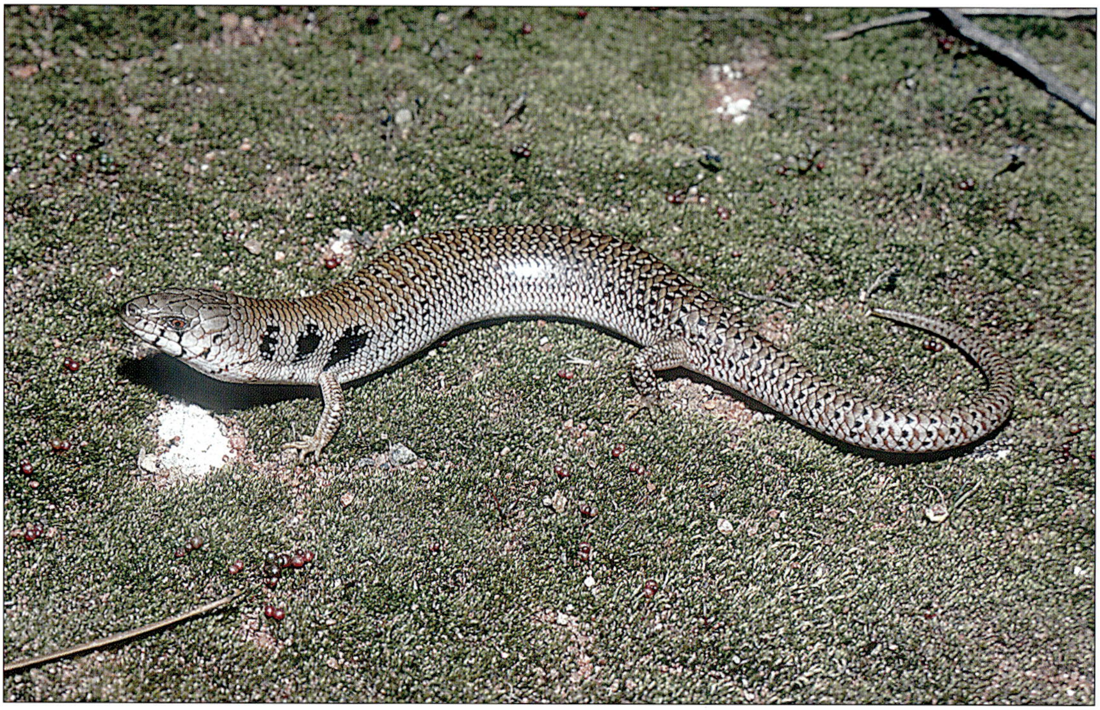

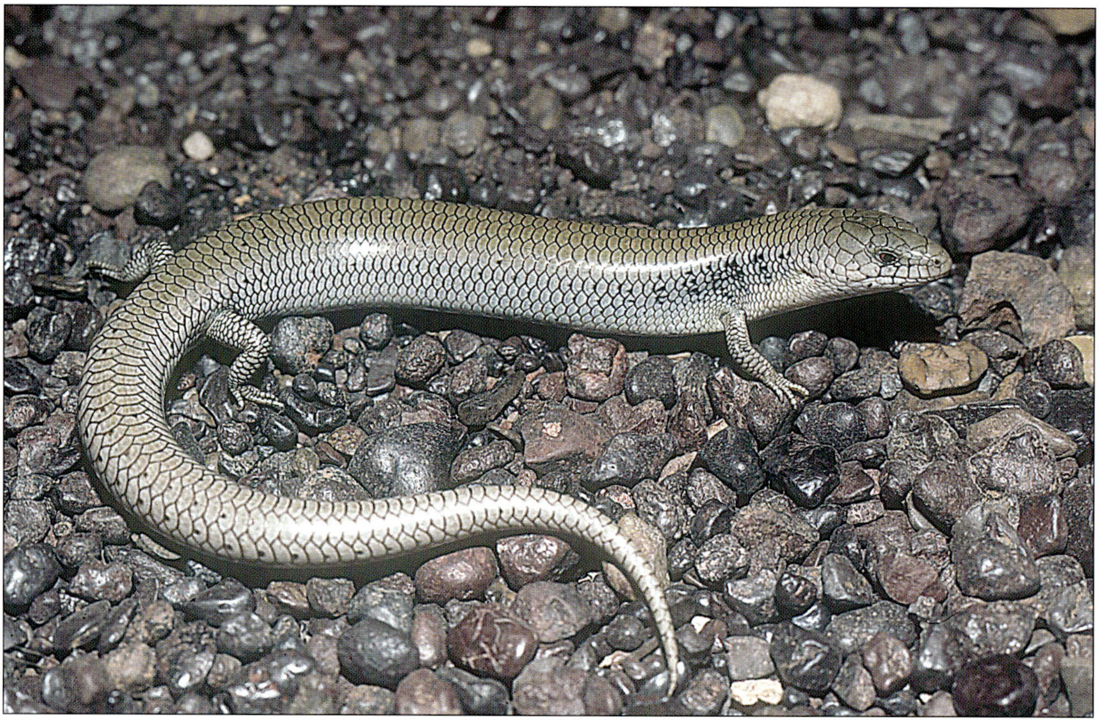

**Fig. 3** *Cyclodomorphus melanops melanops,* juvenile, from Kennedy Ranges, WA          Photograph:  G. Shea

soils farther north, in the vicinity of the common border between South Australia, New South Wales and Queensland, extending east to the Cunnamulla district in Queensland. These populations are currently regarded as eastern gill-necked skinks, although further studies may find that they are distinct.

The most widespread member of the *C. branchialis* complex is *Cyclodomorphus melanops.* Throughout most of its range, this species inhabits spinifex *(Triodia),* a type of grass that forms clumps in which the outward-pointing needle-like leaves form a dense matrix. The slender body, short limbs and thick smooth scales of the skink are ideally suited to movement through the spaces between needles in these tussocks, and the skinks rarely emerge from the tussocks into the open ground between them. The northern spinifex slender bluetongue, *C. melanops melanops,* occurs in spin-

ifex habits in the Pilbara and Kimberley regions, and Great Sandy Desert of western Australia, eastwards into central Australia. The southern spinifex slender bluetongue, *C. melanops elongatus,* occurs in spinifex habitats in the Western Australian Goldfields region, the Great Victorian Desert, and east and

**Fig. 4** *Cyclodomorphus melanops elongatus,* adult, from Comet Vale, WA          Photograph: G. Shea

Opposite from above
**Fig. 1** *Cyclodomorphus branchialis,* adult, from Galena, WA
**Fig. 2** *Cyclodomorphus venustus,* adult, from Sturt National Park, NSW          Photographs: G. Shea

north into central Australia, with isolated populations in eastern South Australia, south-western New South Wales, and western Queensland. In central Australia, where both subspecies occur, the distributions appear to interdigitate, and the differences between the subspecies become less distinct in the east.

The two subspecies may be distinguished by coloration and the arrangement of the temporal scales on the side of the head. The northern subspecies is generally paler in color (yellowish or reddish), with dark spots on dorsal and ventral scales, and has the primary and lower secondary temporal scales in contact, while the southern subspecies is darker in color (usually olive green), lacks dark markings, and has the primary and lower secondary temporal scales separated by the upper segment of the last supralabial.

Farther south, along the southern margin of the Nullarbor Plain, the Nullarbor slender bluetongue, *C. melanops siticulosus,* occurs. This subspecies is generally similar to the southern spinifex slender bluetongue, but is shorter-bodied, with fewer paravertebral scales, and shelters under limestone slabs in low heath habitats. The southwestern slender bluetongue, *Cyclodomorphus celatus,* occurs along the coastal plain from Perth north to Lake McLeod, extending inland in the Yuna district. It therefore occurs both north and south of the western gill-necked skink, although there is no known contact between the two species. In the south of the distribution, it lives in coastal heaths on limestone sands, where it shelters in loose sand and leaf litter, and under blocks of limestone. In the north, it inhabits spinifex clumps, as well as grassy coastal dunes. The south-western slender bluetongue differs from other members of the *C. branchialis* complex in usually having only 22 or fewer midbody scales, a pattern of short dark streaks on the body scales, and a small ear opening partially concealed by large overhanging scales.

**Fig. 5** *Cyclodomorphus celatus* from Ledge Point, WA    Photograph: M. Peterson

**Fig. 6** Habitat of *Cyclodomorphus celatus,* 36.4 km NE of Tamala H.S., WA     Photograph: M. Peterson

The final member of the *C. branchialis* complex is the Kimberley slender bluetongue, *C. maximus.* This species differs from the other species in its much greater size (SVL up to 231 mm, while the next largest species, *C. melanops,* attains a maximum SVL of only 132 mm). It inhabits rocky plateaus with vine forest and spinifex in the tropical north Kimberley.

All members of the *C. branchialis* complex for which data are available have male and female gonadal cycles peaking in spring, and give birth in mid to late summer. Most species give birth to from one to five young, although the only litter reported for *C. maximus* is of seven young. The young are about 40 mm SVL at birth, except for *C. maximus,* in which the young have a SVL of over 60 mm.

Slender bluetongues of the *C. branchialis* complex do well in terraria provided they have access to basking sites, a loose sandy or gravelly substrate in which they can burrow, and low dense grass tussocks in which they can hide. They will often warm themselves at basking sites while still hidden under the gravel or inside tussocks. Although they are found in semi-arid or desert habitats, these slender bluetongues inhabit microhabitats with relatively high humidities in these areas, and should be given access to water at all times. Like the Sheoak skinks, they are aggressive, both to each other and to other species, and should be kept solitary. This aggressive nature has led to them being colloquially called "garbage guts" among Western Australian herpetologists, as they eat anything held with them.

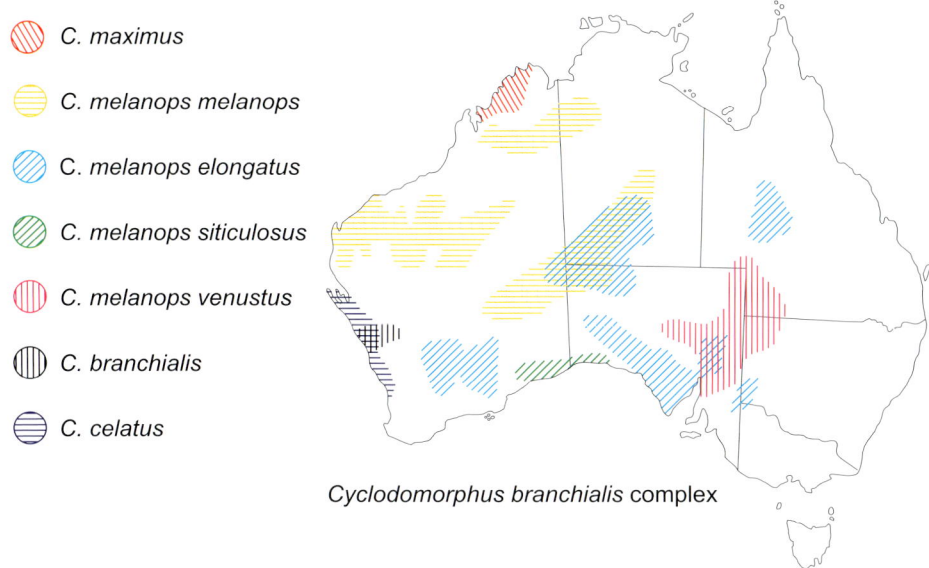

C. *maximus*

C. *melanops melanops*

C. *melanops elongatus*

C. *melanops siticulosus*

C. *melanops venustus*

C. *branchialis*

C. *celatus*

*Cyclodomorphus branchialis* complex

**Fig. 9** Geographical distribution of the species of the *Cyclodomorphus branchialis* complex

The natural diet of most species in the *C. branchialis* complex is arthropods, including insects and spiders. However, stomach contents of the few *C. maximus* have included remains of terrestrial snails, suggesting that this species, which has a large crushing tooth in each jaw, may specialise in snails, like the pinktongue. Captive animals of all species have eaten a wide range of insects and commercial pet foods.

**Literature**

LOVERIDGE, A. (1938): On some reptiles and amphibians from the central region of Australia. – Transactions of the Royal Society of South Australia 62(2): 183–191.

MITCHELL, F.J. (1950): The scincid genera *Egernia* and *Tiliqua* (Lacertilia). – Records of the South Australian Museum 9(3): 275–308.

SHEA, G.M. & B. MILLER (1995): A taxonomic revision of the *Cyclodomorphus branchialis* species group (Squamata: Scincidae). – Records of the Australian Museum 47(3): 265–325.

STORR, G.M. (1976): The genus *Omolepida* (Lacertilia, Scincidae) in Western Australia. – Records of the Western Australian Museum 4(2): 163–170.

Opposite from above
**Fig. 7** *Cyclodomorphus maximus,* juvenile, from Barnett River, WA
**Fig. 8** *Cyclodomorphus maximus,* adult, from Barnett River, WA          Photographs: G. Shea

Author's address
Dr. Glenn M. Shea
Faculty of Veterinary Science
University of Sydney
New South Wales 2006, Australia

# Sheoak skinks (*Cyclodomorphus casuarinae* complex)

GLENN M. SHEA

**Key words: Reptilia: Sauria: Scincidae:** *Cyclodomorphus casuarinae, C. michaeli, C. praealtus,* **systematics, distribution, natural history, reproduction**

Sheoak skinks are slender, elongate lizards with bodies of even diameter, short limbs (hindlimbs about 15-20% of snout-vent length, forelimbs a little shorter), and a relatively thick tapering tail. The color is variable, with red-brown, olive green and blue-gray individuals common. The common name for this complex refers to the scientific name of the first described species. Sheoak trees belong to the genus *Casuarina.* However, the name is not due to any direct association between the skink and the trees, but to a relationship between the lizard and a ship. The type specimen of the Tasmanian sheoak skink was collected by the Baudin Expedition to Australia (1801-04), on Bruny Island. That expedition had as one of the naturalists (the only one to survive to write about the voyage) Francois PÉRON, and one of the ships, the schooner Casuarina, purchased in Sydney during the expedition for inshore exploration. The expedition stopped over at Bruny Island, on the east coast of Tasmania, in January 1802. Of this visit, PÉRON (1807) wrote of "quelques beaux lézards analogues aux Scinques, différant toutefois essentiellement des animaux de celle famille par l'élégance des formes et le rapport des proportions", presumably referring to the sheoak skink. PÉRON died before being able to formally name the reptiles collected by the expedition, but the collections were sent to the Muséum national d'Histoire Naturelle in Paris. Here, a medical doctor, Jean-Théodore COCTEAU, was working on skinks, and examined PÉRON's collections for a major monograph he was writing on the family. Unfortunately, COCTEAU too died before being able to publish, but his names (in this case,

Keneaux de la Casuarina) were remembered when André-Marie-Constant DUMÉRIL and Gabriel BIBRON finally formally described the species in their "Erpétologie Générale" in 1839.

Sheoak skinks are patchily distributed along the coast and ranges of southeastern mainland Australia and Tasmania. Until recently, only a single species was recognized. However, studies of patterns of geographic variation in this species (SHEA 1995) resulted in it being divided into three species, which are geographically disjunct.

The Tasmania sheoak skink, *Cyclodomorphus casuarinae,* is restricted to Tasmania and to Betsy, Bruny, Maria and Tasman Islands along its east coast. On the main island of Tasmania, it is found from sea level to the central plateau, at altitudes of up to about 1200 m. There are few records from southwestern Tasmania, although this may simply reflect the difficulty of access to collectors of this remote area. The Tasmanian sheoak skink differs from other sheoak skinks in commonly having a complex color pattern with dark edges, streaks and blotches on the scales (although some individuals are unpatterned), a tail of about the same length as the body (shorter in juveniles), and usually 24 midbody scales. It is encountered in wet and dry sclerophyll forests, woodlands and grasslands, where it may be found sheltering under logs and flat objects of rubbish (such as corrugated iron sheets) on the ground, and in leaf litter.

The Northern sheoak skink, *Cyclodomorphus michaeli,* occurs in the form of several isolated populations along the coastal plain from north-

**Fig. 1** *Cyclodomorphus casuarinae,* from Mt. Wellington, Tasmania          Photograph: G. Shea

eastern Victoria to the central coast of New South Wales, with higher altitude populations in the Blue Mountains west of Sydney, the Barrington Tops region north of Newcastle, and farther north near Tenterfield. It differs from the Tasmanian sheoak skink in usually lacking a complex pattern (usually either plain or with dark lateral margins to scales forming a series of stripes), usually having 22 midbody scales, and a tail about a third to a half longer than the body (shorter in juveniles). Like the Tasmanian species, the northern sheoak skink occurs in wet and dry sclerophyll forests, woodlands and grasslands, especially tussock grasslands near swampy country, and also inhabits coastal heaths. It is secretive by nature, most often found sheltering under large flat objects on the ground by day.

The Alpine sheoak skink, *Cyclodomorphus praealtus,* has the most limited distribution, found only above 1500 m altitude in the Australian Alps, from Mt. Hotham in Victoria to Kiandra in New South Wales, a distance of only 175 km. It has a very short tail, less than three-quarters of body length, and is relatively short-bodied and smaller than the other two species. Compared to the northern sheoak skink, to which it is geographically closest, it has a greater number of scales at midbody (24-26 vs. usually 20-22). The Alpine sheoak skink inhabits alpine tussock grasslands, shrublands and woodlands, where it has been observed basking on, and being active within, grass tussocks. Individuals have been recorded sheltering under flat rocks and within bull-ant (*Myrmecia*) nests. Although knowledge is limited, it ap-

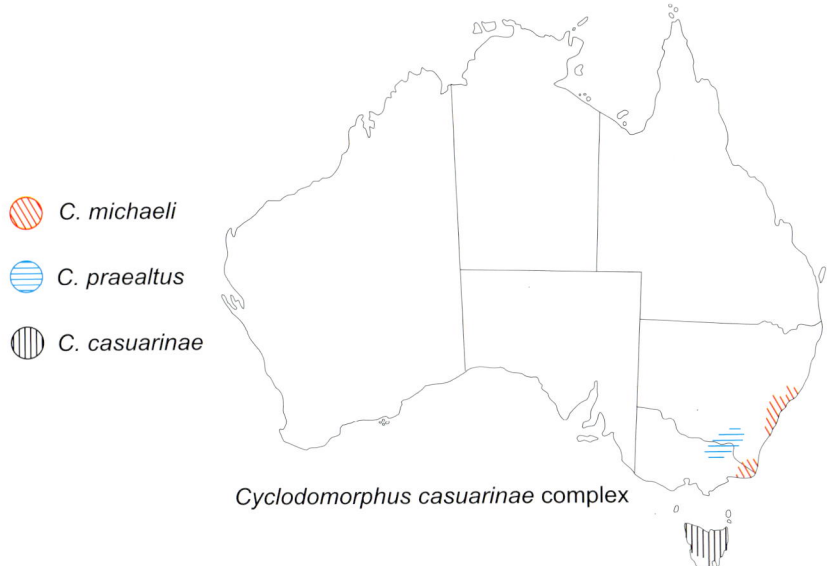

C. michaeli

C. praealtus

C. casuarinae

*Cyclodomorphus casuarinae* complex

**Fig. 4** Geographical distribution of the species of the *Cyclodomorphus casuarinae* complex

pears to be absent from very wet or closed habitats in the alpine region.

Sheoak skinks eat a variety of insects and terrestrial molluscs, with a higher proportion of insects in *C. casuarinae*, and snails and slugs in *C. michaeli* (SHEA 1988).

In all species of sheoak skinks, females attain much larger sizes than males, with the largest females of the two more widespread species (*C. casuarinae, C. michaeli*) reaching snout-vent lengths of 174 mm, about 37% longer than the largest males. In these two species, maturity is reached at a SVL of just over 100 mm for females, and between 74 mm (*C. michaeli*) and 85 mm SVL (*C. casuarinae*) for males. Mating probably occurs in spring, when testes are largest (at least in *C. michaeli,* the best-studied species), and ovulation occurs between mid-spring and early summer. Young are usually born in mid to late summer (possibly a little later in *C. praealtus*), after a gestation period of about three months.

Litter sizes are 4-14 (average 8) for *C. casuarinae,* 4-19 (average 8) for *C. michaeli* and 2-9 (average 5) for the smaller *C. praealtus.* Young are small at birth, between 40 and 46 mm SVL. Two independent observations of parturition indicate that this may extend over at least two days (PALMER 1888, TIMMS 1977).

Sheoak skinks are easily kept in captivity, and are potentially long-lived. One northern sheoak skink held by the author was adult when captured, and lived for another sixteen years, showing signs of age, such as body wasting, in its last year of life. Other adults of this species have been successfully kept in captivity for over five years on a regular basis. Juveniles have proven more difficult to maintain, due to their susceptibility to dehydration.

Opposite from above

**Fig. 2** *Cyclodomorphus michaeli,* juvenile, from Mt. Victoria, NSW          Photograph: G. Shea
**Fig. 3** *Cyclodomorphus michaeli,* adult, from Hazelbrook, NSW          Photograph: R. Hoser

Sheoak skinks are extremely aggressive, both to other animals and their own kind (MEBS 1974, PETERS 1967, RANKIN 1973, TIMMS 1977, SWANSON 1976, SWAN 1990). One wild-caught specimen had swallowed a white-lipped snake *(Drysdalia coronoides)* longer than its own body (SHEA 1988), and one captive animal killed three juvenile red-bellied black snakes *(Pseudechis porphyriacus)* (MEBS 1974). When disturbed, sheoak skinks will initially raise their heads and rapidly flicker the tongue, resembling a snake ready to strike (RANKIN 1973, TIMMS 1977, GREER 1989), and with further provocation, will lunge with an open mouth and bite. Captives housed together may repeatedly bite each other, sometimes breaking off tails and damaging scales. They will also bite and sometimes eat other smaller reptiles in the same enclosure. Not only the bitten lizard suffers in these encounters. Captive lizards which bite others repeatedly may suffer damage to the jaws, and cases of osteomyelitis have been observed. Consequently, sheoak skinks should be housed solitary.

A terrarium with leaf litter, wood chips or other loose substrate and flat items under which the animal can shelter is preferable. Sheoak skinks, like other bluetongues, bask, and a suitable basking site should be provided. Field body temperatures of active animals are around 33°C (RAWLINSON 1974), and the preferred body temperature of a captive Alpine sheoak skink was between 28 and 33°C (BENNETT & JOHN-ALDER 1986).

**Fig. 4** *Cyclodomorphus michaeli,* adult, from Katoomba, Blue Mountains, NSW          Photograph: R. Hoser

In the wild, sheoak skinks aestivate over winter. The habitat of the Alpine sheoak skink is snow-covered in winter, and frosts and snow are common in the range of the Tasmanian sheoak skink. Although snow is rare in the natural range of the northern sheoak skink, winter air temperatures average about 10°C (PARKINSON 1986). Captive animals will also aestivate over winter if given the opportunity. In captivity, sheoak skinks eat a variety of food. Natural items are insects and small snails and slugs, but they will also eat fish, raw meat, canned pet food and some fruit (MEBS 1974, PETERS 1967, pers. obs.).

## Literature

BENNETT, A.F. & H. JOHN-ALDER (1986): Thermal relations of some Australian skinks (Sauria: Scincidae). – Copeia 1986(1): 57–64.

DUMÉRIL, A.M.C. & G. BIBRON (1839): Herpétologie Générale ou Histoire Naturelle Complète des Reptiles. Vol. 5. – Librairie Encyclopédique de Roret, Paris. 854 S.

GREER, A.E. (1989): The Biology and Evolution of Australian Lizards. – Surrey Beatty & Sons, Chipping Norton. xvi + 264 pp.

MEBS, D. (1974): Haltungserfahrungen mit *Tiliqua casuarinae* (Sauria, Scincidae). – Salamandra 10(3/4): 104–106.

PALMER, E. (1888) in: Notes and exhibits. – Proceedings of the Linnean Society of New South Wales (2)3(1): 400–402.

PARKINSON, G. (ed.) (1986): Atlas of Australian Resources (Third series). Vol. 4. Climate. – Division of National Mapping, Canberra. 60 pp.

PÉRON, F. (1807): Voyage de Découvertes aux Terres Australes, exécuté par ordre de Sa Majesté l'Empereur et Roi, sur les Corvettes le Géographe, le Naturaliste, la Golette et le Casuarina, pendant les Années 1800, 1801, 1802, 1803 et 1804. Vol. I. – Imprimerie Impériale, Paris. 496 S.

PETERS, U. (1967): *Tiliqua gerardii* und *Tiliqua casuarinae*, zwei wenig bekannte Echsen. – Monatsschrift für Ornithologie und Vivarienkunde. Ausg. B. Aquarien Terrarien 14(3): 94–96.

RANKIN, P.R. (1973): Lizard mimicking a snake – juvenile *Tiliqua casuarinae* (DUMÉRIL and BIBRON). – Herpetofauna (Sydney) 5(4): 13–14.

RAWLINSON, P.A. (1974): Biogeography and ecology of the reptiles of Tasmania and the Bass Strait area. – Pp. 291–338 in WILLIAMS, W.D. (ed.). Biogeography and Ecology in Tasmania. Monographiae Biologicae (25). – W. Junk, The Hague, 498 pp.

SHEA, G.M. (1988): On the diet of the Sheoak Skink, *Cyclodomorphus casuarinae*. – Herpetofauna (Sydney) 18(1): 7–8.

– (1995): A taxonomic revision of the *Cyclodomorphus casuarinae* complex (Squamata: Scincidae). – Records of the Australian Museum 47(1): 83–115.

SWAN, G. (1990): A Field Guide to the Snakes and Lizards of New South Wales. – Three Sisters Publications, Winmalee, 224 pp.

SWANSON, S. (1976): Lizards of Australia. – Angus & Robertson, Sydney, 80 pp.

TIMMS, B.V. (1977): Notes on the Sheoak Skink. – Hunter Natural History 9(2): 99–102.

Author's address
Dr. Glenn M. Shea
Faculty of Veterinary Science
University of Sydney
New South Wales 2006
Australia

# Husbandry, status and protection - bluetongues past and present

HEIKO WERNING

**Key words: Reptilia: Sauria: Scincidae: *Tiliqua, Cyclodomorphus,* history, conservation, legislation**

## A look at the past

The unique fauna of the Fifth Continent has puzzled Europeans and Americans ever since it was discovered, and Australia's reptiles always ranked among the favorites of terrarium keepers the world over. Impressive, bizarre, or just particularly attractive species such as the frill-necked lizard, carpet and diamond pythons, Australian water dragons, and also blue-tongued skinks and shinglebacks, soon became some of the most sought-after terrarium animals. Already in the early days of the terrarium hobby, which came to experience its first boom right then (for a historical review see, e.g. MASURAT 2000), the large Australian skinks became corner stones in the range offered by dealers and therefore common inhabitants of private terraria.

In his milestone of terrarium literature, Johann VON FISCHER described five species of bluetongues for the terrarium already in 1884: *Cyclodus Casuariae* (today *Cyclodomorphus casuarinae*), *Cyclodus Nigroluteus* (today *Tiliqua nigrolutea*), *Cyclodus Boddaertii* (today *Tiliqua gigas* and *Tiliqua scincoides,* respectively), as well as *Trachysaurus Rugosus* (today *Tiliqua rugosa rugosa*) and *Trachysaurus Asper* (today *Tiliqua rugosus aspera*). All five could at that time be commonly found in the pet trade, and *von Fischer* noted for *C. Boddaertii* (in translation): "This last species is most commonly brought to London and easily obtained from there". As far as shinglebacks are concerned he noted: "Both species arrive in England every year in fairly constant numbers, and can be conveniently obtained in summer from Jamrach or Abrahams for modest prices (10-30 M. a head)". Further on he enthuses: "They belong to the most undemanding and most placid inhabitants of a warm dry terrarium, in which they thrive marvellously if they are provided with the necessary warmth, which next to their food is their main requirement (...). They become very tame, and because they are by nature everything but shy, they soon come to get used to being touched by their keeper.". It is therefore no surprise that these lizards very quickly ranked among the particularly popular terrarium animals.

Over the following decades - interrupted by World War I and the times of crisis it brought about - blue-tongued skinks (in particular *Tiliqua rugosa,* but also *T. scincoides, T. gigas* and *T. nigrolutea*) remained steadfast representatives in the terraria. An especially lively terrarium scene existed in Berlin at the beginning of the 20th century. The aquarium and terrarium association "Triton" - founded in 1888 as the second German society of this nature and still in existence today - provided a forum for the enthusiasts of that time. They were "supplied" by the company "Scholze & Pötschke" which imported a range of reptiles and amphibians on a regular basis (MASURAT 2000). On occasion of the 25th anniversary celebrations of "Triton", held in the "Karl-Haverlands-Festsäle" in Berlin in 1913, "Scholze & Pötschke" exhibited a desert terrarium "in which a variety of tortoises, shingleback lizards etc. led a calm life in an environment according to nature" (CONRAD 1913). SACHS (1931) reported on an import received from Australia by "Scholze & Pötschke": "More lizards had made the trip. Beautiful spiny skinks, *Egernia depressa,* which, as we know, are just as easily kept as blue-tongued skinks, of which a female had given birth to a number of charming young during transport". Almost in a bored manner, he also noted: "Also the usual shingleback lizards were again included.".

In 1929, HERRMANN reported on the successful breeding and raising of the blue-tongued skink *T. scincoides* in the Aquarium of the Zoological Gardens at Halle, Germany, and in 1936, MITSCH stated in his husbandry report on the same species: "*Tiliqua scincoides,* the bluetongue or smooth-scaled lizard from Australia and Tasmania, belong to the core stock of the advanced terrarium keeper, albeit the rare imports and the somewhat elevated price hinder a wide distribution. These animals must certainly offer a lot of interesting traits, for they, unlike many a species, have not vanished from the terraria of the enthusiasts. It is right to count *Tiliqua scincoides* among the most intelligent inhabitants of the terrarium available to us.".

Other references dealing with the early keeping of bluetongues in terraria are quoted in the chapter "History and systematics" by SHEA in this book.

With the terrarium hobby gaining momentum again during Germany's "economic miracle" after World War II, blue-tongued skinks and shinglebacks were once more kept more regularly. The species *T. rugosa, T. scincoides, T. nigrolutea* and *T. gigas,* and occasionally also the pink-tongued skink (then *Tiliqua gerrardii*), appeared constantly on dealers' lists up to 1974. Their prices depended on the size of an individual and ranged from 21 to 150 Deutschmarks in the early 60', to between 85 and 320 Deutschmarks in the early 70'. They were also dedicated extensive chapters in all books on terrarium keeping written during this period.

Up to the mid-seventies, the demand by keepers was covered exclusively by wild caught material imported from Australia. Australia actually experienced a genuine run on its natural resources in the 20th century. Large numbers of blue-tongued skinks were also caught for scientific research within Australia, but the majority were used to supply the Australian and European pet markets with live specimens (see the chapter "History and systematics" by SHEA in this book). Once the devastating repercussions of the "sell out" for the entire fauna of Australia became apparent, the Australian legislative imposed export stops for most Australian animals and plants, irrespective whether these were considered threatened in their continued existence or not.

The consequences of this measure were that the numbers of blue-tongued skinks kept in terraria outside of Australia diminished substantially. The husbandry of these so-called "easy" animals was still riddled with problems, attempts to breed them were unsuccessful more often than not, and keepers had by then dismally failed to build up sufficiently large terrarium populations. The low reproduction rates, in particular of the shingleback, must also be seen as a contributing factor that led to this situation. Prices for Australian blue-tongued skinks skyrocketed, and saw, depending on the species, several hundreds to 1500 Deutschmarks being demanded for one specimen.

The only species that was still regularly imported during the 70' and 80' was *Tiliqua gigas* from Indonesia. Animal dealers then to everybody's surprise discovered populations of *Tiliqua scincoides* and animals resembling *T. scincoides* on Indonesian territory in 1992. Until then the scientific community was entirely unaware of the existence of these large and certainly not inconspicuous lizards outside of Australia.

Meanwhile the pains taken by serious terrarium keepers were beginning to pay off, and by now, many blue-tongued skinks are bred successfully. With some patience and at a price, they are again available to the enthusiast as captive bred specimens.

## Status and protection

Except for *T. adelaidensis* bluetongues of the genus *Tiliqua* are not considered endangered in their existence. As far as Australia is concerned, EHMANN (1992) indicated all large species of *Tiliqua* to be "common/abundant". SHEA (in litt.) also considered none of the large species as threatened in Australia. One reason for this is certainly the biotopes in which the skinks live, which are widespread on the one hand, and which as yet have not fallen victim to rampant destruction on the other. To this can be added the adaptability of the skinks which often enables them to cope with man-made alterations of their natural habitats and has labelled them commensals. If an area offers the basic structures, they will even re-colonize gardens within the perimeter

Opposite from above

**Fig. 1** *Tiliqua gigas* is the only blue-tongued skink that has been imported regularly since after WW II

**Fig. 2** It was not before 1992 that Indonesian animal dealers discovered the existence of skinks similar to *T. scincoides*                     Photographs: F.B. Yuwono

of Australian cities (ACT Herpetological Association 1997).

The species *Tiliqua gigas* and *T. scincoides* are native to New Guinea and adjacent islands. YUWONO (1998) pointed out that both species are present on various islands (Moluccas, Tanimbar, Aru) and several regions of Irian Jaya (Vogelkop, Merauke) in forms that still require to be investigated taxonomically. With the descriptions of *Tiliqua scincoides chimaerea* SHEA, 2000, and *T. s. evanescens* SHEA, 2000 (see the relevant chapters in this book), the situation has become somewhat clearer, and another overview is given by HITZ & HAUSCHILD (in this book). However, the systematics of Indonesian bluetongued skinks are probably not comprehensively finalized at this stage.

As far as the population status of these two species is concerned, the situation appears to be not much different from that in Australia, despite the fact that there are no fundamental studies on the subject. In his work on the Indonesian portion of New Guinea (Irian Jaya) YUWONO (1998) placed them in his category "A" which means "abundant (thousands can be collected if needed)". This situation is probably again based on the ability of both forms to live as commensals that have managed to successfully conquer plantations and other areas influenced by humans (YUWONO in litt.). The continuous destruction of natural habitats does therefore not affect them as much as other animals. On the other hand are these skinks considered venomous in Irian Jaya and Maluku. Native people fear them and kill them on sight. For this reason the pet trade employs migrant workers from Java to catch them (YUWONO in litt.).

Nevertheless, *Tiliqua gigas* was granted a protected status by Indonesian law in 1978 (YUWONO in litt.), and in an updated version of his 1998 publication available on the Internet, YUWONO now indicates

this species only as "common" which is defined as "always available in adequate numbers" (YUWONO 1999). This categorization is, however, based on the availability to the pet trade, *T. gigas* is in fact now as before very common where it occurs (YUWONO in litt.).

## Endangered blue-tongued skinks

The dwarf bluetongue, *T. adelaidensis,* is the only species of the genus *Tiliqua* that is in danger to become extinct. It was already considered extinct until relict populations were eventually discovered in 1992. The thrilling story of its myth and the spectacular rediscovery of this species is told in the contribution by HUTCHINSON & MILNE in this book.

The cause of *T. adelaidensis* being endangered is mainly the destruction of its natural habitat. Dwarf bluetongues inhabit steppe regions of South Australia which used to cover vast stretches of land extending into the neighboring states of New South Wales and Victoria. By now some 98% of this region have undergone massive alterations for agricultural purposes. Just by ploughing of the original steppes many dwarf bluetongues were killed directly, but far worse was the resulting change to their biotopes. These skinks have adapted to a solidified soil that enables certain spiders to excavate burrows, and such type of ground is only found where no ploughing has taken place. Owing to their fascinating adaptation to certain soil characteristics the skinks simply cannot survive if the ground has been altered (see chapter by HUTCHINSON & MILNE). To this are added the loss of habitat through an expanding urbanization radiating from Adelaide and possibly negative secondary effects through agriculture, industries, and general pollution (TSN 1998). Another problem for the protection of this species is that the remaining populations of *T. adelaidensis* do not live on public land (owned by the state), or even inside protected areas, but on privately owned land (COGGER et al. 1993).

*T. adelaidensis* is listed in the Australian "Endangered Species Protection Act" of 1992 as an endangered species (EDGAR & STEPHENS 1993). The law distinguishes between two categories, and *T. ade-*

**Fig. 3** The only endangered species of *Tiliqua:* the pigmy bluetongue *T. adelaidensis*   Photograph: M. Hutchinson

*laidensis* was given the higher one, i.e. the status of "endangered". One consequence of this is that a "species recovery plan" had to be established (COGGER et al. 1993). Due to the fact that the knowledge of the ecology of this enigmatic species was insufficient for establishing a purposeful protection plan, the "recovery plan" had to start off with initiating a research program. At the same time, the Adelaide Zoo in collaboration with the South Australian Museum were entrusted with starting a preservation breeding program which unfortunately has so far been unsuccessful. The major task is to establish a basis of cooperation with the respective land owners in order to prevent negative influences on the remaining habitats of the species.

Starting in 1998, the "recovery plan" has been focusing on the following major tasks (TSN 1998):

– Continued research of the biology and ecology of the species
– Development of measures to expand the presently existing, sequestered distribution localities, e.g. by creating artificial burrows in suitable habitats
– Study of the genetical variability of the populations
– Education of the public

– Development of guide lines for land owners on whose grounds the populations live.

*Tiliqua adelaidensis* is furthermore listed with the status "endangered" in the "SA National Parks and Wildlife Act" of 1972, and as particularly protected species in Appendix I of the "Wildlife Protection (Regulation of Exports and Imports) Act" of 1982, with the latter being intended to also draw international attention to the problem (EDGAR & STEPHENS 1993).

As far as the sheoak skinks of the genus *Cyclodomorphus* are concerned, it is far more difficult to evaluate population situations and their possible endangerment. This is primarily due to the fact that, until recently, their systematic situation was entirely unresolved - nobody really knew how many species there were and where they lived. Older evaluations of their status are therefore very questionable. Only the works published by SHEA have now shed some light on this matter (see the two chapters on *Cyclodomorphus* by SHEA in this book). In the framework provided by the "action plan for Australian reptiles" *Cyclodomorphus* sp. (Samphire, SA) was categorized as "vulnerable" (no longer secured) (CAMERON 1993).

*C. venustus* is currently regarded as "rare or insufficiently known" at Australian federal level, *C.*

*branchialis* is considered "relevant for species protection" in Western Australia, *C. praealtus* is "protected" in Victoria, and the same is to be expected to happen in New South Wales in the near future (SHEA in litt.).

## Trade

**Papua New Guinea and Indonesia:** Papua New Guinea has imposed an complete ban on the export of wild animals (SHEA in litt.), and no information exists about possible illegal exports of bluetongues from there. In contrast, Indonesia pursues a policy of controlled exports of animals and plants (see the various contributions in ERDELEN 1998). Annual quotas are set for every species every year stipulating how many specimens may be exported. On this basis collecting permits are issued for certain numbers of specified species. The transport within Indonesian territory from one province into another requires a transport permit that is issued upon presentation of the collecting permit.

Since 1978 *Tiliqua gigas* is officially protected in Indonesia by the edict 327/Kpts/um/5/1978 issued by the Ministry of Agriculture which states that these animals may only be exported in the form of captive bred specimens (YUWONO in litt.). *T. scincoides chimaerea* is not subjected to any particular protection.

The Indonesian "Association of Amphibian and Reptile Exporters" set quotas of 1900 heads of *Tiliqua* each for the years 1997 and 1998, and one of 1350 for 1999 (YUWONO in litt.). These represent maximum export quotas; the numbers of actually exported animals may be lower. A substantially lower quota was being discussed for the year 2000 at the time this manuscript was prepared. The demand for bluetongues from Indonesia is "surprisingly low" (YUWONO in litt.). This has possibly to do with the fact that *Tiliqua gigas* were exported mainly from Seram in the past. These skinks have a reputation for being aggressive and less attractive, they were kept under insufficient conditions during transit, and therefore often reached the terraria of enthusiasts in desolate condition. Indonesian animal dealers have been exporting *T. scincoides chimaerea* and skinks resembling *T. scincoides* since the early nineties. In this connection a bizarre chain of events unfolded in the Netherlands (NUYT verb. comm.): since the discovery of *T. scincoides* by Indonesian animal dealers, the Dutch animal dealer Frek NUYT had been importing these skinks on a regular basis. Then, in 1995, the Dutch Attorney General had about 30 blue-tongued skinks confiscated from him, and charges were laid against NUYT. The argumentation was that *T. scincoides* would not occur on Indonesian territory, and therefore the animals must either have been smuggled illegally from Australia, or they were incorrectly declared *T. gigas*. Since *T. gigas* was a protected species in Indonesia, these could not have possibly been imported into the Netherlands legally. This point of view was then even confirmed by a highly repudiated Dutch herpetologist during the hearing of evidence. The resulting legal case has meanwhile taken some peculiar, twisted turns, with the confiscated animals disappearing under hitherto unknown circumstances, it has still not been heard before a court of law, and no verdict has as yet been handed down.

**Australia:** Australia is a federation of states, and all matters relating to the export of wild animals are controlled by the state for all of Australia in the same manner. Questions of collecting, keeping in captivity, or trading within the country, however, are dealt with by the individual state governments in different ways (see below).

No reptiles may be legally exported from Australia since the seventies. The law relevant to the export of animals today is the "Wildlife Protection (Regulation of Exports and Imports) Act" of 1982, and the executive office is "Environment Australia". The laws are enforced mainly by the Australian Customs Office, but also by the Federal Police. Legal disputes are heard before the "Administrative Appeals Tribunal". The act of 1982 was implemented in May 1984 and has since been subjected to three major alterations in the form of the "Wildlife Protection (Regulation of Exports and Imports) Amendment Act" of 1986 (number 120 of 1986), "Wildlife Protection (Regulation of Exports and Imports) Amendment Act" of 1991 (number 133 of 1991), and "Wildlife Protection (Regulation of Exports and Imports)

Amendment Act" of 1995 (number 121 of 1995) (Committee 1998). The most relevant core statement of the "Wildlife Protection (Regulation of Exports and Imports) Act" of 1982 is here, that animals cannot be exported legally from Australia. Although the law makes provision for exceptions for a number of species and for some special cases, but these do not include blue-tongued skinks.

Legal exports can only be effected through cooperation with zoological gardens or to mainly non-commercial scientific institutions which have proved their ability to reach their projected research goals in the past and have published their results. There are no exceptions for a commercial utilization.

In March 1998 the Australian Federal Government began a project aimed at rearranging the laws regulating environmental laws and those relating to species protection. The goal is to consolidate the various, scattered laws and edicts. The intention is to combine the new act and other laws relevant to species protection in the complex "Biodiversity Conservation Legislation" with the goal to "... promote the conservation and sustainable use of Australia's biodiversity". Given this framework of rearrangement the complex "sustainable use" of wild animals has again been tabled and is being reconsidered. At present the general opinion appears to tend towards a relaxation of the currently absolute export ban and facilitate a trade with captive bred specimens of certain species under certain conditions. The committee of the Senate of the Australian Parliament has recommended discussions to this effect, and the governments of most states (with the exception of Victoria) have voiced their support for such a relaxation (Committee 1998).

The summary of the hearing before the Committee of the Australian senate (Committee 1998) gives an indication that in the long run an export of captive bred offspring of certain species may become possible. The results of the discussion make it likely that this may also include some species of *Tiliqua*.

## Smuggle

Since it is possible to export blue-tongued skinks legally from Indonesia, there seems to be no serious smuggling problem in New Guinea. What is notable though, is that *T. gigas,* which may be exported from Indonesia only in the form of captive bred specimens, are occasionally wrongfully declared as *T. scincoides* which are not subjected to export regulations (YUWONO in litt.). It also appears probable that wild caught *T. gigas* are wrongfully declared as bred in captivity and then exported with permits.

The ban of exports of indigenous animals from Australia has been in place for about 30 years. Nevertheless a substantial population of Australian animals exists outside of Australia which, consequently, must have been smuggled out of that country illegally at one stage or another. New species also keep on popping up on dealers' lists, with various dwarf monitors and species of knob-tailed geckos (*Nephrurus* sp.) being recent examples. The export ban reduced the availability of Australian animals significantly and simultaneously send their prices skyrocketing. An often heard argument is that this measure has actually initiated increased smuggling activities. As the extent of smuggling is by nature unknown, the only indications are found in the statistics of uncovered attempts of smuggling and in the numbers of Australian animals traded outside of Australia. These estimations sum up to about 2000 reptiles being smuggled out of Australia on an annual basis (Committee 1998).

Table 1 gives an overview of the numbers of reptiles officially confiscated between 1984 and 1996. A particularly often smuggled species is the shingleback *Tiliqua rugosa* (Committee 1998, AULIYA in prep.). One of these cases was illustrated by ANONYMOUS (1986): the terrarium enthusiast Dieter BOXHEIMER tried to smuggle altogether 62 lizards, mainly blue-tongued skinks and shinglebacks, from Australia. He was arrested by customs officials at Tullamarine Airport near Melbourne and released after two days in jail on paying a fine of 30,000 Deutschmarks plus legal fees. Since then I have obtained information about other cases where considerably harsher fines were handed down for similar attempts.

As to how the smuggling activities are to be evaluated has become a debate where Australian officials are at loggerheads (Committee 1998). One side argues that the existence of Australian animals in terraria overseas would prove that smuggling must be going on at a significant level. The small numbers of uncovered smuggling attempts would therefore show that controls were insufficient. They demand more controls. The other side argues that the partly substantial efforts to identify and apprehend individual smugglers would be like trying to break butterflies on a wheel - the actual effect would be way too small for the costs involved. The estimated 2000 smuggled reptiles would make up some 0.0005% of the annual reptile mortality in Australia (Committee 1998).

**Legislative regulations in Australia**

Besides the federal laws mentioned above, regulations regarding the protection, collection, trade, and captive

**Table 1** Number of confiscated reptiles (number of detected smuggling attempts in parentheses) after McDowell (1997).

| Year | Number of confiscated reptiles (number of cases) |
|------|--------------------------------------------------|
| 1984 | 11 (1) |
| 1985 | 34 (2) |
| 1986 | 135 (1) |
| 1987 | 61 (2) |
| 1988 | 0 |
| 1989 | 11 (1) |
| 1990 | 1 (1) |
| 1991 | 43 (2) |
| 1992 | 145 (5) |
| 1993 | 0 |
| 1994 | 34 (3) |
| 1995 | > 60 (3) |
| 1996 | > 6 (3) |

keeping of animals lie in the competence of the individual states. These regulations are partly very different and should therefore be lined out briefly in the following. The laws are often very strict and are at present hotly debated in Australia (Committee 1998).

Even the transport of blue-tongued skinks from one Australian state into another requires both an export and an import permit issued by the relevant authorities of the two states involved. These are normally granted only in the case of captive bred specimens. No reptiles whatsoever may be transported from the Australian mainland to Tasmania.

The traditional utilization of reptiles by the Aborigines (e.g. as food) is permissable with certain restrictions. The **Australian Capital Territory** around Canberra, ACT, is autono-

**Fig. 4** Shinglebacks (here: *Tiliqua rugosa aspera*) are particularly often smuggled out of Australia
Photograph: O. Daniel

mous and has its own legislation (ACT undated, WILLIAMS 1993). All reptiles occurring in the ACT are protected by the "Nature Conservation Act" of 1980. No animals may be removed from nature for private purposes. The law distinguishes the species of reptiles for keeping in terraria according to four categories, and all regulations refer to captive bred animals only. "Exceptional species" may be kept and traded without permits; herein included are *Tiliqua scincoides* and *T. nigrolutea.* Category A includes *T. rugosa* and requires a permit which is also granted to beginners. Category B does not include any bluetongues. Category C, finally, lists *T. multifasciata, T. occipitalis,* and *Cyclodomorphus gerrardii.* Applicants for these permits are required to prove at least two years of experience with category A animals and one year experience with category B animals. Different regulations are in effect for scientific and educational purposes.

By **New South Wales'** laws all reptiles are under protection as well. For a long time only registered stock was permitted to be kept, and captive bred specimens could only be passed on to other licensed terrarium keepers. As it was impossible for a newcomer to obtain a permit terrarium keeping was practically outlawed. This system was changed only in 1997, and now every citizen of the state is entitled to apply for a keeping permit. The various species are listed in three categories which require different licences. Category 1 includes *Tiliqua scincoides, T. nigrolutea* and *T. rugosa.* A keeping permit is valid for two years and costs 40 Australian Dollars. Category 2 is irrelevant for bluetongues. A licence for category 3 animals is issued only to those terrarium keepers who have had a category 1 licence for at least two years. It is valid for one year and costs 120 Australian Dollars. Every transaction involving a category 3 animal (e.g. sale, acquisition) has to be applied for at least 10 days prior with the respective authorities. All licensed terrarium keepers have to supply reports to the authorities on an annual basis in April stating what has been happening to their collections.

Most of the reptiles native to **Northern Territory** are considered not endangered, notwithstanding all species are protected by law (Territory Parks and Wildlife Conservation Act 1978; Territory Wildlife Regulations). The legislation regarding this animal group is relatively liberal (GRAEME et al. 1993, HORNER in litt.): like many species of frogs and lizards, *Tiliqua multifasciata* and *T. scincoides* may be collected from outside of nature conservation areas, and be kept and traded without restrictions. The collecting and keeping of, or the trading in, other species requires permits. If their legal origin can be proved, permits are normally also issued for the other species of skinks.

Until recently, **Tasmania** was the only Australian state in which most of the reptiles, including the native blue-tongued skink *Tiliqua nigrolutea* and the sheoak skink *Cyclodomorphus casuarinae,* were not protected by law (ROUNSEVELL & SWAIN 1993). This has, however, changed in the meantime (SHEA in litt.), and all reptiles are now protected by law, and any commercial trading in them is prohibited. Private keepers have to prove their ability to look after their animals properly and will then be issued a "herpetology permit". This permit allows its bearer to keep reptiles, to swap them with other permit holders, and to catch up to six specimens per species in the wild.

In **Queensland** all terrestrial reptiles have been under protection since the early seventies. According to the "Fauna Conservation Regulation 1989", the collecting in the wild of representatives of 37 species native to Queensland was permissable with certain restrictions; a fee of between 25 and 200 A\$ was charged per specimen. The "Nature Conservation Act 1992" came into effect in May 1992. It rearranged nature conservation legislation of the state, also with the goal to address the acute problem of habitat destruction. A list of particularly endangered species was compiled, which does, however, not include any blue-tongued skinks. The usage of reptiles in the form of keeping them in terraria is in principle permissable as long as such usage is of a lasting character. This was more precisely specified by bringing into effect a new "Nature Conservation Regulation" in the mid-nineties which now made provision for a three-level permit system (similar to that of New South Wales) for private keeping. Besides some "exception species" which may be kept (but not traded) without permits under certain circumstances, there are two permit classes which also take into consideration the level experience of the keeper and the housing of the animals concerned.

The legal basis for the protection of reptiles in **South Australia** (BARRINGTON & CORNS 1993) is the "National Parks and Wildlife Act" of 1972. A permit system was also established in this state in 1993, listing reptiles in four categories. The first of these is made up of "exception species" which may be collected and kept without permits; it does not include any blue-tongues. Category 2 lists commonly kept animals with secured populations in nature and includes *Tiliqua nigrolutea, T. scincoides* and *T. rugosa*. Single individuals of animals in this category may be kept without permit, but if more than one specimen is kept, a permit is required which is usually issued without a problem. Trading is also permissable as long as it can be proved that the animals originate from a legal source. The keeper is required to keep a record book for his collection and report back to the "Resource Protection Branch" once every year. Category 2 contains species where a demand might cause damage to the natural populations and includes *Tiliqua multifasciata* and *Cyclodomorphus gerrardii*. The regulations are quite the same as for Category 1 animals, but written reports are required twice every year. A Category 3 permit is necessary for all other animals, and the requirements are much more strict (e.g., the authorities may physically inspect the husbandry installations).

In the state of **Victoria** three sets of laws affect reptiles: the "Conservation, Forest and Lands Act" of 1987, the "Wildlife Act" of 1975, and the Flora and Fauna Guarantee Act" of 1988 (MANSERGH et al. 1993). All reptiles are under protection in Victoria, and none may be collected, traded, or kept without a respective permit. The "Wildlife Regulations" of 1992 lie down the conditions for obtaining a licence for private keeping and trading. In the case of not particularly protected species permits may be issued for private keeping as well as trading. The only skink species currently with a "particularly protected" status is *Cyclodomorphus praealtus* (SHEA in litt.).

**Western Australia** has the most restrictive laws (EDGAR & STEPHENS 1993, PEARSON in litt.). The "WA Wildlife Conservation Act" of 1950 places all reptiles of this state under protection. *Tiliqua rugosa konowi* is particularly protected, as it is endemic to the nature conservation area of Rottnest Island. Collecting and keeping reptiles in captivity requires respective permits from the Department of Conservation and Land Management (CALM). Such permits are issued only to zoos and universities, a private individual does not stand a chance. This practically renders the private keeping of reptiles, including blue-tongued skinks, illegal in Western Australia, and contraventions have in the past been brought to court. The result is that many terrarium enthusiasts have gone underground and obviously do not publish their observations and study results.

This situation is expected to change soon (PEARCE in litt.), as CALM, in cooperation with the WA Society for Herpetologists, are presently engaged in designing a permit system based on the one in effect in New South Wales so that the keeping of captive animals will become possible. It may therefore be expected that at least some blue-tongued skinks will be included in the lowest category (reptiles well suited for keeping in captivity and easy to feed).

## International conventions

At present no representatives of the genera *Tiliqua* and *Cyclodomorphus* are protected by CITES (Convention on International Trade in Endangered Species of Wild Flora and Fauna).

In a study for TRAFFIC-Europe, however, AULIYA (in prep.) noted that *Tiliqua* spp. and *Cyclodomorphus gerrardii* are of relevance for the international trade. In his "Recommendations" he suggests that a protection status, i.e. listing in Appendix II, should be considered and implemented for these species (AULIYA in litt.).

The "species protection ordinance" of the European Union (EU), in force since June 1, 1997, lists the three species *Tiliqua gigas, T. scincoides* and *Cyclodomorphus gerrardii* (as *Tiliqua gerrardii*) in its Appendix D. This appendix names those species whose import into the EU justifies monitoring in order to possibly implement further protection measures at a later stage. A concrete protection level is

**Table 2** Imports and confiscations of blue-tongued skinks in Germany according to information received from "Bundesamt für Naturschutz" (in litt.)

| Reported imports | | | | |
|---|---|---|---|---|
| Year of import | Species | Number (heads) | Country of origin | Type |
| 1988 | T. nigrolutea | 2 | Switzerland | captive bred |
| | T. rugosa | 15 | Australia | wild caught |
| 1990 | T. nigrolutea | 1 | Switzerland | captive bred |
| 1991 | C. gerrardii | 5 | CSSR | captive bred |
| 1992 | C. gerrardii | 12 | CSSR | captive bred |
| | T. rugosa | 2 | Australia | wild caught |
| 1993 | T. gigas | 10 | Indonesia | wild caught |
| | T. scincoides | 20 | Indonesia | wild caught |
| 1994 | T. scincoides | 6 | Indonesia | wild caught |
| 1995 | T. gigas | 10 | Indonesia | wild caught |
| 1997 | T. scincoides | 9 | Indonesia | wild caught |
| 1998 | T. scincoides | 73 | Indonesia | wild caught |
| 1999 | T. scincoides | 9 | Indonesia | wild caught |
| | C. gerrardii | 4 | Czech Rep. | captive bred |
| Confiscations | | | | |
| 1996 | Tiliqua spp. | 2 | Switzerland | unknown |
| 1997 | T. scincoides | 2 | Czech Rep. | unknown |

not attached to this. Imports of Appendix D animals must only be reported to the relevant authorities, but no permits are required or issued.

The numbers of imported blue-tongued skinks registered (including confiscations) at the German "Bundesamt für Naturschutz" (BfN) from 1988 through 1997 is shown in Table 2; until EU regulations came into effect, the German "Bundesartenschutzverordnung" prescribed that all imports of *Tiliqua* spp. had to be recorded.

## Laws relative to terrarium keeping outside of Australia

No particular restrictions exist for the keeping of blue-tongued skinks in the US. Species, also from outside the US, which are not permissable in the free trade are listed in the "Endangered Species Act", but no representative of blue-tongued skink is included there.

In Germany, skinks of the genus *Tiliqua,* as well as *Cyclodomorphus gerrardii,* used to be particularly protected by the "Bundesartenschutzverordnung"

(BArtSchV) of 1986 and were listed in its Appendix 1. With the coming into effect of the EU Regulation No. 338/97 in June 1997 and only three species of blue-tongued skinks being listed in Appendix D, this protection has practically ceased. The revised version of the "BArtSchV", that came into effect in October 1999, was amended to be in accordance with this EU regulation. It resulted in blue-tongued skinks being no longer particularly protected by the "BArtSchV".

Also in Germany, complying with the "Gutachten über Mindestanforderungen an die Haltung von Reptilien" ("expert opinion of minimum requirements for the keeping of reptiles") (BML 1997) has become obligatory. It defines certain minimum specifications for the captive keeping for all groups of reptiles. Although it does at present not have a force of law, as it is neither a law or legal ordinance nor anchored in any laws, it is indirectly effective since the law against cruelty to animals prescribes an appropriate keeping of animals. In a case before a court of law it is most likely that the court would evaluate the "appropriate keeping conditions" on the basis of this opinion so that it would exert a binding effect indirectly (RÖSSEL 2000). On the other hand is this "opinion" merely a rough guideline that does explicitly not take into account factors such as raising conditions, resting phases, day/night rhythms, and makes provision for a tolerance in the furnishing and sizing of a terrarium. In the case of blue-tongued skinks of the genus *Tiliqua* (*Cyclodomorphus gerrardii* is listed there as *Tiliqua,* and *Tiliqua rugosa* appears as *Trachydosaurus*), the prescriptions shown in Table 3 are applicable. The dimensions of the terrarium ("enclosure size" - length x width x height) always refer to the keeping of one pair and have to be multiplied by the snout-vent length of the animals. An additional 15% of the surface area have to be added for every additional specimen.

The other skinks of the genus *Cyclodomorphus* have not been explicitly mentioned in the "expert opinion" since they are rather irrelevant for the German

**Table 3** Minimum requirements for the keeping of reptiles in Germany (BML 1997)

| Species | Habitat requirements | Enclosure size | Basic temperature | Local temperature | Social composition | Remarks |
|---------|---------------------|----------------|-------------------|-------------------|-------------------|---------|
| *C. gerrardi* | arboreal | 4 × 3 × 6 or 5 × 3 × 4 | 25-30 °C | 40 °C | 1,× | high humidity, tropical-moist substrate |
| *T. rugosa* | subtropical arid regions | 6 × 4 × 3 | 22-28 °C | 40 °C | ×,× | hiding places, one of which moist |
| other species of Tiliqua | subtropical / tropical, mainly arid regions | 6 × 4 × 3 | 25-30 °C | 40 °C | sometimes solitary | hiding places, one of which moist |

terrarium scene. As a rough guideline these would fall into the category "other skinks" that would require a terrarium of 4 × 4 × 5 or 5 × 4 × 4 times the snout-vent length of the individuals.

## Acknowledgements

My thanks go to Andree Hauschild for his suggestions relative to this contribution, as well as to Klaus Henle (Leipzig) and Robert Hitz (Thal). I am particularly indebted to Mark Auliya (Bonn), Frek Nuyt (The Netherlands), Glenn M. Shea (Sidney), M. Sterz (Bundesamt für Naturschutz, Bonn), and Frank Bambang Yuwono (Indonesia) for their answers to my questions and numerous details, as well as Gerhard Hallmann (Dortmund) and Werner Rieck (Berlin) for their scrutinizing and making available of numerous historical documents.

## Literature

ACT (undatiert): Reptile Policy. – ACT Government, Ref. 88/11741, Canberra; im Internet: http://www.act.gov.au/environ/REPPOL.html.

ACT Herpetological Association (1997): The herp friendly garden. –http://aerg.canberra.edu.au/pub/aerg/herps/actha/ha_home.htm

ANONYMUS (1986): Für 62 Echsen ins Gefängnis. – Ein Herz für Tiere, München, 3/1986: 20.

AULIYA, M. (in prep.): The European Union Trade with Live Reptiles. – TRAFFIC-Europe.

BARRINGTON, D. & T. CORNS (1993): Fauna laws in South Australia. – Pp. 356–358 in LUNNEY, D. &

D. AYERS (Hrsg.): Herpetology in Australia – a diverse discipline. – Trans. Royal Zool. Soc. New South Wales (Surry Beatty & Sons), Chipping Norton, 414 pp.

BML [Bundesministerium für Ernährung, Landwirtschaft und Forsten]: Gutachten über Mindestanforderungen an die Haltung von Reptilien vom 10. Januar 1997. – Sonderausgabe der DGHT, Rheinbach, 78 S.

BURBIDGE, A. & G. WYRE (1993): Conservation of reptiles and frogs in Western Australia. – Pp. 43–48 in Lunney, D. & D. Ayers (Hrsg.): Herpetology in Australia – a diverse discipline. – Trans. Royal Zool. Soc. New South Wales (Surry Beatty & Sons), Chipping Norton, 414 pp.

CAMERON, E. (1993): The development of „The action plan for Ausralian reptiles". – Pp. 109–119 in Lunney, D. & D. Ayers (Hrsg.): Herpetology in Australia – a diverse discipline. – Trans. Royal Zool. Soc. New South Wales (Surry Beatty & Sons), Chipping Norton, 414 pp.

COGGER, H.G., E.E. CAMERON, R.A. SADLIER & P. EGGLER (1993): The Action Plan for Australian Reptiles. – Australian Nature Conservation Agency Endangered Species Program No. 124, Austral. Nature Conserv. Agency, Canberra.

COMMITEE [Rural and Regional Affairs and Transport References Committee] (1998): Commercial Utilisation of Australian Native Wildlife. – Commonwealth of Australia, Canberra, ISBN 0 642 26781 2.

CONRAD, A. (1913): Die Jubiläumsausstellung des „Triton", Berlin. – Blätter für Aquarien- und Terrarien-Freunde: 457.

DAVIS, G.W., D.J. HEARD & R.E. CHATTO (1993): Legislation in relation to herpetofauna in the Northern Territory. – Pp. 333–336 in Lunney, D. & D. Ayers (Hrsg.): Herpetology in Australia – a diverse discipline. – Trans. Royal Zool. Soc. New South Wales (Surry Beatty & Sons), Chipping Norton, 414 pp.

EDGAR, B. & S. STEPHENS (1993): Commonwealth legislation relevant to reptiles and amphibians. – Pp. 39–42 in LUNNEY, D. & D. AYERS (Hrsg.): Herpetology in Australia – a diverse discipline. – Trans. Royal Zool. Soc. New South Wales (Surry Beatty & Sons), Chipping Norton, 414 pp.

ERDELEN, W. (1998): Conservation, Trade and Sustainable Use of Lizards and Snakes in Indonesia. – Mertensiella, Rheinbach, 9: 144 Pp.

FISCHER, J. von (1884): Das Terrarium, seine Bepflanzung u. Bevölkerung. – Frankfurt/M (Verlag von Mahlau & Waldschmidt) [Reprint 1989, Berlin, BINA Verlag für Biologie und Natur]: 296–301.

HERRMANN, J. (1929): Beobachtungen über die Fortpflanzung der Blauzunge (*Tiliqua scincoides*). – Blätter für Aquarien- und Terrarienfreunde: 115–116.

MANSERGH, I., G. DAVEY & P. ROBERTSON (1993): Reptiles and amphibians of Victoria – legislation. – Pp. 373–376 in Lunney, D. & D. Ayers (Hrsg.): Herpetology in Australia – a diverse discipline. – Trans. Royal Zool. Soc. New South Wales (Surry Beatty & Sons), Chipping Norton, 414 pp.

MASURAT, G. (2000): Chamäleons in menschlicher Obhut – Rückblick und heutiger Stand. –DRACO, Münster, 1(1): 34–51.

McDOWELL, D. (1997): Wildlife Crime Policy and the Law – An Australian Study. – AGPS, Canberra: 171–184.

MITSCH, H. (1936): *Tiliqua scincoides* White. – Wochenschrift für Aquarien- und Terrarienkunde, Braunschweig: 487–488.

PHILLIPS, S. (1993): Conserving the herpetofauna of Queensland – a look at the Nature Conservation Act 1992. – Pp. 377–381 in LUNNEY, D. & D. AYERS (Hrsg.): Herpetology in Australia – a diverse discipline. – Trans. Royal Zool. Soc. New South Wales (Surry Beatty & Sons), Chipping Norton, 414 pp.

RÖSSEL, D. (2000): Rechtsfragen bei der Haltung von Reptilien. – in Rauh, J. (2000): Grundlagen der Reptilienhaltung. – Münster (Natur und Tier - Verlag).

ROUNSEVELL, D. & R. SWAIN (1993): Current issues in the conservation of the terrestrial herpetofauna of Tasmania. – Pp. 71–74 in Lunney, D. & D. Ayers (Hrsg.):

Herpetology in Australia – a diverse discipline. – Trans. Royal Zool. Soc. New South Wales (Surry Beatty & Sons), Chipping Norton, 414 pp.

SACHS, W. B. (1931): Australien-Import. – Blätter für Aquarien- und Terrarien-Freunde

Shea, G.M. (2000a): Der Sunda-Blauzungenskink *Tiliqua scincoides chimaerea* subsp. nov. – S. 157-160 in HAUSCHILD, A., R. HITZ, K. HENLE, G.M. SHEA & H. WERNING (Hrsg.): Blauzungenskinke. Beiträge zu *Tiliqua* und *Cyclodomorphus*. – Münster (Natur und Tier-Verlag), 287 S.

– (2000b): Die Neuguinea-Blauzunge, *Tiliqua gigas* (SCHNEIDER, 1801): Ökologie und Übersicht über die Unterarten nebst Beschreibung einer neuen Unterart, *Tiliqua gigas evanescens* subsp. nov. – S. 177-189 in HAUSCHILD, A., R. HITZ, K. HENLE, G.M. SHEA & H. WERNING (Hrsg.): Blauzungenskinke. Beiträge zu *Tiliqua* und *Cyclodomorphus*. – Münster (Natur und Tier-Verlag), 287 S.

TSN [Threatened Species Network] (1998): Pygmy Bluetongue Lizard Species Profile Sheet. –http://www.nccnsw.org.au/member/tsn/context/profiles/224.html

WILLIAMS, K.D. (1993): Legislation and protection of reptiles and frogs in the ACT. – P. 58 in LUNNEY, D. & D. AYERS (Hrsg.): Herpetology in Australia – a diverse discipline. – Trans. Royal Zool. Soc. New South Wales (Surry Beatty & Sons), Chipping Norton, 414 pp.

YUWONO, F.B. (1998): The Trade of Live Reptiles in Indonesia. – Pp. 9–16 in: ERDELEN, W. (ed.): Conservation, Trade and Sustainable Use of Lizards and Snakes in Indonesia. – Mertensiella 7, Rheinbach

– (1999): The Trade of Live Reptiles in Indonesia. – http://www.geocities.com/RainForest/6785/paper.htm

Author's address
Heiko Werning
Seestr. 101
13353 Berlin, Germany

# Synonymy of the genera *Cyclodomorphus* and *Tiliqua*

GLENN M. SHEA

**Key words: Reptilia: Sauria: Scincidae: Lygosominae:** *Cyclodomorphus, Tiliqua,* **synonyms**

## *Cyclodomorphus* FITZINGER, 1843

*Cyclodomorphus* FITZINGER, 1843: 23. Type species, by original designation: *Cyclodus casuarinae* DUMÉRIL & BIBRON, 1839
*Omolepida* GRAY 1845a: 71, 87. Type species, by monotypy: *Cyclodus casuarinae* DUMÉRIL & BIBRON, 1839
*Hemisphaeriodon* PETERS, 1867: 24. Type species, by monotypy: *Hinnulia gerrardii* GRAY, 1845
*Homolepida* LÜTKEN, 1863: 294. Incorrect subsequent spelling of *Omolepida* GRAY
*Omolepidota* FROST & LUCAS, 1894: 227. Incorrect subsequent spelling of *Omolepida* GRAY

## *Cyclodomorphus branchialis* (GÜNTHER, 1867)

*Hinulia branchialis* GÜNTHER, 1867: 47. Lectotype: British Museum of Natural History, London, 1946.8.19.48, Champion Bay, Western Australia (F.H. DUBOULAY); lectotype designation by WELLS & WELLINGTON (1985: 28)

## *Cyclodomorphus casuarinae* (DUMÉRIL & BIBRON, 1839)

*Cyclodus casuarinae* DUMÉRIL & BIBRON, 1839: 749. Lectotype: Muséum national d'Histoire naturelle, Paris, 7131, Bruny I., Tasmania ("Australia" in original description) (F. PÉRON & C.A. LESUEUR); lectotype designation based on presumed monotypy by GUIBÉ (1954: 101)
*Cyclodus nigricans* PETERS, 1874: 621. Holotype: Zoologisches Museum, Berlin, ZMB 8193, Australia (W.H. FLOWER)
*Hemisphaeriodon tasmanicum* FROST & LUCAS, 1894, 227. Lectotype: Museum of Victoria, Melbourne, D2087, Lake St. Clair, Tasmania (W.B. SPENCER, donated by C. FROST); lectotype designation by SHEA (1995: 89)

## *Cyclodomorphus celatus* SHEA & MILLER, 1995

*Cyclodomorphus celatus* SHEA & MILLER, 1995: 272. Holotype: Western Australian Museum, Perth, R93111, Ledge Point, Western Australia (M. PETERSON, G. SHEA & B. COULSON)

## *Cyclodomorphus gerrardii* (GRAY, 1845)

*Hinnulia gerrardii* GRAY 1845b: pl. 9. Holotype: British Museum of Natural History, London, xv.5a, Australia
*Hinulia picta* MACLEAY, 1885: 65. Holotype: Macleay Museum, Sydney (lost), Herbert River, Queensland (A.J. BOYD)
*Tiliqua longicauda* DE VIS, 1888: 816. Lectotype: Queensland Museum, Brisbane, J1187, Rockhampton, Queensland (JAGGARD); lectotype designation by WELLS & WELLINGTON (1985: 30)

## Cyclodomorphus maximus (Storr, 1976)

*Omolepida maxima* Storr, 1976: 169. Holotype: Western Australian Museum, Perth, R27760, Kalumburu, Western Australia (W.H. Butler)

## Cyclodomorphus melanops melanops (Stirling & Zietz, 1893)

*Lygosoma melanops* Stirling & Zietz, 1893: 173. Lectotype: South Australian Museum, Adelaide R2732 (lost), between Everard Range, South Australia, and Barrow Range, Western Australia (Elder Expedition); lectotype designation, by considering the adult specimen as holotype, by Mitchell (1950: 304)

*Lygosoma gastrostigma* Boulenger, 1899: 918. Holotype: British Museum of Natural History, London, 1946.8.9.87, Sherlock River, Nicol Bay, Western Australia (E. Clement)

## Cyclodomorphus melanops elongatus (Werner, 1910)

*Lygosoma (Lygosoma) muelleri* Peters, 1878: 191. Lectotype: Zoologisches Museum, Berlin, 9373, Murray River (Krauss); lectotype designation by Shea & Miller (1995: 303). A subjective junior homonym of *Scincus muelleri* Schlegel, 1839

*Lygosoma (Homolepida) branchiale elongatum* Werner, 1910: 479. Holotype: Zoologisches Museum, Hamburg, R03961, Boorabbin (W. Michaelsen & R. Hartmeyer)

*Lygosoma (Homolepida) petersi* Sternfeld, 1919: 81. Replacement name for *Lygosoma muelleri* Peters, 1878

*Lygosoma (Homolepida) woodjonesii* Proctor, 1923: 80. Lectotype: British Museum of Natural History, London, 1946.7.17.97, St. Francis I., Nuyts Archipelago, South Australia (F. Wood-Jones); lectotype designation by Wells & Wellington (1985: 28)

## Cyclodomorphus melanops siticulosus Shea & Miller, 1995

*Cyclodomorphus melanops siticulosus* Shea & Miller, 1995: 308. Holotype: South Australian Museum, Adelaide, R26399, 15 km west of "Nullarbor" homestead, South Australia (K. Casperson)

## Cyclodomorphus michaeli Wells & Wellington, 1984

*Cyclodomorphus michaeli* Wells & Wellington, 1984: 89. Holotype: Australian Museum, Sydney, R 111948, Mt. Victoria, New South Wales (C.R. Wellington)

## Cyclodomorphus praealtus Shea, 1995

*Cyclodomorphus praealtus* Shea, 1995: 105. Holotype: Museum of Victoria, Melbourne, D39148, Three Mile Dam, Kiandra, New South Wales (W.A. Rawlinson)

## Cyclodomorphus venustus Shea & Miller, 1995

*Cyclodomorphus venustus* Shea & Miller, 1995: 312. Holotype: South Australian Museum, Adelaide, R18869, Port Germein, South Australia (T.D. Schwaner)

## Tiliqua Gray, 1825

*Tiliqua* Gray, 1825: 201. Type species, designated by Cogger et al. (1983: 188): *Lacerta scincoides* Hunter, 1790

*Trachydosaurus* Gray, 1825: 201. Type species, by monotypy: *Trachydosaurus rugosus* Gray, 1825

*Trachysaurus* Gray, 1827: 430. Incorrect subsequent spelling of *Trachydosaurus* Gray

*Cyclodus* WAGLER, 1828: pl. 6. Type species, by monotypy: *Cyclodus flavigularis* WAGLER, 1828

*Brachydactylus* SMITH, 1835: 144. Type species, by monotypy: *Brachydactylus typicus* SMITH, 1835

*Tiligua* DUMÉRIL, 1837: 16. Incorrect subsequent spelling of *Tiliqua* GRAY

*Keneaux* DUMÉRIL, 1837: 16. A nomen nudum (originally proposed without inclusion of species, the name taken from an unpublished manuscript by J. COCTEAU)

*Tachydosaurus* GRAY, 1838: 288. Incorrect subsequent spelling of *Trachydosaurus* GRAY

## *Tiliqua adelaidensis* (PETERS, 1863)

*Cyclodus adelaidensis* PETERS, 1863: 232. Lectotype: Zoologisches Museum, Berlin, 4710 (the larger of two specimens with the same number), Buchsfelde, South Australia (R. SCHOMBURGK); lectotype designation by WELLS & WELLINGTON (1985: 39)

## *Tiliqua gigas gigas* (SCHNEIDER, 1801)

*Scincus Gigas Amboinensis* BODDAERT, 1783: 15. A nomen nudum. Holotype: "Museum Physiophilorum" (unlocated)

*Lacerta Scincoides* HOUTTOUYN, 1787: 22. Holotype: Museum Houttuinianum (unlocated; the collection was broken up and sold at auction in 1787). Senior objective homonym of *Lacerta scincoides* HUNTER, 1790; name suppressed by the International Commission on Zoological Nomenclature (ICZN) (HEMMING 1956)

*Scincus gigas* SCHNEIDER, 1801: 202. Neotype: Nationaal Natuurhistorisch Museum, Leiden, 5197 (the larger of two specimens with this number), Ambon, Indonesia (F. KOPSTEIN); neotype designation by SHEA (2000c, i.e. the original edition of this book)

*Cyclodus flavigularis* WAGLER, 1828: pl. 6. Holotype: WAGLER's collection (whereabouts unknown), no locality indicated, but probably from the southern Moluccas, Indonesia

*Cyclodus Boddaertii* (in part) DUMÉRIL & BIBRON, 1839: 752. Syntypes: Muséum national d'Histoire naturelle, Paris, 1000, Ambon, Indonesia (J. QUOY & P. GAIMARD), and 3025, Java, Indonesia (H. KUHL & J. VAN HASSELT), and 3027, Port Jackson, New South Wales (in error) (J. QUOY & P. GAIMARD)

*Cyclodus carinatus* GÜNTHER, 1863: 59. Syntypes: British Museum of Natural History, London, 1946.8.10.1-2, North Seram, Indonesia

*Cyclodus petersi* STRAUCH, 1866: 454. Holotype: Zoological Institute, St. Petersburg, 368, no locality data, but probably from the southern Moluccas, Indonesia

## *Tiliqua gigas evanescens* SHEA, 2000

*Tiliqua gigas evanescens* SHEA, 2000c: 181. Holotype: Australian Museum, Sydney, R116664, Port Moresby, Papua New Guinea (J. PERNETTA)

## *Tiliqua gigas keyensis* OUDEMANS, 1894

*Tiliqua gigas keyensis* OUDEMANS, 1894: 138. Lectotype: Zoologisch Museum, Amsterdam, 10991, Key Islands, Indonesia (WERTHEIM); lectotype designation by DAAN & HILLENIUS (1966: 136)

*Tiliqua gigas keiensis* ROUX, 1910: 236. Incorrect subsequent spelling of *Tiliqua gigas keyensis* OUDEMANS

## *Tiliqua multifasciata* STERNFELD, 1919

*Tiliqua multifasciata* STERNFELD, 1919: 79. Lectotype: Senckenberg Museum, Frankfurt/M., 14037, Hermansburg Mission, Northern Territory (M. VON LEONHARDI), lectotype designation by MERTENS (1967: 78)

*Tiliqua occipitalis nossiteri* GLAUERT, 1923: 59. Lectotype: Western Australian Museum, Perth, R1013, Wallal, Western Australia (C. NOSSITER); lectotype designation by WELLS & WELLINGTON (1985: 40)

*Tiliqua occipitalis auriculare* KINGHORN, 1931: 88. Holotype: Australian Museum, Sydney, R10080, Broome, Western Australia (H. CLARK & A. LIVINGSTONE)

## Tiliqua nigrolutea (QUOY & GAIMARD, 1824)

*Scincus nigro-luteus* QUOY & GAIMARD, 1824: 176. Lectotype: Muséum national d'Histoire naturelle, Paris, 7134, Blue Mountains, New South Wales (J. QUOY & P. GAIMARD); lectotype designation by WELLS & WELLINGTON (1985: 40)

*Lacerta tarda* ANDERSON, 1967: 793.Holotype: painting by J. WEBBER, in the Department of Prints & Drawings, British Museum, London, from Adventure Bay, Tasmania. This name is unavailable, as it was first published as a junior synonym of *Tiliqua nigrolutea* (QUOY & GAIMARD, 1824), although it had been created in a manuscript written in 1777 but not published until 1967.

*Tiliqua milleri* WELLS & WELLINGTON, 1985: 40. Holotype: Australian Museum, Sydney, R92696, Port MacDonnell rubbish tip, South Australia (A. GREER)


## Tiliqua occipitalis (PETERS, 1863)

*Cyclodus fasciatus* LÜTKEN, 1863: 292. Holotype: Zoologisk Museum, Universitets Kjfbenhavn, Copenhagen, R47563, Australia (Captain MÖLLER). A subjective junior homonym of *Tiliqua fasciata* GRAY, 1839

*Cyclodus occipitalis* PETERS, 1863: 231. Holotype: Zoologisches Museum, Berlin, 4709, Buchsfelde, South Australia (R. SCHOMBURGK)

*Tiliqua occidentalis* WAITE, 1920: 24. A lapsus for *Tiliqua occipitalis* (PETERS)


## Tiliqua rugosa rugosa (GRAY, 1825)

*Trachydosaurus rugosus* GRAY, 1825: 201. Holotype: British Museum of Natural History, London, 1946.8.5.1, Australia (P. KING)

*Scincus peronii* WAGLER, 1830: 163. A nomen nudum (introduced in the synonymy of *Trachydosaurus rugosus*)

*Trachysaurus peronii* WAGLER, 1833: Tafel 36. Replacement name for *Trachydosaurus rugosus* GRAY

*Brachydactylus typicus* SMITH, 1835: 144. Syntypes: statusnot clear; one possibly an unregistered specimen in the British Museum of Natural History, London, from Australia (A. SMITH); second syntype presumed lost; listing of the specimen in the British Museum of Natural History, London, as the holotype by COGGER et al. (1993) is problematic (SHEA in prep.)


## Tiliqua rugosa aspera (GRAY, 1845)

*Trachydosaurus asper* GRAY, 1845a: 103. Lectotype: British Museum of Natural History, London, 42.6.29.58, Adelaide (C. FORTNUM); lectotype designation by WELLS & WELLINGTON (1985: 40)

*Lacerta ecaudata* CUNNINGHAM, 1925: 499. Syntypes?: none designated, from the Cudgegong River region, New South Wales (A. CUNNINGHAM); name unavailable because published as a junior synonym of *T. rugosa*


## Tiliqua rugosa konowi (MERTENS, 1958)

*Trachydosaurus rugosus konowi* MERTENS, 1958: 52. Holotype: Western Australian Museum, Perth, R12721, Rottnest I., Western Australia (G. KONOW)


## Tiliqua rugosa palarra SHEA, 2000

*Scincus tropisurus* PÉRON, 1807: 118. A nomen oblitum. Syntype: Nationaal Natuurhistorisch Museum, Leiden, 2842, Nouvelle Hollande (F. PÉRON); second syntype presumed lost

*Scincus pachyurus* GRAY, 1831: 67. A nomen nudum; introduced in the synonymy of *Trachydosaurus rugosus*, but based on the same material as PÉRON's *Scincus tropisurus*

*Tiliqua rugosa palarra* SHEA, 2000a: 106. Holotype: Australian Museum, Sydney, R133199, "Tamala" homestead rubbish tip, Western Australia (A. GREER et al.)

### *Tiliqua scincoides scincoides* (HUNTER, 1790)

*Lacerta scincoides* HUNTER, 1790 in WHITE: 242. Syntypes: presumed lost, New South Wales (J. WHITE)

*Scincus crotaphomelas* LACÉPÈDE, 1804: 209. Syntypes: Muséum national d'Histoire naturelle, Paris, presumed lost, Australia (F. PÉRON)

*Scincus tuberculatus* MERREM, 1820: 73. Replacement name for *Lacerta scincoides* HUNTER

*Tiliqua whitii* GRAY, 1831: 67. Replacement name for *Lacerta scincoides* HUNTER

*Cyclodus Boddaertii* (in part) DUMÉRIL & BIBRON, 1839: 752. Syntype: Muséum national d'Histoire naturelle, Paris, 3026, Port Jackson, New South Wales (J. QUOY & P. GAIMARD)

*Tiliqua whitei* GRAY, 1841: 423. Incorrect subsequent spelling of *Tiliqua whitii* GRAY

*L[acerta] scincoides* var. *australis* GRAY, 1845a: 104. A nomen nudum, introduced in the synonymy of *Cyclodus gigas*, manuscript name of G. SHAW

*L[acerta] variegata* CUNNINGHAM, 1925: 499. Syntypes?: none designated, from the Cudgegong River region, New South Wales (A. CUNNINGHAM)

*Tiliqua macroscincoides* WELLS & WELLINGTON, 1985: 39. Holotype: Australian Museum, Sydney, R68469, 10 km east of Mt. Carbine, Queensland (W. HOSMER)

### *Tiliqua scincoides chimaerea* SHEA, 2000

*Tiliqua scincoides chimaerea* SHEA, 2000b: 155. Holotype: Nationaal Natuurhistorisch Museum, Leiden, 5198 (the holotype is the only one of the four specimens under this number with a complete, original tail), Samlaki, Tanimbar Islands, Indonesia (F. KOPSTEIN)

### *Tiliqua scincoides intermedia* MITCHELL, 1955

*Tiliqua scincoides intermedia* MITCHELL, 1955: 393. Holotype: South Australian Museum, Adelaide, R3095, Yirrkala Mission, Northern Territory (R.R. MILLER)

## Literature

ANDERSON, W. (1967): A Journal of a Voyage in His Majestys Sloop Resolution. – Pp. 723–986 in: BEAGLEHOLE, J.C. (ed.). The Journals of Captain James Cook on his Voyages of Discovery. Vol. III. The Voyage of the *Resolution* and *Discovery* 1776–1780. Part Two. – Cambridge (Cambridge University Press and Hakluyt Society), 1647 pp.

BODDAERT, P. (1783): Specimen Novae Methodi distinguendi Serpentia. – Nova Acta Physico-Medica Academiae Caesareae Leopoldino Carolinae Naturae Curiosorum, 7: 12–16.

BOULENGER, G.A. (1899): Third report on additions to the lizard collection in the Natural-History Museum. – Proceedings of the Zoological Society of London 1898(4): 912–923.

COGGER, H.G., E.E. CAMERON & H.M. COGGER

(1983): Zoological Catalogue of Australia. Vol. 1. Amphibia and Reptilia. – Canberra (Australian Government Publishing Service), 313 pp.

CUNNINGHAM, A., in LEE, I. (1925): Early Explorers in Australia. From the Log-books and Journals, including the Diary of ALLAN CUNNINGHAM, Botanist, from March 1, 1817, to November 19, 1818. – London (Methuen & Co.), xii+651 pp.

DAAN, S. & D. HILLENIUS (1966): Catalogue of the type specimens of amphibians and reptiles in the Zoological Museum, Amsterdam. – Beaufortia 13(158): 117–144.

DE VIS, C.W. (1888): A contribution to the herpetology of Queensland. – Proceedings of the Linnean Society of New South Wales, (2)2(4): 811–826.

DUMÉRIL, A.M.C. (1837): Rapport sur un ouvrage manuscrit de M. le docteur Cocteau, ayant pour le titre: Tabulae synopticae Scincoideorum. – Comptes Rendus hebdomadaires des séances de l'Académie des Sciences, Paris, 4(1): 14–17.

DUMÉRIL, A.M.C. & G. BIBRON (1839): Erpétologie Générale ou Histoire Naturelle Complète des Reptiles. Vol. 5. – Paris (Librairie Encyclopédique de Roret), 854 S.

FITZINGER, L. (1843): Systema reptilium. Fasciculus primus Amblyglossae. – Vindobonae (Braumüller et Seidel), 106 + ix pp.

FROST, C. & A.H.S. LUCAS (1894): On a new skink lizard from Tasmania. – Proceedings of the Linnean Society of New South Wales, (2)8(2): 227–228.

GLAUERT, L. (1923): Contributions to the Fauna of Western Australia. – No. 3. Annotated List of Lizards from Wallal. – Journal of the Royal Society of Western Australia, 9(1): 57–60.

GRAY, J.E. (1825): A Synopsis of the Genera of Reptiles and Amphibia, with a Description of some new Species. – Annals of Philosophy, (2)10(3): 193–217.

– 1827: Reptilia. – Pp. 424–434 in: KING, P.P.: Narrative of a Survey of the Intertropical and Western Coasts of Australia. Performed between the Years 1818 and 1822. Vol. 2. – London (John Murray), 637 pp.

– (1831): A Synopsis of the Species of the Class Reptilia. – Pp. 1–110 in: GRIFFITH, E. & E. PIDGEON: The Animal Kingdom Arranged in Conformity with its Organization, by the Baron Cuvier, Member of the Institute of France. With Additional Descriptions of all the Species hitherto Named, and of many not before Noticed. Vol. 9. The Class Reptilia Arranged by the Baron Cuvier, with specific Descriptions. – London (Whittaker, Treacher, & Co.), 481 + 110 pp.

– (1838): Catalogue of the slender-tongued saurians, with descriptions of many new genera and species. – Annals and Magazine of Natural History, ser 2., 2(10): 287–293.

– (1841): A Catalogue of the Species of Reptiles and Amphibia hitherto described as inhabiting Australia, with a Description of some new Species from Western Australia, and some Remarks on their geographical Distribution. – Pp. 422–449 in: GREY, G.: Journals of two Expeditions of Discovery in North-west and Western Australia, during the Years 1837, 38, and 39, under the Authority of Her Majesty's Government. Vol. 2. – London (T. & W. Boone), 482 pp.

– (1845a): Catalogue of the Specimens of Lizards in the Collection of the British Museum. – London (Edward Newman), xxviii + 289 pp.

– (1845b): Reptiles. – Pp. 1–8 + pl. 1–4, 8–9, 12–14, 20 in RICHARDSON, J. & J.E. GRAY (eds.) (1844–1875): The Zoology of the Voyage of H.M.S. Erebus and Terror, under the Command of Captain Sir JAMES CLARK ROSS, R.N., F.R.S., during the Years 1839 to 1843. – London (Longman, Brown, Green & Longmans).

GUIBÉ, J. (1954): Catalogue des types de lézards du Muséum National d'Histoire Naturelle. – Bayeux (Colas), 119 pp.

GÜNTHER, A. (1863): Contribution to the herpetology of Ceram. – Proceedings of the Zoological Society of London, 1863: 58–60.

– (1867): Additions to the knowledge of Australian reptiles and fishes. – Annals and Magazine of Natural History, (3)20(115): 45–68.

HEMMING, F. (1956): Opinion 380. Suppression for nomenclatural purposes under the Plenary Powers of the catalogue of the collection of animals formed by Martinus Houttuyn prepared under the title *Animalium Musaei Houttuiniani Index* in connection with the sale of the collection in 1787. – Opinions and Declarations Rendered by the International Commission on Zoological Nomenclature, 12(1): 1–32.

HOUTTUYN, M. (1787): Catalogus Van eene uitmuntende Verzameling van allerley Soort van Dieren en Dierlyke Zaaken, Tot opheldering der Natuurlyke

Historie In meer dan dertig jaaren vergaderd en, volgens het Samenstel van den wydberoemden Linnaeus, in orde geschikt. – Amsterdam, viii + 170 pp.

HUNTER, J. in WHITE, J. (1790): Journal of a Voyage to New South Wales with Sixty-five Plates of Non Descript Animals, Birds, Lizards, Serpents, curious Cones of Trees and other Natural Productions. – Picadilly (J. Debrett), 299 pp. + 35 pl.

KINGHORN, J.R. (1931): Herpetological notes. No. 2. – Records of the Australian Museum, 18(3): 85–91.

LACÉPÈDE, B.G.E. (1804): Mémoire sur plusiers Animaux de la Nouvelle-Hollande dont la description n'a pas encore été publiée. – Annales du Muséum national d'Histoire naturelle, Paris, 4: 184–211.

LÜTKEN, C. (1863): Nogle nye Krybdyr og Padder. – Videnskabelige Meddelelser fra den naturhistoriske Forening i Kjobenhaun, 1862(20–22): 292–311.

MACLEAY, W. (1885): On some Reptilia lately received from the Herbert River district. – Queensland. – Proceedings of the Linnean Society of New South Wales, 10(1): 64–68.

MERREM, B. (1820): Versuch eines Systems der Amphibien. Tentamen Systematis Amphibiorum. – Marburg (Johann Christian Kreiger), 191 S.

MERTENS, R. (1958): Neue Eidechsen aus Australien. – Senckenbergiana biologica, 39(1/2): 51–56.

– (1967): Die herpetologische Sektion des Natur-Museums und Forschungs-Institutes Senckenberg in Frankfurt a.M. nebst einem Verzeichnis ihrer Typen. – Senckenbergiana biologica, 48(A): 1–106.

MITCHELL, F.J. (1950): The scincid genera *Egernia* and *Tiliqua* (Lacertilia). – Records of the South Australian Museum, 9(3): 275–308 + pl. xxiii.

– (1955): Preliminary account of the Reptilia and Amphibia collected by the National Geographic Society-Commonwealth Government-Smithsonian Institute Expedition to Arnhem Land (April to November, 1948). – Records of the South Australian Museum, 11(4): 373–408 + pl. xxxvii.

OUDEMANS, J.T. (1894): Eidechsen und Schildkröten. – Pp. 127–146 in: SEMON, R., Zoologische Forschungsreisen in Australien und dem Malayischen Archipel. Band 5. – Denkschriften der Medicinisch-Naturwissenschaftlichen Gesellschaft zu Jena, Vol. 8, 778 pp. + lxvii pl.

PÉRON, F. (1807): Voyage de Découvertes Aux Terres Australes, exécuté par ordre de Sa Majesté l'Empereur et Roi, Sur les Corvettes le Géographe, le Naturaliste, et la Goelette le Casuarina, Pendant les Années 1800, 1801, 1802, 1803 et 1804. Vol. I. – Paris (Imprimerie Impériale), 496 pp.

PETERS, W. (1863): Eine Übersicht der von Hrn. Richard Schomburgk an das zoologische Museum eingesandten Amphibien, aus Buchsfelde bei Adelaide in Südaustralien. – Monatsberichte der Königlichen Preussischen Akademie der Wissenschaften zu Berlin, 1863: 228–236.

– (1867): Herpetologische Notizen. – Monatsberichte der Königlich Preussischen Akademie der Wissenschaften zu Berlin, 1867: 13–37.

– (1874): Über neue Amphibien (*Gymnopis, Siphonops, Polypedates, Rhacophorus, Hyla, Cyclodus, Euprepes, Clemmys*). – Monatsberichte der Königlich Preussischen Akademie der Wissenschaften zu Berlin, 1874: 616–624 + pl. i–ii.

– (1878): Zwei Scincoiden aus Australien und einer neuen *Amphisbaena* von Westafrika. – Sitzungs-Berichte der Gesellschaft Naturforschender Freunde zu Berlin, 1878: 191–192.

PROCTOR, J.B. (1923): The flora and fauna of Nuyts Archipelago and the Investigator Group. No. 5. - The lizards. – Transactions of the Royal Society of South Australia, 47: 79–81.

QUOY, J.R.C. & P. GAIMARD (1824): Zoologie. – In DE FREYCINET, L.: Voyage autour du monde, Entrepris par Ordre du Roi, sous le ministère et conformément aux instructions de s. exc. M. le vicomte du Bouchage, secrétaire d'état au Département de la Marine, Exécuté sur les corvettes de S.M. l'Uranie et la Physicienne, pendant les années 1817, 1818, 1819 et 1820. – Paris (Pillet Aîné, Imprimeur-Libraire, de l'Imprimerie Royale), 712 S.

ROUX, J. (1910): Reptilien und Amphibien der Aru- und Kei-Inseln. – Abhandlungen der Senckenbergischen Naturforschenden Gesellschaft, 33(3): 211–247 + pl. xiii–xiv.

SCHNEIDER, J.G. (1801): Historiae Amphibiorum naturalis et literariae. Fasciculus Secundus continens Crocodilos, Scincos, Chamaesauras, Boas, Pseudoboas, Elapes, Angues, Amphisbaenas et Caecilias. – Jena (F. Frommann), 364 pp.

SHEA, G.M. (1995): A taxonomic revision of the *Cyclodomorphus casuarinae* complex (Squamata: Scincidae). – Records of the Australian Museum,

47(1): 83–115.

– (2000a): Die Shark-Bay-Stutzechse *Tiliqua rugosa palarra* subsp. nov. – S. 108-112 in HAUSCHILD, A., R. HITZ, K. HENLE, G.M. SHEA & H. WERNING (Hrsg.): Blauzungenskinke. – Münster (Natur und Tier - Verlag), 287 S.

– (2000b): Der Sunda-Blauzungenskink *Tiliqua scincoides chimaerea* subsp. nov. – S. 157-160 in HAUSCHILD, A., R. HITZ, K. HENLE, G.M. SHEA & H. WERNING (Hrsg.): Blauzungenskinke. – Münster (Natur und Tier - Verlag), 287 S.

– (2000c): Die Neuguinea-Blauzunge, *Tiliqua gigas* (SCHNEIDER,1801): Ökologie und Übersicht über die Unterarten nebst Beschreibung einer neuen Unterart, *Tiliqua gigas evanescens* subsp. nov. – S. 177-189 in HAUSCHILD, A., R. HITZ, K. HENLE, G.M. SHEA & H. WERNING (Hrsg.): Blauzungenskinke. – Münster (Natur und Tier - Verlag), 287 S.

SHEA, G.M. & B. MILLER (1995): A taxonomic revision of the *Cyclodomorphus branchialis* species group (Squamata: Scincidae). - Records of the Australian Museum, 47(3): 265–325.

SMITH, A. (1835): [Untitled]. – South African Quarterly Journal, 2(2): 143–144 + pl.

STERNFELD, R. (1919): Neue Schlangen und Echsen aus Zentralaustralien. – Senckenbergiana, 1(3): 76–83.

STIRLING, E.C. & A. ZIETZ (1893): Vertebrata. – Transactions of the Royal Society of South Australia, 16(2): 154–176.

STORR, G.M. (1976): The genus *Omolepida* (Lacertilia, Scincidae) in Western Australia. – Records of the Western Australian Museum, 4(2): 163–170.

STRAUCH, A. (1866): Über die Arten der Eidechsengattung Cyclodus Wagl. – Bulletin de l'Académie Impériale des Sciences de St-Pétersbourg, 10: 449–462.

WAGLER, J. (1828): Descriptiones et icones amphibiorum. Part 1. – Monachii, Stuttgartiae, Tubingae (J.G. Cottae).

– (1830): Natürliches System der Amphibien, mit vorangehender Classification der Säugthiere und Vögel. – München, Stuttgart, Tübingen (J.G. Cotta).

– (1833): Descriptiones et icones amphibiorum. Part 3. – Monachii, Stuttgartiae, Tubingae (J.G. Cottae).

WAITE, E.R. (1920): List of donations to the Museum during the year ended June 30th, 1920. – Pp. 23–24 in: Report of the Board of Governors of the Public Library, Museum, and Art Gallery of South Australia for 1919–20. – Adelaide (Government Printer), 25 pp.

WELLS, R.W. & C.R. WELLINGTON (1984): A synopsis of the class Reptilia in Australia. – Australian Journal of Herpetology, 1(3–4): 73–129.

– (1985): A classification of the Amphibia and Reptilia of Australia. – Australian Journal of Herpetology, Supplementary Series, (1): 1–61.

WERNER, F. (1910): Reptilia (Geckonidae und Scincidae). – Pp. 451–493 in MICHAELSEN, W. & R. HARTMEYER (eds.): Die Fauna Südwest Australiens. Ergebnisse der Hamburger südwest-australischen Forschungsreise 1905 herausgegeben von Prof. Dr. W. MICHAELSEN und Dr. R. HARTMEYER, Vol. 2. – Jena (Gustav Fischer), 493 S.

Author's address

Dr. Glenn M. Shea
Faculty of Veterinary Science
University of Sydney
New South Wales 2006
Australia

# A guide to the literature on the genera *Tiliqua* and *Cyclodomorphus*

## Robert Hitz and Klaus Henle

**Key words:** Reptilia: Sauria: Scincidae: *Tiliqua, Cyclodomorphus,* bibliography

## Introduction

The scientifically working herpetologist as well as the interested terrarium enthusiast cannot possibly do without a study of facts already known and published by others for their work or for optimizing the husbandry conditions for the respective animals, whatever the case. Until recently, this knowledge was available exclusively in the form of printed matters, photographs, or film. Today, a lot of information can also be found in the world wide web (www), the Internet, where most of it is accessible free of charge.

This chapter is intended to provide some hints on how to locate literature on the genera *Tiliqua* and *Cyclodomorphus.* It also includes a collection of references that represents a complete list of the literature used for this book plus other, complementary works.

## The bibliography contained in the dissertation of G.M. Shea (literature before 1992)

This is a truly unique bibliography of the genera *Tiliqua* and *Cyclodomorphus* Shea compiled for his dissertation, finalized in 1992. The third volume of this treatise contains on pages 639-1054 a collection of 2200 references dealing with the genera *Tiliqua* and *Cyclodomorphus,* ranging from the earliest written records of the 18th century to the year 1992. Shea took great care to especially record all relevant primary literature without any omissions. When studying this bibliography it becomes apparent that, besides the countless scientific works, also articles published in amateur periodicals and terrarium books have been taken into consideration.

Each set of data consists of the complete reference, and is complemented by key words relating to the genera, species, localities and other important subjects dealt with in the respective text. It is most unfortunate that Shea's dissertation remained unpublished and therefore is difficult to access. The material can only be purchased in the form of microfiches from the library of the University of Sydney.

## Literature published after 1992

In order to catalogue the literature published after the completion of the dissertation by Shea, the senior author initiated searches for the period between January 1992 and May 1999 in the data banks "Biological Abstracts" and "Zoological Record" maintained by the company BIOSIS. These unearthed a total of 88 works that contained information on *Tiliqua* and *Cyclodomorphus* and were mainly of scientific character, a majority of which were published by Australian universities. The yield of terrarium related publications obtained by this search was very low, the reason probably being that BIOSIS usually ignores publications of national societies of herpetology and terrarium enthusiasts and journals in languages other than English.

## "Hidden herpetology" (Shea 1993c)

The headline "Hidden herpetology" refers to the fact that numerous works are authored at universities the world over for academical degrees (e.g. BSc, MSc, and PhD dissertations) every year that remain unpublished. If the respective authors then fail to have their results published in scientific periodicals, the information remains hidden from the public. Whoever wants to work on a scientific subject is therefore advised to search for such unpublished works in university libraries. That this effort may reveal real treasures is clearly demonstrated by the dissertation by SHEA (1992)! In his article on herpetology in Australia this author also pointed to this problem (SHEA 1993c) and listed a total of 470 works from the period between 1970 to mid-1993, of which about 40 deal with information on the genus *Tiliqua*.

## The Internet as a source of knowledge

The world wide web (Internet) is home to vast amounts of information which can be located through the use of search engines. This is easily done by simply typing a key word (e.g. "Tiliqua") in the field provided and clicking "Go" or "Search". There are a number of search engines which access varying numbers of home pages or web pages (information pages) uploaded on the Internet. The greatest yield could be achieved by using the search engine "Altavista" which, in early July 1999, listed the following numbers of web pages found for "Cyclodomorphus" - 19, "Tiliqua" - 347, and "Trachydosaurus" - 60. These webpages can then be accessed individually from the lists appearing on the screen and studied for their contents. Quality ranges from insignificant to extremely interesting, and from amateur to highly scientific. Data may refer to dealers' pricelists, photo galleries, chatrooms for the exchange of experiences, husbandry descriptions (care sheets), to publications from museums and university institutions. By using e-mail, contacts are usually easily established with the authors of such web pages. Although this type of locating and exchanging knowledge is still in its infant stages, it is nevertheless no longer science fiction. It can only be recommended to every enthusiast and scientist.

## Reference collection for the genera *Tiliqua* and *Cyclodomorphus*

The following collection of references is a complete bibliography of the present book. The authors involved have referred to 348 publications, to which 144 works relative to the subject have been added

here; the latter are each marked with an *. This collection therefore includes 492 works in total which should represent the major portion of the relevant literature on the genera *Tiliqua* and *Cyclodomorphus* at this stage.

ABRAHAM, G. (1980): Kopulationsbeobachtungen bei *Tiliqua gerrardii*. – Sauria, Berlin, 2(2): 34.

ACT (undatiert): Reptile Policy. – ACT Government, Ref. 88/11741, Canberra; im Internet: http://www.act.gov.au/environ/REPPOL.html.

ACT Herpetological Association (1997): The herp friendly garden. –http://aerg.canberra.edu.au/pub/aerg/herps/actha/ha_home.htm

*ADLER, K.K. ( 1958 ): Observations on the Australian genera *Egernia* and *Tiliqua* in captivity. – Ohio Herp. Soc., 1(3): 9–12.

ALEXANDER, W.B. (1921): Aboriginal names of the animals of the Lyons River district. – J. Proc. Roy. Soc. Western Aust., 6(1): 37–40.

–*(1922): The vertebrate fauna of the Houtman's Abrolhos (Abrolhos Islands): Western Australia. – J. Linn. Soc. Zool., 34: 457–486.

ANDERSON, W. (1967): Appendix 1 – A journal of voyage in His Majestys Sloop Resolution. – Pp. 723–986 in BEAGLEHOLE, J.C. (ed.): The Journals of Captain James Cook on his Voyages of Discovery. Vol. III: The Voyage of the Resolution and Discovery 1776–1780. Part Two. – Cambridge (Cambridge University Press & Hakluyt Society), 1647 pp.

ANONYMUS (1986): Für 62 Echsen ins Gefängnis. – Ein Herz für Tiere, München, 3/1986: 20.

ARMSTRONG, G., J. REID & M.N. HUTCHINSON (1993): Discovery of a population of the rare scincid lizard, *Tiliqua adelaidensis* (PETERS). – Rec. South Aust. Mus. 26: 153–155.

ARNOLD, E.N. (1988): Caudal autotomy as a defense. – Pp. 235–273 in GANS, C. & R.B. HUEY: Biology of the Reptilia. – New York (Alan R. Liss).

*ARNOLD, V.H. (1971): Amphibians and reptiles. – Victorian Yearbook, 85: 1–36.

AULIYA, M. (in prep.): The European Union Trade with Live Reptiles. – TRAFFIC-Europe.

*BAARSLAG, A. ( 1980 ): Captive breeding of the Australian skink *Tiliqua gerrardii*. – Proc. 4th Annual Reptile

Symposium on Captive Propagation and Husbandry, Louisiana, ZCl Publ., 1980: 40–42.

BAEHR, M. (1976): Beiträge zur Verbreitung und Ökologie tasmanischer Reptilien. – Stuttgarter Beitr. Naturk., Ser. A (Biol.), Stuttgart, 292: 1–24.

BAMFORD, M.J. (1980): Aspects of the population biology of the Bobtail Skink, *Tiliqua rugosa* (GRAY). – Perth (BSc thesis, School of Environmental and Life Sciences, Murdoch University), 184 pp.

BANNERT, B. (1993): Erfahrungen zur Überwinterung von Eidechsen. – elaphe (N.F.), 1(2): 11–14.

BARBOUR, T. (1912): A contribution to the zoogeography of the East Indian islands. – Mem. Mus. Comp. Zool., 44(1): 1–203 + 8 pl.

*BARDEN, W. ( 1995 ): „Mobbing" behaviour. – Bird Observer, 752.

BARNETT, B. (1977): Additional notes on new-born Centralian Bluetongues (*Tiliqua multifasciata*). – Vict. Herp. Soc. Newsletter, 1: 10.

*BARRETT, C.(1927): Reptilienleben in Australien. – Blätter für Aquarien, Stuttgart, 38: 163–165.

BARRINGTON, D. & T. CORNS (1993): Fauna laws in South Australia. – Pp. 356–358 in LUNNEY, D. & D. AYERS (Hrsg.): Herpetology in Australia – a diverse discipline. – Trans. Royal Zool. Soc. New South Wales (Surry Beatty & Sons), Chipping Norton, 414 pp.

BARTHOLOMEW, J. & SON (1971): The Times Atlas of the World. – Zürich (Ex Libris).

BARTLETT, R.D. (1984): Notes on the captive reproduction of the Australian skink, *Tiliqua nigrolutea*. – Brit. Herpetol. Soc. Bull., 10: 34–35.

*BATEMAN, G.C. (1897): The Vivarium, being a practical guide to the construction, arrangement, and management of vivaria, containing full information as to all reptiles suitable as pets, how and where to obtain them, and how to keep them in health. – London (L. Upcott Gill), 424 pp.

BAUDIN, N.-T. (1974): The Journal of Post Captain Nicolas Baudin Commander-in-Chief of the Corvettes Géographe and Naturaliste assigned by Order of the Government to a Voyage of Discovery. – Adelaide (Libraries Board of South Australia), xxi + 609 pp.

BAVERSTOCK, P.R. & S.C. DONNELLAN (1990): Molecular evolution in Australian dragons and skinks: a progress report. – Mem. Queensland Mus., 29(2): 323–331.

BELS, V.L., M. CHARDON & K.V. KARDONG (1994): Biomechanics of the hyolingual system in squamata. – Adv. Comp. Environm. Physiol., 18: 197–236.

BENNETT, A. F. & H. JOHN-ALDER (1986): Thermal relations of some Australian skinks, Sauria: Scincidae. – Copeia, (1): 57–64.

BENNETT, G. (1834): Wanderings in New South Wales, Batavia, Pedir Coast, Singapore, and China. – Being the journal of a naturalist in those countries, during 1832, 1833, and 1834. Vol. I. – London (Richard Bentley), 440 pp.

*BENTLEY, P.J. (1959): Studies on the water and electrolyte metabolism of the lizard *Trachydosaurus rugosus* (GRAY). – J. Physiol., 145: 37–47.

BERG, J. (1897): Zur Kenntnis der Stummelschwanzechse (*Trachysaurus rugosus*). – Der Zoologische Garten, Frankfurt, 38(9): 277–279.

BIRD, D.M. & S.K. HO (1976): Nutritive values of whole animal diets for captive birds of prey. – Raptor Res., 10: 45–49.

BODDAERT, P. (1783): Specimen novae methodi distinguendi serpentia. – Nova Acta Physico-Medica Academiae Caesareae Leopoldino Carolinae Naturae Curiosorum, 7: 12–16.

BÖHME, W. (1988): Zur Genitalmorphologie der Sauria: funktionelle und stammesgeschichtliche Aspekte. – Bonn. zool. Monogr., 27: 1–176.

– (1995): Hemiclitoris discoverd, a fully differentiated erectile structure in female monitor lizards (*Varanus spp.*) (Reptilia: Varanidae). – J. Zool. Syst. Evol. Res., 33: 129–132.

BONNEMAINS, J., E. FORSYTHE & B. SMITH (1988): Baudin in Australian Waters. The Artwork of the French Voyage of Discovery to the Southern Lands 1800–1804. – Melbourne (Oxford University Press), 347 pp.

BOULENGER, G.A. (1887): Catalogue of Lizards in the British Museum (Natural History). Vol. III. Lacertidae, Gerrhosauridae, Scincidae, Anelytropidae, Dibamidae, Chamaeleontidae. – London (Trustees of the British Museum), 575 pp + xl pl.

– (1914): Reptiles and batrachians. – London (J.M. Dent & Sons), 278 pp.

*BOURNE, A.R. (1972): Reproductive endocrinology of the viviparous lizard *Tiliqua rugosa*. – Adelaide (PhD Thesis, University of Adelaide), 171 pp., Appendix, 49 pp.

*– (1980): Progesterone-like activity in the plasma of the viviparous skink *Trachydosaurus rugosus*. – Melbourne Herp. Symp., 14–16.

*– (1981): Blood metabolites of injected (14c) progesterone in the lizard *Tiliqua rugosa*. – Comp. Biochem. Physiol., 70 B: 661–664.

*– (1984): Occurence of 20b-hydroxysteroid oxidore-ductase activity in the kidney and liver of the lizard *Tiliqua rugosa*. – Comp. Biochem. Physiol., 77 B: 221–222.

*BOURNE, A.R. & R.F. SEAMARK (1973): The synthesis of corticosterone by the adrenal tissue of the lizard *Tiliqua rugosa*. – Comp. Biochem. Physiol., 45 B: 275–277.

– (1975): Seasonal changes in 17b-hydroxysteroids in the plasma of a male lizard (*Tiliqua rugosa*). – Comp. Biochem. Physiol., 50 B: 515–536.

– (1978): Seasonal variation in steroid biosynthesis by the testis of the lizard *Tiliqua rugosa*. – Comp. Biochem. Physiol., 59 B: 363–367.

BOURNE, A.R., B.J. STEWART & T.G. WATSON (1986): Changes in blood progesterone concentration during pregnancy in the lizard *Tiliqua (Trachydosaurus) rugosa*. – Comp. Biochem. Physiol., 3: 581–583.

*BOURNE, A.R., J.L. TAYLOR, B.J. STEWART & T.G. WATSON (1984): Seasonal variation in epitestosterone in the lizard *Tiliqua rugosa*. – J. Endocrinol., 102, Suppl.

*BOURNE, A.R., J.L. TAYLOR & T.G. WATSON (1985): Identification of epitestosterone in the plasma and testis of the lizard *Tiliqua (Trachydosaurus) rugosa*. – Gen. Comp. Endocrin., 58(3): 394–401.

– (1986): Annual cycles of plasma and testicular androgens in the lizard *Tiliqua (Trachydosaurus) rugosa*. – Gen. Comp. Endocrin., 61: 278–286.

*BRAAK, C. (1931): Klimakunde von Hinterindien und Insulinde. Band IV, Teil R. – in KÖPPEN, W. & R. GEIGER (Hrsg.): Handbuch der Klimatologie in fünf Bänden. – Berlin (Kraus).

BRADSHAW, S.D. (1986): Ecophysiology of Desert Reptiles. – Sydney (Academic Press).

*BRAUER, P. (1980): *Tiliqua scincoides*. Haltung und Zucht des Blauzungenskinks. – Sauria, 2(2): 5–12.

*BRAYSHER, M. (1971): The structure and function of the nasal salt gland from the Australian sleepy lizard *Trachydosaurus* (formerly *Tiliqua*) *rugosus*. – Physiol. Zool., 44(3): 129–136.

BREHM, A.E. (1883): Brehms Thierleben. Allgemeine Runde des Thierreichs. Dritte Abtheilung. Kreichthiere, Lurche und Fische. Erster Band. – Leipzig (Bibliographisches Institut), 673 S.

*BRENT, M.G. & M. HALPERN (1991): Discrimination of self from conspecific chemical cues in *Tiliqua scincoides* (Sauria: Scincidae). – J. Herpetol., 25(1): 125–126.

*BRISBANE, K. (1994): Deformities in blotched blue-tongue lizards *Tiliqua nigrolutea* after presumed dichlorous (pest strip) poisoning. – Monitor, Vic. Herp. Soc., 6(2): 55–57.

BRONGERSMA, L.D. (1933): Herpetological notes IX. Contribution to the herpetology of the Babber-islands. – Zool. Meded., 16(1–2): 27–29.

BROWN, G.W. (1991): Ecological feeding analysis of southeastern Australian scincids (Reptilia: Lacertilia). – Aust. J. Zool., 39: 9–29.

BULL, C.M. (1978): Dispersal of the Australian reptile tick *Aponomma hydrosauri* by host movement. – Aust. J. Zool., 26(4): 689–697.

– (1987): A population study of the viviparous Australian lizard, *Trachydosaurus rugosus* (Scincidae). – Copeia, 3: 749–757.

– (1988): Mate fidelity in an Australian lizard *Trachydosaurus rugosus*. – Behav. Ecol. Sociobiol., 23(1): 45–49.

– (1990): Comparisons of displaced and retained partners in a monogamous lizard. – Aust. Wildl. Res., 17(2): 135–140.

– (1994): Population dynamics and pair fidelity in sleepy lizards. – Pp. 159–174 in L.J. VITT & E.R. PIANKA (eds.): Lizard Ecology. Historical and Experimental Perspektives. – Princeton (Princeton University Press), 403 pp.

– (1995): Population ecology of the sleepy lizard, *Tiliqua rugosa*, at Mt Mary, South Australia. – Aust. J. Ecol., 20(3): 393–402.

BULL, C.M. & B.C. BAGHURST (1998): Home range overlap of mothers and their offspring in the sleepy lizard, *Tiliqua rugosa*. – Behav. Ecol. Sociobiol., 42(5): 357–362.

BULL, C.M., G.S. BEDFORD & B.A. SCHULTZ (1993): How do sleepy lizards find each other? – Herpetologica, 49(3): 294–300.

BULL, C.M., D. BURZACOTT & R.D. SHARRAD (1989): No competition for resources between two tick species at their parapatric boundary. – Oecologia 79: 558–562.

*BULL, C.M., S.J.B. COOPER & B.C. BAGHURST (1998): Social monogamy and extra-pair fertilization in an Australian lizard, *Tiliqua rugosa*. – Behav. Ecol. Sociobiol., 44(1): 63–72.

BULL, C.M., M. DOHERTY, L.R. SCHULZE & Y. PAMULA (1994): Recognition of offspring by females of the Australian skink, *Tiliqua rugosa*. – J. Herpetol. 28(1): 117–120.

BULL, C.M., A. MCNALLY & G. DUBAS (1991): Asynchronous seasonal activity of male and female sleepy lizards, *Tiliqua rugosa*. – J. Herpetol., 25(4): 436–441.

BULL, C.M. & Y. PAMULA (1996): Sexually dimorphic head sizes and reproductive success in the sleepy lizard *Tiliqua rugosa*. – J. Zool., London, 240: 511–521.

*– (1998): Enhanced vigilance in monogamous pairs of the lizard, *Tiliqua rugosa*. – Behav. Ecol., 9(5): 452–455.

BULL, C.M., Y. PAMULA & L. SCHULZE (1993): Parturition in the sleepy lizard, *Tiliqua rugosa*. – J. Herpetol., 27: 489–492.

BULL, C.M. & R. SATRAWAHA (1981): Dispersal and social organisation in *Trachydosaurus rugosus*. – P. 24 in BANKS, C.B. & A.A. MARTIN (eds.): Proceedings of the Melbourne Herpetological Symposium. – Melbourne (Zoological Board of Victoria).

BUNDESMINISTERIUM FÜR ERNÄHRUNG, LANDWIRTSCHAFT UND FORSTEN, REFERAT TIERSCHUTZ (1997): Gutachten über Mindestanforderungen an die Haltung von Reptilien, vom 10. Januar 1997. – Unveränderte Sonderausgabe der Deutschen Gesellschaft für Herpetologie und Terrarienkunde (DGHT) e.V., 77 S.

BURBIDGE, A. & G. WYRE (1993): Conservation of reptiles and frogs in Western Australia. – Pp. 43–48 in LUNNEY, D. & D. AYERS (Hrsg.): Herpetology in Australia – a diverse discipline. – Trans. Royal Zool. Soc. New South Wales (Surry Beatty & Sons), Chipping Norton, 414 pp.

*BUSH, B., B. MARYAN, R. BROWNE-COOPER & D. ROBINSON (1995): A Guide to the Reptiles and Frogs of the Perth Region. – Nedlands, (University of Western Australia Press), 226 pp.

*BUSTARD, H.R. (1968): The reptiles of Merriwindi State Forest, Pilligar West, Northern New South Wales, Australia. – Herpetologica, 24(2): 131–140.

BUSTARD, R. (1970): Australian Lizards. – Sydney, London (William Collins Ltd.), 158 pp.

*CABANAC, H.P. & H.T. HAMMEL (1971a): Comportement thérmorégulateur du lézard *Tiliqua scincoides*: Réponses au froid. – J. Physiol., 63: 222–225.

*– (1971b): Peripheral sensitivity and temperature regulation in *Tiliqua scincoides*. – Int. J. Biometeor., 15: 239–243.

CAMERON, E. (1993): The development of „The action plan for Ausralian reptiles". – Pp. 109–119 in LUNNEY, D. & D. AYERS (Hrsg.): Herpetology in Australia – a diverse discipline. – Trans. Royal Zool. Soc. New South Wales (Surry Beatty & Sons), Chipping Norton, 414 pp.

CAMP, C (1923): Classification of the lizards. – Bull. Amer. Mus. Nat. Hist., 48: 289–481.

CARD, W. (1993): Natural history and husbandry of the shingleback skink (*Trachydosaurus rugosus*) and the blotched blue-tongued skink (*Tiliqua nigrolutea*). – The Vivarium, Lakeside, American Federation of Herpetoculturists, 6(3): 26–27.

CARPENTER, C.C. & G.W. FERGUSON (1977): Variation and evolution of stereotyped behavior in reptiles. – Pp. 335–554 in C. GANS & D.W. TINKLE (eds.): Biology of the Reptilia Vol. 7. – New York (Academic Press).

CARPENTER, C.C. & J.B. MURPHY (1978): Tongue display by the common bluetongue (*Tiliqua scincoides*) (Reptilia, Lacertilia, Scincidae). – J. Herpetol., 12: 428–429.

CASARES, M. (1995): Untersuchung zum Fortpflanzungsgeschehen bei Riesenschildkröten (*Geochelone elephantopus* und *G. gigantea*) und Landschildkröten (*Testudo graeca* und *T. hermanni*) anhand von Ultraschalldiagnostik und Steroidanalysen im Kot. – Zool. Garten N. F., 65(1): 50–76.

*CHAUMONT, F. (1963): Meine Beobachtungen bei der Geburt kleiner Blauzungenskinke. – DATZ,16(5): 151–152.

– (1964): Die Aufzucht der jungen Blauzungenskinke. – DATZ, 17: 28–29.

CHRISTIANE, U. & H. WICKE (1994): West-Australien natürlich. – Hürth (VERBE Verlag und Beratung), 431 S.

*COGGER, H.G. (1967): Australian Reptiles in Colour. – Honolulu (East-West Center Press), 112 pp.

– (1979): Reptiles and Amphibians of Australia, Revised edition 1979. – Sydney (Reed), Hollywood, USA (Ralph Curtis Books), 608 pp.

*– (1980): A biogeographic study of the Arnhem Land herpetofauna. – Pp. 148–155 in BANKS, C.B. & A. A. MARTIN (eds): Proceeedings of the Melbourne Herpetological Symposium. – Melbourne (Zoological Board of Victoria).

– (1992): Reptiles and Amphibians of Australia, 5th edition. – Chatswood (Reed International Books), Ithaca, New York (Cornell University Press), 775 pp.

*COGGER, H.G., E.E. CAMERON & H.M. COGGER (1983): Zoological Catalogue of Australia. – Vol. I: Amphibia & Reptilia – Canberra (Australian Government Publishing Service), 313 pp.

COGGER, H.G., E.E. CAMERON, R.A. SADLIER & P. EGGLER (1993): The Action Plan for Australian Reptiles. – Australian Nature Conservation Agency Endangered Species Program No. 124, Austral. Nature

Conserv. Agency, Canberra.

COMMITTEE [Rural and Regional Affairs and Transport References Committee] (1998): Commercial Utilisation of Australian Native Wildlife. – Commonwealth of Australia, Canberra, ISBN 0 642 26781 2.

CONRAD, A. (1913): Die Jubiläumsausstellung des „Triton", Berlin. – Blätter für Aquarien- und Terrarien-Freunde: 457.

COOPER, S.J.B., C.M. BULL & M.G. GARDNER (1997): Characterization of microsatellite loci from the socially monogamous lizard *Tiliqua rugosa* using a PCR-based isolation technique. – Molecular Ecol., 6: 793–795.

COOPER, W.E. (1994): Prey chemical discrimination, foraging mode and phylogeny. – Pp. 15–16 in VITT, L.J. & E.R. PIANKA (eds.): Lizard Ecology. Historical and Experimental Perspectives. – Princeton (Princeton University Press).

*COOPER,W.E., M.T. MENDONCA & J. VITT (1987): Induction of orange head coloration and activation of courtship and agression by testosterone in the male broad-headed skink (*Eumeces laticeps*). – J. Herp., 21(2): 96–101.

COPE, E.D. (1896): On the hemipenes of the Sauria. – Proc. Acad. Nat. Sci. Philadelphia, 48: 461–467.

*COPLAND, S.J. (1947): Reptiles occuring above the winter snowline at Mt. Kosciusko. – Proc. Linn. Soc. New South Wales, 72(1/2): 69–72.

CREWS, D.P. (1975): Psychobiology of reptilian reproduction. – Science, 189: 1059–1065.

*DALE, F.D., (1973): Forty Queensland Lizards. – Brisbane (Queensland Museum). 64 pp.

DAMPIER, L. (1729): A Voyage to New Holland, & c. In the year 1699. – London (J & J Knapton), pp. 85–86.

DAVIS, G.W., D.J. HEARD & R.E. CHATTO (1993): Legislation in relation to herpetofauna in the Northern Territory. – Pp. 333–336 in LUNNEY, D. & D. AYERS (Hrsg.): Herpetology in Australia – a diverse discipline. – Trans. Royal Zool. Soc. New South Wales (Surry Beatty & Sons), Chipping Norton, 414 pp.

*DE ROOIJ, N. (1909): Reptilien. (Eidechsen, Schildkröten und Krokodile). – S. 375–383 in A. WICKMANN (Hrsg.): Uitkomen der Nederlandsche Nieuw-Guinea-Expeditie in 1903. – Leiden (E.J. Brill, Ltd.).

– (1915): The Reptiles of the Indo-Australian Archipelago. I. Lacertilia, Chelonia, Emydosauria. – Leiden (E.J. Brill, Ltd.). [Reprint, 1970. – Vaals (A. Asher & Co.), 384 pp.]

– (1917): The Reptiles of the Indo-Australian Archipelago. II. Ophidia. – Leiden (E.J. Brill, Ltd.), xiv + 314 pp.

*DE RUITER, M. (1993) : Adelaide-Blauzunge: (Noch) nicht ausgestorben. – DATZ, 46(9): 619.

*DE VIS, C.W. (1888): A contribution to the herpetology of Queensland. – Proc. Linn. Soc. New. South Wales, Ser. 2, 2: 811–826.

*– (1892): Vertebrata. – Ann. Qld. Mus, 2: 3–12.

*DELL, J. & A. CHAPMAN (1977): IV. Reptiles and frogs of Cockleshell Gully Reserve. – Rec. West. Aust. Mus, Perth,(4): 75–87.

*DEMARZ, H. (1955): Die Tannenzapfenechse (*Trachydosaurus rugosus* GRAY) – DATZ., 8(8): 216–217.

DENNERT, C. (1997): Untersuchungen zur Fütterung von Schuppenechsen und Schildkröten. – Hannover (Diss. Tierärztl. Hochschule), 190 S.

DÖBELI, M., M. RÜHLI, M. PFEIFFER, A. RÜBEL, R. HONEGGER & E. ISENBÜGEL (1992): Preliminary results on faecal steroid measurements in tortoises. – The First International Symposium on Faecal Steroid Monitoring, 73–83.

DOMEIER, I. (1993): Akkulturation bei den westlichen Aranda in Zentralaustralien. – Mundus Reihe Ethnologie, Bd. 63. – Bonn (Holos Verlag), 404 S.

DONNELLAN, S.C. (1991): Chromosomes of Australian lygosomine skinks (Lacertilia: Scincidae) I. The *Egernia* group: C-banding, silver staining, Hoechst 33258 condensation analysis. – Genetica, 83(3): 207–222.

DORIA, G. (1874): Enumerazione dei rettili raccolti dal dott. O. BECCARI in Amboina, alle isole Aru ed alle isole Kei durante gli anni 1872–73. – Ann. Mus. Civico Storia Nat. Genova, 6: 325–357 + pl. x–xi.

DOUGLAS, A.M. & W.D.L. RIDE (1962): Reptiles. – Pp. 113–119 in FRASER, A.J. (ed.): The Results of an Expedition to Bernier and Dorre Islands, Shark Bay, Western Australia in July, 1959. – Western Australian Fisheries Department Fauna Bulletin, 2: 1–131.

DOUGLAS, M. & D. OLDMEADOW (1972): Across the Top and other Places. – Adelaide (Rigby), 200 pp.

DUBAS, G. & C.M. BULL (1991): Diet choice and food availability in the omnivorous lizard *Trachydosaurus rugosus*. – Wildl. Res., East Melbourne, 18(2): 147–155.

DUBAS, G. & C.M. BULL (1992): Food addition and home range size of the lizard *Tiliqua rugosa*. – Herpetologica, 48(3): 301–306.

DUBOIS, A. (1988): The genus in zoology: A contribution to the theory of evolutionary systematics. – Mém. Mus. nat. Hist. nat., Paris, (Zool.), 140: 1–122.

DUMÉRIL, A.M.C. & G. BIBRON (1839): Erpétologie Générale ou Histoire Naturelle Complète des Reptiles. Vol. 5. – Paris (Librairie Encyclopédique de Roret), 854 pp.

DUNBAR, G.K. (1943–44): Notes on the Ngemba tribe of the central Darling River, western New South Wales. – Mankind 3(5): 140–148, (6): 172–180.

DUVALL, D., L.J. GUILLETTE & R.E. JONES (1982): Environmental control of reptilian breeding cycles. – Pp. 201–231 in GANS, C. & B. HUE (eds.): Biology of the Reptilia. Vol. 13. – New York (Alan R. Liss).

EDEN, W. (1787): The History of New Holland, from its First Discovery in 1616, to the Present Time. With a Particular Account of its Produce and Inhabitants. and a Description of Botany Bay: Also a List of the Naval, Marine, Military, and Civil Establishment. To which is Prefixed, an Introductory Discourse on Banishment, 2nd Edn. – London (John Stockdale), 254 pp.

EDGAR, B. & S. STEPHENS (1993): Commonwealth legislation relevant to reptiles and amphibians. – Pp. 39–42 in LUNNEY, D. & D. AYERS (Hrsg.): Herpetology in Australia – a diverse discipline. – Trans. Royal Zool. Soc. New South Wales (Surry Beatty & Sons), Chipping Norton, 414 pp.

EDWARDS, A. & S.M. JONES (2001): Changes in plasma testosterone, estrogen, and progesterone concentrations throughout the annual reproductive cycle in male viviparous blue-tongued skinks, Tiliqua nigrolutea, in Tasmania. - Journal of Herpetology, 35(2): 293-299.

*EHMANN, H. (1982): The natural history and conservation status of the Adelaide pigmy bluetongue lizard Tiliqua adelaidensis. – Herpetofauna, 14(1): 61–76.

– (1992): Encyclopedia of Australian Animals. Reptiles. – The National Photographic Index of Australian Wildlife (R. STRAHAN, series ed.). – Pymble ( Angus & Robertson), 495 pp.

ERDELEN, W. (1998): Conservation, trade and sustainable use of lizards and snakes in Indonesia. – Mertensiella, 9: 1–144.

ESTES, R. (1984): Fish, amphibians, and reptiles from the Etadunna Formation, Miocene of South Australia. – Aust. Zool., 21(4): 335–343.

*EVARTS, P.W. & P. DRAGON (1979): The captive propagation of blue-tongued skinks. Fact or fantasy? – Annual Reptile Symposium on Captive Propagation and Husbandry. ZCI Publications, 2: 26–30.

FAIRBRIDGE, R.W. (1953): The Sahul Shelf, northern Australia; its structure and geological relationships. – J. Roy. Soc. West. Aust. 37: 1-33.

FERGUSSON, B. & D. ALGAR (1986): Home range and activity patterns of pregnant female skinks, Tiliqua rugosa. – Aust. Wildl. Res., 13(2): 287–294.

*FERGUSSON, B. & S.D. BRADSHAW (1991): Plasma arginine, vasotocin, progesterone, and luteal development during pregnency in the viviparous lizard Tiliqua rugosa. – Gen. Comp. Endocrin., 82: 140–151.

*– (1992): In vitro uterine contractions in the viviparous lizard Tiliqua rugosa: Effects of gestation and steroid pretreatment in vivo. – Gen. Comp. Endocrin., 86: 203–210.

*FIELD, R. (1980): The pink-tongued skink (Tiliqua gerrardii) in captivity. – Herpetofauna, 11(2): 6–10.

*FIRTH, B.T. & I. BELAN (1998): Daily and seasonal rhythms in selected body temperatures in the Australian lizard Tiliqua rugosa (Scincidae): Field and laboratory observations. – Physiol. Zool., 71(3): 303–311.

*FIRTH, B.T., D.J. KENNAWAY & M.A.M. ROZENBILDS (1979): Plasma melatonin in the scincid lizard, Tachydosaurus rugosus: diel rhythm, seasonality, and the effect of constant light and constant darkness. – Gen. Comp. Endocrin., 37: 493–500.

*FISCHER, J. von (1882): Die Stummelschwanz-Eidechse (Trachydosaurus asper) in der Gefangenschaft. – Zool. Garten, Frankfurt, 23(7): 206–210.

– (1884): Das Terrarium, seine Bepflanzung u. Bevölkerung. – Frankfurt/M (Verlag von Mahlau & Waldschmidt) [Reprint 1989, Berlin, BINA Verlag für Biologie und Natur]: 296–301.

*FLEMMING, A.F. & J.H. VAN WYK (1992): The female reproductive cycle of the lizard Cordylus p. polyzonus (Sauria: Cordylidae) in the Southwestern Cape Province, South Africa. – J. Herpetol., 26(2): 121–127.

FLINDERS, M. (1814): A Voyage to Terra Australis. Undertaken for the Purpose of Completing the Discovery of that Vast Country, and Prosecuted in the Years 1801, 1802, and 1803, in His Majesty's Ship the Investigator, and Subsequently in the Armed Vessel Porpoise and Cumberland Schooner. With an Account of the Shipwreck of the Porpoise, Arrival of the Cumberland at Mauritius, and Imprisonment of the Commander during Six Years and a Half in that Island. Vol. I. – London (G. & W. Nicol), cciv + 269 pp.

FLYNN, T.T. (1923): On the occurrence of a true allantoplacenta of the conjoint type in an Australian lizard. – Rec. Aust. Mus., 14(1): 72–77.

*FRANK, W.(1969): Regenerationsvermögen beim

Blauzungenskink (*Tiliqua scincoides*). – Salamandra, 5(1/2): 15–17.

FRASER, L. (1862): List of Vertebrated Animals Living in the Gardens of the Zoological Society of London. – London (Longman, Green, Longman and Roberts), v + 100 pp.

*FREAKE, M.J. (1998): Variation in homeward orientation performance in the sleepy lizard (*Tiliqua rugosa*): effects of sex and reproductive period. – Behav. Ecol. Sociobiol. 43(4,5): 339–344.

FRENCH, R.J., W.E. MATHESON & A.L. CLARKE (1968): Soils and agriculture of the nothern and York Peninsula regions of South Australia. – Dept. Agriculture, South Australia Special Bull. No. 1.68. – Adelaide (Government Printer), 72 pp.

FRIEDERICH, U. & W. VOLLAND (1992): Futtertierzucht, 2. Aufl. – Stuttgart (Ulmer Verlag), 188 S.

FRYE, F.L. (1991): Nutrition. A practical guide for feeding captive reptiles . – In FRYE, F.L. (ed.): Reptile Care. An Atlas of Diseases and Treatments. – Neptune City (T.F.H. Publications), 325 pp.

FYFE, G. (1981): Predation on reptiles by the brown falcon (*Falco berigora*). – Herpetofauna, Sydney, 13(1): 31.

– (1983): Some notes on the sympatry between *Tiliqua occipitalis* and *Tiliqua multifasciata* in the Ayers Rock region and their associations with aboriginal people of the area. – Herpetofauna, 15(1): 18–19.

GANS, C., F. DE VREE & D. CARRIER (1985): Usage pattern of the complex masticatory muscles in the shingleback lizard, *Trachydosaurus rugosus*: a model for muscle placement. – Amer. J. Anat., 173: 219–240.

GEIGY, J.R. (1968): Wissenschaftliche Tabellen. – Basel (J.R. Geigy Pharma), 798 S.

*GEISER, F., B.T. FIRTH & R.S. SEYMOUR (1992): Polyunsaturated dietary lipids lower selected body temperature of a lizard. – J. Comp. Physiol. B, 162: 1–4.

*GENTILLI, J. (1971): Climates of Australia and New Zealand. – World Survey of Climatology, Vol.13. – Nedlands, W.A. (University of Western Australia), 371 pp.

GEVERS, A. (1787): Museum Geversianum sive index rerum naturalium continens instructissimam copiam pretiosissimorum omnis generis ex tribus regnis naturae objectorum quam dum in vivis erat magna diligentia multaque cura comparavit vir amplissimus. – Rotterdam (P. & J. Holsteyn), iv + 659 pp.

GIBSON, D.B. & J.R. COLE (1988): A biological survey of the northern Simpson Desert. – Conserv. Comm. North. Terr. Tech. Rep., 40: 1–205.

GIDDINGS, S. (1984): An observation of parturition of a blotched-bluetongue (*Tiliqua nigrolutea*). – South Aust. Herp. Group Newsletter, May: 4.

*GLASBY, C.J., G.J.B. ROSS & P.L. BEESLEY (1993): Fauna of Australia, Vol. 2A: Amphibia & Reptilia. – Canberra (Australian Government Publishing Service), 439 pp.

GLAUERT, L. (1929): Contributions to the fauna of Rottnest Island. No. 1: Introduction and vertebrates. – J. Roy. Soc. West. Aust., 15: 37–46.

GORSEMAN, P.D. (1998): *Tiliqua gigas*, de Nieuw-Guinea-blauwtongskink. – Lacerta, 57(2): 54–63.

*GRAVES, B.M. & M. HALPERN (1991): Discrimination of self from conspecific chemical cues in *Tiliqua scincoides* (Sauria: Scincidae). – J. Herpetol., 25(1): 125–126.

GRAY, J.E. (1825): A synopsis of the genera of reptiles and amphibia, with a discription of some new species. – Ann. Philos., Ser. 2, 10 (3): 193–217.

– (1827): Reptilia. – Pp. 424–434 in KING, P.P. (ed.): Narrative of a Survey of the Intertropical and Western Coasts of Australia. Performed between the Years 1818 and 1822. Vol. II. – London (John Murray), 637 pp.

– (1831): A Synopsis of the Species of the Class Reptilia. – Pp. 483–600 in GRIFFITH, E. & E. PIDGEON (eds.): The Animal Kingdom Arranged in Conformity with its Organization, by Baron CUVIER, Member of the Institute of France, & c. with Additional Descriptions of all the Species Hitherto Named, and of many not before Noticed. Volume 9. The Class Reptilia Arranged by the Baron CUVIER, with Specific Descriptions. – London (Whittaker, Treacher & Co.).

– (1838): Catalogue of the slender-tongued saurians, with descriptions of many new genera and species. – Ann. Mag. Nat. Hist., ser. 2, 2(10): 287–293.

– (1841): A Catalogue of the species of reptiles and Amphibia hitherto described as inhabiting Australia, with a description of some new species from Western Australia, and some remarks on their geographical distribution. – Pp. 422–449 in GREY, G. (ed.): Journals of two Expeditions of Discovery in North-west and Western Australia, during the years 1837, 38, and 39, Under the Authority of Her Majesty's Government. Vol. 2. – London (T. & W. Boone), 482 pp.

*– (1843): Descriptions of the reptiles and amphibians hitherto observed in New Zealand. – Pp. 202–206 in DIEFFENBACH, E. (ed.): Travels in New Zealand. Vol. 2.

– London (Murray).

*– (1845): Catalogue of the Specimens of Lizards in the Collection of the British Museum. – London (Trustees of the British Museum), 289 pp.

*GRAY, J.E. & A. GÜNTHER (1995): The Lizards of Australia and New Zealand. With an introduction by GLENN M. SHEA. – St. Louis (Society for the Study of Amphibians and Reptiles.), 29 pp.

*GREEN, D.(1973): The reptiles of the outer North-Western suburbs of Sydney. – Herpetofauna, Sydney, 6(2): 2–5.

GREEN, D. (1995): A comparison of three litters in the shingleback lizard, *Trachydosaurus rugosus*. – Herpetofauna, 25(1): 42–43.

GREENBERG, N. (1977): A neuroethological study of the display behavior in the lizard *Anolis carolinensis* (Sauria Iguanidae). – Amer. Zool., 17: 191–201.

GREENE, H.W. (1994): Antipredator mechanisms in reptiles. – Pp. 1–152 in GANS, C. & R.B. HUEY (eds.): Biology of the Reptilia. Vol. 16. – Ann Arbor (Branta Books).

GREER, A.E. (1970): A subfamilial classification of scincid lizards. – Bull. Mus. Comp. Zool., Cambridge, Mass., 139(3): 151–183.

– (1979): A phylogenetic subdivision of Australian skinks. – Rec. Aust. Mus., 32(8): 339–371.

– (1986): Lygosomine (Scincidae) monophyly: a third, corroborating character and a reply to critics. – J. Herpetol., 20(1): 123–126.

– (1989): The Biology and Evolution of Australian Lizards. – Chipping Norton, NSW (Surrey Beatty), 264 pp.

– (1990): The *Glaphyromorphus isolepis* species group (Lacertilia: Scincidae): diagnosis of the taxon and description of a new species from Timor. – J. Herpetol., 24: 372–377.

*GRIFFITHS, K. (1984): Reptiles and Frogs of Australia. – Sydney, (View Prod.), 96 pp.

*– (1987): Reptiles of the Sydney Region. – Winmalee, NSW (Three Sisters Productions), 120 pp.

*– (1997): Frogs & Reptiles of the Sydney Region. – Sydney (University of NSW Press), 125 pp.

*GRIMM, H.D. (1965): Die Blauzunge. – DATZ: 243–244.

GROSS, J. (1989): Pflege, Geschlechtsbestimmung und Zucht der Tannenzapfenechse. – DATZ, 42(10): 612–613.

GRÜNEWALD, G., E. HÖLLER & D. STRANZ (1982): Brockhaus Texte und Tabellen – Länder und Klima – Asien, Australien. – Wiesbaden (F.A. Brockhaus) & Hamburg (Interpress Übersee-Verlag), 240 S.

*GRZIMEK, B. (1980): Grzimeks Tierleben. Enzyclopädie des Tierreiches. Kriechtiere. – München (Deutscher Taschenbuch Verlag GmbH & Co. KG), 609 S.

*GUILLETTE, L.J. (1985): The evolution of egg retention in lizards: a physilogical model. – Pp. 379–386 in GRIGG, G., R. SHINE & H. EHMANN (eds.): Biology of Australasian Frogs and Reptiles. – Chipping Norton, (Surrey Beatty & Sons).

*HAACKE, W.(1883): Zur Naturgeschichte der Stummelschwanzeidechsen. – Der Zoologische Garten, Frankfurt, 24(8): 225–227.

HÄFELI, W. (1994): Endoskopische Geschlechtsbestimmung juveniler Schildkröten. – Verh. Ber. Erkrankung Zootiere, 36: 159–162.

HALPERN, M. (1992): Nasal chemical senses in reptiles: structure and function. – Pp. 423–524 in GANS, C. & D. CREWS (eds.): Biology of the Reptilia. Vol. 18. Physiology E. – Chicago (University of Chicago Press).

HALVERSON, J. (1990): Avian sex identification by recombinant DNA technology. – Proc. Ann. Meet. Assoc. Avian Vet., Phoenix, AZ, 256–262.

HAMMEL, H.T., F.T. CALDWELL & R.M. ABRAMS (1967a): *Tiliqua scincoides*: Temperature-sensitive units in lizard brain. – Science, 158: 1050–1051.

*– (1967b): Regulation of body temperature in the blue-tongued lizard. – Science, 156: 1260–1262.

HANCOCK, L.J. & M.B. THOMPSON (1997): Distributional limits of eastern blue-tongue lizards *Tiliqua scincoides*, blotched blue-tongue lizards *T. nigrolutea* and shingleback lizards *T. rugosa* (GRAY) in New South Wales. – Aust. Zool., 30(3): 340–345.

HARTERT, E. (1901): On the birds of the Key and South-East Islands, and of Ceram-Laut. – Novitates Zool., 8(1): 1–5.

HAUCHECORNE, F. (1929): Zuchterfolge bei der Blauzunge (*Tiliqua scincoides*) im Zoologischen Garten zu Halle. – Zool. Garten, Frankfurt, 2(1/3): 50–51.

HAUSCHILD, A. (1988): Bemerkungen zu Haltung und Nachzucht des Schneckenskinkes *Tiliqua gerrardii* (GRAY, 1845). – Salamandra, Bonn, 24(4), 248–257.

HAUSCHILD, A. & P. GAßNER (1995): Skinke im Terrarium. – Hannover (Landbuch Verlag), 197 S.

HAUSCHILD, A., R. HITZ, K. HENLE, G.M. SHEA & H. WERNING (Hrsg.) (2000): Blauzungenskinke. Beiträge zu *Tiliqua* und *Cyclodomorphus*. – Münster (Natur und Tier-Verlag), 287 S.

*HEDIGER, H.(1934): Beitrag zur Herpetologie und Zoogeographie Neu Britanniens und einiger umliegender Gebiete. – Zool. Jahrb., Jena, 65(5–6): 389–582.

*HENLE, K. (1988): Population Ecology and Life History Evolution of a Lizard Community in Arid Australia. – Canberra (Aust. Nat. Univ., Unveröff. Diss.), 197 S.

– (1989): Ecological segregation in an assemblage of diurnal lizards in arid Australia. – Acta Œcol. Œcol. Gener., 10: 19–35.

– (1990): Notes on the population ecology of the large herbivorous lizard, *Trachydosaurus rugosus*, in arid Australia. – J. Herpetol., Oxford, 24(1): 100–103.

HENLE K. & C.J.J. KLAVER (1986): *Podarcis sicula* (RAFINESQUE-SCHMALTZ, 1810) – Ruineneidechse. – S. 254–342. in BÖHME, W. (Hrsg.): Handbuch der Reptilien und Amphibien Europas. Bd. 2/II: Echsen (Sauria) III: Lacertidae III: *Podarcis*. – Aula, Wiesbaden.

*HERREL, A., P. AERTS & F. DE VREE (1998a): Static biting in lizards: Functional morphology of the temporal ligaments. – J. Zool., London, 244(1): 135–143.

*– (1998b): Ecomorphology of the lizard feeding apparatus: a modelling approach. – Netherlands J. Zool., 48(1): 1–25.

*HERRMANN, F. ( 1929): Beobachtungen über die Fortpflanzung der Blauzunge *Tiliqua (scincoides)*. – Blätter für Aquarien- und Terrarienkunde, Stuttgart, 40(7): 115–116.

HERRMANN, J. (1929): Beobachtungen über die Fortpflanzung der Blauzunge (*Tiliqua scincoides*). – Blätter für Aquarien- und Terrarienfreunde: 115–116.

*HERRMANN, J.M. ( 1997): Haltung und Nachzucht des Schneckenskinks *Tiliqua gerrardi*. – elaphe, 5 (3): 16–18.

HITZ, R. (1983): Pflege und Nachzucht von *Trachydosaurus rugosus* (GRAY, 1827) im Terrarium. – Salamandra, Bonn, 19(4), 198–210.

– (1984): Geschlechtsbestimmung bei Echsen der Gattungen *Tiliqua* und *Trachydosaurus* mittels der Sondenmethode (Sauria: Scincidae). – Salamandra, Bonn, 20(1): 39–42.

*HOCHLEITHNER, M. (1995): Isoflurane (Florane). Anaesthesia in birds and reptiles. – Europ. J. Companion Anim. Practice, 5(1): 37–41.

*HOLMES, R. & A. LIGHT (1983): A serendipitous age estimation of a lizard, *Tiliqua rugosa* (Lacertilia: Scincidae). – West. Aust. Nat., 15(7): 159–160.

HONEGGER, R.E. (1978): Geschlechtsbestimmung bei Reptilien. – Salamandra, 14(2): 69–79.

*HONEGGER, R.E. & C.R. SCHMIDT (1964): Herpeto-

logisches aus dem Züricher Zoo. 1.Beiträge zur Haltung und Zucht verschiedener Reptilien. – DATZ, 17: 339–342.

HORN, H.-G. (1980): Bisher unbekannte Details zur Kenntnis von *Varanus varius* auf Grund von feldherpetologischen und terraristischen Beobachtungen (Reptilia: Sauria: Varanidae). – Salamandra, 16(1): 1–18.

HORNER, P. (1992): Skinks of the Northern Territory. – Northern Territory Mus. Arts Sci., Darwin (Handbook Series No. 2), 174 pp.

HOSER, R.T. (1989): Australian Reptiles & Frogs. – Mosman NSW (Pierson & Co.), 238 pp.

*– (1996a): A prey record of the common brown snake *Pseudonaja textilis* for the eastern blue-tongue *Tiliqua scincoides*. – Monitor, Melbourne., 8(2): 85–86.

– (1996b): Reptiles encountered collecting in the Pilbara – Australia. – Reptilian, 4(2): 25–35.

HOUBA, J. (1959): *Tiliqua rugosa* (GRAY). – Aquarien Terrarien, 6: 176–177.

*HOUTMAN, H.(1988): De verzorgin en voortplanting van Gerrards blauwtongskink (*Tiliqua gerrardii*): – Lacerta, Utrecht,46(6): 92–95.

HOUTTUYN, M. (1787): Catalogus van eene uitmuntende Verzameling van allerley Sorrt van Dieren en Dierlyke Zaaken, Tot opheldering der Natuurlyke Historie. In meer dan dertig jaaren vergaderd en, volgens het Samenstel van den wydberoemden Linnaeus, in orde geschikt. – Amsterdam, viii + 170 pp.

*HOW, T.L. & C.M. BULL (1998): Lacertilia: *Tiliqua rugosa* (sleepy lizard). Mating behaviour and necrophilia. – Herpetol. Rev., 29(4): 240.

*HUF, P.A., A.R. BOURNE & T.G. WATSON (1989): The in vitro biosynthesis of epitestosterone and testosterone from C19 steroid precursors in the testis of the lizard *Tiliqua rugosa*. – Gen. Comp. Endocrin., 75: 280–286.

HULBERT, J.A. & C.A. WILLIAMS (1988): Thyroid function in a lizard, a turtle, and a crocodile compared with mammals. – Comp. Biochem. Physiol., 90A: 41–48.

HUNTER, J. (1790): The Scincoid, or Skinc-formed Lizard. – Pp. 242–243 in WHITE, J. (ed.): Journal of a Voyage to New South Wales with Sixty-five Plates of non Descript Animals, Birds, Lizards, Serpents, Curious Cones of Trees and other Natural Productions. – Piccadilly (J. Debrett).

HUTCHINSON, M.N. (1980): The systematic relationships of the genera *Egernia* and *Tiliqua* (Lacertilia: Scincidae). A review and immunological reassessment. – Pp. 176–193 in BANKS, C.B. & A.A. MARTIN (eds.): Proceeedings of the Melbourne Herpetological Symposium. – Melbourne (Zoological Board of Victoria).

– (1993a): Family Scincidae. – Pp. 261–279 in GLASBY, C.J., G.J.B. ROSS & P.L. BEESLEY (eds.): Fauna of Australia, Vol. 2A, Amphibia & Reptilia. – Canberra (Australian Government Publishing Service).

– (1993b): Return of the pygmy bluetongue. – Xanthopus, Nature Conservation Society of South Australia, 148: 10.

– (1994): Rare and endangered: the Adelaide pygmy bluetongue. – Aust. Nat. Hist., 24(8): 18–19.

HUTCHINSON, M.N., T. MILNE & T. CROFt (1994): Redescription and ecological notes on the pygmy bluetongue, *Tiliqua adelaidensis* (Squamata: Scincidae). – Trans. Roy. Soc. S. Aust., 118(4): 216–27.

HYDE, M. (1995): The Temperate Grasslands of South Australia: Their Composition and Conservation Status. – Sydney (World Wide Fund for Nature), 339 pp.

ILGENSTEIN, G. (1990): Die Steinzeitmenschen von Australien. – Jena (Fischer), 111 S.

IVERSON, J.B. (1980): Colic modifications in iguanine lizards. – J. Morphol., 163: 79–93.

JACOBSHAGEN, E. (1937): Mittel- und Enddarm. Rumpfdarm. – S. 563–724 in BOLK, L., E. GÖPPERT, E. KALLIUS & W. LUBOSCH (Hrsg.): Handbuch der vergleichenden Anatomie der Wirbeltiere; Bd. 3. – Berlin, Wien (Urban & Schwarzenberg), 1018 S. – Nachdruck, 1967, Amsterdam (A. Asher & Co.).

JENKINS, R. & R. BARTELL, (1980): A Field Guide to Reptiles of the Australian High Country. – Melbourne (Inkata Press), 278 pp.

JOGER, U., E. WALLIKEWITZ & A. HAUSCHILD (1986): Hormon- und serochemische Untersuchungen zur Bestimmung des Geschlechtes und zur Überprüfung des Gesundheitszustandes bei *Trachydosaurus rugosus* (GRAY, 1827). – Salamandra, Bonn, 22(1): 21–28.

JOHNSTON, T.H. (1932): The parasites of the „stumpy-tail" lizard, *Trachydosaurus rugosus*. – Trans. Roy. Soc. S. Aust., 56: 62–70.

– (1943): Aboriginal names and utilization of the fauna in the Eyrean region. – Trans. Roy. Soc. S. Aust., 67(2): 244–311.

JONES, S. (1987): A report on a reproducible and sustainable system for the captive propagation of the genus *Tiliqua* GRAY, 1825. – Pp. 17–25 in COOTE, J. (ed.): Reptiles. – Proceedings of the 1986 U.K. Herpet. Societies Symposium on Captive Breeding. – London (British Herpet. Soc.).

JONGSMA, D. (1970): Eustatic sea level changes in the Arafura Sea. – Nature, 228: 150–151.

– (1974): Marine geology of the Arafura Sea. – Commonwealth Aust. Dept. Minerals Energy, Bur. Mineral Res., Geol. Geophysics Bull., 157: 1–73.

JORGENSEN, L. & J.B.S.V. WELCH (1953): Pregnancy test: Australian reptiles as test animals. – Med. J. Aust., 40(II)(15): 564–565.

*KEAST, A. (1959): The Reptiles of Australia. – Pp. 115–135 in.KEAST, A., R.C. CROCKER & C.S. CHRISTIAN (eds.): Biogeography and Ecology in Australia. – Den Haag (W. Junk).

KIENE, T.L., K.V. KARDONG & V.L. BELS (1996): Evolution of lizard feeding systems: testing a model. – Amer. Zool., 36: 116A.

*KING, M. (1973): Chromosomes of two Australian lizards of the families Scincidae and Gekkonidae. – Cytologica, 38: 205–210.

KLINGELHÖFFER, W. (1957): Terrarienkunde. 3.Teil. Echsen (2. vollständig neubearbeitete Aufl.). – Stuttgart (Alfred Kernen Verlag), 264 S.

KOPSTEIN, F. (1926): Reptilien von den Molukken und den benachbarten Inseln. – Zool. Meded., Leiden, 9(2/3): 71–112.

KREGER, M.D. (1993): Physiological and behavioral effects of handling and restraint in the ball python (*Python regius*) and the blue-tongued skink (*Tiliqua scincoides*). – Appl. Anim. Behav. Sci., 38: 323–336.

LAMBIRIS, A.J. (1966): Observation on Rhodesian reptiles. – J. Herpet. Assoc. Africa, 2: 33–34.

*LANDERT, H.(1961): Was liegt vor? – DATZ, 14: 62.

LAPTHORNE, T.A. & A.A. LAPTHORNE (1987): Some notes on the captive reproduction of the New Guinea bluetongued skink. – South Western Herpetol. Soc. J., 1(1): 32–33.

LASZLO, J. (1977): Practical methods of inducing mating in snakes, using extended daylengths and darkness. – Proc. Amer. Assoc. Zool. Parks Aquar. Regional Conf., 1977.

LAWLOR, R. (1993): Am Anfang war der Traum. – München (Droemer Knaur), 451 S.

*LE BRETON, M. (1990): Reproductive notes on the eastern blue–tongued lizard *Tiliqua scincoides*. – Herpetofauna, 20(1): 30–32.

LE SOUEF, D. (1918): The blue-tongued lizard. – Vict. Nat., 35(1): 15.

LICHT, P. (1972): Environmental physiology of reptilian breeding cycles: role of temperature. – Gen. Comp.

Endocrin., Suppl. 3: 477–488.

LICHT, P., W.R. DAWSON, V.H. SHOEMAKER & A.R. MAIN (1966): Observations on the thermal relations of Western Australian lizards. – Copeia, l: 97–110.

LIMBERGER, M. (2000): Topographische Anatomie der inneren Organe des Rumpfes bei Skinken der Gattungen *Tiliqua* und *Corucia* (Reptilia: Lacertilia: Scincidae) unter Verwendung der Kernspintomographie als Methode in der Wirbeltieranatomie. Dissertation, TU Darmstadt, 140 Seiten.

*LITH DE JEUDE, T.W. VAN (1897): Reptiles and batrachians from New Guinea. – Notes Leyden Mus., 18: 249–257.

LONGLEY, G. (1939): The blue-tongued lizard (*Tiliqua scincoides*). – Proc. Roy. Zool. Soc. New South Wales, 1938/39: 39–42.

– (1941): Notes on some Australian lizards. – Proc. Roy. Zool. Soc. New South Wales, 1940–1941: 30–35.

– (1944): Notes on a hybrid blue tongue lizard. – Proc. Roy. Zool. Soc. New South Wales, 1943–44: 23–24.

*LONGMORE, R. & P. LEE (1981): Some observations on techniques for assessing the effects of fire on reptile populations in Sturt National Park. – Aust. J. Herp., 1: 17–22.

LOVERIDGE, A. (1938): On some reptiles and amphibians from the central region of Australia. – Trans. Roy. Soc. S. Aust., 62(2): 183–191.

– (1946): Reptiles of the Pacific World. – Cambridge (Museum of Comparative Zoology), 259 pp.

– (1948): New Guinean reptiles and amphibians in the Museum of Comparative Zoology and United States National Museum. – Bull. Mus. Comp. Zool., 101(2): 305–430.

*LUNNEY, D. & J. BARKER (1986): Survey of reptiles and amphibians of the costal forest near Bega, NSW. – Aust. Zool., 22(3): 1–9.

MACMILLEN, R.E., M.L. AUGEE, & B.A. ELLIS (1989): Thermal ecology and diet of some xerophilous lizards from western New South Wales. – J. Arid Environ., 16(2): 193–201.

MAIN, A.R. & C.M. BULL (1996): Mother-offspring recognition in two Australian lizards, *Tiliqua rugosa* and *Egernia stokesii*. – Anim. Behav., 52: 193–200.

MAJUPURIA, T.C. (1970): The muscles, blood vessels and nerves of the cloaca and copulatory organs of *Uromastyx hardwickii*, GRAY, together with the mode of eversion of the hemipenis, the copulation and the sexual dimorphism. – Zool. Anz., 184: 48–60.

MANSERGH, I., G. DAVEY & P. ROBERTSON (1993): Reptiles and amphibians of Victoria – legislation. – Pp. 373–376 in Lunney, D. & D. Ayers (Hrsg.): Herpetology in Australia – a diverse discipline. – Trans. Royal Zool. Soc. New South Wales (Surry Beatty & Sons), Chipping Norton, 414 pp.

*MATHER, P.B. (1979): An examination of the reptile fauna of Wyperfeld National Park using pitfall trapping. – Vict. Nat., 96: 98–101.

MATTISON, C. (1991): Keeping and Breeding Lizards. – Poole (Blandford Press), 224 pp.

*MATZ, G.(1968): Les scinques australiens. – Aquarama, Straßburg, 2(18): 27–29.

*– (1972a): Einige Australische Skinke der Gattungen *Egernia* und *Tiliqua*. – Aquar. Terrar. Z., 25(4): 136–139.

*– (1972b): Les scinques australiens II. *Egernia* GRAY, 1838 et *Tiliqua* GRAY, 1825. – Aquarama, 6(17): 45–47.

– (1973): Biologie et reproduction de *Tiliqua gerrardii*. – Bull. Soc. Zool. France, 98(4): 5900.

*– (1974a): Données sur la reproduction et l'élevage de Scincidae (Reptilia, Lacertilia). – Bull. Soc. Zool. France, 99(4): 798–799.

*– (1974b): Sur la réproduction des reptiles en captivité – Aquarama, 8(27): 49–53.

– (1984): La réproduction des reptiles et les facteurs de son induction. – Acta Zool. Pathol. Antverpiensia, 78: 33–68.

MATZ, G. & M. VANDERHAEGE (1980): BLV Terrarienführer. – München, Wien, Zürich (BLV Verlagsgesellschaft), 360 S.

MCCARTHY, F.D. (1976): Rock art of the Cobar pediplain in central western New South Wales. – Aust. Aboriginal Studies. Res. Reg. Studies, (7): 1–163 + 78 figs.

MCDOWELL, D. (1997): Wildlife Crime Policy and the Law – An Australian Study. – AGPS, Canberra: 171–184.

MEBS, D. (1974): Haltungserfahrungen mit *Tiliqua casuarinae* (Sauria, Scincidae). – Salamandra, Frankfurt, 10(3/4): 104–106.

*MEMBERS, A.H.S. & G.M. SHEA (1982): Observations on some members of the Genus *Tiliqua*. – Herpetofauna, 13(2): 18–19.

*MERTENS, R.(1934): Die Insel-Reptilien, ihre Ausbreitung, Variation und Artbildung. – Zoologica, Stuttgart, 32(84): 1–209.

– (1950): Über Reptilienbastarde. – Senckenbergiana, 31(3–4): 127–144 + pl. i–iii.

– (1958a): Neue Eidechsen aus Australien. – Senckenb.

biol., 39(1/2): 51–56.

*– (1958b): Quer durch Australien. Biologische Aufzeichnungen über eine Forschungsreise. – Frankfurt/Main (Kramer), 200 S.

MERTON, H. (1910): Forschungsreise in den südöstlichen Molukken. – Abh. Senckenb. Naturforsch. Ges., 33(1–2): 1–208.

MEYER, H. & E. HECKÖTTER (1986): Futterwerttabellen für Hunde und Katzen (2. Aufl.). – Hannover (Schlütersche), 48 S.

MILANI, A. (1894): Beiträge zur Kenntnis der Reptilienlunge, 1. Teil (Lacertilia). – Zool. Jb., Abt. Anat., Vol. 7, Heft 1.

MILES, T. (1973): Measurements and notes on adult and juvenile pink tongue skinks (Tiliqua gerrardi). – Herpetofauna, Sydney, 6(1): 116–117.

MILNE, T.I. & M.N. HUTCHINSON (1997): Draft Recovery Plan for the Pygmy Bluetongue Lizard (Tiliqua adelaidensis). – Canberra (Environment Australia), 27 pp.

MITCHELL, F.J. (1950): The scincid genera Egernia and Tiliqua (Lacertilia). – Rec. S. Aust. Mus., 9(3): 275–308 + pl. Xxiii.

– (1955): Preliminary account of the Reptilia and Amphibia collected by the National Geographic Society. – Commonwealth Government – Smithsonian Expedition to Arnhem Land (April to November, 1948). – Rec. S. Aust. Mus., 11: 373–408.

*– (1964): Reptiles and amphibians of Arnhem Land. – Pp. 309–343 in SPECHT, R.L. (ed.): Records of the American-Australian Scientific Expedition to Arnhem Land. Vol. 4: Zoology. – Melbourne (Univ. Press).

MITSCH, H. (1936): Tiliqua scincoides White. – Wochenschrift für Aquarien- und Terrarienkunde, Braunschweig: 487–488.

MORTON, J. (1991): Black and white totemism: conservation, animal symbolism. – Pp. 21–52 in CROFT, D.B. (ed.): Australia´s People and Animals in Todays Dreamtime. – New York (Praeger).

MOUNTFORD, C.P. (1965): Ayers Rock, its People, their Beliefs and their Art. – Sydney (Angus & Robertson), 216 pp.

MUDRACK, W. (1969): Einiges über Pflege und Zucht von Blauzungenskinken im Zimmerterrarium. – DATZ, Stuttgart, 6(2): 23–24.

– (1974): Der Rosazungenskink, eine terraristische Kostbarkeit. – Das Aquarienmagazin, 8(10): 407–411.

MÜLLER, M.J. (1987): Handbuch ausgewählter Klimastationen der Erde. – Trier (Forschungsstelle Bodenerosion, Univ. Trier), 346 S.

*MÜNSCH, W. (1979): Erschreckendes Ergebnis bei der Zucht der Blauzunge Tiliqua scincoides. – Das Aquarium, Minden, 125: 526–527.

– (1980): Erfahrungen mit dem Schneckenskink Tiliqua gerrardii. – Das Aquarium, Minden, 133: 371–374.

*– (1982): Männliche Tannenzapfen- oder Stutzechse sucht Weibchen. – Das Aquarium, Minden, 153: 145–147.

*MYHRE, K. & H.T. HAMMEL (1969): Behavioral regulation in internal temperature in the lizard Tiliqua scincoides. – Amer. J. Physiol., 217: 1490–1495.

NICHOLAS, F.W. & J.M. NICHOLAS (1989): Charles Darwin in Australia. – Cambridge (Cambridge University Press), 175 pp.

NIETZKE, G. (1978): Die Terrarientiere 2 (2. Aufl.). – Stuttgart (Eugen Ulmer), 322 S.

NIND, S. (1832): Description of the natives of King George's Sound (Swan River Colony) and adjoining country. – J. Roy. Geogr. Soc. London, 1: 21–51.

O´SHEA, M. (1991): The reptiles of Papua New Guinea. – Brit. Herpetol. Soc. Bull., 37: 15–32.

*– (1994): The herpetofauna of coconut husk piles on Kar Kar Island, Madang Province, Papua New Guinea. – Assoc. Study Rept. Amph. J., 1994: 51–72.

OBST, F.J., K. RICHTER & U. JACOB (1984): Lexikon der Terraristik. – Hannover (Landbuch Verlag), 465 S.

*OLMO, E. (1986): Reptilia. – Pp. 1–101 in BERNARD, J. (ed.): Animal Cytogenetics. Vol. 4. – Berlin (Gebrüder Borntraeger).

OUDEMANS, J.T. (1894): Eidechsen und Schildkröten. – S. 127–146 in SEMON, R. (Hrsg.).: Zoologische Forschungsreisen in Australien und dem Malayischen Archipel. Band 5. – Denkschr. Medic.-Naturwiss. Ges. Jena, 8: 1–778 + lxvii pl.

OWEN, R. (1840–1845): Odontography or a Treatise on the Comparative Anatomy of the Teeth, their Physiological Relations, Mode of Development, and Microscopic Structure, in the Vertebrate Animals (2 Vols.). – London (Hippolyte Bailliere), 655 pp + 150 pl.

PALMER, E. (1888): Notes and exhibits. – Proc. Linn. Soc. New South Wales, (2)3(1): 400–402.

PARKINSON, G. (1986): Atlas of Australian Resources (Third series). Vol. 4: Climate. – Canberra (Division of National Mapping), 60 pp.

PERNETTA, J.C. (1983): The wildlife of the Purari catchment. – Pp. 253–268 in PETR, T. (ed.): The Purari Tropical Environment of a High Rainfall River Basin. – The Hague (W. Junk: Monographiae Biologicae 51).

PÉRON, F. (1807): Voyage de Découvertes aux Terres Australes, exécuté par ordre de Sa Majesté l'Empereur et Roi, sur les Corvettes le Géographe, le Naturaliste, et la Goelette la Casuarina, pendant les Années 1800, 1801, 1802, 1803 et 1804. Vol. I. – Paris (Imprimerie Impériale), 496 pp.

PESANTES, O.S. (1994): A method for preparing the hemipenis of preserved snakes. – J. Herpetol., 28 (1): 93–95.

PETERS, U. (1967): *Tiliqua gerrardii* und *Tiliqua casuarinae*, zwei wenig bekannte Echsen. – Aquarien Terrarien, Jena/Leipzig/Berlin, 14(3): 94–96.

*– (1969): Australische Skinke. – DATZ, 22(2): 53–55.

– (1986): Australische Skinke. Acht Arten werden vorgestellt. – Das Aquarium, Minden, 20(206): 436–440.

*PETERS, W. (1864): Übersicht der von Hrn. Richard Schomburgk an das zoologische Museum eingesandten Amphibien, aus Buchsfelde bei Adelaide in Südaustralien. – Monatsber. Königl. Preuss. Akad. Wiss. Berlin 1863: 228–236.

– (1867): Herpetologische Notizen. – Monatsber. Königl. Preuss. Akad. Wiss. Berlin, 24: 13–37.

*PETNEY, T.N. & C.M. BULL (1984): Microhabitat selection by two reptile ticks at their parapatric boundary. – Aust. J. Ecol., 9(3): 233–239.

PETTIT, R. (1985): Australien. Tier- und Pflanzenwelt. – Hannover (Landbuch-Verlag), 176 S.

*PHILLIPS, J.A. (1986): Ontogeny of metabolic processes in blue-tongued skinks, *Tiliqua scincoides*. – Herpetologica, 42(4): 405–412.

PHILLIPS, S. (1993): Conserving the herpetofauna of Queensland – a look at the Nature Conservation Act 1992. – Pp. 377–381 in Lunney, D. & D. Ayers (Hrsg.): Herpetology in Australia – a diverse discipline. – Trans. Royal Zool. Soc. New South Wales (Surry Beatty & Sons), Chipping Norton, 414 pp.

*PIANKA, E.R. (1969): Habitat specificity, speciation, and species density in Australian desert lizards. – Ecology, 50: 498–502.

*– (1994) : The Lizard Man Speaks. – Austin (University of Texas Press), 179 pp.

PORTER, K.R. (1972): Herpetology. – Philadelphia, London (Saunders), 524 pp.

QUOY, J.R.C. & P. GAIMARD (1824): Zoologie. – Pp. 176–178, pl. 41 in DE FREYCINET, L. (ed.): Voyage autour du monde, entrepris par ordre du Roi, sous le ministère et conformément aux instructions de s. exc. m. le vicomte du Bouchage, secrétaire d'état au Département de la Marine, éxécuté sur les corvettes de S. M l'Uranie et la Physicienne, pendant les années 1817, 1818, 1819 et 1820. – Paris (Pillet Aîné, Imprimeur-Libraire, de l'Imprimerie Royale), 712 pp.

RANKIN, P.R. (1973): Lizard mimicking a snake-juvenile. *Tiliqua casuarinae* (DUMERIL & BIBRON). – Herpetofauna, Sydney, 5(4): 13–14.

RAU, A.S. (1924): Observations on the anatomy of the heart of *Tiliqua scincoides* and *Eunectes murinus*. – J. Anat., London, 59: 60–71.

*RAWLINSON, P.A. (1967): The vertebrates of the Bass Strait Islands: The Reptilia of Flinders and King Islands. – Proc. Roy. Soc. Vict., 80(2): 211–224.

*– (1969): The reptiles of East Gippsland. – Proc. Roy. Soc. Vict., 82(1): 113–128.

*– (1971): The reptiles of West Gippsland. – Proc. Roy. Soc. Vict., 84(1): 37–52.

*– (1974): Biogeography and ecology of the reptiles of Tasmania and the Bass Strait area. – Pp. 291–338 in WILLIAMS, W.D. (ed.): Biogeography and Ecology in Tasmania. – The Hague (W. Junk: Monographiae Biologicae 25), 498 pp.

*REBER, U.(1982): Blauzungen – Interessante Echsen vom 5. Kontinent. – Aquaria, St. Gallen, 29(5): 83–84.

RHODIN, A.G.J. (1994): Chelid turtles of the Australasian Archipelago: II. A new species of *Chelodina* from Roti Island, Indonesia. – Breviora, 498: 1–31.

RICHES, B. (1988): Unplanned breeding of blue-tongue skinks. – The Herptile, 13(2): 52–54.

RIDE, W.D.L. (1962): Narrative. – Pp. 10–18 in FRASER, A.J. (ed.): The Results of an Expedition to Bernier and Dorre Islands, Shark Bay, Western Australia in July, 1959. – West. Aust. Fish. Dept. Fauna Bull., 2: 1–131.

RIPPEY, E. & N. MARCHANT (ohne Datum): Rottnest Island Plants. – Rottnest Island Authority.

RIX, C.E. (1978): Royal Zoological Society of South Australia 1878–1978. – Adelaide (Royal Zoological Society of South Australia), 247 pp.

*ROBERTS, B. (1984): Predation of the Mediterranean beetle *Blaps polychresta* by the western bluetongue lizard *Tiliqua occipitalis*. – Herpetofauna, 15(2): 50.

*ROBERTS, J. & P. MIRTSCHIN (1991): An uncommon prey record for the common brown snake *Pseudonaja textilis*. – Herpetofauna, 21(1): 36.

ROBERTSON, G., J. SHORT & G. WELLARD (1987): The environment of the Australian sheep rangelands. – Pp. 14–34 in CAUGHLEY, G., N. SHEPHERD & J. SHORT (eds.): Kangaroos, their Ecology and Management in the Sheep Rangelands of Australia. – Cambridge (Cambridge Univ. Press).

ROBERTSON, P. (1980): Captivity mating of pink tongue skinks (*Tiliqua gerrardii*). – Vict. Herp. Soc. Newsletter, 18: 11–12.

*ROESCH, K.E. (1956): Ein Beitrag zur Fortpflanzung und Aufzucht der Stutz-Eidechse (*Tiliqua rugosa*). – Aquar.-Terrar.-Zeitschr., Stuttgart, 9(10): 270–273.

RÖSSEL, D. (2000): Rechtsfragen bei der Haltung von Reptilien. – in Rauh, J. (2000): Grundlagen der Reptilienhaltung. – Münster (Natur und Tier - Verlag).

ROGERS, D.C. (1967): The structure of the carotid bifurcation in the lizards *Tiliqua occipitalis* and *Trachydosaurus rugosus*. – J. Morph., 122: 115–130.

ROGNER, M. (1994): Echsen: Haltung, Pflege und Zucht im Terrarium. Bd. 2. – Stuttgart (Ulmer), 270 S.

ROOM, P.M. (1974): Lizards and snakes from the nothern district of Papua New Guinea. – Brit. J. Herpetol., 5(3): 438–447.

ROSE, S. (1985): Captive breeding of Cunningham's Skink. – The Vipera (South Western Herpetol. Soc., U.K.), 1(8): 14–22.

*ROSE, T.A. (1992): Husbandry and succesfull breeding of the New Guinea blue-tongued skink. – ASRA (Assoc. Study Reptilia Amphibia) Monogr., 2(2): 22–28.

ROSS, R.A. & G. MARZEK (1994): Riesenschlangen – Zucht und Pflege. – Ruhmannsfelden (bede Verlag), 245 S.

ROUNSEVELL, D. & SWAIN, R. (1993): Current issues in the conservation of the terrestrial herpetofauna of Tasmania. – Pp. 71–74 in Lunney, D. & D. Ayers (Hrsg.): Herpetology in Australia – a diverse discipline. – Trans. Royal Zool. Soc. New South Wales (Surry Beatty & Sons), Chipping Norton, 414 pp.

ROUX, J. (1910): Reptilien und Amphibien der Aru- und Kei-Inseln. – Abh. Senckenberg. Naturforsch. Ges., 33(3): 211–247 + pl. xiii–xiv.

SACHS, W. B. (1931): Australien-Import. – Blätter für Aquarien- und Terrarien-Freunde

– *(1961): Terrarien-Pflege leicht gemacht. – Stuttgart (Kosmos – Franckhsche Verlagshandlung), 76 S.

*SAINT GIRONS, H. (1982): Reproductive cycles of male snakes and their relationships with climate and female reproductive cycles. – Herpetologica, 38(1): 5–16.

SAMOUR, H.J., D. RISLEY, T. MARCH, B. SAVAGE, O. NIEVA & D.M. JONES (1984): Blood sampling techniques in reptiles. – Veterinary Rec., 12: 472–476.

SARRE, S., T.D. SCHWANER & A. GEORGES (1990): Genetic variation among insular populations of the sleepy lizard, *Trachydosaurus rugosus* GRAY (Squamata: Scincidae). – Aust. J. Zool., 38:603–616.

SARRE, S. & J.M. DEARN (1991) : Morphological variation and fluctuating asymmetry among insular populations of the sleepy lizard, *Trachydosaurus rugosus*. – Aust. J. Zool., 39: 91–104.

SATRAWAHA, R. (1980): Ecology and Activity Patterns of the Lizard *Trachydosaurus rugosus*. – Adelaide (M. Sc. Thesis, The Flinders University of South Australia), 136 pp.

SATRAWAHA, R. and C.M. BULL (1981): The area occupied by an omnivorous lizard, *Trachydosaurus rugosus*. – Aust. Wildl. Res., 8(2): 435–442.

SAUVAGE, E. (1875): De quelques reptiles d'Australie. – La Nature, 3(II)(106): 22–26.

– (1879): Les Cyclodes. – La Nature, 7(I)(310): 367–368.

SAVAGE, J.M. (1997): On terminology for the description of the hemipenes of squamate reptiles. – Herpetol. J., 7: 23–25.

*SCHADE, W. (1980): *Tiliqua gigas* (Riesenskink). Meine ersten Erfahrungen mit Pflege und Nachzucht. – Sauria, Berlin, 2(3): 23–24.

SCHILDGER, B.-J. (1995): Endoskopische Untersuchungen des Urogenitaltraktes bei Reptilien. – Verh. Ber. Erkrg. Zootiere, 37: 305–308.

SCHILDGER, B.-J., R. BAUMGARTNER, W. HÄFELI, A. RÜBEL & E. ISENBÜGEL (1993): Narkose und Immobilisation bei Reptilien. – Tierärztl. Prax., 21: 361–376.

SCHILDGER, B.-J., M. KRAMER, H. SPÖRLE, M. GERWING & R. WICKER (1993): Vergleichende bildgebende Ovardiagnostik bei Echsen am Beispiel des Chuckwallas (*Sauromalus obesus*) und des Arguswarans (*Varanus panoptes*). – Salamandra, Bonn, 29(3/4): 240–247.

SCHILDGER, B.-J. & R. WICKER (1987): Endoskopische Geschlechtsbestimmung bei *Trachydosaurus rugosus* (GRAY, 1827). – Salamandra, Bonn, 23(2/3): 97–105.

– (1989): Sex determination and clinical examination in reptiles using endoscopy. – Herpetol. Rev., 20(1): 9–10.

– (1992): Endoskopie bei Reptilien und Amphibien – Indikationen, Methoden, Befunde. – Der praktische Tierarzt, 1992/6: 516–526.

SCHMIDA, G. (1985): The Cold-Blooded Australians. A Unique Photographic Study of Australia's Reptiles, Amphibians and Freshwater Fish. – Lane Cove, NSW (Doubleday Australia), 208 pp.

SCHMIDT, A. (1979): Opdraet af *Tiliqua gigas*. – Nordisk Herpetologisk Forening, 22(10): 238–245.

*SCHMIDT, K.P. & R.F. INGER. (1957): Knaurs Tierreich in Farben. Reptilien. – Zürich (Buchclub Ex libris); München/Zürich (Droemersche Verlagsanstalt Th. Knaur Nachf.), 311 S.

*SCHNEE, P.(1900): Kleine Mitteilungen über das Freileben einiger australischer Reptilien. – Zool. Garten, Frankfurt, 41(1): 17–19.

SCHNEIDER, J.G. (1801): Historiae Amphibiorum naturalis et literariae. Fasciculus Secundus continens Crocodilos, Scincos, Chamaesauras, Boas, Pseudoboas, Elapes, Angues, Amphisbaenas et Caecilias. – Jena (F. Frommann), 364 S.

SCHNEIDER, K.M. (1941): Über Fettlager im Schwanz der Krusten- (Heloderma WIEGM.) und Stutz-Echse (Trachydosaurus GRAY). –Zool. Garten, 13(3/4): 236–247.

SCHODDE, R. & S.J. MATHEWS (1977): Contributions to Papuasian Ornithology V. Survey of the Birds of Taam Island, Kai Group. – Canberra (CSIRO Div. Wildl. Res. Tech. Pap., 33: 1–29.

SCHOOLDERMAN, G. (1994): Verzorging en voortplanting van de Australische Blauwtongskink (Tiliqua scincoides intermedia). – Lacerta, 52(4): 91 – 94.

*SCHROEDER, R. & H. BAUTZMANN (1956): Vergleichende Studien über Bau und Funktion des Amnions. Das Amnion der Reptilien bei Tropidonotus, Mabuia, Egernia Tiliqua, Alligator und Gecko. – Zeitschr. Zellforsch. mikr. Anat., 44(1): 1–13.

SCHWENK, K. (1988): Comparative morphology of the lepidosaur tongue and its relevance to squamate phylogeny. – Pp. 569–598 in R. ESTES & G. PREGILL (eds.): Phylogenetic Relationships of the Lizard Families. – Stanford (Stanford University Press).

SCROBOGNA, B. (1980): Die Pintubi. Am Ende der Steinzeit. – Berlin, Frankfurt/M., Wien (Ullstein), 246 S.

SERVENTY, V. (1970): Dryandra. The Story of an Australian Forest. – Sydney (A.H. & A.W. Reed), 205 pp.

SHARRAD, R.D. (1995): Necrophilia in Tiliqua rugosa: a dead end in evolution? – West. Aust. Nat., 20(1): 33–35.

*SHEA, G.M. (1981): Notes on the reproductive biology of the eastern blue-tongue skink, Tiliqua scincoides (SHAW). – Herpetofauna, 12(2): 16–23.

– (1982): Insular range extensions for the New Guinea bluetongue, Tiliqua gigas (BODDAERT) (Lacertilia: Scincidae). – Herpetofauna, 13(2): 7–12.

– (1988): On the diet of the sheoak skink, Cyclodomorphus casuarinae. – Herpetofauna, Sydney, 18(1): 7–8.

– (1989): Diet and reproductive biology of the Rottnest Island bobtail, Tiliqua rugosa konowi (Lacertilia, Scincidae). – Herpetol. J., 1: 366–369.

– (1990): The genera Tiliqua and Cyclodomorphus (Lacertilia: Scincidae): Generic diagnoses and systematic relationships. – Mem. Qld. Mus., 29(2): 495–519.

– (1992): The Systematics and Reproduction of Bluetongue Lizards of the Genus Tiliqua (Squamata: Scincidae) (4 Vols.) – Sydney (Unpubl. Ph.D. thesis, University of Sydney).

– (1993a): The male reproductive cycle of the eastern bluetongued lizard Tiliqua scincoides scincoides (Squamata: Scincidae). – Pp. 397–403 in LUNNEY, D. & D. AYERS (eds.): Herpetology in Australia, a Diverse Discipline. – Sydney (Surrey Beatty), 414 pp.

– (1993b): The anatomist John Hunter (1728–1793), the eastern bluetongue skink Tiliqua scincoides (Squamata: Scincidae), and the discovery of herbivory in skinks. – Arch. Nat. Hist., 20(3): 303–306.

– (1993c): Hidden herpetology: a list of theses in Australian universities to mid-1993. – Pp. 1–15 in LUNNEY, D. & D. AYERS (eds.): Herpetology in Australia, a Diverse Discipline. – Sydney (Surrey Beatty), 414 pp.

– (1995): A taxonomic revision of the Cyclodomorphus casuarinae complex (Squamata: Scincidae). – Rec. Aust. Mus., 47(1): 83–115.

– (1997): Reptiles, Lizards / Skinks, Blue-tongued Skinks. – Pp. 339 in: Encyclopedia of Australian Wildlife. – Surrey Hills (Readers Digest, Australia).

– (1998): Blue tongued lizards in New South Wales. – http://www.austmus.gov.au/is/sand/bluetoun.html.

– (2000a): Die Shark-Bay-Tannenzapfenechse Tiliqua rugosa palarra subsp. nov. – S. 108-112 in HAUSCHILD, A., R. HITZ, K. HENLE, G.M. SHEA & H. WERNING (Hrsg.): Blauzungenskinke. Beiträge zu Tiliqua und Cyclodomorphus. – Münster (Natur und Tier-Verlag), 287 S.

– (2000b): Der Sunda-Blauzungenskink Tiliqua scincoides chimaerea subsp. nov. – S. 157-160 in HAUSCHILD, A., R. HITZ, K. HENLE, G.M. SHEA & H. WERNING (Hrsg.): Blauzungenskinke. Beiträge zu Tiliqua und Cyclodomorphus. – Münster (Natur und Tier-Verlag), 287 S.

– (2000c): Die Neuguinea-Blauzunge, Tiliqua gigas (SCHNEIDER, 1801): Ökologie und Übersicht über die Unterarten nebst Beschreibung einer neuen Unterart, Tiliqua gigas evanescens subsp. nov. – S. 177-189 in HAUSCHILD, A., R. HITZ, K. HENLE, G.M. SHEA & H. WERNING (Hrsg.): Blauzungenskinke. Beiträge zu Tiliqua und Cyclodomorphus. – Münster (Natur und Tier-Verlag), 287 S.

SHEA, G.M. & M.N. HUTCHINSON (1992): A new species of lizard (*Tiliqua*) from the Miocene of Riversleigh, Queensland. – Mem. Qld. Mus., 32(1): 303–310.

*SHEA, G.M. & D.S. KENT ( 1988 ): Albinism in blue-tongued lizards (Sincidae: *Tiliqua*). – Herpetofauna, 18 (2): 3–4.

SHEA, G.M. & B. MILLER (1995): A taxonomic revision of the *Cyclodomorphus branchialis* species group (Squamata: Scincidae). – Rec. Aust. Mus., 47(3): 265–325.

SHEA, G. M. & M. PETERSON (1981): Observations on sympatry of the social lizards *Tiliqua multifasciata* (STERNFELD) and *T. occipitalis* (PETERS). – Aust. J. Herp., 1(1):27–28.

*SHINE, R. (1985): The reproductive biology of Australian reptiles: a search for general patterns. – Pp. 297–303 in GRIGG, G., R. SHINE & H. EHMANN (eds.): Biology of Australasian Frogs and Reptiles. – Sydney (Surrey Beatty).

*SHOEMAKER, V.H., P. LICHT & R.W. DAWSON (1966): Effects of temperature on kidney function in the lizard *Tiliqua rugosa*. – Physiol. Zool., 39(3): 244–252.

SMITH, J. & P. SMITH (1990): Fauna of the Blue Mountains. – Kenthurst (Kangaroo Press), 95 pp.

SOUCI, S.W., W. FACHMANN & H. KRAUT (1993): Die Zusammensetzung der Lebensmittel. Nährwert-Tabellen (4. Aufl.) – Stuttgart (Wissenschaftliche Verlagsgesellschaft), 1091 S.

SPECHT, R.L: (1972): The Vegetation of South Australia. – Adelaide (Government Printer), 328 pp.

SPELLERBERG, I.F. (1972): Temperature tolerances of southeast Australian reptiles examined in relation to reptile thermoregulatory behavior and distribution. – Oecologia, 9: 23–46.

*SPÖRLE, H. (1991): Sonographische Graviditäts- und Ovarialdiagnostik bei Schlangen. – Der praktische Tierarzt, 1991(4): 286–292.

*SPRACKLAND, R.G. (1992) : Grossechsen. – Ruhmannsfelden (bede Verlag), 288 S.

*– (1992) : Giant Lizards. – Brookvale (T.F.H., Australia), 288 pp.

STAMPS, J.A. (1983): Sexual selection, sexual dimorphism and territoriality. – Pp. 169–204 in HUEY, R.B., E.R. PIANKA & T.W. SCHOENER (eds.): Lizard Ecology. – Cambridge (Harvard University Press).

STANBURY, P.J. & G. PHIPPS (1980): Australia's Animals Discovered. – Sydney (Pergamon Press), 120 pp.

STEPHENSON, G. (1977): Notes on *Tiliqua gerrardii* in captivity. – Herpetofauna, 9(1): 4–6.

*STERNFELD, R.(1918): Zur Tiergeographie Papuasiens und der pazifischen Inselwelt. – Abh. Senckenberg. Naturforsch. Ges., Frankfurt, 36(4): 375–436.

STETTLER, P.H. (1953): Die kalte Überwinterung südaustralischer Grossechsen. – Aquarien- Terrar.-Zeitschr., Stuttgart, 6(12): 321–324.

– (1978): Handbuch der Terrarienkunde. Terrarientypen, Tiere, Pflanzen, Futter. – Stuttgart (Kosmos – Franckh´sche Verlagshandlung), 228 S.

STEWART, J.R. & D.G. BLACKBURN (1988): Reptilian placentation: structural diversity and terminology. – Copeia, 1988(4): 839–852.

STORR, G.M. (1976): The genus *Omolepida* (Lacertilia, Scincidae) in Western Australia. – Rec. West. Aust. Mus., 4(2): 163–170.

*STORR, G.M. & T.M.S. HANLON (1980): Herpetofauna of the Exmouth Region, Western Australia. – Rec. West. Aust. Mus., 8(3): 423–439.

*STORR, G.M., T.M.S. HANLON & J.N. DUNLOP (1983): Herpetofauna of the Geraldton Region, Western Australia. – Rec. West. Aust. Mus., 10(3): 215–234.

STORR, G.M. & G. HAROLD (1978): Herpetofauna of the Shark Bay region, Western Australia. – Rec. West. Aust. Mus., 6(4): 449–467.

*– (1980): Herpetofauna of the Zuytdorp Coast and Hinterland, Western Australia. – Rec. West. Aust. Mus., 8(3): 359–375.

– (1984): Herpetofauna of the Lake Mac Leod Region, Western Australia. – Rec. West. Aust. Mus., 11(2): 173–189.

STORR, G.M., L.A. SMITH & R.E. JONSTONE (1981): Lizards of Western Australia, Vol. I: Skinks. – Nedlands (University of Western Australia Press), 200 pp.

SUHR, E. (1967): Ein seltener Australier, leicht zu pflegen: *Tiliqua gerrardii*. – Aquarien Terrarien, Jena/Leipzig/Berlin, 14(8): 52–53.

SUKANTO, M. (1969): Chapter 4: Climate of Indonesia. – Pp. 215–229 in ARAKAWA, H. (ed.): Climates of Northern and Eastern Asia. – In: World Survey of Climatology, Vol. IIX. – Amsterdam, London, New York (Elsevier).

SWAN, G. (1990): A Field Guide to the Snakes and Lizards of New South Wales. – Winmalee(Three Sisters Productions), 224 pp.

*– (1995) : A Photograghic Guide to Snakes & other Reptiles of Australia. – Frenchs Forest (New Holland Publishers), 144 pp.

SWANSON, S. (1976): Lizards of Australia. – North Ryde (Angus & Robertson), 142 pp.

Swanson, S. (1987): LIZARDS OF AUSTRALIA. – NORTH RIDE (ANGUS & ROBERTSON BOOK), 160 PP.

*SWITAK, K.H. (1984): Tannenzapfenechsen in der freien Natur und im Terrarium. – Das Aquarium, 176: 89–94.

– (1986): Zwei Echsen aus Australien: Tannenzapfen- und Blauzungenskink. Verhalten und Pflegeansprüche. – Aquarienmagazin, Stuttgart, 20(7): 296–299.

*– (1994): Die Tannenzapfenechse, *Trachydosaurus rugosus*. Pflege und Zucht. – DATZ, 47(8): 496–500.

*– (1997): Shingle-backed skinks. – Reptiles, February 1997, 48–69.

THROCKMORTON, G., S.J. DE BAVAY, W. CHAFFEY, B. MERROTSKY, B.S. NOSKE & R. NOSKE (1985): The mechanism of frill erection in the bearded dragon *Amphibolurus barbatus* with comments on the jacky lizard *A. muricatus* (Agamidae). – J. Morphol., 183: 285–292.

TIMMS, B.V. (1977): Notes on the she-oak skink. – Hunter Nat. Hist., 9(2): 99–102.

*TOFOHR, O. (1908): Riesenglattechsen im Terrarium. – Bl. Aquar. Terrarienk., Stuttgart, 19(5): 49–50.

TREMPER, R.L. (1985): An improved technique for sexing skinks of the genus *Tiliqua*. – 9th Intern. Herp. Symp. on Capt. Prop. & Husb., San Diego: 171–174.

TREVOR, C. (1977): Notes on centralian bluetongues (*Tiliqua multifasciata*). – Newsletter Vict. Herp. Soc., 1:8–9.

TSN (Threatened Species Network( (1998): Pygmy Bluetongue Lizard Species Profile Sheet. –http://www.nccnsw.org.au/member/tsn/context/profiles/224.html

TURNER, G. (1996): Some litters of the eastern blue-tongued skink *Tiliqua scincoides scincoides* (Scincidae). – Herpetofauna, 26(2): 39–47.

TYLER, M.J. (1962): Unusual observations on the lizard *Tiliqua* (*Trachysaurus*) *rugosa* (GRAY). – South Aust. Nat., 37(2): 22–23.

TYLER, M.J., G.F. GROSS, C.E. RIX & R.W. INNS (1976): Terrestrial fauna and aquatic vertebrates. – Pp. 121–129 in TWIDALE, C.R., M.J. TYLER & B.P. WEBB (eds.): Natural History of the Adelaide Region. – Adelaide (Royal Society of South Australia), 189pp.

UNDERWOOD, G. (1971): A modern appreciation of Camp's "Classification of the Lizards". – Introduction to reprint (Soc. Study Amph. Rept.).

*VALENTIC, R. (1996): A prey record of the eastern blue-tongue *Tiliqua scincoides* for the common brown snake *Pseudonaja textilis*. – Monitor (Vict. Herp. Soc.), 8(2): 84.

VANCOUVER, G. (1798): A Voyage of Discovery to the North Pacific Ocean, and round the World, in which the Coast of North-west America has been Carefully Examined and Accurately Surveyed. Undertaken by His Majesty's Command, Principally with a View to Ascertain the Existence of any Navigable Communication between the North Pacific and North Atlantic Oceans. And Performed in the Years 1790, 1791, 1792, 1793, 1794, and 1795, in the Discovery Sloop of War, and Armed Tender Chatham, under the Command of Captain George Vancouver (3 Vols.) – London (G.G. & J. Robinson).

VERON, J.E.N. (1969): The reproductive cycle of the water skink, *Sphenomorphus quoyi*. – J. Herpetol., 3: 55–63.

*VITT, L.J. & E.R. PIANKA (1994): Lizard Ecology. Historical and Experimental Perspectives. – Princeton (University Press).

*VOGT, T. (1912): Beitrag zur Amphibien- und Reptilienfauna der Südsee-Inseln. – Ges. Naturforsch. Freunde Berlin, Sitzungsber. 1: 1–13.

VON FISCHER, J. (1882): Die Stummelschwanz-Eidechse (*Trachydosaurus asper*) in der Gefangenschaft. –Zool. Garten, 23(7): 206–210.

WAGLER, J. (1830): Natürliches System der Amphibien, mit vorangehender Classifikation der Säugthiere und Vögel. – München, Stuttgart und Tübingen (J.G. Cotta), 354 S.

WAGNER, E. & D. RICHARDSON (1988): Breeding the shingleback skink, *Trachydosaurus rugosus*. – The Vivarium, California (American Federation of Herpetoculturists), 1(2): 40–41.

WAITE, E.R. (1929): The Reptiles and Amphibians of South Australia. – Adelaide (Government Printer), 270 pp.

WAKEFIELD, N.A. (1956): Blue-tongued lizards and instinct. – Vict. Nat., 72:143–144.

*WALKER, H. (1994): The care and breeding of pink-tongue skinks, *Tiliqua gerrardii*. – Herptile (J. Int. Herpetol. Soc.), 19(4): 148–150.

WALLS, J.G. (1995): Skinke im Terrarium. – Neptune City, New Jersey (T.F.H. Publications); Ruhmannsfelden (bede Verlag), 65 S.

– (1996): Blue-tongued Skinks: Keeping and Breeding them in Captivity. – Neptune City, New Jersey (T.F.H.

Publications), 64 pp.

*WARBURG, M.R. (1965): The influence of ambient temperature and humidity on the body temperature and water loss from two Australian lizards *Tiliqua rugosa* (GRAY) (Scincidae) and *Amphibolurus barbatus* (CUVIER) (Agamidae). – Aust. J. Zool., 13: 331–350.

WEBB, G.A. & J.A. SIMPSON (1985): Some unusual food items for the southern blotched blue-tongue lizard *Tiliqua nigrolutea* (QUOY & GAIMARD) at Bombala, New South Wales. – Herpetofauna, 16(2): 44–45.

WEEKES, H.C. (1935): A review of placentation among reptiles with particular regard to the function and evolution of the placenta. – Proc. Zool. Soc. London., 2: 625–645.

WEIGEL, J. (1989): Care of Australian Reptiles in Captivity (Reprint). – Gosford (Reptile Keepers Association), 144 pp.

WEIS, P. (1998): Care Sheets – Blue-Tongued Skinks. – Internet, 1998, www.herp.com/care/wr_bts.html

WELLS, R.W. & C.R. WELLINGTON (1985): A classification of the Amphibia and Reptilia of Australia. – Aust. J. Herpetol., Suppl. Ser., 1: 1–61.

WERNER, F. (1909): Neue oder seltenere Reptilien des Musée Royal d'Histoire naturelle de Belgique in Brüssel. – Zool. Jahrb., Abt. Syst. Geogr. Biol. Tiere, 28(3): 263–288.

– (1910): Reptilia (Geckonidae und Scincidae). – S. 451–493 in MICHAELSEN, W. & R. HARTMEYER (Hrsg.): Die Fauna Südwest Australiens. Ergebnisse der Hamburger südwest-australischen Forschungsreise 1905. Band 2. – Jena (Gustav Fischer), 493 Seiten.

WHITLEY, G.P. (1970): Early History of Australian Zoology. – Sydney (Royal Zoological Society of New South Wales), 75 pp.

WILLIAMS, K.D. (1993): Legislation and protection of reptiles and frogs in the ACT. – P. 58 in LUNNEY, D. & D. AYERS (Hrsg.): Herpetology in Australia – a diverse discipline. – Trans. Royal Zool. Soc. New South Wales (Surry Beatty & Sons), Chipping Norton, 414 pp.

WILSON, S.K. & D.G. KNOWLES (1988): Australia's Reptiles. A Photographic Reference to the Terrestrial Reptiles of Australia. – Sydney (Collins Publishers), 447 pp.

WOLF, S. (1933): Zur Kenntnis von Bau und Funktion der Reptilienlunge. – Zool. Jb. Anat., Jena, 57: 139–190.

WOLTER, W. (1980): Unternehmen Kopfjäger. – Stuttgart (Pietsch Verlag), 189 S.

WORRELL, E. (1963): Reptiles of Australia. – Sydney (Angus & Robertson), 207 pp.

YEATMAN, E.M. (1988): Resource partitioning by three congeneric species of skink (*Tiliqua*) in sympatry in South Australia. – Adelaide (Unpubl. Ph.D. thesis, Flinders University of South Australia), 459 pp.

YUWONO, F.B. (1998): The trade of live reptiles in Indonesia. – S. 9–15 in ERDELEN, W. (ed.): Conservation, Trade and Sustainable Use of Lizards and Snakes in Indonesia. – Mertensiella 9: 1–144.

– (1999): The Trade of Live Reptiles in Indonesia. – http://www.geocities.com/RainForest/6785/paper.htm

ZAHN, U. (1984): Diercke-Universalatlas. – Braunschweig (Georg Westermann), 447 S.

ZIEGLER, T. & W. BÖHME (1996a): Neue Erkenntnisse zur Geschlechtsunterscheidung bei squamaten Reptilien. – Kleintierpraxis, 41(8): 585–590.

– (1996b): Zur Hemiclitoris der squamaten Reptilien: Auswirkungen auf einige Methoden der Geschlechtsunterscheidung. – herpetofauna, Weinstadt, 18(101): 11–19.

– (1997): Genitalstrukturen und Paarungsbiologie bei squamaten Reptilien, speziell den Platynota, mit Bemerkungen zur Systematik. – Mertensiella 8: 1–210.

ZIMMERMANN, E. (1983): Das Züchten von Terrarientieren: Pflege, Verhalten, Fortpflanzung. – Stuttgart (Kosmos – Franckh'sche Verlagshandlung), 238 S.

ZWART, P. (1995): Echsen. – S. 809–858 in GABRISCH, K. & P. ZWART (Hrsg.): Krankheiten der Heimtiere. – Hannover (Schlütersche), 1000 S.

*ZWINENBERG, A.J.(1974): Australische Reptilien: Scincidae. – Lacerta, Utrecht, 32(12): 195–200.

– (1976): Der Schneckenskink *Tiliqua gerrardii* (GRAY). – Aquaria, St. Gallen, 23(8), 123–126.

Authors' addresses
Dr. Robert Hitz
Am Mülibach 8
CH-9425 Thal, Switzerland

Dr. Klaus Henle
Department of Conservation Biology and Natural Resources, Centre for Environmental Research, UFZ Leipzig-Halle
Permoserstr. 13
D-04318 Leipzig, Germany

# Glossary and conversion table

## compiled by ANDREE HAUSCHILD

**abdominal** – relating to the venter
**adspection** – medical inspection, evaluation
adult – grown-up
**allometric** – different growth rates showing in relation to body size or individual organs
**allopatric** – distribution ranges that do not overlap
**anatomy** – science of the structure of the body, including both external and internal structures
**anterior** – in front, in the front
**apex** – tip, highest or most prominent point of an organ
**apical** – situated at the apex; here: the top or anteriormost area of external genital structures (hemipenis and hemiclitoris, respectively) of squamates
**apical lobes** – elongated protrusions of the apex
**apomorphic** – presence of morphological traits which, if commonly present, permit to deduce cladistic relationships
**arboreal** – living on trees
**arid** – dry, desert-like
**arthroscope** – optical device with a fine tube for the adspection of joints (here: of the body cavity) that causes only minimal injury to the covering tissue
**asulcal** – situated on the side opposite the sperm groove
**asymmetric** – not the same on both sides
**autapomorphy** – the derived (autapomorphous) appearance of a trait typical for a certain taxon or a certain group of taxa
**autotomy** – the ability to lose parts of the body (e.g., the tail) under physical stress as a defense mechanism
**basal** – belonging to the base, situated low or near the base

**biochemistry** – science of the chemical properties of animated matter
**biomechanic** – science of the laws of mechanics according to which biological processes unfold
**blood protein** – protein components of the blood
**chemoreception** – the recognition of chemical cues
**chorioallantois** – fusion, junction of the two embryonic membranes chorion and allantois
**chromosome** – the carrier of genetic (hereditary) information
**clinal variance** – variation of traits that parallels a geographical continuance
**compartment** – a specified sector, area
**conical** – cone-shaped
**craniodorsal** – towards above and forward, situated towards the dorsal head region
**cuttle fish shell** – calcium-rich endoskeleton of marine cephalopods
**demographic** – descriptive research of the economical and sociopolitical changes within a population
**divergent** – development into opposite directions
**dorsal** – relating to the back, situated on the back, above
**dorsolateral** – on the side of the back
**dorsoventral** – in the direction from the back to the belly
**ecology** – science of the interaction among organisms and between these and their environment
**ectopterygoid** – piece of bone in the ossified roof of the mouth of vertebrates
**enzymatic** – action caused by enzymes
**ethology** – science of behavior
**evertible** – protrudable, extrudable

**everted** – protruded, extruded

**evolutionary** – by development, by advancement

**exterior** – on the outside, on the outer surface

**external morphology** – structural traits on the outside

**fecal steroid patterns** – ratio of (steroidal) sexual hormones to each other contained in feces

**frontal** – scale on the forehead

**genitals** – external sexual organs

**genital morphology** – description of the outer sexual organs and their structures

**gonads** – inner, primary sexual organs

**gravidity** – pregnancy, in the process of developing eggs or young

**habitat** – biotope, environment in which an organism typically lives

**HCL** – hemiclitoris length

**hemiclitoris** (Pl.: hemiclitores) – external sexual organ of female squamates

**hemipenis** (Pl.: hemipenes) – external sexual organ of male squamates

**hemipenis exuviae** – shedding of the hemipenes

**herbivorous** – feeding on plant matter

**hexagonal** – with six angles/planes

**hibernation** – resting period during winter, overwintering

**holotype** – the reference specimen used to describe and establish a taxon

**HPL** – hemipenis length

**hybrid** – bastard, the product of parents representing two different taxa

**hybridization** – the cross breeding of two species or subspecies that are genetically compatible enough to produce offspring

**immune** – insensitive, impervious to a substance or pathogen

**immunological electrophoresis** – splitting of protein compounds by biophysical and biochemical means aided by antigen/antibody reactions

**immunology** – science of the interactions between micro–organisms or biological substances (antigens) and the defense products (antibodies) produced by higher life forms

**infertile** – unable to reproduce; not fertilized

**incompatible** – antagonistic, inharmonious

**intermediary** – positioned between the original forms (species or parental specimens)

**interparietals** – small scales situated between the scales on the crown of the head

**invertebrates** – organisms without a vertebral column

**inverted** – retracted

**irreversible** – cannot be undone

**isofluran** – anesthetic in the form of gas that is breathed in

**juvenile** – not yet sexually mature

**laterite** – red erosion soil

**lectotype** – a "substitute" holotype

**lobe** – elongated flap or protrusion

**loreals** – "bridle shields", scales between nasal and preocular shields

**maxilla** – upper jaw bone

**median** – situated in the middle or center

**melanistic** – colored black

**metabolite** – metabolic product

**Miocene** – geological epoch 23 million years ago

**monogamous** – living together with only one sexual partner

**monomorphous** – with an equal appearance (referring to the sexes)

**morphology** – science of the appearance of organisms

**nasal** – scale pierced by the nostril

**occipital** – larger shield on the rear side of the head (occiput) bordering the crown shield (parietal)

**olfactory** – by sense of smell

**omnivorous** – feeding on both meat and plant matter

**ontogenesis** – development of an individual over time

**osteomyelitis** – inflammation of the bone marrow

**Outback** – the inhospitable, arid interior of Australia

**ovary** – the female organ in which egg cells are produced

**oviduct** – a tube–like structure attached to an ovary

**ovulation** – release of an egg cell ready to be fertilized from the ovary

**paratype** – a preserved reference specimen next to the holotype representing the same taxon

**paravertebral** – situated next to the midline of the back

**paravertebrals** – scales along the longitudinal midline of the back, counted from the posterior margin of the parietal / interparietal to the last scale anterior to the line formed by the anterior edge of the hind legs when these are positioned at a right angle to the longitudinal axis of the body

**parietal** – shield on crown of head

**pathological** – changed by disease

**pedicel** – basal, or lowest, section of the external genital structures (hemipenes or hemiclitores) of squamates

**phenotype** – outer appearance as the result of genetical and environmental influences

**pholidosis** – entirety of scalation traits by which a taxon is diagnosed and identified

**phylogenetic** – evolutionary relationships

**physiology** – science of ordinary life processes

**Pleistocene** – geological epoch some 2 million years ago

**plica** – fold; here: the ridge–like fold ornamentation of the external sexual organs of squamates

**plica compartment** – section of folds

**posterior** – in the back, behind

**postsuboculars** – posterior scales below the eyes, first row of scales behind the eye

**predator** – natural "enemy" feeding on this organism

**presuboculars** – anterior scales below the eye

**primary sexual organs** – interior sexual organs (testes / ovaries)

**reduction** – regress, retrogress development of a trait

**receptive** – able to be fertilized

**Sauria** – suborder containing the lizards

**secondary** – "in second place"; here: on the outside

**secondary** sexual organs – exterior sexual organs (hemipenes / hemiclitores)

**Serpentes** – suborder containing the snakes

**serum-immunological electrophoresis** – splitting of proteins comprising the blood serum by biophysical and biochemical means aided by antigen/antibody reactions

**serum testosterone evaluation** – analysis of the content of male sexual hormone (testosterone) in the blood serum

**sex-correlated** – typical for a sex

**sexual dimorphism** – differences in the appearance of males and females of the same species

**skeleton chronology** – identification of the age of an individual based on bone growth

**sonography** – graphic diagnostic process using ultrasonic technology

**Squamata** – order containing lizards and snakes

**squamosum** – temporal bone

**subcaudal** – on the underside of the tail

**subcaudals** – scales covering the underside of the tail, counted from the posterior margin of the preanal shield to the tip of the tail

**subdigital lamellae** – lamella–like scales on the underside of the toes: in the case of *Tiliqua* the fourth toe is used for evaluation

**sulcal** – situated on the side of the sperm groove

**sulcus** – sperm groove

**sulcus spermaticus** – sperm groove bordered by lips of the exterior genitals of male squamates

**supraciliary** – "eye brow" scale

**supralabial** – scale covering the upper lip

**supraocular** – "eye lid" scale, scale above the eye ball

**SVL** – snout–vent length; standard measurement taken on the ventral side from the tip of the snout to the posterior edge of the preanal scale

**sympatric** – occurring in the same geographical region

**synopsis** – comparative compilation

**taxon** (Pl.: taxa) – systematic unit at various categories (subspecies, species, genus etc.)

**taxonomy** – science of identification and description of organisms using scientific nomenclature

**temporal** – shield covering the temple

**testis** (Pl.: testes) – "testicle", sperm producing organ

**TL** – tail length

**tracheal tube** – tube that is inserted into the windpipe to administer anesthetic gas

**truncus** – trunk, truncal or mid–section of the external genital structures (hemipenes, hemiclitores) of squamates

**truncus arteriosus** – here: truncal or mid–section (central trunk) of the external genital structures (hemipenes, hemiclitores) of squamates

**turgid** – under increased tissue pressure; here: swollen or erect condition of the external genitals of squamates

**type locality** – the point of collection of the holotype

**upper lip** – site of transition from the inner to the outer side of the mouth on the upper jaw

**urbanization** – conversion of natural land into town land

**ventral** – situated on the belly, underside

**vertebrals** – scales situated immediately above and along the vertebral column

**viviparous** – giving birth to fully developed young

**ZFMK** – Zoologisches Forschungsinstitut und Museum Alexander Koenig

## Literature

HADORN, E. & R. WEHNER (1972): Allgemeine Zoologie. Begründet von Alfred Kühn. – Stuttgart (Georg Thieme), 474 S.

HENTSCHEL, E. & G. WAGNER (1986): Zoologisches Wörterbuch. – Jena (Gustav Fischer), 672 S.

KABISCH, K. (1990): Wörterbuch der Herpetologie. – Jena (Gustav Fischer), 478 S.

KRÜGER, G. (1968): Veterinärmedizinische Terminologie. – Leipzig (S. Hirzel), 784 S.

MACKENSEN, L. (1990): Das Wörterbuch für jeden Tag. – Hamburg (Merit), 699 S.

STEINER, G. (1988): Wort-Elemente der wichtigsten zoologischen Fachausdrücke. – Stuttgart (Gustav Fischer), 31 S.

TEXTOR, A.M. (1971): Auf deutsch – das Fremdwörterlexikon. – rororo handbuch. – Reinbek bei Hamburg (Rowohlt Taschenbuch), 342 S.

ULBER, T., W. GROSSMANN, J. BEUTELSCHIESS & C. BEUTELSCHIESS (1989): Terraristisch / Herpetologisches Fachwörterbuch. – Berlin (Terrariengemeinschaft Berlin e.V.), 176 S.

## Conversion table

1 mm (millimeter) = 0.039 in. (inches)
1 cm (centimeter) = 0.39 in. (inches)
1 m (meter) = 39.5 in. (inches)
1 km (kilometer) = 0.62 mi. (miles)
1 m$^2$ (square meter) = 1.196 sq. yds. (square yards)
1 ha (hectare) . 2.5 acres
1 g (gram) = 0.04 oz. (ounces)
1 kg (kilogram) = 2.2 lb. (pounds)
1 l (liter) = 0.264 gal. (American gallons)
1 °C (degree Celsius) = 2.63 °F (degrees Fahrenheit)

Author's address
Andree Hauschild,
Narzissenweg 7
D–41516 Grevenbroich, Germany

# The authors of the bluetongue book
## (in alphabetical order)

Prof. Dr. Wolfgang **Böhme** is 56 years of age. He is the curator of the herpetological section of the Zoologisches Forschungsinstitut und Museum Alexander Koenig in Bonn, Germany, and its Assistant Director. His major field of research is the evolution of squamates.

Dr. Carolin **Dennert** is a practizing veterinarian with emphasis on reptiles. Her PhD dissertation was entitled "Research into the feeding of squamates and testudines".

Peter **Ferger** was born on 12.01.1943 in Giessen, and now lives in Niederdorf, Switzerland. He is a biology technician by profession and works in an industrial laboratory. For over 30 years his passion has been the keeping, observation and breeding of Australian skinks and dwarf tortoises.

Dr. Paul **Gassner** is 36 years of age, married, with a son, resident in Münster, Germany. He is a biologist by profession, specializing in reproductive medicine. Being a terrarium keeper since childhood he has been focusing on the keeping and breeding of giant skinks (genera *Corucia, Egernia* and *Tiliqua*) for 15 years. His core collection also includes Russian and Moorish tortoises.

Andree **Hauschild** is a public servant. He is 51 years of age. Being an enthusiastic terrarium keeper and author, his major interest is skinks. He is the main editor of the German edition of this book and initiator of the project. By managing to unite all renowned "skink professionals" to participate, and so create a unique collection of information on *Tiliqua* and *Cyclodomorphus,* a dream has come true for him.

Dr. Klaus **Henle** is 46 years of age. He studied biology at the University of Stuttgart/Hohenheim, graduated in Australia on the ecology of lizards, habilitated at the University of Mainz with the topic "Animal ecologic fundamentals for a methodical, conceptional and theoretical advancement of the research into nature". He is at present manager of the project group "Near-natural landscapes and rural regions" at the environmental study center at Leipzig-Halle, Germany, and responsible for the organization of multilateral projects relating to nature conservation and utilization of land. He is honorary secretary of the periodical "Salamandra" published by the DGHT. His interests are herpetology, natural history, population ecology, Central Europe, countries of the Mediterranean, Australia, and New Zealand. Hobbies: table tennis, windsurfing, travelling, and photography.

Dr. Anthony **Herrel** was born in Belgium in 1970. He graduated at the University of Antwerp in 1998 on the subject "herbivorous lizards". Since then he has been working in a Belgian post-doctorate position, and is partly based in Arizona. His most important hobby is sports, particularly mountaineering, cave exploration and the catching of lizards and snakes (almost a sport ...). While keeping lizards and snakes used to be his hobby, it has now become part of his profession.

Dr. Robert **Hitz**, born on 03.07.1951, lives in Thal, Switzerland. Married to Rösli Hitz, with two children, he is a veterinarian with his own praxis. For the past 25 years he has been keeping and breeding various species of *Tiliqua* and been engaged in studying the literature on this genus. He was the first to breed *T. rugosa aspera* in Europe in 1983. Other interests: herpetology and terrarium keeping in general, identification of sexes in monomorphous lizard species, biology and husbandry of tarantulas, animal photography.

Paul **Horner** is 54 years of age. He works as the curator of the "Museum and Art Gallery of the Northern Territory" in Darwin, Australia, and is responsible for the terrestrial vertebrate fauna. His particular interest is the taxonomy and biogeography of the skinks living in the northern parts of Australia.

Dr. Mark **Hutchinson**, born 1954 in Melbourne, Australia, graduated at the La Trobe University, where his research began to be focused on the evolution of lizards. He was elected curator of amphibians and reptiles at the South Australian Museum in Adelaide in 1990, where he since has continued his research into the systematics, phylogenetics, and conservation of Australian lizards.

Markus **Limberger** is 33 years of age, not married, and lives in Seligenstadt, Germany. Having studied at the Technical Highschool Darmstadt from 1989 through 1994, he has been working on the completion of a dissertation on the anatomy of giant skinks. Next to this he has been studying veterinarian medicine at the University of Giessen since 1995.

Beate **Löhr** lives in Bad Dürkheim, Germany, is 52 years of age, and a technical draughtswoman by profession. She has been an active terrarium keeper for 25 years and dedicates much of her time to the breeding of pink-tongued skinks. She has also gained a name in high esteem for her continuously successful propagation of spiny-tailed agamas. Her hobbies include needlework, backpack travelling, succulent plants, and tennis.

Dr. Tim **Milne** authored his PhD dissertation on the subject of endangered dwarf blue-tongued skinks at Flinder University of South Australia in 1999. He is an enthusiastic herpetologist and used to be president of the South Australian Herpetology Group. His major research interest is the conservation of biodiversity, especially of reptiles. He is currently employed by the Nature Conservation Society of South Australia.

Heidrun **Röhe**, born 25.07.1947, married to Uwe Röhe, lives in Hamburg, Germany. By profession she is an editorial secretary. Her hobbies include dinghy sailing, photography, and, for more than 20 years, the keeping and breeding of livebearing skinks. For the last few years she has been focusing on studying behavioral patterns of species of *Tiliqua.*

Dr. Glenn M. **Shea** is 40 years of age and resides in Sydney, Australia. He is a lecturer in veterinary anatomy at the University of Sydney. His major interests are herpetology in general, and the systematics, biology, and captive husbandry of blue-tongued skinks in particular.

Dr. med. Thomas **Unverzagt** lives in Duisburg, Germany. He is married, 38 years of age, and works as a surgeon at the Düsseldorf City Hospital. He owned a terrarium already when he was ten, and today his focus is on Australian blue-tongued skinks and shinglebacks. Other hobbies include travelling and biking.

Heiko **Werning** was born in 1970 and lives in Berlin and Münster. He is chief editor of the periodicals Reptilia and Draco, working as lector, journalist, and author. He is studying technical nature conservation centring around subjects such as nature conservation and species protection. Privately he keeps lizards, mainly water dragons and iguanas, but he also composes songs which he performs if the occasion arises.

Dr. Thomas **Ziegler**, born 1970 in Bonn, is biologist. Since 1994 he published more than 50 scientific publications dealing mainly with herpetological faunistics and systematics, especially of reptiles. His focus is on diversity studies in South East Asia and Vietnam, respectively, as well as on monitor lizards and on genital morphology.

# Index